LINE OF ADVANTAGE

LINE OF
ADVANTAGE

JAPAN'S GRAND STRATEGY IN
THE ERA OF ABE SHINZŌ

MICHAEL J. GREEN

Columbia University Press
New York

Columbia University Press
Publishers Since 1893
New York   Chichester, West Sussex
cup.columbia.edu

Library of Congress Cataloging-in-Publication Data
Names: Green, Michael J, author.
Title: Line of advantage: Japan's grand strategy in the era of Abe Shinzō
/ Michael J Green.
Description: First Edition. | New York: Columbia University Press, [2022] |
Includes bibliographical references and index.
Identifiers: LCCN 2021047783 | ISBN 9780231204668 (Hardback)
| ISBN 9780231204675 (trade paperback) | ISBN 9780231555630 (eBook)
Subjects: LCSH: Political leadership—Japan. | Abe, Shinzō, 1954- |
Geopolitics—Indo-Pacific Region. | Indo-Pacific Region—Strategic
aspects. | Japan—Politics and government—21st century. | National security—
Japan—History—21st century. | Japan—Economic conditions—21st century. |
Japan—Foreign relations—1989-
Classification: LCC JQ1681.G74 2022 | DDC 306.20952—dc23/eng/20211206
LC record available at https://lccn.loc.gov/2021047783

Cover photograph: Getty Images / Kent Nishimura
Cover design: Julia Kushnirsky

In memory of Okamoto Yukio and Professor Ezra Vogel,
who made the U.S.-Japan alliance what it is today
and mentored so many of us over the years. May we
all aspire to their high standards of patriotism,
scholarship, and integrity.

CONTENTS

ACKNOWLEDGMENTS

I n 2014, Al Song of the Smith Richardson Foundation reached out
to me proposing that I write a new book on Japan's strategy toward
China. It was the centennial of the First World War, and the Smith
Richardson board was interested in supporting studies that would help
illuminate ways that Asia could avoid the conflagration that had over-
taken Europe in 1914. I was still working on my history of U.S. strategy in Asia, *By More than Providence*, and hesitated to launch a new
book project so soon, but Al and his colleagues at Smith Richardson
were characteristically patient, persistent, and generous in their support
and encouragement.[1] With help from the indefatigable Teraoka Ayumi,
Georgetown Master of Arts in Asian Studies (MASIA) grad and now
doctoral student at Princeton, I launched the new project with a three-
day gathering of American and Japanese diplomatic historians to consider Japan's options in the face of the China challenge. Warren Cohen,
Peter Feaver, Will Inboden, Jonathan Steinberg, and Phil Zellikow joined
me in Hakone, Japan, along with Hosoya Yuichi, Iokibe Makoto, Kitaoka
Shiinichi, Sakamoto Kazuya, Nakanishi Hiroshi, and Shiraishi Takashi.
It was a bilateral dream team of strategic thinkers, all of whom truly
helped me to frame the overall approach to the book by drawing out
important lessons from Japan's past and the statecraft of other powers
throughout history.

I had excellent research assistants at Georgetown University and the Center for Strategic and International Studies (CSIS) over the six years of the project, including Hannah Fodale, Kato Ryoko, Nakano Tomoaki, Nishimura Rintaro, Elliot Silverberg, Lauren Sun, and Alexis Ayano Terai. I also had the opportunity to test my work in scholarly roundtables supported by the Laboratory Program for Korean Studies through the Ministry of Education of the Republic of Korea and the Korean Studies Promotion Service of the Academy of Korean Studies (AKS-2016-LAB-2250001), the Reischauer Institute at Harvard, and the 21st Century Japan Politics and Society Initiative at the University of Indiana. I am grateful to the organizers of those sessions and all the participants. Several friends and colleagues read chapters or whole iterations of the manuscript. Jeffrey Hornung and Nick Szechenyi made important suggestions based on their own cutting-edge research on Japan's defense policies. CSIS visiting fellow Suzuki Hiroyuki gave me important context for my chapter on regional order with respect to development finance. Charles Lake made me smarter, as he always does, on questions of Japanese history and economic policy. Hosoya Yuichi and Kato Yoichi helped me tease out the larger historical argument of the book. The anonymous reviewers chosen by Columbia University Press gave the last important vector checks before Caelyn Cobb and her team at the press put the book into production. Sincere thanks are also due to Victor Cha and David Kang, who lead this excellent series on East Asia for Columbia.

I would never have finished this or my earlier books if my wife Eileen Pennington and my children Xander and Virginia had not been so tolerant of my frequent cloistering in the study to write. "Quiet. . . . your father is writing!" is a refrain many authors will appreciate and for which I owe my entire family a great deal.

As a scholar practitioner I try to convey through my work a sense of appreciation for those who have toiled in the policy world before us and a sense of inheritance and purpose for those who will follow. For those who write at the intersection of history and political science, however, it is also important not to obscure failures, tragedies, and biases. Being an idealistic realist is a tough balancing act that I hope I have achieved in these pages.

A NOTE ON TRANSLITERATION OF JAPANESE WORDS AND NAMES

I have relied on the Hepburn romanization standard for transliterating Japanese names and words, using macrons for long vowels (for example, Abe Shinzō). Macrons are skipped for words commonly used in English, such as "Tokyo." Family names come first for Japanese, Korean, and Chinese individuals referenced in the text as they would be in the original. If Japanese authors publish or are cited in English with their given name first or without the use of macrons, that is how they will appear in citations.

LINE OF ADVANTAGE

INTRODUCTION

There are two ways to secure national independence and defense. The first is to protect the line of sovereignty. The second is to protect the line of advantage (riekisen). *The line of sovereignty means the nation's border and the line of advantage includes the area closely related to the safety of the line of sovereignty. There is no country that does not try to defend both lines.*

—YAMAGATA ARITOMO, 1890

Japan is back.

—PRIME MINISTER ABE SHINZŌ, CENTER FOR STRATEGIC AND INTERNATIONAL STUDIES, WASHINGTON, DC, FEBRUARY 2013

ABE'S RETURN

On February 22, 2013, Prime Minister Abe Shinzō stepped up to the podium at the Center for Strategic and International Studies (CSIS) to celebrate his triumphant return to Washington after six years in the political wilderness. His first twelve-month tenure as prime minister had ended abruptly in September 2007 after his ruling coalition lost control of the Upper House of the Japanese Diet and Abe himself was struck down by a debilitating intestinal illness. In the intervening years Japan had changed prime ministers six times, and the country had been repeatedly humiliated by friends and foes alike as Chinese paramilitary ships contested the Japanese-administered Senkaku Islands and an exasperated President Barack Obama disparaged one of his confused Japanese counterparts, Hatoyama Yukio, as "loopy."[1] In 2010 the International Monetary Fund (IMF) announced that China had surpassed Japan to become the world's second largest economy, and then in March 2011 Japan was struck by the deadliest earthquake and tsunami of the postwar period. While the Japanese people responded with stoic courage, the political leaders of the ruling Democratic Party of Japan (DPJ) stumbled badly. After the decisive role played by Prime Minister Koizumi Junichiro on the world stage from 2001 to 2006, Japan once again seemed truly adrift, an object of derision and pity unable to manage its own affairs, let alone shape regional and global developments.

Months before Abe's speech at CSIS, a bipartisan group of veteran American Asia policy experts led by former deputy secretary of state Richard Armitage and former assistant secretary of defense Joseph Nye had sounded the alarm at Japan's drift in a new report on the U.S.-Japan alliance. In a deliberately provocative line, the report concluded by asking whether Japan intended to remain a "tier one power."[2] Abe had read the report and shared the same concern. Speaking in English and looking directly at Armitage and the other authors in the audience, including me, the prime minister gave his answer: "Japan is not now *and will never be* a tier two power!"[3] Over the next eight years, Abe realigned his country's institutions and alliances to prove just that.

A NEW GRAND STRATEGY

Nation-states deploy new grand strategies when structural changes in the balance of power coincide with the emergence of strong-willed leaders who seize that moment to shape rather than be shaped by the new environment. Harry S. Truman, Dean Acheson, and those "present at the creation" in the early Cold War provide one such example of this convergence of structure and agency in modern American history.[4] In the 1980s leaders such as Ronald Reagan, Margaret Thatcher, and Helmet Kohl led a similar generational change in strategies for prevailing in the Cold War. Japan's own postwar grand strategy was defined by the legacy of Prime Minister Yoshida Shigeru and his doctrine of minimizing geopolitical risk, relying on the United States for security, and seeking autonomy and freedom of maneuvering through a single-minded focus on the economy. Abe's transformation of Japan's grand strategy from 2012 to 2020 was as profound as any of these examples. It marked the end of the Yoshida doctrine and the beginning of a new era in Japanese statecraft.

The core challenge for Abe upon his resumption of power in 2012 was how to respond to China's intensifying drive for regional hegemony under Xi Jinping. Indeed, Abe's own political comeback was largely fueled by public alarm at China's increasing use of coercion against Japan and the belief among Liberal Democratic Party (LDP) leaders that Abe alone possessed the experience and clarity of thinking to restore Japan's position in Asia and the U.S. trust needed to counter China's moves.[5]

International relations scholars have long posited that under such conditions of deteriorating relative power vis-à-vis an adversary, states like Japan have three broad options: they can *bandwagon* with the rising power; they can engage in *external balancing* to build alliances to restore a favorable balance of power; or they can pursue *internal balancing* to maximize their own relative military, economic, or other strengths.[6] Abe's statement at CSIS that Japan "is not now and will never be a tier two power" was an emphatic rejection of bandwagoning as an option. Indeed, Japan has not accepted Chinese hegemony in the thirteen centuries since the first emperor of Japan was declared a descendant of the Sun Goddess Amaterasu and imbued with divine legitimacy equal to China's older imperial line. Instead, Abe used his unprecedented seven-plus years as prime minister to embark on deliberate external and internal balancing strategies to restore a more favorable equilibrium vis-à-vis China.

In terms of external balancing, Abe revised Japan's long-standing ban on collective self-defense to allow intimate joint planning and military operations with the United States and other security partners like Australia for missions beyond the direct defense of Japan. He then announced a "Free and Open Indo-Pacific (FOIP)" strategy to counter Chinese hegemonic ambitions in Asia through increased diplomacy, military capacity building, and infrastructure financing for the region. When the Trump administration was searching for a framework and a title for its still unformed Asia policy in 2017, it borrowed the FOIP strategy as its own—as did the Biden administration four years later—while Australia and India signed on with the United States to Abe's earlier proposal for a "Quad" of the major maritime democracies in Asia.[7] European states concerned about China also began adopting the "Indo-Pacific" approach.[8]

If Abe was engaging in the kind of external balancing that realists would expect, however, it was external balancing with decidedly liberal internationalist characteristics. Under Abe, Japan invested in major multilateral trade and diplomatic agreements in order to reinforce rulemaking that might shape China's future behavior, rather than seeking to exclude China from regional cooperation. When the Trump administration withdrew from the Trans-Pacific Partnership (TPP), for example, Japan stepped in to complete the agreement and cement global trading norms in Asia (hoping for the United States' eventual return) while simultaneously concluding an intraregional trade agreement inclusive of China called the Regional Comprehensive Economic Partnership (RCEP). These moves prompted the Australian Lowy Institute to conclude in a 2019 review of regional power and influence that Japan had emerged as "the leader of the liberal order in Asia."[9]

This external balancing strategy was supplemented by internal balancing. Though Abe pushed through modest increases in Japan's defense budget, his effort was defined more by *qualitative* than *quantitative* balancing, which is to say that he drew primarily on organizational reform and unity of effort within Japan to align limited resources for maximum impact. Abe put in place the first fully functioning national security establishment in Japan's postwar history. This included establishing a new U.S.-style National Security Staff and official *National Security Strategy* document; enhancing the power of the Prime Minister's Office to guide personnel and policy decisions; empowering the uniformed military and Coast Guard in the policymaking process and conduct of operations; strengthening interoperability among the services and with the Coast Guard; and unifying intelligence analysis and security of information. Abe also attempted to squeeze more material power out of Japan's languishing economy by targeting reform in underperforming sectors, particularly tourism (which tripled under his tenure); stock market returns (with revised indexes to better reflect return on equity), and women's participation in the economy (which surpassed the U.S. level during Abe's tenure).

The overall results have not been uniformly successful, to be sure. Relations with neighboring Korea deteriorated and outreach to Russia faltered, leaving dangerous holes in Abe's external balancing strategy. His "Abenomics" delivered impressive returns in easily reformed sectors of the economy, but much growth resulted from monetary easing and stimulus packages that were less likely to sustain high economic performance over the longer term without deeper market-based structural reforms. With defense spending in Japan still below 1 percent of GDP in 2020, the new goals for strategic planning and joint military operations were not fully resourced.

Nevertheless, at a time when the United States was just beginning to debate a long-term strategy for competition with China, Japan had already defined its own. Four years before the Trump administration announced a focus on strategic competition with China in the 2017 *National Security Strategy of the United States of America*, Japan had already articulated a comprehensive approach to competition with China in its own 2013 *National Security Strategy*.[10] When President Joe Biden's future national security advisor Jake Sullivan and top Indo-Pacific coordinator Kurt Campbell argued in 2019 that Trump's approach was too zero sum and the United States had to find a strategy toward China of "competition without catastrophe," Japan was already implementing one.[11] As foreign policy scholars Hal Brands and Zack Cooper have noted, no other U.S. ally is engaged in *all* the aspects of strategic competition with China the way Japan is—from technology trade to military deterrence, values, diplomacy, and infrastructure.[12] While no senior American policymaker is self-consciously modeling U.S. strategy on Japan's example, the numerous points of convergence around Japan's approach are unmistakable.

CONSIDERING THE COUNTERARGUMENTS

Yet even as organizations like the Lowy Institute point to Japan as the new leader of the liberal international order in Asia and both the Trump and Biden administrations have adopted the key pillars of Japanese statecraft as their own, there is still residual doubt about Japan's actual capacity for successfully developing and executing a grand strategy. A generation of American foreign policy leaders with primary experience in Europe or the Middle East is still conditioned to view Japan as an adjunct to U.S. strategy rather than an increasingly successful thought leader in its own right. When I explain to senior U.S. foreign policy figures or members of Congress that no country has had more influence on U.S. China strategy in recent years than Japan, they are initially taken aback—but then usually agree after some reflection. It was telling that the lead article on Japan after Abe's resignation in the November/December 2020 issue of *Foreign Affairs* was titled, "The Underappreciated Power" and that the author, Brookings scholar Mireya Solís, had to once again remind readers why Japan has had such an impact on the entire world's approach to China and the maintenance of an open liberal order in the Indo-Pacific.[13]

Three negative assumptions about Japan's capacity and trajectory have been particularly pernicious. While they do not undermine the core argument of this book that Abe transformed Japanese statecraft, they do help to define some of the limitations Japan faces and therefore merit consideration at the outset.

The first source of skepticism is that Japan is hobbled by too many endogenous structural challenges to be able to shape its external security environment. Once seen as an unstoppable economic juggernaut set to overtake the United States, Japan is now often portrayed as a crippled giant with a declining population and an overly conservative business culture. There is no doubt that Japan faces serious demographic challenges, with the country's population aged seventy-five and over set to increase by 20 percent from 2020 to 2040.[14] However, the recent underestimation of Japan is as inaccurate as the earlier overestimation of Japanese power in the 1980s and 1990s. More to the point, Japan's inability to rely on economic growth alone as a source of national influence is precisely what has forced deliberate application of other previously underutilized instruments of national power, including the military, women's empowerment, soft power, trade negotiations, and external alliances and partnerships.[15] Other sources of power, such as immigration, may yet follow. Indeed, if relative economic power were the only measure of strategic influence, one would be hard pressed to explain how the United States remained the world's leading power after its share of global economic output dropped from 50 percent to 25 percent between 1945 and 1970 or how Britain retained global preeminence for over a century with a global share of economic output that never surpassed 10 percent (Japan's current share today is about 7 percent). The answer, in short, is *statecraft*. Still, even as Japan is skillfully doing more with less, the strategy will be bound by the fact that the denominator is not growing as it once did.

The fact that shortfalls in relative power are forcing smarter choices helps to address the second source of skepticism—that Japan or any democracy is capable of a "grand strategy." As I noted in my history of American statecraft in Asia, *By More than Providence*, the checks and balances, contestation, and transparency necessary for democratic governance confound the disciplined, secretive, and patient pursuit of national objectives that most scholars associate with a grand strategy.[16] Japan's story has been even more complicated by a postwar culture of pacifism in which Japanese politicians and scholars for decades eschewed the very word "strategy" as sounding too militaristic. Japan scholars have also noted for years the tendency for Japan's prewar and postwar bureaucracy to obscure the national direction in policymaking through polite subterfuge and factional infighting.[17] As Secretary of State

George Schultz lamented during the Cold War, with Japan you quickly went from "grand strategy to fruit puree."[18]

To the extent that American scholars saw an emerging competitive strategy in Japan after the Cold War, they tended to focus on economic strategy or "techno-nationalism" aimed primarily at challenging U.S. preeminence. However, that perspective fell into disfavor when Japan's economic miracle hit a wall in the 1990s.[19] It was in that context that I argued in *Japan's Reluctant Realism* (2001) that beneath the thick layers of postwar pacifism and democratic contestation, Japan remained a nation-state acutely aware of power, hierarchy, and prestige in the international system and was therefore responding to changes in the balance of power vis-a-vis China with a more proactive foreign policy.[20]

In a way, putting the word "grand" before strategy implies an elegance when the word is merely intended to posit comprehensive use of all instruments of national power beyond just military means. There is no doubt that major democracies act on perceived changes to structural changes in the international system no less than nondemocracies. However, they do so in what political scientist Richard Betts calls a "metaprocess that links ends and means effectively if not efficiently."[21] That metaprocess began in Japan over two decades ago in what I described at the time as "reluctant realism." It accelerated in different ways under both LDP and opposition DPJ governments. The debates within and among these parties are important, and postwar pacifism still shapes and constrains government choices in significant ways.[22] Japan does not and will not soon have the full national security toolkit of countries like the United States or Britain—if ever. However, the general trajectory of Japan's proactive counterbalancing vis-à-vis a rising China is clear. Japan is reluctant no more. For all its flaws, and despite ongoing debates on issues from technology decoupling to human rights, Japan arguably has the clearest conceptualization, consensus, and implementation of a grand strategy of any of the democracies confronting Chinese hegemonic ambitions in the Indo-Pacific. That does not mean, of course, that U.S. officials will not sometimes be frustrated by uniquely Japanese aspects of bureaucratic politics and political posturing—and the feeling is often mutual. Even at its strongest, the U.S.-UK "special partnership" had no shortage of such bureaucratic friction.[23] It was the clarity of strategic direction and common purpose—rather than the lack of friction—that made that relationship "special."

The third point of skepticism is that Abe was the exception rather than the rule—that his individual strategic attributes will not be repeated as Japan slides back into a more passive and reactive mode in his wake. There is no doubt, as we will see, that Abe prepared himself in unique ways to lead Japan at a moment of uncertainty and peril.[24] He took an unusual interest in history and strategy and learned from his failed tenure as prime minister in 2006–2007 when reconstituting his policies six years later. It may be some time before Japan has another decisive and strategically focused leader comparable to Abe. The Japanese public clearly recognized Abe's transformational legacy after he stepped down—an *Asahi Shimbun* survey found that 71 percent of the public approved of Abe's tenure, with a plurality pointing specifically to foreign affairs and defense as his greatest legacy.[25] In the Lowy Institute's 2018 *Asia Power Index*, Abe was ranked as the most effective leader in the entire region.[26] Indeed, there is even reason to wonder whether Japan might slide into another series of short-term prime ministers as it did after strong leaders like Nakasone Yasuhiro in the 1980s and Koizumi Junichiro in the 2000s.

However, the strategic trajectory that was consolidated under Abe is not likely to change soon. In part this is because the metaprocess that led to Abe's own grand strategy was well over a decade in the making. Abe pulled together the pieces, but he did not invent all of them. As we shall see, Abe's immediate predecessor from the DPJ, Noda Yoshihiko, attempted to pursue many of the same changes to Japan's defense and trade policies as Abe but was hamstrung by collapsing public support for the DPJ and internal fights in his coalition. Abe's successor in 2020, Suga Yoshihide, then pledged to continue Abe's security policies, while none of the rivals vying to replace Suga within the LDP proposed alternative strategic visions, emphasizing instead that they would be better at competing with China. The sharpest departure from Abe's foreign policy vision when he stepped down came from Edano Yukio, leader of the Constitutional Democratic Party (CDP) of Japan, who promised a somewhat more dovish foreign policy, but his party enjoyed only 15 percent in the polls in 2020 and had only 109 of 465 seats in the more powerful Lower House of the Diet.[27] Moreover, Edano's CDP chose not to challenge Abe or Suga on the core pillars of their strategy to push back against China's hegemonic ambitions, a point Edano and other party leaders have emphasized to me. Equally important, Abe's successors will all utilize and be bound by the changes in Japan's national security bureaucracy instituted between 2012 and 2020, including new authority for the prime minister and greater unity of the bureaucracy under the National Security Council (NSC). None of Abe's aspiring successors have said they would throw away those new tools of prime-ministerial strategy making.

Of course, if Japan's external environment dramatically changes, so will the current strategic framework. We will consider some of those black swan scenarios at the end of the book. We will also examine the major contenders for leadership in Japan to illuminate some of the variations that might be expected in the future. Absent major exogenous shocks, however, none are likely to put in place a grand strategy as transformative as Abe's. What is now in place is a grand strategy for the era of Abe Shinzō—not just the tenure of Abe Shinzō.

THE HISTORICAL CONTEXT: DEFINING THE LINE OF ADVANTAGE

An additional reason to expect that the broad contours of Abe's grand strategy will endure lies in an appreciation of Japanese geography and history. This is not the first time that Japanese leaders have been forced to realign institutions and foreign policy strategies to compete in a newly competitive geopolitical environment. In fact, if one looks for a strategy to contrast with the Yoshida doctrine, there are elements of Japan's position in the nineteenth century that resonate with the current situation. Faced with a collapsing Qing Empire in China and the rapacious expansion of Russia and the European imperial powers, Meiji leader Yamagata

Aritomo declared in 1890 that Japan had to think beyond its immediate territorial defense to consider where to draw the "line of advantage" (*riekesen*) to shape the external environment and prevent a rival power from controlling critical access points to Japan.[28]

Though Abe did not use the same words as Yamagata, his new proactive foreign and defense policies represent a similar search for the right "line of advantage" in the twenty-first century—but with one very important difference. Yamagata's first priority was to establish a naval buffer, but his line of advantage was soon drawn on the *continent* of Asia, beginning with dominance over the Korean peninsula, and then extending to Manchuria and China until finally Japan found itself choosing between war with the Anglo-American maritime democracies or retreat from China. Japan chose war with the maritime powers and suffered calamitous defeat as a result.[29] Abe's line of advantage, in contrast, is decidedly *maritime* and draws from an alternate vision of Japanese grand strategy from Yamagata's era that receded as the army, militarists, and continentalists came to dominate decision making in Tokyo in the early twentieth century. This alternate vision was championed by the young firebrand modernizer Sakamoto Ryoma in his 1867 Eight-Point Program for the Emperor Meiji, which called for a strong navy, alignment of Japan's currency with the silver standard, and convergence with international commercial norms and implicitly with the maritime powers.

As we will see in this volume, Abe and his government consistently and deliberately framed Japan's new grand strategy in maritime and cosmopolitan terms—as one can detect in the formulation of the Quad and the Free and Open Indo-Pacific vision. And while Abe's new line of advantage was deliberately rooted in a geographic concept—the importance of the seas to an island nation—it is also about competing to lead the agenda for rulemaking and norm setting regionally and globally, as befits a nation dependent on commerce. Abe's "proactive contribution to peace" aimed to defend the access points to Japan—from sea lanes to cyberspace—but through a contest of ideas, investment, alliances, and diplomacy rather than the strategies of preemptive military conquest of prewar Japan.[30]

Despite these important differences, the evocation of Sakamoto and earlier periods of Japanese history is helpful to our understanding of Japan's new grand strategy for three reasons. First, it proves that Japan can compete as a tier one power without defaulting to the brutal militarism of the 1930s and 1940s. The academic study of postwar Japanese foreign and security policy has been constrained for too long by the premise that Japan is trapped in a binary choice between pacifism and becoming a "normal" state with a full military repertoire. To be sure, Japan's anti-militarist culture since 1945 has been the focus of important theory building about the impact of norms on states' security policies, but those norms can also change in response to the structure of international politics—and in Japan's case they have in significant ways.[31] The Abe grand strategy does not avoid military instruments, but neither does it preference them over diplomatic, economic, and ideational tools. The misunderstanding on this point when Abe came to power led to a flurry of warnings about Japan's return to militarism.[32] But Abe's maritime and cosmopolitan framing of his strategy helped: Japan is now seen not as a revisionist state, but as one of the most important defenders of the international liberal order.

Second, a historical reflection on Japan's maritime strategy illuminates the natural priorities of an island nation. It is now well recognized that Japan's expansion of the line of advantage across the continent of Asia in the 1930s and 1940s represented a colossal misallocation of resources and risk for a nation dependent on the seas. It was not only morally wrong—it was strategically foolish. For Japan today, a strategy focused on alignment with other maritime powers aimed at reinforcing global standards for commerce and protection of the sea lanes has a logic that explains why Abe's legacy will likely endure and why advocates of alternate strategies to align with China or defy the United States have fallen into obscurity. The fact that the United States, Australia, and other maritime democracies have gravitated toward the same strategy and the construct of the "Indo-Pacific" will further reinforce the continuity of this framing. The early emergence, collapse, and then gradual postwar reemergence of maritime strategy therefore put important historical tailwinds behind Abe's transformation of Japan's foreign policies.

And third, while the maritime framing explains how Japan is effectively mustering its strengths around defense of sea lanes and global standards, it also helps to explain some of the persistent shortcomings in the new strategy. Japan has largely retreated from trying to shape the geopolitics of the Korean peninsula—the very target of Yamagata's original line of advantage. As we will see, the self-defeating drift in Japan's approach to South Korea cannot be explained by historical grievances or domestic politics alone. Under the maritime outlook, the Korean peninsula has clearly fallen in importance in Japan's grand strategy. Japan responded to the U.S.–Democratic People's Republic of Korea (DPRK) crisis in 2017 with alacrity but has not attempted to shape the geopolitics of the Korean peninsula for years—this is arguably the behavior of a maritime state consolidating its position offshore.

History thus provides critical context—but not just the history of the interwar years that has been used by political scientists as a contrast with Japan's postwar pacifism. As the Yoshida doctrine is replaced with a new grand strategy, Japan is making far better choices than it did a century ago. Through the maritime framing of his more proactive statecraft, Abe attempted to prove that the early twentieth century was the aberration in Japan's history and not the norm. This formulation does not absolve Japan of the damage it caused across Asia in the 1930s and 1940s, but it does provide a longer historical arc for understanding some of the enduring drivers Japan faces by dint of geography. For this reason, this book will place each aspect of Japanese statecraft in a broader historical context, beginning with choices made before Japan's descent into militarism.

ORGANIZATION OF THE BOOK

The following pages explain the logic, durability, and shortcomings of Abe's grand strategy by placing it in the context of Japanese geography and history; illuminating comparable strategic approaches by other powers in similar circumstances; tracing Japan's own choices from earlier periods of history to the present; and then detailing how Abe transformed Japan's diplomacy, defense, and economic policies for new circumstances.

Chapter 1 examines the geographic setting and national narratives that shaped Japan's search for security and prestige from the earliest recorded exchanges with China through Japan's confrontation with the West and modern reemergence as Asia's most active and effective champion of Western values. The chapter sets the broad historical context for debates about China, Korea, and the West but also focuses on definitions of Japan's role as a maritime power that began emerging as early as the seventeenth century. This intellectual lineage is important because it forms the basis for the maritime strategic framework behind Abe's approach to the U.S.-Japan alliance, the Quad, and the Free and Open Indo-Pacific.

Chapter 2 examines Japan's relationship with China—the greatest threat to Japanese sovereignty and security and the driver behind Abe's return to power in 2012, but also an economic partner that contributed to Japanese economic growth and thus Abe's own hold on power. This complex mix of interdependence and fierce geopolitical rivalry between what Council on Foreign Relations scholar Sheila Smith calls two "intimate rivals" sets the parameters for the elements of Japan's grand strategy in subsequent chapters.[33]

Chapter 3 turns to Japan's most important answer to the challenge posed by China—which is the U.S.-Japan alliance. After decades of avoiding entrapment in U.S. strategies of containment in Asia, Japan has embraced tighter security cooperation with the United States and accepted the risks of entrapment in Asian conflicts that this entails—all with the vision of keeping the United States locked in to the defense of the western Pacific. Too often Japan's renewed embrace of the U.S.-Japan alliance is portrayed as reluctant hedging against a rising China—or external pressure (*gaiatsu*) from Washington—when it would be better understood as proactive shaping of *U.S. choices* in order to counter China. As U.S. opinion polls illustrate and this chapter will explain in more detail, Abe was hugely successful in this endeavor.

Chapter 4 examines Japan's strategy for shaping regional order in what Tokyo and much of the world now call the Indo-Pacific. Here the earlier tracing of maritime strategy in chapter 1 becomes important to understanding the conceptual framework for competition with China over alignment, infrastructure, values, and institutions that will define the future of the region.

Chapter 5 tries to explain the Achilles heel in Japan's regional shaping strategy—relations with the two Koreas. The legacy of Japan's colonization of Korea obviously helps to explain the counterproductive standoff between Seoul and Tokyo at a time when both need closer alignment to manage shifting geopolitics in the region, but so too does the growing maritime strategy bias in Japan's regional outlook.

Chapter 6 ends the detailed case studies with an examination of Japan's efforts at internal balancing, focusing in particular on the establishment of a more centralized national security state that will define the tools available to—and the expectations of—future Japanese leaders.

The volume concludes with observations on the importance of Japan's choices for the preservation of stability and prosperity in Asia and a consideration of how leadership changes at home or unexpected structural changes abroad—such as U.S. retrenchment or Chinese liberalization— might change the trajectory of Japanese strategic thinking.

Abe's transformation of Japanese grand strategy is one of the most important developments in the modern international relations of Asia. Understanding where it came from and how it happened will help us all better assess the prospects for competition without catastrophe as China becomes more dominant in the twenty-first century.

1

THE HISTORIC ROOTS OF MODERN JAPANESE GRAND STRATEGY

China is mirroring Japan's mistake in the last century, only this time it is a continental power engaged in the folly of seeking maritime conquest.

—FORMER PRIME MINISTER ASO TARO TO THE AUTHOR, 2020

J apan is burdened by the ghosts of the first half of the twentieth century: by memories of brutal conquest across Asia that caused tens of millions of deaths, including millions of Japanese; by unresolved domestic debates about whether some Japanese leaders at the time—including Abe Shinzō's own grandfather Kishi Nobusuke—had nobler intentions; and by the continued insistence in the national narratives of China and the two Koreas that Japan remains dangerously unrepentant, even as polls show that the rest of Asia trusts Japan more than any other nation.[1]

Scholars of Japan also bend under these burdens of the past. The steady shift in Japanese thinking toward a more deliberate balance-of-power strategy vis-à-vis China has been accepted as the new normal, but it continues to be interpreted by many through the lens of Japan's past militarism—as a tug-of-war between Japan's postwar pacifist culture and external geopolitical pressures. This dialectical framing is not wrong and helps us to measure the pace of change and the constraints on Japan's national security toolkit. However, it tells us relatively little about the trajectory of Japanese strategy or Japan's agency in the international system—perpetuating aspects of the "reactive state" model of Japanese statecraft long after Japan has emerged, among the major democracies, as the most proactive shaper of regional order in Asia.[2]

Abe's intellectual allies have sought to liberate thinking on Japan's role in the world from the constraining box of the 1930s and 1940s. In *Rekishi no Kyōkun* (The lessons of history), for example, Abe's former deputy national security advisor Kanehara Nobukatsu urges readers to consider Japan's current responsibility to actively uphold democratic norms in precisely the context of the collapsing world order that precipitated Japan's descent into militarism and defeat eight decades ago.[3] Rather than presenting militarism as Japan's original sin and pacifism as the antidote, Kanehara argues that Japan made tragically flawed choices in the 1930s that almost destroyed the world order and thus has a particular responsibility to make strategic choices today that will save the liberal world order at a time of renewed opportunity and peril. Kanehara's use of the longer sweep of history may appear as a convenient retort to criticism of Abe's foreign policies from the left, but that is not his primary purpose. He seeks not to avoid Japan's dark past but instead to apply the lessons in a new way to strategic choices going forward.

Historians will debate the advantages of this larger contextualization of the twentieth century in terms of understanding the root causes of Japanese prewar militarism, but viewing contemporary Japanese policy choices in the longer sweep of history has important advantages for those trying to understand the roots and durability of Japan's current strategy. As was noted in the introduction, Japan's choices today are defined by geography as much as by wartime experience. Faced with the same geography over a century ago, Japanese leaders made the wrong choices—but it is important to remember that they had choices.

GEOGRAPHY AND JAPANESE STRATEGIC CHOICES

> *Geography helps determine whether a given polity will find itself relatively free from threat or surrounded by potential adversaries. Historical experience creates preconceptions about the nature of war and politics and may generate irresistible strategic imperatives. And ideology and culture shape the course of decision-makers and their societies in both conscious and unconscious ways.*
>
> —WILLIAMSON MURRAY

Japan's geography has always been inextricably intertwined with its strategic culture—for 1,500 years and still today. With the four main islands of Hokkaido, Honshū, Kyūshū, and Shikoku and another 6,800 smaller

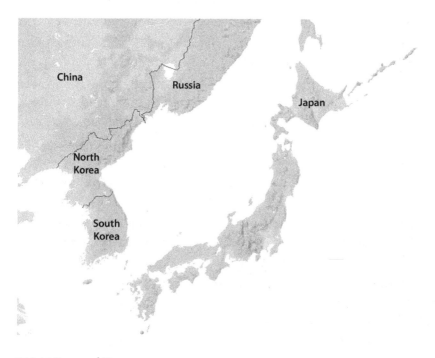

MAP 1.1 Japan and Korea

islands, the Japanese archipelago is slightly larger than the British Isles. But in contrast to Britain and other major maritime powers, Japan lacks arable land and navigable waterways. Covered with uninhabitable steep mountains, volcanoes, rivers, and forests, only 12 percent of Japanese land is arable, and over half of the population lives on 6 percent of the land around what are today Tokyo, Osaka, and Nagoya. Internal navigation in Japan is hampered by steep, shallow rivers descending from the mountains—useful only for irrigation and power generation but not navigation like the Thames or the Mississippi. For over a millennium, ocean navigation in Japan took place almost entirely along the inland seas between the main islands of Honshū, Shikoku, and Kyūshū. While the English built seagoing ships of powerful oak, the Japanese mariners found the lighter *hinoki* (cypress tree) both plentiful and adequate for inland navigation.[4]

At the same time, premodern Japan had far greater security from the seas than Britain enjoyed. The part of the Korean peninsula closest to Japan is 190 kilometers away (see map 1.1), a stark contrast to the English Channel, which separates Britain from continental Europe by a mere 21 kilometers. The weather over the Sea of Japan can be particularly harsh and unforgiving, as the Mongols found when their invading fleet was destroyed by typhoons (*kamikaze* or "divine wind") in 1274. Further afield, the closest point in China is 800 kilometers away, with rough seas half the year. Russian Sakhalin is only 45 kilometers from Japan's northern island of Hokkaido but is separated by even harsher seas and was populated by the Russians only in the last few centuries. The Western Hemisphere is 9,000 kilometers away. Nineteenth-century technologies—especially steam power—transformed Japanese thinking about the vulnerability of their home islands to the sea. But this happened centuries after Britain became the world's dominant maritime power. As with all things in its history, Japan was forced to catch up.

Meanwhile, the same archipelagic geography shaped Japan's internal political development. The patchwork of isolated valleys and islands with limited arable land contributed to collectivism and strong competition among local clans to the detriment of central leadership. This topography also vexed invaders, from the Toi in the eleventh century to the Mongols in the thirteenth century and the United States in 1945. In contrast to neighboring Korea, where clans and princedoms could be easily exploited by invaders to divide and conquer the peninsula, Japan's clans could engage in mutual warfare and competition without rendering the archipelago vulnerable to external conquest. Indeed, it has been a recurring feature of Japanese clan and factional strife that competition is exported—whether in the form of invasions of the Korean peninsula, the imperial army and navy's decision to fight both China and the Americans rather than resolve internal conflicts, or in the postwar era the decision to export excess manufacturing rather than allow competition to force the merger of major industrial groupings (*keiretsu*) at home.[5]

Not unlike Britain, Japan's geography and internal clan rivalries created a political culture that gave the sovereign *legitimacy* but also gave the nobility considerable *power*. The prince regent Shōtoku Taishi enshrined the rights of the Japanese nobility vis-à-vis the emperor in the "Twelve Grades of Cap Rank" four centuries before Britain's *Magna Carta*.[6] As a result, Japan—like Britain and America—changed regimes by restoring the rights of the conservative elite against overbearing sovereigns (Britain in 1688, America in 1776, and Japan in 1868). Peasant revolutions are the stuff of large continental powers like Russia, France, and China. Island nations are more fundamentally conservative.

It is also important to emphasize that despite its geographic distance and political insularity, Japan enjoyed constant interaction with continental Asia throughout recorded history. The Korean peninsula is just close enough that Japan could usually afford to import superior foreign technology or culture without the risk of political delegitimization. Chinese records show that the Yayoi people, who dominated Honshū and Kyūshū from 300 BCE until about 250 CE, knew of Chinese and Korean superiority and imported key technologies such as irrigated wet rice cultivation.[7] Later Han Chinese political culture, writing, and art, as well as Buddhism, flowed through the Korean peninsula to Japan. The threat of a major invasion, however, did not materialize until the Mongols took Korea more than a thousand years after the Yayoi began importing technologies from the continent through the peninsula. Japan therefore became adept at adapting and adopting external technologies and cultures to serve Japanese self-strengthening without the same devastating effect on regime legitimacy suffered by continental China and Korea. It was that fear of external technologies' being exploited by internal rivals that prompted the Tokugawa shogun to close Japan to the outside world after his consolidation of power with the Battle of Sekigahara in 1600.[8] When Japan opened again in the mid-nineteenth century, the Meiji reformers rallied to the four-character slogan "Wakon yōsai" ("Japanese spirit with Western learning") in an effort to harness the external technologies and reinforce Japan's autonomy from the West.

This distanced attention to continental Asia ensured that Japanese leaders were closely attuned to the nature of order, hierarchy, and competition in the outside world. This was *possible* as a matter of grand strategy because separation from the continent left time for observation, analysis, and consensus building. The focus on order and hierarchy was *necessary* because threats would build on the peninsula—and later in the northern islands and the western Pacific approaches—and because Japanese leaders' own legitimacy still derived from advances made using superior technologies from abroad. From the beginning, geography determined that Japan would compete in a hierarchical and often anarchic region.

JAPAN IN THE SINOCENTRIC ORDER

Attention to rank and autonomy inevitably meant that Japan would define its strategic coordinates relative to China, the historic center of East Asian civilization. Japan developed a political culture that stood on the edge of sinocentric Asia: respectful yet autonomous, seeking legitimacy from Chinese culture yet standing alone in its insistence on symbolic parity with China.

The eighth-century *Nihon Shoki* (Chronicles of Japan) survives as the second oldest book of Japanese classical history and the first to situate Japan within Asia. The *Chronicles*, written in part in classical Chinese, expressed respect for Chinese culture and borrowed Confucian concepts that the ruler's legitimacy is based on a divinely inspired hierarchical order.[9] Indeed, in the period leading up to the *Chronicles*, the Yamato Dynasty (250–710) had built its capital city of Nara and its penal and civil codes on Chinese Tang Dynasty models of planning and governance, which were recognized as superior. Yet the Yamato Dynasty also was the only dynasty in Asia to claim an imperial line similar to China's, using "emperor" (*tennō*) to describe its divine leader rather than "king" (*ō*). Channeling this chauvinism, the powerful prince Shōtoku angered the emperor of the Sui Dynasty by sending a message at the turn of the seventh century introducing himself as a regent of "the country where the sun rises" and characterizing China as "the country where the sun sets."[10]

Japanese cartographers and scholars continued seeking ways to define Japan's autonomy and prestige within a sinocentric international order even as Japan continued looking to China for art and cultural excellence. In the fourteenth century, the aristocrat Kitabatake Chikafusa elaborated on the earlier *Chronicles* with a new *Jinnō Shōtōki* (Chronicle of gods and sovereigns), which noted that "Japan is the divine country. The heavenly ancestor it was who first laid its foundations, and the Sun Goddess left her descendants to reign over it forever and ever. This is true only in our country, and nothing similar may be found in foreign lands. That is why it is called the divine country."[11] By the early eighteenth century this chauvinism toward China was represented in the writings of scholars like geographer Nishikawa Joken, who argued that isolation from China was itself the source of Japanese superiority: "Our country is the eastern crown of the myriad nations, the land upon which the morning sun first shines, the first to feel its invigorating rays, the land from which thunder and lightning powerful arise. The name *Nihon* ('Source of the Sun') is most fitting."[12]

The search for legitimacy in a sinocentric world was also popularized by authors such as Hiraga Gennai, whose 1763 satirical novel *Fūryū Shidōken Den* (The stylish life of Shidōken) mocked Chinese customs:

> The customs of China are not like those of Japan. Their emperors are like vagabonds; when people tire of them, they are replaced by violent

overthrow, accompanied by a lot of big talk about the realm belonging to all under heaven and not merely one man. It being such a rascally country, the sages emerged to give instruction to it. In Japan, if the emperor were abused in this way even tiny children would be outraged and unable to remain silent, as we are a country of steadfast loyalties. That is why our emperors have no equal in any of the countries of the world.[13]

It is striking how much Japan's emerging identity as an island state paralleled distant Britain's own journey in the same period; Nishikawa and Hiraga were proclaiming Japan's purity and uniqueness, British parliamentarians and pamphleteers in London were similarly constructing a pure and industrious "British" identity in opposition to the slovenly "Catholic and French other" on the continent of Europe.[14] There were important differences, however. Britain's regal line came from Hanover in Germany and before that from the House of Orange in the Netherlands. British politics and strategy were thus deeply enmeshed in the politics of continental Europe, whereas Japan's politics and strategy were not yet intertwined with China and the continent of Asia. Japan also rarely faced a maritime threat from imperial China the way Britain did from imperial Spain or France (the exception for Japan being the Mongol invasion from Korea in the late thirteenth century, after which the Mongol Empire collapsed). Britain established itself as the most powerful maritime nation on earth in large part because of the need to defeat these threats at sea, but Japan was able to retreat from even its modest seagoing traditions by the seventeenth century to focus on containing internal threats because China retreated from the oceans after the fourteenth century. And Britain and Japan faced continental power distributions that were fundamentally different: Britain was able to shape the balance of power in a multipolar European continent plagued by competition among the Habsburgs, Hohenzollerns, and Bourbons, among others, whereas Japan usually faced a unipolar imperial power on the continent of Asia.

At the same time, Japan retained a sharp interest in developments on the Korean peninsula, much as Britain endeavored to prevent a continental hegemon from dominating the Low Countries and gaining easy access across the Channel. While, in the premodern era, Japan only rarely reached beyond the peninsula to affect the balance of power within the continent the way British diplomats did through alliances or war, Japanese leaders nevertheless attempted to shape the balance of power on the Korean peninsula for reasons of self-defense or self-validation. Like the British in Flanders, Japan resorted to direct invasion of Korea when opportunity or necessity dictated.

Indeed, Korea was a "dagger aimed at the heart of Japan" long before the Meiji-era leader and founder of Japan's national army, Yamagata Aritomo, famously borrowed that phrase in the late nineteenth century from a Prussian staff officer to describe the dangers of Russia or the other imperial powers controlling the peninsula in the waning years of the Qing Empire.[15] The *Chronicles of Japan* described how the Yamato Dynasty had consolidated its political base in the southern island of Kyūshū by the early fourth century and then expanded onto the southern tip of the Korean peninsula in pursuit of more sophisticated means of production for pottery and ironwork. By the end of the fourth century, the Yamato had successfully established a governing body to control the Gaya Kingdom around the modern Korean city of Gimhae. When the powerful Goguryeo Kingdom to the northeast began expanding southward into the third kingdom of Baekje in 399, the Baekje and Gaya requested 50,000 Yamato "naval infantry" (*suigun*) to help repel the invaders. The Goguryeo prevailed and the Japanese withdrew—only to return in 663 in an unsuccessful attempt to help restore the Baekje. Defeated by the combined armies of the Silla Kingdom and the rising Tang Dynasty in China, the Japanese retreated home once again.[16]

This pattern repeated itself for centuries. When China was weak, Japan expanded onto the peninsula. When China was strong, Japan retreated from the peninsula. The Korean kingdoms' intramural rivalry—and later factional intrigue within the Korean court—drew in Japanese and Chinese intervention and accelerated collisions caused by the shifting balance of power among the two larger powers. Distracted by internal warfare, Japan did not mount a major invasion of Korea again until the late sixteenth century, when the powerful warlord Toyotomi Hideyoshi struck in the waning days of China's Ming Empire. His invasions ultimately failed, but they also contributed to the Ming's imperial over-reach and demise a few years later at the hands of the Manchu invaders from the north. As the Manchu's Qing Empire rose to power, Japan retreated in isolation under the Tokugawa Shogunate's closed state (*sakoku*) period and only returned to the peninsula when the Qing Empire began to collapse under the pressure of encroaching European powers two centuries later. Korean factionalism and Sino-Japanese rivalry evoke these same dynamics for historians in Japan, South Korea, and China today, as we shall see.[17]

Yet in the eighteenth century, Japan still enjoyed natural buffers from the sea that protected the archipelago from the ravages suffered by continental Asia. As the geographer Nishikawa put it in 1791, reflecting the prevailing view of the Tokugawa leaders: "The defenses of Japan are superior to those of any country in the world. Small countries bordering on great ones are almost always forced to submit to the larger country or are even absorbed it in the end. Japan is geographically close to a great power, but the two are separated by a rough sea that keeps them relatively distant from one another. Thus, Japan has never suffered the misfortune of having to submit to a great power, much less be annexed by one."[18] This splendid isolation would not last.

WESTERN IMPERIALISM AND THE FIRST EMERGENCE OF MARITIME STRATEGY

Decades before the arrival of Commodore Matthew Perry's "Black Ships" in Edo Bay in 1853—and about the same time that Nishikawa boasted of Japan's superior geographic position vis-à-vis the continent—a small group of Japanese scholars began warning that their archipelago was in fact highly vulnerable to the encroaching European maritime powers. In 1791 military theorist Hayashi Shihei (1738–1793) warned in *Kaikoku Heidan* (Discussion concerning military matters of a maritime nation) that "from Nihonbashi in Edo to China and the Netherlands, there are no visible borders but just waterways," and thus "our adversaries can attack whichever coast they like with their ships. Therefore, we cannot simply rest on advantages of an island nation."[19] Hayashi advocated ship-building, forging of cannons, and modern military drill (as opposed to individual mastery of the sword then prevalent): all of which were for-bidden by the Tokugawa Shogunate. These notions, which would later define Japanese grand strategy, were still treasonous. The woodblocks used for Hayashi's publication were confiscated by officials and disap-peared until naval strategists in the Meiji period reprinted his works to great acclaim a century later.

Nevertheless, these new maritime defense theories (*kaibōron*) con-tinued to spread. The Anglo-French victory over the Qing Empire in the First Opium War (1839–1842) fueled interest in the permissible study of Western knowledge around the small Dutch trading outpost at Dejima near Nagasaki. One of the leading scholars of the so-called Dutch School, Sakuma Shōzan (1811–1864), argued that it was time for Japan to absorb "not theories of government and ethics, but highly ingenious techniques and machinery, borrowed so that we might be prepared to ward off indignities from the West."[20] The major lesson of Western learning, explained the Mito lord Tokugawa Nariaki in 1846, was that "for a maritime nation (like Japan), warships should be the first line of defense."[21] As Hotta Masayoshi, who headed the shogun's council at the time of Japan's negotiations with the United States, put it in 1857, "Military power always springs from national wealth" and that wealth is "principally to be found in trade and commerce." Thus Japan should "conclude friendly alliances, send ships to foreign countries everywhere and conduct trade, copy the foreigners where they are at their best and repair our own shortcomings, foster our national strength and complete our armaments."[22] The Dutch School modernizer and founder of Keio University, Fukuzawa Yukichi, echoed these sentiments when he urged emulation of Britain's grand strategy to "expand the navy so that we can achieve purposes as a country built on commerce."[23]

Yet at the same time that these cosmopolitan maritime defense theo-ries emerged, other intellectuals were arguing that technological mod-ernization should instead be used to reinvigorate the traditional martial prowess that had distinguished Japan from China. The seas had made

Japan vulnerable—it was true—but most of the Meiji leaders who led Japan's modernization in the second half of the nineteenth century saw army expansion as more essential to establishing a new national identity and restoring confidence in the Japanese martial virtue that had been lost when the West asserted its dominance over China.[24]

One of the earliest expressions of this view was the scientist Satō Nobuhiro's 1823 treatise *Kondō Hisaku* (Secret strategy for expansion), which argued that Japan could counter the European threat only by developing an authoritarian form of government and harnessing Western technology to conquer East Asia before the West did. Satō advocated the invasion of Manchuria, Korea, and Southeast Asia—foreshadowing what would become Japan's 1940 Greater East Asia Co-Prosperity Sphere.[25] Later, the Chōshū samurai Yoshida Shōin (1830–1859), an intellectual godfather to several of the leaders of the Meiji Restoration before he was executed by the Tokugawa Shogunate as a rebel in 1859, similarly argued that Japan needed *continental* buffers. "Taking advantage of favorable opportunities," he said, "we will seize Manchuria, thus coming face to face with Russia; regaining Korea, we will keep watch on China; taking the islands to the South, we will advance on India."[26]

The contrasting strategic choices facing Japan as it entered the world stage were later captured in the liberal writer Nakae Chōmin's treatise, *Discourse by Three Drunkards on Government*.[27] In the discourse, one of the three drunkards is identified as a "man of Western learning" who is hopelessly naive and idealistic and calls for Japan to "shame" the European powers by embracing small-power liberalism, foreswearing arms, and establishing an egalitarian democracy. His red-faced chauvinistic antagonist, the "Champion of the East," argues that war and expansion are inevitable, declaring that "there is a large country [China]. . . . it is vast and rich in natural resources . . . however, it is very weak. . . . Why shouldn't we go and tear off a half or a third of that country? If we issue an imperial decree summoning all the able-bodied men of our nation, we should be able to gather at least four or five hundred thousand men. . . . Our small nation will instantly change into a Russia or a Great Britain." Master Nankai, the inebriated voice of "sweet reason," rejects both extremes but offers no path of his own, a reflection of Nakae

Chōmin's own recognition of the unresolved tensions in Japan's emerging national identity and strategic choices.

One finds these same tensions in the career of one of the leading protagonists of the Meiji Restoration, the ambitious young *rōnin* Sakamoto Ryōma. A master swordsman and early advocate of anti-Western resistance under the slogan "sonnō jōi [revere the emperor, expel the barbarian]," the swashbuckling Sakamoto set out in 1862 to assassinate the Tokugawa government's leading naval expert and proponent of opening, Katsu Kaishū. Instead of killing Katsu, however, Sakamoto became so intrigued by the Tokugawa bureaucrat's brilliance that he became his protégé and a leading voice for maritime strategy among the new Meiji Restoration forces. In 1865 Sakamoto established Japan's first trading company and began smuggling guns by sea to the Chōshū Clan forces battling the shogunate. The next year he successfully brokered an alliance between Chōshū and its rival Satsuma Clan, which led to the collapse of Tokugawa power and positioned Sakamoto as a central figure in the negotiations for restoration of imperial rule. In those negotiations he presented a strategic vision for the modernization of Japan in his 1867 Eight-Point Program, which called for a strong navy, alignment of Japan's currency with the silver standard, and convergence with international commercial norms. Only three months before the succession of Emperor Meiji to power, Sakamoto was assassinated at the age of thirty-one, but his Eight Points were incorporated in new imperial decrees and set the template for a modernizing Japan.[28] (When Japan's *Asahi Shimbun* newspaper asked 200 leading executives and intellectuals in 1999 what historical figure modern Japan needed the most, Sakamoto topped the list.)[29]

Despite the successful adoption of Sakamoto's vision by the new Meiji government, however, the original divisions over national strategy were embedded in the contrasting cultures of the Chōshū and Satsuma statesmen now in charge. The more powerful Chōshū Clan, which had been the first in Japan to form a conscript army of nonsamurai (the *kiheitai*) in 1863, dominated the new imperial army. The weaker Satsuma Clan, which had a pronounced maritime orientation because of its nominal suzerainty over the Ryukyu Kingdom (Okinawa) since 1609, sourced the nascent navy.[30] For Chōshū leaders like Yamagata Aritomo, the highest priority after the restoration of imperial rule in 1868 was suppression of the more than one hundred revolts and peasant uprisings against the new government and the establishment of a shared patriotism through a national army that touched all provinces of Japan. The navy had a more difficult time winning support for its mission, having fought only one minor battle for the new government off Awaji Island in 1868 and drawing its recruits from more limited geographic locations.

When the navy finally established its own status as a separate ministry in 1873, it was fortunate to have as the first minister none other than Katsu Kaishū. Katsu was a truly renaissance figure, and it is not entirely surprising that he charmed the assassin Sakamoto and won him to his cause. Born Katsu Yoshikuni in 1823 to a minor samurai, Katsu took the nickname "Kaishū" (Ocean Ship) after graduating as the first midshipman of the Dutch-taught naval academy that was established in Nagasaki after the arrival of Commodore Matthew Perry's black ships. Fluent in Western languages and an expert on naval architecture, Katsu had commanded the Dutch-built sail and steam corvette *Kanrin-Maru* on Japan's first diplomatic mission to the United States in 1860.[31] As navy minister, Katsu inculcated a spirit of internationalism and technological prowess but was hobbled by his status as a former Tokugawa Shogunate official and by his service's inability to articulate a compelling mission to the other army-oriented Meiji leaders. Initially the navy ministry tried to justify increased spending by arguing for a South Seas colonial empire, much as strategists in the newly ambitious imperial German and U.S. navies were proposing at the same time.[32] Katsu and his successors made little traction until the imperial Japanese army suddenly took an interest in the Qing Empire's naval buildup in the late 1880s. For Yamagata and the army, naval power was suddenly necessary to secure access to the Korean peninsula, where internal political intrigues and great-power rivalry were putting into play the "dagger aimed at the heart of Japan."

The navy now rapidly modernized with the introduction of British and French warships and training in gunnery and tactics from the British Royal Navy. When the fleet of Admiral Itō Sukeyuki faced the larger Chinese *Beiyang* fleet at the mouth of the Yalu River in the opening of the Sino-Japanese War in 1894, Japan's "Flying Squadron" of fast cruisers led the main battle fleet at high speed around the Chinese fleet, sinking most of the imperial Chinese navy's capital ships and ensuring Japanese domination over the Yellow Sea until final victory in 1895. Ten years later, Admiral Tōgō Heihachirō's fleet defeated Russian admiral Zinovy Rozhetsvensky's fleet in a similarly brilliant tactical strike at Tsushima (crossing Rozhetsvensky's "t" like Tōgō's hero Nelson had at the Battle of Trafalgar a century earlier). Japan was now recognized as one of the world's leading naval powers. As an excited Theodore Roosevelt wrote to Captain Alfred Thayer Mahan, who had been advocating an alignment of the United States, Britain, and Japan to safeguard the Pacific against the more authoritarian continental powers, "Japan is playing our game!"[33]

THE FOLLY OF CONTINENTAL EXPANSION

The U.S. Naval War College historian S. C. M. Paine argues in her study of Japanese prewar strategy that the victories over China and Russia were shaped primarily by maritime strategic approaches and secondarily by the objectives for ground conquest on the continent.[34] After the Battle of Tsushima the imperial Japanese navy's prestige and influence were at an all-time high. The view of internationalists in the navy and some political leaders like Itō Hirobumi was captured by "Japan's Alfred Thayer Mahan," the naval theorist and captain (later vice admiral) Satō Tetsutarō, who argued in 1908 that Japan's victory over Russia had secured for the nation a "first-tier" status and that Japan now needed to follow the example of its new ally Britain, which had achieved security for the homeland only after shedding its continental holdings in Europe.[35] The British naval historian G. A. Ballard observed in his 1921 study, *The Influence of the Sea on the Political History of Japan*, that after losing battles larger than Trafalgar to Korea in the sixteenth century because of a tendency to view the maritime domain as ancillary to land campaigns, Japan had finally developed a maritime strategic outlook. Japan, Ballard declared, was now the third maritime power in the world after

Britain and the United States, with, he hoped, comparable "moderation, restraint, and political sagacity" to ensure that "the North Pacific is not likely to carry the rumble of heavy gunfire in our time if self-control and reasoned sense prevail."[36]

Yet this vision of a respected maritime power—securing the ocean approaches for commerce and self-defense while skillfully engaging in offshore balancing and alignment alongside the other leading maritime powers—was already colliding with a new strategy of continental expansion emanating from the imperial Japanese army and hypernationalists in the political realm. The structure of domestic and international politics would conspire against the maritime thinkers and collapse Japanese strategic culture into the dark recesses represented by Nakae Chōmin's red-faced "Champion of the East." In the second decade of the twentieth century, the Meiji oligarchs died off (beginning with Itō Hirobumi, who was assassinated in Harbin in 1909), leaving political parties too weak to sustain political control; the European powers destroyed themselves in the fields of Flanders, creating a power vacuum in Asia; America turned inward; and China began to restore its own national autonomy as a republic, igniting the angst of the continental expansionists in the imperial Japanese army. Then global financial calamity in 1929 dealt a blow to the premise that national security and prestige could be achieved through economic convergence with the West and open global commerce.[37]

The imperial Japanese navy was not innocent in the subsequent descent toward militarism, but, as the historian W. G. Beasley notes in his classic study of Japanese imperialism, the navy leadership "had the reputation of being moderates, that is, less concerned than their army colleagues with opportunities for territorial acquisition, more interested than them in trade and emigration. This made them natural allies as a rule of those groups in Japanese society whose influence and ambitions derived from the growth of national wealth."[38]

The army was the more powerful service, of course, and more radicalized from within by the impact of economic displacement in the 1930s and Japan's precarious position on the continent vis-à-vis both Chiang Kai-shek's Chinese nationalists and the Soviet Union. Within the army, the "Imperial Way Faction" (Kōdōha) agitated for preemptive war against the Soviets and expansion into China. When young officers of the Imperial Way Faction attempted a bloody coup on February 26, 1936, the faction was disbanded, but officers in the Kwantung Army in China seized the initiative the next year to precipitate a war for conquest on the mainland that propelled Japan toward direct confrontation with the United States and Britain.

In late 1941 Prime Minister Tōjō Hideki's army-dominated cabinet concluded that Germany would win the war in Europe, allowing Japan to knock out the United States, Britain, and the Netherlands in a lightning strike to preserve Japanese control over China and establish autarky in East Asia. The navy leadership, most notably Admiral Yamamoto Isoroku, harbored profound doubts about the chances of success but nevertheless led the assaults against the Anglo-American strongholds in Hawaii, the Philippines, and Singapore in December 1941.[39] The British admiral Ballard had warned in 1921 that if he was wrong about Japan's future, the Pacific could "become the highway to one of the most sanguinary racial conflicts that ever convulsed the world."[40] He may have underestimated the devastation. Having known little but military victories for generations, the Japanese people suffered the greatest military defeat in their history. As the historian Iokibe Makoto observed decades later in the preface to his *Diplomatic History of Postwar Japan*, his country's slide toward ruinous war in the twentieth century was the direct result of a maritime power foolishly choosing to gain security through expansion on the continent.[41]

THE POSTWAR SEARCH FOR STRATEGY

For a Japan destroyed in material, political, and spiritual terms, after the war there was little room for grand strategic debates about how to defend against Western powers or maximize autonomy within Asia. Instead, Japan's early postwar debates focused on national survival and recovery. The political left gravitated to socialism or communism, which had been banned before the war and offered pacifist neutralism but no path to recovery. For the conservatives, who still constituted the majority of the ruling elite thanks to American occupation, there were two broad camps that reflected—but did not replicate—the prewar schisms in Japanese politics. As political scientist Richard Samuels explains, the mainstream conservatives (*hoshu honryū*) generally held the view that economic recovery through aligning with great powers was a prerequisite to strengthening national security. They rejected military spending and "accepted unequal alliance with the United States and used it as a shield behind which they could regenerate prosperity."[42] These mainstream conservatives were opposed by the so-called *anti*-mainstream conservatives (*hoshu-boryu*), who cast the mainstream as overly subservient to the West and argued that they themselves were "imbued with traditional nationalist (though not ultranationalist) sentiments, [and] held to an organic vision of Japan as a unique 'national polity' (*kokutai*), distinguished primarily by its imperial institution and neo-Confucian values, which emphasize unity and sacrifice for the national order."[43] The anti-mainstream conservatives advocated rewriting Japan's pacifist 1947 constitution and pursuing a more independent yet equal Japanese security and foreign policy role, though they differed over whether that would come through more shared regional security responsibilities with the United States or greater autonomy through normalization with China and Russia.

While the anti-mainstream leader Hatoyama Ichirō became the first leader of the Liberal Democratic Party (LDP) in 1955, which ruled without interruption until the end of the Cold War, it was the mainstream conservatives who defined the agenda and dominated the party thereafter. The architect of their approach was Yoshida Shigeru, prime minister in 1946–1947 and then 1948–1955. Yoshida established the contours of a foreign and economic policy that proved unassailable for decades: Japan would ally with the United States for protection, markets, and technology and to avoid debilitating domestic debates about rearmament; Japan would focus above all else on economic recovery; Japan would engage in minimal rearmament to ensure that it was not abandoned by the United States; and Japan would defy the anti-mainstream conservatives' call for revising the constitution and would keep Article Nine as a check against entrapment by the United States in future wars in Asia.[44] A former ambassador to Britain and nemesis to the wartime Tōjō government, Yoshida recentered Japanese foreign policy on convergence with the maritime powers while seeking new tools to preserve and enhance Japanese autonomy by ensuring economic recovery, minimizing defense obligations, and rehabilitating relations with Asia.

Yoshida's vision for a broad and inclusive agenda worked. The socialists hardened ideologically on the left in opposition to the U.S.-Japan alliance and constitutional reform, and many anti-mainstream conservatives hardened on the right in favor of constitutional reform and more security independence. This left most of the LDP positioned to occupy the center, where they could keep the focus on economic growth, the Japanese peoples' highest priority.[45] Earlier ideological divisions moved below the surface. Mainstream conservative heirs to the prewar Liberal Party under Yoshida formed the dominant faction within the LDP, later forming governments under Satō Eisaku, Tanaka Kakuei, Takeshita Noboru, and Obuchi Keizō—many of these noted for pork barrel scandals as their faction gained control of national budgets but also for their equitable distribution of growth to the countryside. A second strand of mainstream conservatives gravitated to the factions led by Ikeda Hayato, Ōhira Masayoshi, Suzuki Zenkō, and Miyazawa Kiichi, all noteworthy for their technocratic emphasis on economic performance over security policy and their relatively clean reputations. The anti-mainstream conservatives formed governments under Abe Shinzō's grandfather, Kishi Nobusuke, and then Fukuda Takeo. Other anti-mainstream conservatives followed the line from Kōno Ichirō to the government of Nakasone Yasuhiro in the 1980s.

Kishi in those early years experimented with many of the ideas that would later animate his grandson Abe Shinzō. Kishi was profoundly anticommunist and suspicious of the left. He believed that Japan's own security depended on the fate of the Western camp as a whole and not just Asia. He wanted Japan to take greater risk in support of the U.S.-led international order but also to establish Japan as a more equal partner of the United States within that order. He was drawn to India as a symbol of Japan's legitimate views of anti-imperialism and Asian solidarity, and he believed that some restoration of nationalism was healthy for Japan.[46]

Other anti-mainstream politicians followed his lead, propelling Japan toward the strategic outlook we associate with Abe—but this only proved politically sustainable for brief periods, with the mainstream factions and the Yoshida doctrine inevitably returning to define Japan's overall strategy. After Kishi pushed through the revised mutual security treaty with the United States in 1960, his successors eschewed geopolitics and pledged instead to double Japan's national income. After Nakasone pledged that Japan would be America's "unsinkable aircraft carrier" against the Soviets in the 1980s, his successors retreated from geopolitics and then stumbled badly when the United States called on Japan for assistance in the 1990–1991 Gulf War.[47] With wartime memories so recent for a generation of political leaders and Japan's economic miracle so successful, there seemed little utility in proactive geopolitical strategies.

REALIST THEORIES OF PEACE

Outside the glare of national politics, however, a small group of self-proclaimed national security realists in Japanese universities began searching for a new grand strategy that would rely on neither idealistic postwar pacifism nor discredited prewar militarism. While these scholars were drawn to the assumptions of prominent realists in the United States like Hans Morgenthau, they were also constrained by the Japanese peoples' anti-militarism and lingering memories of ruinous war. As a result, they turned to what international relations scholar Kamiya Matake (a progeny of one of those early realists) calls a realistic liberalism, in which

- the role of the state is still paramount but in an interdependent world;
- the role of military power is a critical determinant in the hierarchy of international relations but is not always the most important factor;

- military power is essential to the maintenance of peace and order but less important to statecraft overall as economic and cultural power become key; and
- international organizations reflect the real balance of power but are also important forums to incorporate the interests, prosperity, and security of less powerful states.[48]

In short, postwar Japanese realists sought to justify a focus by the nation's leaders and public on power politics in the international system while recognizing that Japan's toolkit would be severely restrained and dependent on alignment with the United States.

The postwar realists also sought examples from earlier liberals and internationalists in Japanese history that would legitimize the "Japaneseness" of their strategic views while offering a clear break from the darker elements of the prewar debate. For example, one of the most influential postwar realist intellectuals, Kōsaka Masataka of Kyoto University, had learned international relations and philosophy from his famous father, Kōsaka Masaaki of the prewar "Kyōto School," which had turned to German philosophy in the 1930s to construct an ideology in Japan of national socialism around the uniqueness of Japanese culture and history. Kōsaka the younger often complained of being forced to learn Johann Herder and Martin Heidegger in German as a boy, but he also concluded that he could not ignore the role of nationalism and national identity in his own postwar studies on Japanese strategy.[49] His concern was that postwar Japanese had lost their sense of national purpose. He sought a new philosophy that would reflect both national interest and internationalism, in the spirit of Nitobe Inazō, the early-twentieth-century diplomat and scholar who had championed the League of Nations while writing the book *Bushido* to explain the unique essence of the Japanese national character to the West.[50] It was particularly important for the postwar realists to frame Japan's strategy in terms that preserved a unique role and identity apart from the United States within Asia, while reinforcing the credibility of the U.S.-Japan alliance and Japan's commitment to universal norms.

The realists were isolated and under siege from a Japanese media and academic world that largely viewed the concept of alliance and activism in international security with revulsion. The leading critic of the realists was Tokyo University professor Maruyama Masao, a survivor of the Hiroshima bombing who attacked the U.S.-Japan alliance system for perpetuating the hypernationalism of the prewar era.[51] Other scholars on the left, like Maruyama's Tokyo University colleague Sakamoto Yoshikazu, acknowledged the anarchic nature of the international system but called for Japan to place its defense forces directly under the United Nations to ensure independence from the United States and an adequate break from militarism.[52] In many respects, intellectuals of the left harnessed self-determination and nationalism in a way that the outnumbered center-right realists found far more difficult to counter in the antimilitarist environment of the early postwar decades.[53]

After leftist professors encouraged their students to join in massive civil protests against the 1960 revision of the U.S.-Japan Security Treaty, the realists became even more prolific and began attracting supporters from among anti-mainstream political leaders—and not a few mainstreamers as well. Kamiya's father, the scholar Kamiya Fuji, wrote at the time that the Japanese public must understand that "the essence of international politics is the intersection of power politics and national interests."[54] The Kyoto University professor Inoki Masamichi, who taught the younger Kōsaka and later emerged as a major advisor on national security to Japanese prime ministers like Nakasone in the 1980s, attacked the progressives for their fascination with Marxist dictatorships and their utopian pacifism.[55]

Initially the postwar realists engaged in a fight to defend the very concept of "national interest" as a legitimate topic of scholarly discussion, but in the wake of the 1960 antitreaty demonstrations, they began offering ways to think about the direction of postwar Japanese national security strategy. They were motivated in large measure by the changes in the security treaty, which now accepted U.S. bases under Article VI as necessary for the "security of the Far East" and thus implied a role for a sovereign Japan in regional security policy (the original 1951 treaty had been negotiated under U.S. occupation). It was in that context that Kōsaka Masataka wrote his first major essay in 1963, "Genjitsushugisha no Hei-waron" (A realist's views on peace).[56] In the treatise, he sought to establish enduring principles of international relations that applied to Japan rather than slip into the left/right split that he thought had distorted the debate up to that point. Marrying the prevailing intellectual idealism of his day with a hardheaded realism, he asserted that deterrence, alliances, and a balance of power were all necessary strategies on the way to creating the conditions for a more idealistic world of intra-Asian peace and disarmament. Significantly, Kōsaka argued that Japan had the ability to influence the balance of power in Asia based on a combination of economic development, the U.S.-Japan alliance, and technological competitiveness. The postwar order, he saw, was about competition through means other than seizing territory, and Japan had the tools to play that new game without resorting to dangerous prewar militarism.[57] Though he did not say so, Kōsaka was essentially trying to find a new definition of Japan's line of advantage.

For Kōsaka the logical framework for his postwar definition of national interest and identity was a variation of the cosmopolitanism of Japan's early Meiji maritime strategy. In 1965 he wrote *Kaiyō Kokka Nihon no Kōsō* (The concept of Japan as a maritime nation), which argued that Japan relied on the seas for its commerce and security and therefore needed the U.S.-Japan alliance, but that the oceans could also be the source of Japan's independent identity and purpose as a leader in trade, investment, science, and the expansion of international law.[58] He lamented that Prime Minister Ikeda Hayato's vision of "doubling Japan's national income" the year before had no basis in Japanese culture other than as a means to an end, that Japan as a maritime power would never be part of a sinocentric system but could reject neither Asia nor the West, that Japan must be more assertive, and that it could do so peacefully in alliance with the United States from the sea.[59] In effect, Kōsaka turned Japan's unique archipelagic position from a source of isolation and complacency into a raison d'être for standing side by side with the other great democratic powers of the world in support of stability, commerce, and rule of law.

Yet while Kōsaka's vision of a Japanese liberal-realist maritime strategy resonated with growing numbers of his students, public intellectuals, and LDP politicians, it remained a minority view within the larger national discourse. With Japan's economy surging to number two in the world by the 1980s, there was no urgency to the strategic debate. Japan now enjoyed closer commercial ties to China than the United States. With the sudden appreciation of the yen in the 1985 Plaza Accord of the G-7 finance ministers, the value of the yen almost doubled in value, vaulting Japan to the number two spot behind the United States in the United Nations and the international financial institutions of the Bretton Woods system and opening the spigots of Japanese investment in Southeast Asia, Latin America, and the United States itself. Politicians in the 1980s were animated by the concept of "comprehensive national security," which was more of a license to spend money on foreign policy than a competitive strategy, as we shall see.[60] Some of Japan's *means* were obvious, but the *ends* and *ways* of strategy proved elusive.

Nevertheless, within the ruling LDP a small group of midlevel politicians like Shiina Motoo, scion of Kishi-protégé and former foreign minister Shiina Etsusaburō, steadily began winning allies for a more proactive Japanese security role as a member of the Western camp (I worked for Shiina in the Diet from 1987 to 1989 while studying at Tokyo University). Many of the ideas that later animated Abe and his allies were developed in this period by scholar-diplomats around Shiina like Ambassador Okazaki Hisahiko, a veteran of the foreign ministry and defense agency who championed a harder-edged version of geopolitics and argued that Japan's future security would rest almost entirely on the Anglo-Saxon maritime hegemony as China would one day attempt to reassert its centrality in Asia.[61]

The main threat at the time was not China, of course, but the Soviet Union, which was expanding militarily into the Pacific. American strategists immediately recognized that Japan's archipelagic positioning was ideally suited for the Reagan administration's new "maritime strategy" aimed at containing and destroying the Soviet fleet in the event of global war. Senior U.S. officials like Richard Armitage and James Kelly traveled regularly to plan with Shiina, Okazaki, and others in the LDP and foreign ministry and defense agency who shared this vision for rolling back Soviet communism.[62] They won support from more senior leaders like Nakasone and Abe's father, Foreign Minister Abe Shintarō. Decades later Armitage and Kelly returned as senior architects of Asia policy in the George W. Bush administration and as close confidants of Abe Shinzō.

Still, by the late 1980s voices like Okazaki's remained in the minority. East-West competition in the Cold War was losing steam, and rising U.S.-Japan trade friction appeared to signal the future dynamics of international relations. Growing numbers of intellectuals in both the United States and Japan began arguing that the older ways of alignment and statecraft championed by Kōsaka, Okazaki, and their protégés were giving way to a new kind of geopolitics based on the techno-nationalism and economic competition that Japan—it seemed—had mastered.[63]

FROM RELUCTANT REALISM TO THE RESURGENCE OF MARITIME STRATEGY

Then in rapid order the prevailing assumptions about the sources of Japanese power and regional and global order all collapsed. First, in 1990 the Gulf War demonstrated the continuing relevance of advanced military power and the limits of Japan's own ability to shape security issues with economic tools alone. Next, in the fall of 1990 the Japanese Nikkei index plummeted by 40 percent, marking the end of Japan's high-growth "bubble" and the beginning of prolonged stagnation in the economy—the so-called lost decades. As Japan's economic performance failed and the bipolar Cold War structure in international politics collapsed, the underpinnings of Japan's domestic political alignments fell into disarray. The Socialist Party died first with the collapse of the Soviet bloc, and then the LDP was driven from power in 1993 over a series of embarrassing pork barrel scandals. It returned to power two years later but was now able to stay in power only with the help of coalition partners—including, ironically, its erstwhile nemeses in the dying Socialist Party. Finally—and perhaps most importantly—Beijing demonstrated with missile tests around Taiwan in 1995 and 1996 that China would now use its renewed national power coercively without significant regard for economic interdependence with Japan. In a hierarchal Asian order, it was suddenly clear that Beijing had never been prepared to accept Japanese dominance or even coequal status within the system. As former prime minister Asō Tarō later noted, China was mirroring Japan's mistake in the last century, only this time it was a continental power engaged in the folly of seeking maritime conquest.[64] Japan's leadership reluctantly shifted to a renewed focus on balance-of-power logic in an era of uncertain power.

Over the next two decades—first LDP governments, then elements of the opposition Democratic Party of Japan (DPJ) governments, and finally the government of Abe Shinzō—all institutionalized balance-of-power logic vis-à-vis China in their foreign and security policies. Within the LDP, the mainstream conservatives changed course under Hashimoto Ryūtarō (prime minister 1996–1998), heir of the Satō and Tanaka faction line, but himself more of a hawkish thinker on foreign policy and champion of a more effective national security state. Hashimoto was defeated for the presidency of the LDP in April 2001 by Koizumi Junichirō, an iconoclastic third-generation descendant of anti-mainstream political figures. From that point on (with the brief interregnum of the DPJ governments in 2009–2012), the anti-mainstream faction once led by Kishi in 1955 formed the core of every LDP government for two decades. The postwar realism of Kōsaka and Okazaki now represented the mainstream perspective for Japanese political leaders, with Kōsaka's best students emerging as the most influential advisors to Prime Minister Abe, and Okazaki himself preparing Abe for his second term.[65] The intellectual currents shifted more broadly as well, with even left-leaning scholars calling for a more liberal internationalist variant of balance-of-power strategy that tracked much more closely with Kōsaka's realist theory of peace than with the UN neutralism or unarmed pacifism of his rivals Sakamoto Yoshikazu and Maruyama Masao.[66]

ABE CONSOLIDATES THE STRATEGIC FRAMEWORK

Which brings us back to Abe Shinzō. In his first term as prime minister (2006–2007), Abe stumbled as he squandered Koizumi's reforming populism against the old guard of the LDP and instead chose to crusade against his family's old nemeses on the ideological left.[67] Voters saw no advantage to themselves; Abe lost control of the Upper House in his first major election, and then he abruptly resigned as his illness took an unacceptable toll. But Abe learned from those mistakes. In his years out of power, he agonized over his own political demise and Japan's plummeting international influence. In the spirit of Winston Churchill or Richard Nixon, he used his time out of power to study Japan's strategic circumstances—meeting with like-minded officials and conservative foreign policy luminaries from Japan, the United States, and Australia— and steadily rebuilding political capital within the LDP as the man who could best turn out the DPJ and restore Japan's dignity and influence on the world stage. He also regained his physical strength with the release of a new drug that would counter his intestinal disease. In September 2012 he won the LDP presidential race and in November 2012 led the party to a massive victory at the polls.

In his second term as prime minister, Abe tended to those areas that had been his undoing the first time around, appointing the best and brightest bureaucrats to work under him in the Prime Minister's Office and ensuring that—as he put it to me over lunch in 2013—he spent 70 percent of his time on the economy.[68] And while he still entertained associations with the right wing, the main driver in his second term was ensuring Japan's status as a tier one power—a matter of strategy rather than ideology.[69]

For that purpose, he turned to the maritime framework that had evolved from Hayashi Shihei in the Tokugawa period to Katsu Kaishū in the Meiji period and Kōsaka Masataka and Okazaki Hisahiko in the postwar years. In multiple speeches leading up to his return to power and in the years since, Abe evoked Kōsaka's earlier vision of Japan as a responsible maritime stakeholder in contrast to the revisionist and coercive behavior of continental and authoritarian China in East Asia. As Abe's speechwriter and foreign policy brain Taniguchi Tomohiko explained in 2019, previous Japanese governments had a choice of continental or maritime strategies, and under Abe "Japan chose the maritime route, which has allowed the country to play a greater strategic role as part of the U.S. defense policy in Asia."[70]

Japan's 2013 National Security Strategy—the first ever and one modeled on the reports issued by the U.S. National Security Council—began with a clear statement that Japan faces an "increasingly severe security environment" that will require proactive steps to increase deterrence; improve the security environment in partnership with the United States and like-minded states in Asia; and "improve the global security environment and build a peaceful, stable, and prosperous international community by strengthening the international order based on universal values and rules." The maritime strategic predicate was clear throughout the document: "Surrounded by the sea on all sides and blessed with an immense exclusive economic zone and an extensive coastline, Japan as a maritime state has achieved economic growth through maritime trade and development of marine resources and has pursued 'Open and Stable Seas.'"[71] Or as Abe subsequently explained in his 2014 keynote address at the business gathering in Davos, Switzerland:

> The foundation for prosperity comes down to freedom of movement for people and goods. On the sea lanes, in air space, and recently, in outer space and cyber space, freedom of movement must remain secure. The only way to fully keep these indispensable public goods safe and peaceful is to rigorously maintain the rule of law. It is for that purpose that fundamental values like freedom, human rights and democracy must be assured. There is no alternative. If peace and stability were shaken in Asia, the knock-on effect for the entire world would be enormous.[72]

The threat that drove Abe to emphasize the security of the seas and alignment with the other maritime democracies was clearly China.

China had become the single most important influence on Japan's choices regarding alliance with the United States, regional order in the Indo-Pacific, and internal balancing at home. In the eighth century the *Chronicles of Japan* had first defined Japan's strategic choices with reference to her giant continental neighbor. And in 2013 Japan's National Security Strategy did the same.

2

CHINA

COMPETITION WITHOUT CATASTROPHE?

When Abe told his audience at Davos in January 2014 that "if peace and stability were shaken in Asia, the knock-on effect for the entire world would be enormous," he was trying to explain why his new strategy, with its focus on maritime security and universal norms, would help prevent such a conflagration. But for Europeans attending the conference, the air was pregnant with remembrances of the centennial of the First World War and whispers that Japan and China might destroy international peace in their own modern-day conflict over small islands in the East China Sea. Knowing his audience, but not quite well enough, Abe referenced the centennial of the guns of August to highlight the necessity of his approach. However, his pointed criticism of Chinese expansionism diluted whatever reassurance he had hoped to convey about Japan's own "proactive contribution to peace." When a Chinese businessman later haughtily dismissed the problem in his own presentation by saying that China could easily defeat Japan in a quick war, the staid hallways filled with an even deeper sense of foreboding.[1]

As MIT political scientist Taylor Fravel notes in his study of China's rise: "According to variants of power transition theory, conflict is most likely when a rising power, dissatisfied with the status quo, approaches parity with the dominant state in a region or the system and is willing to use force to reshape the system's rules and institutions."[2] In the mid-1990s, then Singaporean prime minister Lee Kwan Yew put it more starkly, warning that Japan and China have rarely been powerful at the same time and that the last time that happened, in the late nineteenth century, there was a catastrophic war.[3]

This is not 1914, however, or 1894 for that matter. Japan and China coexist with a level of mutual economic interdependence that far surpasses Britain and Germany's in 1914 and certainly Japan and China's in 1894. While there is a pronounced military dimension to Sino-Japanese competition today, the prevailing mode of competition for Japan is one of statecraft.

MARITIME POWERS AND THEIR CONTINENTAL RIVALS

But what kind of statecraft? The direction of Japanese diplomacy toward China has constantly shifted throughout history, including in the postwar period. Like Britain lying astride the great continental powers of Europe, Japan has struggled to find the right ways to shape the balance of power from offshore. Britain began the nineteenth century confident in the stability provided by the post-Napoleonic Concert of Europe but prepared to intervene should it fail. As Britain's architect of the concert, Foreign Minister Viscount Castlereagh, understood, Britain could shape the balance of power from offshore, since "our reputation on the Continent as a feature of our strength, power, and confidence is of more real moment than any acquisition."[4] Yet after Castlereagh, Prime Minister George Canning distrusted all the continental powers and retreated from activist foreign policy intervention on the continent, relying instead on the English Channel and the Royal Navy to protect Britain's real commercial and geopolitical interests further afield.[5] As prime minister, Viscount Palmerston then reasserted Britain into the balance-of-influence game in continental Europe in the 1850s, but then after 1865, Foreign Secretary Edward Stanley pulled back again from the continent, arguing that "it is the duty of a Government to abstain from menace if they do not intend to follow that menace by action."[6] By the beginning of the twentieth century, Foreign Minister Sir Edward Grey had lost his predecessors' ability to read the balance of power on the continent and thus intervened too late to deter imperial Germany's gamble for victory over France and Russia.[7] The lesson from 1914 is not that a Sino-Japanese clash is inevitable, in other words, but rather that the agility of Japanese statecraft toward the continent will matter to the peace of Asia no less than Britain's did to the peace of Europe a century ago.

Japan's new maritime strategy is predicated on competition with China through measures to shape the environment around China by reinforcing the ability of the rest of the Indo-Pacific to resist expansionism by Beijing. But for the first time in over a century, Japan's strategy toward China is now animated by Chinese power rather than Chinese weakness. As historian Koshiro Yukiko notes, prewar Japan was intensely focused on China and the "formidable presence of Russia and then the Soviet Union as intermediaries of Western culture and communist ideology" on the continent.[8] It was this intense awareness of Chinese vulnerability and Russian encroachment that led to Yamagata's effort to seek Japan's own "line of advantage" on the continent at the turn of the century. Yamagata was himself contradictory on China strategy. On the one hand, he believed that China's territorial integrity, economic development, and pan-Asian racial solidarity would be important tools for Japan in countering European imperialism. Yet Yamagata also believed that Japan would require some level of conquest on the continent to have "a base for our trade and industry inside China" so that in time of emergency Japan could "hold in its grasp the 'throat of the Far East' and guard against any intrusions by an enemy."[9] Motivated by both fear and greed over China's internal struggles, Japan defined its "line of advantage" ever northward after Yamagata, from the Korean peninsula to Manchuria and then all of China—bringing Japan into an existential clash with the major maritime powers.

After the war, Japan's strategy was again determined by Chinese weakness, but now also Japan's own weakness. Yoshida Shigeru approached China with a fundamental belief, based on his own experience as a diplomat in Manchuria and northern China, that Japan had "special feelings" toward China and an abiding interest in Chinese self-strengthening as an antidote to Western domination of Asia, a view similar in some respects to Yamagata's (or at least *some* of Yamagata's musings).[10] Yoshida was confident that this history, now unencumbered by Japanese militarism, would eventually draw China to seek Japanese support and guidance in modernization and would, in turn, give Japan a more balanced relationship within Asia and reduced dependence on the United States. The premise, of course, was that Japan enjoyed the senior—if benign—position in the relationship. Thus Yoshida pushed constantly for closer ties with Beijing than the United States enjoyed. Even anti-mainstream hawks like Kishi quietly worked to solidify trade relations with Beijing in the late 1950s to stay one step ahead of Washington (in Kishi's case with President Eisenhower's blessings because of the Japanese leader's solid anticommunist credentials).[11] After President Richard Nixon shocked Japan with his opening to China in 1971 and a promise in 1972 to normalize U.S. relations with Beijing, Tokyo rushed to normalize Japan-China relations first. The 1978 Sino-Japanese Treaty of Friendship and Cooperation marked both Japan's restored friendship with China and also a commitment to help China with self-strengthening through generous yen loans.[12] Japan was also the first country to convince the United States to reengage with China after the brutal crackdown in Tiananmen in June 1989.

But if a weak China was a liability for Japan during the Cold War, post–Cold War Japan had to contend with the threatening consequences of restored Chinese power. Recognition that Japan and China had been lying in the same bed with different dreams hit hard in the mid-1990s when China conducted its 1994 nuclear test and sparked a military crisis in the Taiwan Strait in 1995–1996.[13] Over the next two decades China's military ambitions spread to the East and South China Seas and beyond to the Indian and Pacific Oceans, while Chinese diplomatic initiatives sought to displace Japan and eventually the United States as leading powers within Asia. Tokyo came to understand that Japan's "special feelings" and economic interdependence with China might dampen—but clearly would not stop—Beijing's rising ambitions to restore its own hegemonic leadership in the region.

Yet for all the challenges China has presented to Japan—and for all the consensus that Japan must compete in response—few Japanese political leaders are prepared to completely abandon Yamagata's or Yoshida's premise that Japan still has a stake in China's success. Thus while some pundits and politicians in Tokyo muse about the coming collapse of China, a large majority of business and political leaders in Tokyo know that this would be a disaster for Japan.[14] China may be Japan's greatest diplomatic, technological, military, and ideational rival—but China's economy also helps fuel Japan's economy; China's participation in regional multilateral institutions reinforces regional stability; China's control of air pollution protects Japan's environment; and a heavily armed chaotic and illiberal Chinese state would clearly be worse than the current Communist Party for Japanese security. As the United States veered toward zero-sum containment strategies toward China under Donald Trump, Japan remained wedded to a balance-of-power strategy that recognizes this need for a mix of competition and cooperation with Beijing.

The rest of this chapter explores three dimensions of China's geopolitical challenge to Japan—security related, diplomatic, and economic—that forced the search for this balance between competition and cooperation and determined the elements of Japan's new grand strategy.

THE SECURITY CHALLENGE

It was the Chinese security challenge that first impacted Japan's national consciousness. China's nuclear tests and military pressure on Taiwan between 1994 and 1996 not only shook the foundations of Japan-China relations but also accelerated the realignment of internal Liberal

Democratic Party (LDP) politics in Japan. The last time the Japanese public saw the mighty Tanaka Kakuei alive was in April 1992 when TV cameras filmed the visit of Chinese Communist Party general secretary Jiang Zemin to the ailing politician at his Tokyo home. As the cameras rolled, Jiang and his delegation beamed and applauded the architect of Sino-Japanese rapprochement in 1971 while he sat reclined before them, still suffering the effects of an earlier stroke. Presented with a gorgeous Chinese landscape painting, a deeply moved Tanaka murmured, "Wow . . . wow . . . this is nice . . . so nice" before breaking down in tears, unable to continue.[15] The next year Tanaka was dead and with him the era of friendly Japan-China relations.

In the years that followed, the mainstream Tanaka Faction's foreign policy orientation toward China became politically untenable. Ironically, the pivot to the more deliberate balance-of-power strategy that we now associate with Abe actually commenced under one of the last of the Tanaka Faction leaders, Hashimoto Ryūtarō. Hashimoto's hard-headed nationalism was already well known to the American negotiators who had tangled with him as trade minister in 1994–1995. Then, as prime minister, Hashimoto agreed in 1996 to expand U.S.-Japan defense cooperation to "areas surrounding Japan"—an implicit evolution of defense cooperation to deal with China's growing threat to the maritime domain.

Yet Hashimoto also invested in relations with China in parallel with these early balance-of-power moves, particularly in advance of the symbolic twentieth anniversary commemoration of the 1978 Sino-Japanese Treaty of Friendship and Cooperation. Hashimoto's successor, Obuchi Keizō (also from the Tanaka Faction), hosted Jiang for that commemoration in Tokyo in November 1998 with the expectation that Sino-Japanese relations would move forward in concert with the strengthening of the U.S.-Japan alliance. But things went terribly awry. Rather than celebrating a new future together with Japan, Jiang arrived at the elegant state dinner dressed in a Mao jacket and lectured the revered Emperor Akihito on Japan's militarist past, to the horror and embarrassment of the assembled Japanese dignataries.[16] This rude gesture was no accident: Jiang would have none of Japan's efforts to maintain friendly relations at the same time that Japan was deliberately hedging with the Americans and expanding its military role.

When the maverick anti-mainstream politician Koizumi Junichirō seized the leadership of the LDP from the Tanaka Faction in 2001, he had every intention of building on his predecessors' proactive security policy with the United States while continuing efforts to forge understanding with Beijing. But Koizumi poured new salt in Beijing's wounds by pledging the War Bereavement Association (Nippon Izokukai) that he would worship at the controversial Yasukuni Shrine if elected prime minister. Japanese of all political hues pay respects to their dead relatives lost in the war at the large Shinto shrine in downtown Tokyo, but the 1978 secret internment ceremony for Class-A war criminals proved so politically toxic that the emperor himself could no longer pay his respects at the shrine. For Koizumi this was more a matter of political calculation than ideology, since the *Izokukai* had long supported Hashimoto, Koizumi's chief rival in his leadership bid. To soften the blow, during his first visit to China as prime minister in October 2001, Koizumi stopped at the Marco Polo Bridge, where he offered a heartfelt apology and expressed deep remorse at the site where Japan had initiated the 1937 Sino-Japanese War.[17] But the gesture did little good. Koizumi had already visited the shrine in August 2001, and Beijing demanded a commitment that he would make no further visits. Koizumi refused to bow to Chinese pressure. The old ideological issues intertwined with the new geopolitical competition in an impasse the two countries never resolved during his tenure.

Koizumi later told me that he made his subsequent visits to Yasukuni—particularly his last visit on August 15, 2006—precisely to demonstrate that China would no longer be allowed to dictate Japan's foreign or domestic policies and to clear the path for his successors to not feel they had to visit Yasukuni to make that point again. The struggle between Japan and China was not just about history—it was about rank and prestige. And the steady increase in Chinese military pressure on Japan compounded efforts by subsequent Japanese leaders to restore some measure of stability if not amity to Sino-Japanese relations.

RELENTLESS PRESSURE IN THE EAST CHINA SEA

Over the subsequent decades a pattern became all too familiar to Tokyo as diplomats and business leaders worked to repair relations with their counterparts in Beijing, only to have the vague principles of cooperation or deconfliction they had negotiated be ignored with impunity by the People's Liberation Army (PLA). In 2001, for example, the two foreign ministries had agreed to explore joint development around the Senkaku Islands and to provide prior notification of any unilateral exploration to the other side.[18] No concrete scheme for joint development was ever developed, and by 2003 Chinese rigs were spotted drilling in the Xihu Trough in violation of the agreement.[19] Abe's successor in 2007, Fukuda Yasuo, had close ties to Japan's business community and prided himself on his more moderate approach toward China. In a statement issued in May 2008, Fukuda and Hu Jintao agreed to resume joint development efforts and to make the East China Sea a "Sea of Peace, Cooperation and Friendship"—but that effort fared no better.[20] By 2015 the Japanese government had identified sixteen structures China had built for unilateral resource extraction in the supposed "Sea of Peace" (see map 2.1).[21]

When the opposition Democratic Party of Japan (DPJ) came to power in 2009 under the campaign banner "Seiken kōtai" ("change of government"), polls showed that its coalition had a popular mandate to punish the LDP for slipping back into its old corrupt ways in the years since the reforming Koizumi, but no mandate for radical changes in foreign policy.[22] Nevertheless, the tone-deaf DPJ leader Hatoyama Yukio came into office longing to fulfill his grandfather's vision from the 1950s of using the China card against the United States, promising in a press conference in New York in September 2009 to form an "East Asia Community" with China to help Japan stand up to Washington.[23] The stunned Obama administration—which harbored no ill will or protectionist agenda toward Japan—struggled to make sense of Hatoyama's fantasy. Even the Japan experts in Beijing were wary. As one of the leading Japanologists in Beijing told me in 2009, "The DPJ is a leftist government but Japan is a rightist country so the Hatoyama policies will not last."

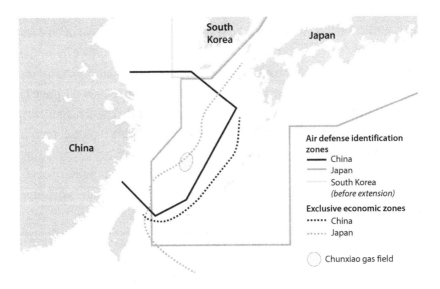

MAP 2.1 Air defense identification zones

Hatoyama's experiment with embracing China to counter the United States backfired badly. On September 7, 2010, a Chinese maritime militia boat deliberately collided with a Japan Coast Guard cutter near the Senkaku Islands, and in response the DPJ government broke precedent by placing the Chinese captain under arrest in preparation for trial under domestic Japanese law. Beijing responded furiously with mercantilist boycotts of rare earth metals and the arrest of Japanese businessmen in China on trumped-up charges of espionage. In Tokyo former socialists in the DPJ clashed with more hawkish members of the party like Foreign Minister Maehara Seiji as the government grasped for a response. Eventually, the Chinese captain was released unconditionally on September 24. The immediate crisis was defused and Chinese incursions into the Senkakus returned to precrisis levels—for the time being.[24]

The DPJ government then tried to reboot Sino-Japanese relations through a previously scheduled China-Japan-Korea trilateral summit in May 2012, in which the three countries agreed to establish a new trilateral secretariat in Seoul (given the oddly generic name "Trilateral

Secretariat" since no government was willing to let either of the others go first on the official name of the office). That respite ended in September 2012 when the third DPJ government in as many years under Prime Minister Noda Yoshihiko frantically arranged to purchase one of the Senkaku Islands from a private Japanese landowner to prevent the nationalistic and anti-Chinese governor of Tokyo, Ishihara Shintarō, from buying the island and using it to foment trouble with Beijing for his own political ends. Noda got the trouble he was trying to avoid anyway, as China dramatically increased its military and paramilitary operational tempo around the islands yet again to punish Japan—this time permanently, as figure 2.1 indicates.[25]

For strategists in Tokyo, the ups and downs in relations with Beijing now contained one steady and continuous feature: Beijing was embarked on a relentless military and paramilitary pressure campaign to undermine Japan's contention that it had sovereignty over the Senkakus by demonstrating Japan's inability to stop Chinese incursions. Tokyo was especially sensitive to this strategy because Secretary of State Warren Christopher had clumsily responded to a Japanese journalist's question

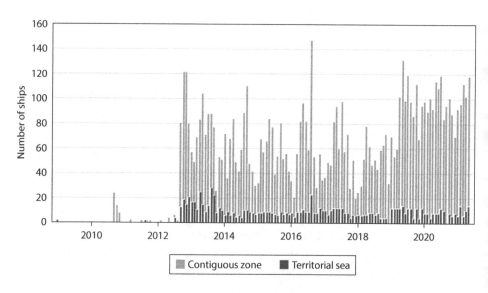

FIGURE 2.1 Number of Chinese government vessels in Senkakus' contiguous zone and territorial sea (2009–2021)

back in 1997 about whether the U.S.-Japan Security Treaty would cover the Senkakus in the event of conflict by urging "restraint" by all parties.[26] The Pentagon later clarified that any attack on Japan around islands administered by Japan would in fact trigger Article V of the security treaty (the State Department maintained that this reflected recognition of Japan's administrative control but not territorial rights). The delicate diplomatic and legal parsing of the U.S. commitment proved a target for Chinese pressure in the view of Japanese officials. Successive U.S. governments reiterated the U.S. commitment under the security treaty all the way up to the level of the president himself.[27] However, every Chinese move to expand paramilitary and military operations in and around the Senkaku Islands since 1997 has been viewed in Tokyo as part of a consistent Chinese strategy of "salami slicing" (or "cabbage peeling" in the Chinese metaphor) to wear down the credibility of Japanese administrative control and to weaken the U.S. security commitment. Japanese experts began using a new phrase to describe the Chinese strategy that would soon enter the lexicon of American national security experts as well—"grey zone" coercion.[28]

"LIKE A SHEEP SHORN OF ITS WOOL"

It was this clear pattern of Chinese expansion and DPJ unsteadiness that helped to revive Abe's political fortunes within the LDP. Abe returned to power raising the alarm about China's security threat and pledging to restore the U.S.-Japan alliance. At the Brookings Institution in 2009 he called on Japan to "invest more into our time-honored alliance, bound by the same set of common values, especially when our great neighbor, China, is undergoing such a shaky transformative period of growth."[29] At the Hudson Institute in Washington in 2010, he accused China of engaging in "lebensraum" and warned that China's goal was to "Finlandize" Japan and Korea.[30] Abe's Churchillian message resonated within the conservative ranks of the LDP, who returned him to the party presidency and then the premiership in his landslide victory over the DPJ in December 2012.

Far from being an outlier from the anti-mainstream ranks of the LDP as he might have been two decades earlier, Abe now stood for the consensus view on China that was evident in both public and elite polling.[31] His 2013 National Security Strategy did not elicit major criticism at home when it stated unequivocally that "China has taken actions that can be regarded as attempts to change the status quo by coercion based on their own assertions, which are incompatible with the existing order of international law, in the maritime and aerial domains, including the East China Sea and the South China Sea."[32]

Meanwhile, Beijing continued with coercive actions that proved that very point. On January 30, 2013, a PLA Navy surface combatant locked its fire control radar onto a Japan Maritime Self-Defense Forces (JMSDF) destroyer. On November 23 of that year, Beijing announced an air defense identification zone (ADIZ) over the East China Sea, including an area that was Japanese administered (and claimed), and threatened to intercept and take necessary defensive measures against any aircraft entering the space.[33] China's operational tempo around the Senkaku Islands remained at the significantly higher level established the year before, and PLA submarines and surface action groups (squadrons of destroyers and frigates) also began exercising regularly on the Pacific side of the Japanese archipelago. By October 26, 2018, the Japan Ministry of Defense white paper was warning that "China's recent activities, including its rapid military modernization and enhancement of operational capabilities, its unilateral escalation of actions in areas around Japan, and with the lack of transparency in the military build-up, present a strong security concern for the region including Japan and the international community."[34] The white paper chronicled repeated overflights and circumnavigation of Japanese territorial waters and regular incursions in the contiguous zone around the Senkaku Islands, including military exercises on the East China Sea and Pacific Ocean sides of Japan, detection of Shang-class submarines, and a grey-hull Jiangkai II-class frigate in the Senkaku Islands contiguous zone (the first confirmed case in which a submerged submarine entered into the contiguous zone). Meanwhile, the Ministry of Defense reported that China's military aircraft flights through the strait between Okinawa and Miyako Island increased from five per year through 2016 to eighteen in 2017 alone.[35] Even as both governments renewed efforts to thaw tensions in 2018 in anticipation of a visit by Xi to Japan on the fortieth anniversary of the 1978 bilateral treaty, the Japan Air Self-Defense Forces (JASDF) had to scramble fighter jets 638 times to respond to PLA Air Force incursions—well above the rate only a year earlier.[36] In July 2020 the Japanese Coast Guard reported that Chinese patrol ships had navigated within the 24-nautical-mile contiguous zone of the Senkaku Islands for one hundred straight days, the greatest number since at least 2012.[37]

At the end of the Cold War, Japan's defense budget had been twice the size of China's. Despite annual increases under Abe, Japan's defense budget was one-fifth the size of China's when he left office in 2020—a fact that the PLA and Chinese Coast Guard were eager to demonstrate to Japan's increasingly stretched Self-Defense Forces and Coast Guard. So alarming was China's maritime expansion and use of military pressure against Taiwan and Southeast Asian states that Japanese political leaders began openly predicting that Japan would play a major role helping Taiwan should it be attacked—an absolutely taboo subject for decades despite the warm feelings the Japanese people have for Taiwan. The 2021 Defense White Paper declared that "stabilizing the situation surrounding Taiwan is important for Japan's security and the stability of the international community" while Deputy Prime Minister Aso and former senior defense officials in Tokyo began explaining for the first time that Japan would likely help in a Taiwan contingency because of the direct threat to Japan's own security in the First Island Chain—and polls in 2021 showed that 74 percent of the public agreed.[38]

There is no doubt that Japanese leaders made tactical missteps as the security environment deteriorated. Koizumi's impasse with Jiang and Hu over visits to Yasukuni froze leader-level diplomatic interactions for years. Then the DPJ bungled strategic messaging to China with the 2010 arrest of the Chinese ship captain and the 2012 purchase of the Senkaku Island from a private landowner. Yet despite these missteps, the larger Chinese intent was unmistakable—and particularly threatening for a maritime power. As former ambassador to the United States Katō Ryōzō put it, China's moves were meant to leave the Japanese archipelago "like a sheep shorn of its wool."[39]

THE DIPLOMATIC CHALLENGE

The Chinese military threat punctured not only the Japanese sense of physical security but also Japan's rank and prestige within Asia. After sleeping in the same bed but with different dreams for decades, the Japanese and Chinese governments discovered their incompatible assumptions about the natural hierarchy in Asia when Japanese foreign minister Kōno Yōhei warned that the 1994 Lop Nur nuclear tests put at risk Japan's generous provision of yen loans, to which the Chinese foreign minister reportedly replied that Japan was only paying the reparations due for its past transgressions against China.[40] That exchange revealed to many observers in Tokyo what subsequent Chinese coercion and propaganda only confirmed: that Beijing's strategy was designed to put Japan back in a smaller box, to demonstrate that Japan and China were not in fact equal powers, and that China had legitimate rights to full military power and regional leadership, while Japan had a historic obligation to remain a partial and incomplete power.

For Chinese leaders the reference points for defining the future of leadership in Asia were the summits at Potsdam and Yalta in 1945, where the "Four Policemen" (the United States, Britain, the Soviet Union, and China) agreed on unconditional surrender and a more punitive approach to postwar Japan (even though Chinese leaders were not present at the actual meetings and the country was led by the Chinese Communist Party's enemy Chiang Kai-shek at the time). For Japanese leaders, the reference point to determine the future of regional order was the 1951 San Francisco conference in which the United States and other democracies agreed on a nonpunitive peace settlement with Japan and the United States signed the bilateral security treaties with Japan, the Philippines, and Australia/New Zealand that underpin U.S. and Japanese strategy in the region to this day. Japan was obviously not included in the wartime Yalta and Potsdam meetings, nor was China included in the San Francisco negotiations, which took place only two years after the communists' victory in China and at the height of the Korean War. Japanese and Chinese journalistic and scholarly accounts of the postwar settlement completely diverge into these two mutually contradictory accounts—a fact little noticed until the post–Cold War emergence of Chinese ambitions and Japanese insecurity. Indeed, conflicting Chinese and Japanese claims to the Senkakus (the *Diaoyu* to Beijing) diverge sharply because of each nation's interpretation of vague and contradictory American commitments made regarding the islands at the Potsdam summit and then the San Francisco peace treaty negotiations. American policymakers frequently fail to understand how U.S. decisions or statements have played into one or another of these narratives about the legitimate basis for postwar order in Asia and the Pacific.[41]

THE COMPETITION SPREADS TO REGIONAL AND GLOBAL FORUMS

With the intensification of bilateral diplomatic competition over core issues of sovereignty and national legitimacy, burgeoning Sino-Japanese cooperation on broader regional economic integration fell victim as well. The high-water mark of that cooperation may have been the 1997–1998 Asian Financial Crisis, when the Japanese finance ministry rallied Asian economies to blunt American and International Monetary Fund (IMF) pressure for painful structural reforms in Thailand, Indonesia, and Korea, while Beijing agreed not to devalue the renminbi, saving those same economies from damaging competitive devaluation across the region.[42] The region's dissonance with Washington propelled interest in forming an East Asia financial arrangement that could step in to provide stabilization funds—primarily through debt swaps—before regional economies would be forced to accept the conditions necessary for IMF funds. That arrangement was finalized by Japan, Korea, and China and the ten member states of the Association of Southeast Asian Nations (ASEAN) in May 2000 and named the Chiang Mai Initiative (CMI) after the northern Thai city where the finance ministry delegations convened.[43]

However, despite pledges to honor debt swaps at various points, the CMI failed to mature into a regional alternative to the IMF. One reason was that the leading lenders—particularly Japan—were wary of accepting the moral hazard of lending without the political and financial backing of the IMF and the other Organisation for Economic Co-operation and Development (OECD) countries in North America and Europe. Though the iconoclastic economic nationalist Sakakibara Eisuke had tried to form an "Asia Monetary Fund" to defy the United States when leading the finance ministry as vice minister in 1997–1998, his successors abandoned his quasi-autarkic vision and were extremely careful to coordinate the new CMI and align its practices with the IMF and the U.S. Treasury Department. However, the more important reason for the failure of the CMI was the growing shadow of Sino-Japanese diplomatic rivalry, which became obvious as the member states struggled to agree on voting rights in the new organization. After a decade of squabbling, the finance ministries agreed in May 2009 that Japan and China would each be able to claim "equal" status by keeping China's voting share below Japan's on its own, but equal to Japan with the inclusion of Hong Kong.[44] Since then the newly renamed CMIM (Chiang Mai Initiative Multilateralization) has never been fully activated in a financial crisis.[45]

The Japan-China diplomatic spats spread to other multilateral forums. At the United Nations, Japan succeeded in organizing a "G-4" effort in 2004 with India, Brazil, and Germany to push for reform and expansion of the UN Security Council (UNSC) to include those four new members on a permanent basis. Beijing then organized each of the G-4's neighboring rivals—countries like Pakistan, Argentina, Italy, and Korea—into an informally named "coffee club" to block UNSC reform.[46] The Japanese foreign ministry was particularly surprised at how effective China was in diluting Southeast Asian support for Japan and how quickly Korea rallied to China's effort. For Japanese officials, who viewed the UN system as a key pillar in Japanese foreign policy and a seat on the Security Council as the ultimate vindication of Japan's recovery from the Second World War (the UN was formed initially to fight Japan and the Axis powers), this was a bitter pill indeed.

Japan and China also collided over the formation of a new East Asia Community, envisioned by a group of regional wise men (the East Asia Vision Group) in the aftermath of the 1997–1998 Asian Financial

Crisis and built around the same member states that formed the CMI as a notional framework for regional integration and influence building vis-à-vis North America and Europe.[47] At the same time that Japanese diplomats battled with Chinese proxies over UNSC reform, they began hearing from their counterparts within ASEAN that Beijing was grabbing control of the agenda for a new East Asia summit proposed by the Vision Group. Senior officials from the more independent-minded member states were alarmed in late 2004 when Cambodia and Laos acted as proxies to table a Chinese proposal that the new summits of regional leaders would be held first in Kuala Lumpur but then in China—with Beijing determining the agenda.[48]

Senior officials from the Ministry of Economy, Trade and Industry (METI) were still generally more sanguine about their ability to work with China in an Asian context than their foreign ministry counterparts, but they soon became anxious about China's growing clout in negotiations for a free-trade agreement comprising the ten ASEAN states, Japan, Korea, and China. Originally intended to fuel regional integration and give greater negotiating leverage vis-à-vis other regions of the world, the "ASEAN plus Three" trade concept morphed into a strategy to shape and integrate China. As one senior METI official told me in 2004, Japan would use the trade talks to "build a cage around China." A year later the same official confessed that the cage was not big enough and that Japan was pushing to include the like-minded democracies India, Australia, and New Zealand to add more heft vis-à-vis China in what eventually became the Regional Comprehensive Economic Partnership (RCEP).[49]

Multilateral diplomacy remains an important part of Japan's diplomatic playbook and will receive more attention in chapter 4. There is no turning away from these institutions for a nation that began its disastrous path to world war by walking out of the League of Nations in 1933. But over the past two decades Sino-Japanese competition has soured many Japanese strategic thinkers on the efficacy of multilateral institution building in Asia. Japanese diplomats and trade and finance officials energetically participate in the ASEAN-centered multilateral meetings that crowd the calendar in East Asia, but they now do so to block China as often as they do to advance regional integration.

When the Center for Strategic and International Studies (CSIS) surveyed Japanese foreign policy elites on regional institution building in 2008, the enthusiasm was still palpable, with 81 percent arguing that East Asia community building was important for Japan. By 2014 the same survey found that 62 percent were pessimistic about the prospects for community building in the region, with Japanese respondents most negative of the ten regional countries surveyed. When asked why they were pessimistic, the top answer given was "uncertainty about a rising China."[50]

ABE OUTFLANKS XI

With Abe's return to power in 2012, Sino-Japanese diplomatic rivalry was on full display. Beijing's effort to delegitimize Japanese leadership and Abe in particular by evoking the glorious days of global alignment against militarist Japan reached a crescendo in late 2013 and early 2014 when Chinese diplomats around the world were instructed to write op-eds accusing Abe of being a revisionist warmonger. The most ludicrous article was written by China's ambassador in London for the *Telegraph* that January, in which he reminded British readers that China had been on Britain's side in the Second World War and then compared Abe to the evil Lord Voldemort from *Harry Potter*.[51]

Abe did not bend to Chinese pressure, but neither did he give up on his goal of eventually stabilizing relations with Beijing. Like his grandfather Kishi, he considered productive economic relations with China an important pillar in Japan's overall economic and foreign policy even as he sought to deter Chinese coercion and compete with China for influence in Asia. In his first unsuccessful term as prime minister in 2006–2007, he had previewed his inaugural visit to China with a speech reaffirming Japan's responsibility for the Second World War based on his predecessors' official statements on August 15, 1995, and 2005 and admitting that Japan's past rule and "invasion" had brought pain to Asia. The speech angered his allies on the right, since only months earlier he had questioned whether Japan's war with China technically qualified as an "invasion" at all.[52]

Yachi Shōtarō, who was Abe's vice foreign minister at the time and then became national security advisor in 2013, has explained that Abe also planned from the beginning of his return to office to improve ties with China after first demonstrating to Beijing that he would not be intimidated.[53] During Beijing's world propaganda campaign to isolate Abe, he encouraged former prime minister Fukuda to travel to Beijing for "personal diplomacy" to keep the political dialogue open and lay the groundwork for eventual stabilization of relations (Chinese diplomats have told me how important the Fukuda connection was during that period of confrontation). Abe himself focused on outflanking Chinese pressure by strengthening ties with Washington, Canberra, and Delhi and across Southeast Asia, Europe, and the Middle East (this combination of external balancing and ideational competition is addressed in subsequent chapters). In his first year in office, Abe held more summit meetings than most postwar prime ministers held in their entire terms. By 2014 polls in the region found that he was generally twice as trusted as Xi Jinping, with even higher margins in Washington, Delhi, and Canberra.[54] Meanwhile, Abe's convincing victory in the July 2013 Upper House elections proved to Beijing that he was not going to fall from power as quickly as his six immediate predecessors had. Japanese business leaders reported to me in meetings in Tokyo the week after the 2013 election that they suddenly received multiple requests for office calls from senior Chinese Community Party (CCP) officials who had previously spurned Japanese overtures.

With Abe standing intact after a year of Chinese pressure, Xi agreed to hold a bilateral meeting on November 2014, dropping his earlier preconditions that Abe acknowledge there was a territorial dispute over the Senkaku Islands and that the Japanese prime minister pledge not to visit Yasukuni. In their awkward summit photo, the two leaders looked like they were "smelling each other's socks," in the words of former deputy secretary of state Richard Armitage. In the two leaders' curt four-point joint statement, Abe acknowledged "different views" on tensions in the

East China Sea without giving in to Beijing's insistence that there was an actual territorial dispute.[55] Nor was there any commitment on Yasukuni, though Abe did not visit the shrine aside from his first and only visit as prime minister in December.

Having blunted China's campaign to isolate Japan diplomatically, Abe now needed to stabilize ties with China to maintain solidarity within his ruling coalition—and to fulfill his pledge to restore Japan's economic growth.

THE ECONOMIC CHALLENGE

Japan's opening to China in the 1970s was strategic at first, with the agreement on yen loans in 1978 designed primarily to cement friendship and strengthen a weak and vulnerable China vis-à-vis the Soviet Union.[56] By 2005, however, Japan's investment in China had reached almost $30 billion and China had become so integrated in supply chains for Japanese manufacturers and Chinese consumers so important for Japanese consumer good exports that economic interests in China were now on a par with geopolitics.[57] Japanese farmers were making small fortunes exporting their high-end sake, strawberries, and melons to the new Chinese middle class, which by 2005 was estimated to be larger than Japan's entire population, while manufacturers like Toyota anticipated faster growth in the Chinese market over the coming decades than in Japan, Europe, or North America.[58] Yet this was precisely the period during which Sino-Japanese political relations were spiraling downward. Tensions were visible to all, punctuated when the Japanese deputy chief of mission's car was attacked by Chinese football hooligans at the 2004 Japan-China Asian Cup game in Beijing on August 7.[59] Citing political uncertainty as well as the rising costs of Chinese labor and uncertainty about intellectual property rights protection in China, Japanese firms began implementing what came to be known as the "China plus-one" strategy to diversify risk away from the Chinese market and

China-based manufacturing and assembly. The primary beneficiaries as "plus ones" were India and Southeast Asia (Vietnam in particular), which later helped Abe's own diplomatic outreach in response to China's strategy of isolating Japan in the region.[60]

With a huge growing market but increasing headwinds from political risk, labor costs, and intellectual property rights theft, the growth in Japanese foreign direct investment (FDI) in China peaked in 2012. It was now evident in the Senkaku disputes that Beijing was prepared to use economic interdependence to punish Japanese business in times of geopolitical confrontation.[61] Japanese industry had hoped for decades to preserve *seikei bunri*—a safe wall between business and political issues in relations with China, but Beijing was clearly no longer willing to honor the tacit understanding that had been in place since 1978.

Nevertheless, the level of Japanese FDI in China remains high, as figure 2.2 indicates.[62] In surveys of business confidence, auto producers in particular have expressed optimism about the Chinese market.[63] In addition, Abe's success in tripling the tourism sector of Japan's economy since coming to power has rested on the twin pillars of internal reform and large numbers of wealthy Chinese tourists eager to see the beautiful historic sites of Kyoto and Nara or to shop in the Ginza district of Tokyo.[64] In preparing for this book, I convened a group of leading Japanese and American historians and foreign policy experts at a hot spring resort in Hakone, Japan, to contemplate the future of strategic competition with China. When we asked the manager of the resort about business demand, he replied that they were doing very well—thanks to all the Chinese tourists we could see enjoying the hot springs and gardens as we debated strategic competition in Asia in the resort's conference room. Abe's own slowness to close Japan to Chinese visitors as COVID-19 shut down Wuhan in 2020 also reflected concerns about damage to the Japanese tourism industry.[65] The ironic reality is that Abe came to power to compete with China, but his political longevity was made possible by decent economic growth and good returns on the Nikkei stock index, fueled in significant measure by Chinese tourists visiting Japan and Japanese exports to China.

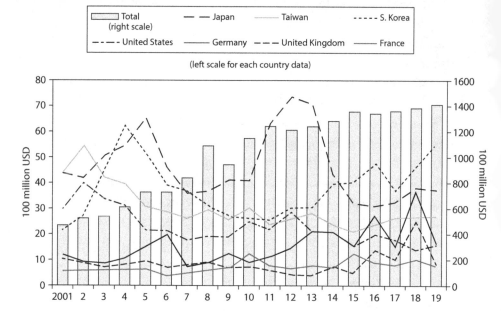

FIGURE 2.2 Value of foreign direct investment in China by country

STABILIZING ECONOMIC RELATIONS . . . ALMOST

The opportunity for Abe to benefit the economy by stabilizing political relations came with the 2018 fortieth anniversary of the Japan-China Treaty of Peace and Friendship. Previous efforts to use the ten-year anniversaries of the treaty had usually ended in failure: the 1998 summit was a disaster for relations after Jiang Zemin lectured the Japanese emperor at a state banquet in Tokyo,[66] and Fukuda's agreement with Hu Jintao in 2008 to turn the East China Sea into a "Sea of Peace, Cooperation and Friendship" had been followed by increased military confrontations. As Xi and Abe approached 2018, they were at an impasse over geopolitics but ready for progress on economic issues—like two exhausted prize fighters hanging off each other's shoulder, both eager for the bell to bring them relief. For his part, Xi faced new pressures and unpredictability from the Trump administration in Washington, while Abe had to prepare for a landmark third term as LDP president by shoring up business support and cementing ties with his pacifist coalition partner the *Komeito* Party and ascendant powerhouses in the ruling LDP like former trade minister Nikai Toshihiro, one of the few remaining LDP leaders eager to improve ties with Beijing.[67] Significant economic players on both sides were also ready for a change. When the two countries' foreign ministries began making plans for reciprocal visits, including visits to Japan by Xi for the G-20 summit in Osaka and a separate state visit with the new Japanese emperor, Japanese business leaders like the chairman of Keidanren (Japan's leading business organization) expressed satisfaction and relief.[68] In business surveys taken subsequent to the new thawing of political relations that year, Japanese executives suddenly reported that the Chinese government was showing a more welcoming attitude toward them as political relations calmed—aided likely by the increasing hostility in U.S.-China trade relations at the same time.[69]

Tokyo and Beijing also muted their confrontation on economic statecraft within Asia. When China announced a new Asia Infrastructure Investment Bank (AIIB) in October 2013, Japan initially joined India and the United States in strong opposition, even as other allies like Britain and Australia decided to join the bank. Tokyo was similarly skeptical of Xi's announcement of the new One Belt One Road (later Belt and Road) Initiative that same year, countering with promises of "quality infrastructure" and later partnering with the United States and Australia under the Free and Open Indo-Pacific (FOIP) vision to offer an alternative (covered in more detail in chapter 4).[70] On the eve of Abe's October 2018 summit with Xi in China, however, the Japan Bank for International Cooperation (JBIC) and the China Development Bank reversed positions somewhat and agreed to find joint projects involving China's Belt and Road Initiative (BRI) and FOIP, with the Chinese side agreeing to all of Japan's conditions for "quality infrastructure" such as debt sustainability.[71] A year later the head of JBIC acknowledged that there had been little progress on identifying joint projects, but the shift in attitude was part of a larger effort to stabilize relations and preserve Japanese economic interests in China.[72] Nevertheless, it was noteworthy that Tokyo and Beijing had a notional agreement to cooperate on development, since 2018 marked the end of Japan's four decades of official development assistance to China.

SHARPENING TECHNOLOGY COMPETITION

Those positive changes in tone and treatment aside, policymakers in Tokyo simultaneously continued to increase economic security measures designed to protect Japan's companies and market from China's undiminished predatory economic behavior in high technology, highlighted by Beijing's alarmingly ambitious "Made in China 2025" report of May 2015.[73] The United States is not alone in at least partially decoupling from economic dependence on China; indeed, no country has tracked more closely with that effort than Japan. Alert to intellectual property theft, Japanese companies continued moving critical R&D out of China even as the investment environment marginally improved. Alarmed at Chinese penetration into Japanese telecommunications after a surprise agreement between Huawei and the Japanese firm SoftBank in July 2015, the Japanese government introduced regulations barring Huawei, ZTE, and other Chinese telecom companies from participating in 5G bandwidth in Japan even as Abe was in China for a summit with Xi in October 2018.[74] Then in 2019 METI gave administrative guidance to Japanese corporate compliance officers not to engage in technology transfers or major business deals with Huawei.[75]

In the same year, the Japanese government commenced revisions to its Foreign Exchange Law that lowered the equity threshold at which certain foreign investors must seek government approval for their investment before taking a stake in strategically important Japanese companies from 10 percent to 1 percent. The companies listed by the Ministry of Finance included most utilities and firms involved in supporting core infrastructure or producing defense-related technologies or certain other technologies related to cybersecurity.[76] Though universal in application, the threat that prompted the change was clearly China. Indeed, U.S. legislators crafting parallel changes to strengthen U.S. investment screening included amendments calling on the U.S. government to coordinate intelligence with Japan on Chinese high-tech investment patterns in order to align the two allies' efforts.[77] Even in its April 2020 massive stimulus package to recover from the economic impact of COVID-19, the Japanese government set aside over $2 billion to help Japanese companies bring supply chains and manufacturing back to Japan to create jobs and protect technology.[78] By July applications for total funding by Japanese firms were over ten times the available funds.[79] Polls in 2020 showed that 80 percent of the Japanese public approved the tightening of sensitive technology exports.[80]

Yet just as U.S. tech companies have grown anxious that investment screening, reshoring of supply chains, and strict export controls vis-à-vis China could hurt their bottom line, so too many Japanese companies have quietly expressed concern at the trend toward increasing restrictions on trade and investment. The *Wall Street Journal* found one reason why in June 2020, when it reported that Japanese tech companies were still making close to $10 billion a year exporting components to Huawei and related Chinese companies for 5G technology despite the tighter government restrictions.[81] In a survey of thought leaders on China policy in August 2020, CSIS found that a large majority of Japanese national security experts wanted to block Chinese penetration of Japan's 5G market, but only 44 percent wanted to cut off supply chains in China.[82] Some Japanese business leaders took an even dimmer view of interrupting supply chains, since companies like Sony would lose an estimated $1 billion in exports to China in 2020 alone due to strict U.S. application of high-tech export controls to third countries.[83] Still, the Japan Center for Economic Research found in a 2020 survey of 3,000 Japanese business leaders that a plurality (46 percent) favored reducing tie-ups with Chinese firms and 48 percent supported the Trump administration's aggressive export control policies against China.[84]

These unresolved tensions in Japan's economic relationship with China will not recede easily. As one Japanese CEO put it to me, Japanese companies are riding the proverbial tiger—with most top-100 companies drawing about a third of their profits from operations in China yet constantly anxious that the tiger will break the leash and devour them. Trading companies and tech companies describe "tapering" their dependence on the China market, while tourism and consumer goods manufacturers fear falling behind in the competition to serve the world's largest middle class. Still, the gap between these sectors appears small indeed compared with the yawning gap between

U.S. financial firms' view of China and the reality that those firms are being hollowed out by China's predatory competition and intellectual property rights theft.

WHITHER JAPAN-CHINA ECONOMIC RELATIONS? TWO COMPETING POLITICAL VIEWS

As Tokyo University's Ito Asei notes, Japan's debates about China are not about competition versus cooperation per se, but rather about how much protection and decoupling of economic activity are necessary to protect Japanese technology while cooperating with a predatory but wealthy China.[85] To the extent that there are two camps, they are well represented in the views of two veteran LDP political leaders who were jostling to set the agenda for economic relations with China after Abe's term. These are classic "kuromaku"—éminences grises who shape policy and political debates in bars in Akasaka and in private offices of the LDP headquarters without aspiring to vault themselves into the top job of prime minister.

The first of these two political giants—Nikai Toshihiro—served as secretary general of the LDP beginning in 2016 and was an early and essential ally for Abe's bid for a third term as party president and prime minister.[86] Nikai got his start in politics as personal secretary to the minister of construction in the 1960s and 1970s as Tanaka Kakuei built his powerful political machine around infrastructure in rural Japan and the convenient kickbacks and favors that went with massive government spending. Like his hero Tanaka, Nikai rose through LDP ranks by going where the money was: leading the powerful *zoku* (caucuses) for transportation and construction, two primary sources of financing for the party. He left the party for a decade in the 1990s but stepped back in under the Koizumi cabinet as powerful as if he had never strayed.

After serving as minister of tourism in the late 1990s, Nikai became the leading champion for tourism, which more than tripled under Abe and became a major driver of growth for rural Japan—the LDP's political bastion. The largest number of foreign tourists now came from

China, and Nikai became the main brake on hostile LDP voices against Beijing as well as the major advocate of reducing tensions with China and setting aside disagreements over the Senkakus.[87] Early in Abe's tenure, former prime minister Fukuda Yasuo had been Abe's preferred private emissary to Beijing, but after 2016 it was Nikai. It was Nikai who led Japan's delegation to China's Belt and Road Forum on June 4, 2017, overruling the more cautious foreign ministry and hawks on Abe's National Security Council (NSC) staff. Nikai's vision for the next stage in Japan-China economic relations was captured in a quote he gave in September 2020 on his expectations for Xi Jinping's planned (but postponed) state visit to Japan: "We would strengthen our determination to achieve world peace and prosperity together," he declared, "with Japan and China playing a central role in the so-called co-creation [kyosō] of the world"—using a line from Fukuda's short-lived attempt at friendly relations with Beijing in 2008.[88] The word went out in the bureaucracy that Abe and the LDP had to listen to the new secretary general. Though Nikai's faction was only the fourth largest in the LDP, it was now number one in terms of fundraising for the party and indispensable to Abe's continued rule.[89]

By 2021, however, an aging Nikai had overstepped. Following the money once again, he drove the Suga administration's stimulus plans to respond to COVID-19 with a major emphasis on tourism.[90] His effort to control the distribution of government funding sparked a political backlash from other factions, and his push for unrestricted tourism in the "Go to Travel" campaign caused a press furor because of the resulting spike in COVID cases.[91] The powerful political figure was also undercut by the CCP's November 2020 five-year plan and flurry of economic nationalist measures, including an emphasis on "dual-circulation" dominance of supply and demand for emerging technologies and new FDI and export controls that threatened Japanese companies.[92] Nikai's influence was waning but not finished. He continued serving as Beijing's most important political interlocutor and the leading political champion of sectors that depended on Chinese tourists and the Chinese market. It was clear by 2021, however, that the winds of political debate on economic relations with China were shifting again in Tokyo.

The beneficiary was Amari Akira, the other éminence grise and Japan's tough-minded negotiator for the Trans-Pacific Partnership (TPP) from 2013 to 2016. As Amari clashed with U.S. trade representative Mike Froman over tariff rates and rice prices, the gift shops in the National Diet featured packs of sweet candies with Amari's image and a label declaring: "When it comes to TPP . . . it's Amari!!" (a pun on his name since *amari* can also mean "not so much" or "no, thank you"). Amari's rise was later interrupted by a campaign finance scandal that knocked him out of contention for the top spot in the LDP but did not necessarily prevent him from having major influence behind the scene. And he built his new power base with a coalition of like-minded LDP politicians who looked to him for a new strategy on economic security—this time vis-à-vis China.[93]

In a series of widely attended sessions within the LDP (one of which I keynoted), Amari pushed Abe to include an economic secretariat on the NSC and then produced an LDP strategic blueprint in December 2020 titled "Toward Developing an 'Economic Security Strategy.'"[94] Amari's strategy advocated a series of measures, including strengthening government security clearances related to technology, expanding strategic investment screening, and working with the United States and Europe to formulate new rules for digital trade, export controls, and economic rulemaking that would prevent theft and domination of the democracies' technology sectors by China.[95] In 2021 these proposals were moving toward a broadly supported comprehensive legislative package on economic security in the Diet.[96]

Where Nikai spoke of mutual understanding and shared interests with China, frequently evoking the name of Tanaka Kakuei and the golden era of Japan-China relations in the 1970s and 1980s, Amari summed up his views to the members of his LDP caucus by stating that while Japan had certainly contributed to China's development, "it had ended in vain" because China is a "dictatorship."[97] Yet the difference in thinking about China between these two LDP heavyweights is not as large as these quotes suggest—nor anywhere near as yawning as the debates over China in the LDP in the 1960s or in other countries in the West more recently. Nikai is a supporter of the U.S.-Japan alliance and did nothing to obstruct Abe's strengthening of security ties with Australia and India, despite Beijing's displeasure with that alignment. For his part, Amari has never advocated complete decoupling the Japanese and Chinese economies—just stricter protection of Japan's technology and continued leadership in international rulemaking following his own work on the TPP. As two battle-scarred and influential political survivors, Amari and Nikai know well the boundaries of responsible debate in Japan—and the need to deter and compete with China without hurting Japan's own economy. Part of the enduring quality of Japan's strategy is precisely this consensus on first principles, despite the inherent tensions in emphasis between Nikai and Amari.

MULTILATERALIZING THE CHINA PROBLEM

The most important overlap in the Nikai and Amari Venn diagrams of economic policy lies in international alignment. Japan does not have the heft to shape China's economic policies or to sustain long-term economic confrontation with Beijing alone. Externalizing and internationalizing the problem is therefore Tokyo's best hope. Both Amari and Nikai know that Japan's economic security policies toward China must be well aligned with the United States and Europe so that Japanese firms are not unfairly handicapped and so that China is more responsive to Japanese entreaties. As Tokyo University professor Ito notes, "The Japanese approach will be effective if consensus can be built among domestic and international actors on the right balance between hedging and conditional engagement with China."[98]

In fact, the Abe government struggled to convince the Trump administration and the European Union to align technology policies toward China, eventually brokering a series of trilateral trade ministers' statements starting in 2019 that included—in addition to the hodgepodge of trans-Atlantic disputes over subsidies, steel tariffs, and the future of the World Trade Organization—language acknowledging the need to discuss "core principles to prevent forced technology transfer policies of third countries."[99] Japan's prospects for striking the right balance between competition and cooperation with China will not succeed without unity among the core democratic countries of the G-7 and the OECD. Disunion in Europe and distraction in the United States have made this effort extremely challenging. But as Amari put it in the 2020 strategy document, Japan must "amplify its voice in international rulemaking," for the sake of Japan's "independence, survival and prosperity from an economic perspective."[100]

THE U.S. FACTOR IN JAPAN'S STRATEGIC COMPETITION WITH CHINA

The fortieth anniversary of the 1978 Japan-China Treaty of Peace and Friendship ushered in a series of reciprocal visits between Xi and Abe that softened the two leaders' earlier friction. Meeting with Xi in Beijing in October 2018, Abe announced the end of Japan's four decades of official development assistance (ODA) to China, marking the end of an era, and Xi officially thanked him, marking a warmer tone than in the previous summits.[101] In December 2019, on the margins of a trilateral agreement with Korea held in Beijing, Abe stood next to Xi at the joint press conference looking considerably less ill at ease than he had at their first summit five years earlier, pledging to elevate Japan-China ties to a "new level."[102]

But the thaw in Japan-China relations was at best measured—a reassuring reminder that there are costs to both countries from excessive confrontation, but not proof that relations had turned a corner. The Japanese public clearly understood this fact. Polls by Genron NPO in 2019 demonstrated that close to half of Chinese respondents—informed by a changed propaganda tone from Beijing because of a deterioration in Sino-American relations—believed that relations with Japan had improved. However, Japanese respondents reading stories in a free press about increasing Chinese incursions around the Senkaku Islands, the arbitrary arrests of close to a dozen Japanese businessmen, crackdowns in Hong Kong, and ideological criticism of democracies and alliances were not so sure: those saying relations with China are "good" barely went up at all from previous years.[103]

The COVID-19 pandemic only worsened trust in Beijing. Despite initial sympathy for the victims of the pandemic in Wuhan and some exchange of medical equipment, Japanese public opinion of China hit the lowest level ever recorded in the wake of Beijing's subsequent aggressive "wolf warrior" diplomacy and threats against countries and firms not sufficiently awed by China's performance on the pandemic.[104] In June 2020 the ruling LDP was set to issue a resolution opposing Xi's expected visit to Japan because of China's new national security law on Hong Kong. Nikai convinced the party rank and file to instead issue the resolution from the party's National Security Commission, one notch below the top leadership, but was still unable to save the summit.[105] Observers of Japan-China relations took note the next month when Tokyo announced that the next ambassador to Beijing would be Tarumi Hideo, a known China hawk who had clashed with Chinese officials over the Senkaku issue in 2012 and was labeled a "spy" in the Chinese media.[106] Japan was responding to China's aggressive postpandemic "wolf warrior" diplomacy with some teeth of its own.

This would be the new normal in Japan-China relations. As Shiraishi Takashi, a leading Asia scholar and former advisor to the DPJ government, noted in the pages of the *Nikkei Asia* review, Abe had brought Japan-China relations to a "more even keel" but one based on a broad consensus that Japan must engage China while deepening the U.S.-Japan alliance and partnerships in the Indo-Pacific in order to blunt Xi's dream of becoming the hegemon of Asia. Abe would leave office in the coming years, Shiraishi concluded, but he had "changed Japan's China policy for a generation."[107] Indeed, Abe's successor, Suga Yoshihide, promised in the fall of 2020 to follow Abe's precedent on foreign policy, implying both strong counterbalancing but also careful attention to Japanese business interests with China. When Suga stepped down in 2021 the four contenders to succeed him as LDP leader all ran on their strategies to counter China through increased defense efforts and external alliance-building while seeking reassurance with Xi Jinping.[108] Though the China challenge was enormous, Abe had left his successors with an enviable relationship with China compared with his predecessors. The United States was now clearly more closely aligned with Japan, while Japan's relationship with China took on relatively more importance to Beijing as China-U.S. relations deteriorated. That left Japan with the potential for closer relations with the United States and China than each had with the other, an advantageous position for a nation that long sought to be a "bridge across the Pacific" even while countering Chinese revisionism within Asia.[109]

There was still one critical dimension, however. At the beginning of the Cold War, Yoshida had viewed China as the independent variable that would help Japan manage dependence on the United States in Asia. Now the United States had become the indispensable variable that Japan needed to manage China. This dependence required Japan to have a strategy to shape American choices.

3

THE UNITED STATES

Only a fool would want to get rid of Article Nine.
—YOSHIDA SHIGERU

For the first time in my career, our forces can prepare to fight
alongside the United States.
—SENIOR MINISTRY OF DEFENSE OFFICIAL, 2015

n the waning days of the Cold War, it was common for scholars and journalists to predict the demise of the U.S.-Japan alliance and the emergence of a new geopolitical rivalry between the United States and Japan. A 1988 Gallup poll found that more Americans feared Japan's economy than Soviet nuclear weapons; a 1992 draft Pentagon planning guidance predicated postwar U.S. defense strategy on geopolitical competition with Japan; and a popular book at the time bore the chilling title *The Coming War with Japan.*[1] The fact that the U.S.-Japan security relationship actually grew stronger over the next three decades is remarkable testament to the resilience of alliances between democratic states. And that resilience was not entirely dependent on a common geopolitical enemy after the Soviets, as theorists thought would be necessary. Poor coordination in a crisis with North Korea in 1994 initially refocused the Pentagon on the drift in the relationship since the end of the Cold War, but the "Nye Initiative" that followed aimed primarily to restore stability and predictability to the alliance and international order rather than to counterbalance a new geopolitical foe.[2] By the late 1990s, however, the rise of Chinese power and ambition emerged as the unmistakable driver behind tighter U.S.-Japan alignment. Faced with declining relative power and absolutely unwilling to accept Chinese hegemony in Asia, Japanese leaders and the Japanese public more broadly embraced a strengthened alliance with the United States as the centerpiece of a new external balancing strategy.

As important as structural explanations are for understanding the revitalization of the U.S.-Japan alliance in this period, however, they can obscure ideational factors and geopolitical countercurrents that remain as wild cards. Alliances enhance a state's material power, but they also matter for reasons of legitimacy and prestige. Mismanagement of these ideational dimensions can do as much damage to alliances as any failure in the material realm. And in terms of geopolitical countercurrents, it is important to recall Thucydides's observation that smaller states aligned with more powerful hegemons face a vexing dilemma between *entrapment* in conflicts they do not seek (the risk inherent in moving too close to the larger power) and *abandonment* in the face of threats not shared by the larger power (the risk inherent in seeking too much autonomy).[3] Dependence on another power for security is not a natural state of affairs for nations with long histories of seeking autonomy in the international system, even if exogenous structural threats leave few good alternatives.

Much of Japan's postwar alliance policy can be understood as the pursuit of tools to escape this Thucydidean dilemma by maximizing autonomy without losing American support. For the most part, these tools worked remarkably well for Japan—so much so that few Japanese strategic experts or political leaders in the late 1980s and early 1990s anticipated the increasing level of dependence Japan would have on the United States for security three decades hence. Yet the dependence is also two-way: Abe and Japan's other conservative leaders approach the alliance with a recognition that the United States now also depends on

Japan much more for its security. Though Abe faced some headwinds from the public's pacifist sentiments, he brought Japan to a place where the risks of entrapment have been accepted in order to avoid the far more consequential risks of abandonment in the face of Chinese expansion. Yet the risks of closer alignment remain—and in some ways are more acute—particularly as U.S. power and purpose have increasingly come into question.

This chapter explains the powerful structural and ideational forces behind U.S.-Japan alignment in the twenty-first century and also the challenges that greater security dependence and integration have presented for Japan. For context, the chapter begins with the lessons from Japan's first formal alliance in modern history, the 1902–1922 Anglo-Japanese alliance, before examining Japan's postwar efforts to preserve autonomy, Abe's more recent decision to "embrace entrapment," and the lingering challenges left by renewed security dependence on the United States.

THE HISTORICAL CONTEXT: ALLIANCES, PRESTIGE, AND THE PURSUIT OF AUTONOMY

Japan's emergence from isolation into a competitive multipolar system of imperial rivalries at the end of the nineteenth century led Meiji leaders to search for partners in the pursuit of prestige and a more favorable balance of power in East Asia. After a millennium of avoiding entangling alliances, Japan's leaders soon embraced alliance with the same vigor they did a modern educational system and armaments industry. The choice of Britain as that ally was logical for a Japan seeking greater freedom of action in Asia, since Britain was also seeking new strategic alignments to free up resources to protect the empire and the home islands in the face of the growing naval power of imperial Russia, Germany, and France (Britain at the turn of the century also considered closer alignment with the United States, but Americans still clung stubbornly to their independent status in world affairs). It was the common Russian threat—particularly after the Russian occupation of parts of Manchuria in 1900—that formed the strongest bond between Japan and Britain. As Yamagata wrote in April 1901 to a more skeptical Itō Hirobumi to convince him of the need for alliance with Britain:

> Relations between Japan and Russia have not yet suffered a major upset but sooner or later a serious collision is inevitable. If Russia uses violence and invades our rightful spheres, we must be prepared to confront her decisively. But, if we are to avoid a collision and prevent war beforehand, we must secure the help of other powers to arrest Russia's southward advance. . . . If the alliance is achieved, we can preserve peace in East Asia, build up our trade, stimulate our industry and revive the economy.[4]

Britain was also the logical choice for Japan in terms of rank and prestige. The British were the first to end the imperial powers' series of unequal treaties with Japan. Anglo-Japanese negotiations ended extra-territoriality and other infringements of sovereignty in 1899 and were followed two years later by the conclusion of a bilateral security treaty between the two fully sovereign states. Five decades later, this pattern was repeated in San Francisco when Japanese envoys signed a peace treaty with the United States ending the postwar occupation of Japan, followed immediately by the first U.S.-Japan Treaty of Mutual Security, which went into effect in 1952. In 1902 Japanese and British newspapers showed front-page portraits of King Edward VII and the Emperor Meiji standing at equal stature, even though the British monarch would have towered over his Japanese counterpart. In 1951 the photographs were of John Foster Dulles hovering over Yoshida with President Harry Truman nowhere in sight—an early sign that establishing real autonomy and an equal partnership with the victorious United States would take more time.

The ideational importance of alignment with Britain went beyond rank and prestige. While Meiji Japan imported German advisors for the army and modeled the parliament (the Diet) on German rather than British parliamentary precedent, it was Britain's maritime posture in the world that had initially set the more important example for early modernizers like Katsu Kaishū and Fukuzawa Yukichi. The Royal Navy seconded officers to the naval academy in Tokyo beginning in 1873, and

Japan's best officers studied in Britain, including Tōgō Heihachirō, who did research on Horatio Nelson's "crossing of the 't'" at Trafalgar, laying the intellectual groundwork for his own victory at Tsushima. In the 1880s and 1890s Fukuzawa Yukichi was "imbued with the spirit of British utilitarianism and liberalism," as historian Ian Nish notes, and gathered around him at Keio University and the *Jiji Shimpō* newspaper strong advocates of the Anglo-Japanese alliance and a cosmopolitan, commercial, and imperial maritime strategy.[5] Completing the package started with geopolitical counterbalancing, rank and prestige, and ideational inspiration was British technology Japan needed to build the fleet that defeated the Chinese and then Russian navies—another precedent that was repeated five decades later when the United States followed the 1951 San Francisco peace and security treaties with the 1954 U.S. and Japan Mutual Defense Assistance Agreement transferring technology to restart Japan's dormant defense industries and economy after the Korean War.[6]

Ironically, it was the United States that insisted on termination of the Anglo-Japanese alliance as part of the Washington Naval Treaty in 1922. The British had attempted to provide assurances that the Royal Navy would not turn on the United States in the event of a U.S. war with Japan, but U.S. Navy planners still feared a two-front war, and after the experiences of August 1914 American politicians and diplomats became convinced that bilateral security treaties were sources of conflict rather than instruments of stability. Backed by unprecedented military and diplomatic power after the First World War, the Americans prevailed and the British agreed to end the Anglo-Japanese alliance in exchange for caps on naval armament, without which the U.S. Navy would have surpassed the Royal Navy to become the largest battle fleet in the world. As noted, other factors, such as the demise of the Meiji oligarchs, the depletion of European imperial power in the First World War, the collapse of the international economy, and the internal consolidation of China, all contributed to Japan's march to militarism and autarky in the interwar years. Yet one important factor in Japan's fateful turn in this period has to be considered: the termination of the Anglo-Japanese alliance and the corresponding rise in influence of the continentalist German school of thought in Japanese grand strategy.

ESCAPING POSTWAR ENTRAPMENT
THROUGH ANTI-MILITARISM

The architect of Japan's postwar foreign policy and alliance with the United States, Yoshida Shigeru, was himself a loyal adherent to the Anglo-Japanese alliance, which had been signed the year he joined the foreign ministry and which shaped his entire diplomatic philosophy. The insuppressible Yoshida wrote to Prime Minister Konoe Fumimaro in 1940 opposing the new Axis pact with Germany and Italy and lecturing the prime minister that "the reason why the China Incident has not been resolved as desired is because [the government] has been counting on Germany and Italy, who are of no help, and has failed to prepare to utilize the power Great Britain and the United States have in China."[7] Yoshida paid a steep professional price for his honesty throughout the war, but he emerged as Japan's most powerful strategic thinker after the war, determined to return to Japan all the advantages of alignment with Britain's replacement as the world's leading maritime power.

Alliance with the United States proved far more complicated for Japan than alliance with Britain. Instead of a multipolar system in which Japan could choose an ally for maximum freedom to maneuver, Tokyo now faced a rigid bipolar system in the face-off with the Soviet Union and near total dependence on the United States for economic growth, security, and technology. The new conservative consolidation in Japan's domestic politics also rested on the shared assumption among disparate political forces in the new LDP that the alternative to alliance with the United States would be neutralism and the ascent of the socialists and communists left at home. Yoshida was fully committed to aligning with the United States for reasons of domestic politics, economic recovery, and international prestige—but he was also constantly on guard to protect Japan's residual autonomy from American hegemony. Throughout his career he retained his prewar Anglophilia and distrust of the idealistic Wilsonian streak in American statecraft that had crippled his beloved alliance with Britain and unhinged Japanese diplomacy before the war.[8]

The brilliance of Yoshida's approach was that he secured the alliance with the United States and consolidated the conservatives at home while diversifying Japan's toolkit for maintaining autonomy in the international system. In fact, most of the tools in that kit followed logically from the very principles behind America's vision for a new postwar order. First, Japan would focus on economic recovery based on import substitution and export-led growth, just as U.S. planners in the late 1940s intended as a bulwark against communist expansion in East Asia. Second, Japan would restore its prestige in the international system by earning ever higher rank in the United Nations system and the multilateral architecture that Japan had tried to destroy in the prewar years, for as international relations scholar John Ikenberry notes, the United States was positioning itself after the war as a "liberal leviathan" that would attract states by allowing them to partially constrain American hegemony through multilateral institutions.[9] Third, Japan would strive—as noted in the previous chapter—to restore a relationship with Beijing that was closer than Washington's if not closer than Japan's connection to the United States. Fourth, Japan would avoid complete dependence on the United States by establishing a national police force (and after 1954 a self-defense forces) to provide minimal defense and to keep U.S. forces out of domestic security issues. And fifth, Japan would wield the antiwar clause written by U.S. authorities into Article Nine of the 1947 Japanese constitution as a perpetual alibi against entrapment in America's Cold War conflicts in Asia.[10] In what must have been sweet revenge, Yoshida turned Wilsonian idealism into a powerful tool to strengthen Japanese autonomy.

While many of those closest to Yoshida believe he did not intend for Japan's pacifist constitution to remain intact forever, at the time he called the opponents of Article Nine "fools" for wanting to remove the nation's most important brake on militarism and entrapment in Cold War conflicts at a time when Japan was weak.[11] American architects of Cold War strategy like Richard Nixon and John Foster Dulles admired Yoshida's realism and anticommunism, but when Dulles proposed a NATO-style Pacific Pact in 1950, Yoshida gave a resounding "no" lest the collective security arrangement obligate Japan to help defend Korea or Taiwan (Yoshida was ultimately saved by Australia and New Zealand, which opposed including Japan in such a pact).[12] Yoshida and his mainstream political successors then took the vaguely worded pacifist language in Article Nine outlawing the right of war to settle international disputes and institutionalized it over the following decades in a series of restrictive policies and precedents aimed at strengthening the nation's alibi against military entrapment. In the 1990s leading scholars of the newly ascendant constructivist school of international relations theory pointed to this phenomenon as evidence that ideas and identity are ultimately more significant shapers of state behavior than the simplistic balance-of-power considerations that realists examine, arguing that Japan went from "sword to chrysanthemum."[13] The constructivists were right about the influence of pacifism in postwar Japanese political culture, but the same history can also be explained with Thucydides's observation that states will seek to escape entrapment if they can. Japan's institutionalization of the anti-militarist norms in the postwar constitution reflected the power of ideas, as constructivists note, but also very old ideas about power, going back to the original ancient Greek realist himself.

THE BAN ON COLLECTIVE SELF-DEFENSE

The most important of these postwar brakes against entrapment was the Japanese government's ban on participation in collective self-defense (*shūdanteki jieiken*), or the use of force to assist another state under attack. The UN Charter guarantees all states that right, as the first U.S.-Japan Security Treaty in 1951 noted explicitly: "The Treaty of Peace recognizes that Japan as a sovereign nation has the right to enter into collective security arrangements, and further, that the Charter of the United Nations recognizes that all nations possess an inherent right of individual and collective self-defense."[14] As legal scholar Murase Shinya has emphasized, there has never been any treaty or constitutional ruling in Japan that explicitly banned the use of collective self-defense. Instead, "the government's decision not to permit the use of collective self-defense was made from a policy perspective."[15] The only judicial test of the constitutionality of the right of collective self-defense came with the 1959 *Sunakawa* case, in which the Supreme Court of Japan ruled that U.S.

bases in Japan and the right of self-defense were not inconsistent with the constitution but were matters of "extremely high political consideration" better left to the cabinet.[16] Rather than pick up the ideological hot potato, the politicians who made up the cabinet then passed the responsibility for ruling on questions of collective self-defense to the career bureaucrats in the powerful and enigmatic Cabinet Legislation Bureau (CLB) (*Naikaku Hōseikyoku*).

Established under the Cabinet Law of 1952, the CLB consists of twenty-four lawyers from across Japan's ministries; the lawyers have five-year terms of service and make a practice of preventing foreign ministry officials from ruling on issues related to security that the bureau oversees.[17] As a result, key decisions on whether specific military operations or commitments to the alliance violate the constitution have been left to specialists from ministries such as agriculture or justice. One of the first and most consequential rulings came in the Diet debate over the new U.S.-Japan Security Treaty in 1960—picking up the same issues in the *Sunakawa* case—when the bureau director, Hayashi Shūzō, determined that the U.S. commitment to defend Japan under the new agreement was consistent with America's right of collective self-defense enshrined in the UN Charter, but in the spirit of Article Nine Japan would *not* act upon its own right of collective self-defense to assist the United States or its allies.[18] Additional CLB rulings specified that this ban on collective self-defense prevented "integration in the use of force" (*buryoku kōshi no ittaika*) with the United States, meaning that Japan's forces could not even arm U.S. warplanes if they went into action against a third state not engaging in direct aggression against Japan.[19] The CLB bureaucrats ensured that the "mutual" aspect of the treaty would essentially be a trade of bases for security protection.

Additional brakes were put on entrapment in the context of regional conflict, particularly with respect to Japan's association with any American use of force deriving from U.S. bases in Japan. The United States was fully utilizing bases in Japan to defend South Korea when the first security treaty was signed in 1951. When Washington insisted that Japan's commitment to host U.S. bases for the "security of the Far East" be made more explicit in the 1960 reversion of the treaty (the 1951 treaty stated only that the United States would station forces "to deter armed attack upon Japan"), the Japanese government agreed, but then the CLB unilaterally defined the Far East to be "the Philippines and northward, Japan and its neighborhood, South Korea and Taiwan." This restrictive geographic definition of the "Far East" excluded Vietnam, of course, forcing U.S. B-52 bomber pilots operating from Anderson Air Force Base in Okinawa a decade later to pretend they did not know where they were going to be flying each day with their planes full of bombs.[20]

These obstacles to integrating U.S. and Japanese military operations proved frustratingly impervious for the American side. After Chinese and North Korean threats prompted the government of Hashimoto Ryūtaro to issue his joint security declaration with President Bill Clinton in April 1996 pledging to revise the earlier bilateral Guidelines for Defense Cooperation, which would include for the first time "cooperation in the areas surrounding Japan that have a direct impact on Japan's security," the CLB ruled—without any consultation with the American side—that the Far East Clause still pertained and that the ban on collective defense would continue to prevent any integration in the use of force outside of the direct defense of Japan.[21] Japanese defense and foreign ministry officials were able to carve out some new missions, such as Japanese seaborne missile defense for U.S. carrier battle groups, that could be defined as defensive (and were high on the Pentagon's action list), but the lingering legal uncertainties made it close to impossible for the Pentagon to consider the kind of joint military planning common in other alliances like NATO or the U.S.-Korea alliance. American efforts to operationalize defense cooperation outside of the narrow defense of Japan once again broke on the rocks of the CLB's rigid interpretation of Article Nine.

The hardening strictures on collective self-defense did not entirely deter anti-mainstream Japanese leaders like Nakasone Yasuhiro from finding other ways to strengthen security cooperation with the United States, however. In the 1980s, for example, Nakasone supplemented the Reagan administration's strategy of containing Soviet expansion in the Far East by increasing Japan's own military capability to turn the home islands into a "shield" while the U.S. Navy and U.S. Air Force went into the Soviet maritime regions to attack with the "spear." While highly risky for Japan in a geopolitical context—Japan might have been implicated in horizontal U.S. escalation against the Soviets in the Far East in the event of war against NATO——the legal basis for Nakasone's strategy was entirely premised on "exclusively defensive defense" (*senshu bōei*)—the basic parameters initially set in 1957 for Japan's military capabilities—and *not* collective self-defense with the United States.[22] As a result, U.S. and Japanese force buildups and military planning happened in parallel but not in unison. As Jim Auer, the top Japan expert in the Pentagon at the time, noted, the two countries were lucky that the Soviets did not really understand how disconnected the U.S. and Japanese militaries would have been in an actual shooting war.[23]

When the George H. W. Bush administration urged Japan to play a similarly proactive role in the 1990–1991 Gulf War a few years later, Nakasone had been replaced by an internally focused puppet of the mainstream Tanaka Faction, Kaifu Toshiki, and Japan no longer had the convenient excuse of contributing by merely defending the home islands. Multiple efforts by the foreign ministry to dispatch transport planes, equipment, and hospitals to Kuwait foundered, and even after Japan contributed over $14 billion instead, the effort was dismissed by observers around the world as selfish, risk-averse "checkbook diplomacy."[24] Too late to actually contribute to the Gulf War, Japan passed legislation in 1992 allowing the Self-Defense Forces to participate with strict restrictions in certain UN peacekeeping operations.[25] This multilateral ticket to shoring up the alliance and Japanese credibility while maintaining a hedge against entrapment proved only marginally helpful, however, since the UN-centered collective security system envisioned by George H. W. Bush at the time of the Gulf War failed to materialize.

In the first major test of the alliance after the 1996 U.S.-Japan Joint Security Declaration and the 1997 revised defense guidelines, Japan was led by another anti-mainstream political figure determined to demonstrate the strength of the U.S.-Japan alliance despite the constraints imposed by the CLB. Koizumi Junichirō responded to the September 11, 2001, terrorist attacks promptly and decisively, writing to President George W. Bush, "I am your friend. . . . I will always be your friend," and passing the next month antiterrorism legislation that allowed Japan to dispatch forces to operate with the U.S. Central Command in the Middle East.[26] The Japan Maritime Self-Defense Forces refueled coalition warships searching for Taliban-related transshipments in the Arabian Sea, and a Japanese engineer battalion was deployed to Samawah in southern Iraq to provide humanitarian assistance and reconstruction capabilities.[27] The deployment was as politically risky for Koizumi as support for U.S. military strategy had been for Nakasone two decades earlier. Had the Self-Defense Forces suffered casualties, Koizumi's government might have fallen (as it happened, the only casualties were two diplomats, one a personal friend named Oku Katsuhiko, while the mustachioed commander of the engineer battalion, Satō Masahisa, returned to Japan as a celebrity and became a successful politician). Koizumi took that enormous political risk because he needed to demonstrate solidarity with the United States in the context of the growing threat posed to Japan in the western Pacific by China and to demonstrate Japan's readiness for a more assertive role in international affairs without American "gaiatsu" (pressure).[28] He succeeded on both fronts, but as a group of frustrated former officials from the Bush Pentagon argued in a report in 2006, the United States and Japan were no better off in terms of their readiness to deal with military contingencies with China in Japan's own backyard.[29]

THE DPJ AND THE DEBATE OVER COLLECTIVE SELF-DEFENSE

When the populist Democratic Party of Japan (DPJ) came to power in 2009, the initial signals from Prime Minister Hatoyama were of dealignment, as he touted his new "East Asia Community" with China and expressed opposition to existing plans for a new U.S. Marine Corps air station in Okinawa, which U.S. and Japanese governments had been trying to move forward since 1995 to relieve pressure on local communities from the existing base at Futenma.[30] The kingmaker behind Hatoyama, former Tanaka Faction strongman Ozawa Ichirō, held deep resentment against the United States and supporters of the alliance in the foreign ministry and made an ostentatious show of bringing hundreds of political supporters to Beijing while studiously ordering new DPJ members not to visit the United States.[31]

Yet among the hodgepodge of former socialists and autarkic nationalists who made up the coalition was also a committed group of national security realists who had more in common with LDP figures like Abe regarding the alliance than they did with their own prime minister, let alone Ozawa. Principal among these were Maehara Seiji, the first DPJ foreign minister, his successor Genba Kōichirō, and the third and last of the three DPJ prime ministers, Noda Yoshihiko. The three were graduates of the Matsushita Institute of Government and Management (*Matsushita Seikeijuku*), established in 1979 by Matsushita Kōnosuke, the visionary founder of Panasonic Corporation, in order to prepare a new class of political leaders based on merit rather than the increasingly hereditary assumption of power evident in the LDP.[32] Had they been the scions of founding members of the LDP like Abe, Asō Tarō, or Kōno Tarō, they would almost certainly have been recruited into the ruling party. Instead they studied, campaigned, and clawed their way into power from the outside, backed financially by other iconoclastic loners in the business community like Kyocera founder Inamori Kazuo. Where Hatoyama had called for moving away from "servile diplomacy for the U.S." and his bombastic coalition partner Kamei Shizuka had argued that Japan should elevate China to the level of U.S. importance in Japanese diplomacy, Maehara, Genba, and Noda spoke out clearly on the Chinese threat and the indispensable role of the alliance with the United States.[33] Cut from the same conservative cloth were other DPJ figures like Nagashima Akihisa, who had studied with alliance expert James Auer at Vanderbilt and wrote a report at the Council on Foreign Relations in 1999 proposing a "host regional support" concept that would have reduced the burden of U.S. bases in Japan by entering into the kind of Pacific Pact Yoshida had rejected in 1951.[34]

Faced with mounting challenges from China stemming from the Senkaku crises of 2010 and 2012, these conservative realists in the DPJ pushed behind the scenes for Japan to finally exercise the right of collective self-defense.[35] Prime Minister Kan Naoto, a populist anti-establishment figure who succeeded Hatoyama, insisted in the Budget Committee of the Upper House of the Diet on August 5, 2010, that the government had no plans to change the interpretation of the constitution with respect to collective self-defense.[36] But that December the government introduced a more flexible "dynamic defense forces concept" in the 2010 update of Japan's National Defense Program Guidelines, and the next January the DPJ actually began examining options to exercise collective self-defense in anticipation of Kan's planned visit to the United States the following spring.[37]

In the interim, a massive tsunami struck Japan on March 11, 2011, and these major defense policy debates came to a halt as the inexperienced Kan struggled to manage the meltdown of the nuclear reactor in Fukushima and the credibility of his government. In response to the tsunami, the U.S. and Japanese militaries mounted a highly successful joint humanitarian response and recovery effort under Operation *Tomodachi* ("Friend"), including trilateral operations with the Royal Australian Air Force that put the U.S.-Japan alliance and the validity of joint and combined operations in a popular new light.[38] When Matsushita Institute alumnus Noda took the premiership from Kan in September 2011, he made it clear that he disagreed with his predecessor's reticent view on collective self-defense and intended to begin preparing for a new interpretation of the constitution to allow Japan to exercise that right.[39] Weighed down by internal ideological divisions in the ruling coalition and his party's failure to respond vigorously to the March 2011 tsunami, however, Noda lost his first election and his job to Abe and the LDP in December 2012. Had they been in the same party, Noda and Abe would have been close political allies on the issue of collective self-defense and alliance with the United States. As it was, Noda faded to the background of Japanese politics as Abe picked up the baton and carried it forward to transform Japan's security policy.

ABE'S NATIONAL SECURITY LEGISLATION

Abe's own resurgence within the LDP in 2012 was made possible by Chinese coercion in the East China Sea, as was noted, but also by DPJ mismanagement of the U.S.-Japan alliance. In closed study groups with security experts like Okazaki Hisahiko and conservative industrial leaders like Kasai Yoshiyuki of the Central Japan Railway Company, Abe had been studying Japan's strategic circumstances and the history of the collective self-defense debate.[40] In speeches in Tokyo and Washington, Abe spoke of the United States and Japan as "the guardians, protecting the order, peace, freedom and prosperity that have made the Pacific the greatest highway for humankind," stressing that "Japan and the US must work together and with like-minded democracies to ensure that the oceans remain free."[41] But where Koizumi had sung Elvis Presley's "I need you, I love you," to George W. Bush and cited his admiration for American toughness as epitomized in Gary Cooper movies, Abe was motivated less by sentimentality and more by hard geopolitical calculations. As his speechwriter and brain trust, Taniguchi Tomohiko, has noted, Abe felt it was his duty to ensure that the United States remained committed to the Indo-Pacific, by "making it easier for the United States to maintain a presence in Japan" and able to count on the alliance with Japan in global diplomacy and regional crises.[42] Abe took nothing for granted with the United States. To shape China, his government needed to first shape Washington's choices.

In his first summit meeting with President Barack Obama on February 22, 2013, in Washington, Abe stunned the White House with an ambitious agenda that included reviewing the 1997 defense guidelines and revising the division of roles and missions between U.S. and Japanese forces. He also declared his readiness for Japan to join the U.S.-led Trans-Pacific Partnership (TPP), which prompted the unprepared U.S. trade representative to ask for more time to lay the groundwork with Congress.[43] Abe and his chief cabinet secretary, Suga Yoshihide, also pledged to make progress on the contentious issue of constructing the new Marine Corps air station to replace Futenma in Okinawa, which Hatoyama had thrown into confusion by pledging to find a new location outside of Okinawa and then just as glibly reversing his position when he confessed not having understood what "deterrence" is.[44] Abe wanted to show a marked departure from the DPJ and a readiness to take on hard problems in the alliance. As he put it in his first speech in Washington in February 2013, "I am back . . . and so shall Japan be!"

Abe's first year in power (for the second time) marked the most consequential reform of Japanese security policy and alliance relations with the United States since 1960, when his grandfather had pushed through the expanded and revised security treaty at the cost of his government. For Abe, this was unfinished family business. In October 2013 the United States and Japan agreed to revise and upgrade the 1997 guidelines for Japan-U.S. defense cooperation, which Secretary of Defense Robert Gates and Minister of Defense Onodera Itsunori pledged to complete by 2015. The Abe government's *National Security Strategy* that December emphasized the centrality of the U.S.-Japan alliance to "peace and stability in the Asia-Pacific region" and announced plans "to reinforce the domestic foundation" for the alliance and the new bilateral defense guidelines with new laws and policies.[45] Specific laws were passed and policies implemented by the end of 2013 to establish the National Security Council (NSC), strengthen protection of sensitive intelligence, and formulate a new five-year defense plan aimed at creating the "Dynamic Joint Defense Forces" needed to respond to asymmetric "grey zone" challenges from China.[46] Planning for the new defense guidelines and roles and missions with the United States would take another two years. In the meantime, the Abe government had to address the stickiest issue of all to ensure that the new agreements with the United States were credible in terms of the actual ability of U.S. and Japanese forces to operate together—the issue of collective self-defense.

REINTERPRETING ARTICLE NINE

While revising the interpretation of the constitution to make explicit the right of collective self-defense would by political necessity require an extensive Diet, national, and even international debate, the initial epicenter of the contest would be the CLB. In August 2013, Abe appointed as director Komatsu Ichirō, a bookish career diplomat with expertise in international law. While serving in the Japanese embassy in Washington in 2001, Komatsu had been the key liaison with me in the Bush White House on 9/11 and had conveyed directly to Prime Minister Koizumi the night of the attack the message that Britain and Australia had both pledged to exercise *their* right of collective self-defense with the United States in response to the terrorist attack.[47] Japan, he explained to Tokyo, was handicapped by its inability to do the same. The real-world implications of the abstract legal arguments he had worked on throughout his career were suddenly illuminated in clear relief, and he brought that searing experience into his new appointment under Abe.

Japanese prime ministers had always had the authority to appoint a foreign ministry diplomat to lead the CLB under the Cabinet Law, but none had faced the urgency or enjoyed the political support within the LDP necessary to make the move. Abe faced no resistance within his party and ensured that Komatsu's appointment signaled clearly that the CLB would now determine that collective self-defense would be permitted.[48] Diagnosed with terminal cancer shortly after his appointment, Komatsu stuck to his post despite Abe's offer to let him step down and focus on treatment. To emphasize procedural continuity, Komatsu held that collective defense could be applied under the so-called basic logic established in 1972 that Japan could take measures in self-defense consistent with Article Nine of the constitution "only when they are inevitable for dealing with imminent unlawful situations where the people's right to life, liberty, and the pursuit of happiness is fundamentally overturned due to an armed attack by a foreign country, and for safeguarding these rights of the people."[49] Komatsu did not change the constraints of the "basic logic" but merely extended them to cover collective self-defense, which was already determined as allowable under the UN Charter consistent with Japan's postwar position that international treaties supersede domestic law. Thus, in response to the "evolving security environment surrounding Japan," the CLB concluded that

> not only when an armed attack against Japan occurs **but also when an armed attack against a foreign country that is in a close relationship with Japan occurs** [emphasis mine] and as a result threatens Japan's survival and poses a clear danger to fundamentally overturn people's

right to life, liberty and pursuit of happiness, and when there is no other appropriate means available to repel the attack and ensure Japan's survival and protect its people, use of force to the minimum extent necessary should be interpreted to be permitted under the Constitution as measures for self-defense in accordance with the basic logic of the Government's view to date.[50]

Based on this new predicate and recommendations of a parallel *Report of the Advisory Panel on Reconstruction of the Legal Basis for Security* led by Kasai, Okazaki, and other scholars and business leaders close to Abe, the cabinet announced its detailed plan for the "Development of Seamless Security Legislation to Ensure Japan's Survival and Protect Its People" on July 1, 2014.[51] With the permissibility of collective self-defense established as a matter of policy, the government announced it would now introduce legislation relaxing restrictions on "integration in the use of force" (*buryoku kōshi no ittaika*) with an ally so that the kind of logistical support could be provided to U.S. forces at sea or from Japan that had been originally envisioned by the U.S. side in the 1997 defense guidelines. The new legislative package would also aim to remove the previous obstacles to the Maritime Self-Defense Forces' "seamless" operations with the Japan Coast Guard and with U.S. forces when responding to "grey zone" coercion by China that did not cross the line of "armed attack" against Japan. And the cabinet pledged to introduce legislation that would reduce restrictions on the use of force by the Self-Defense Forces for the purpose of "coming to the aid of geographically distant units or personnel under attack" (*kaketsuke keigo*) so that Japan's forces would no longer be a liability to fellow militaries deployed together for UN peacekeeping or other similar operations in third countries.[52] Komatsu did not live to see the announcement of the sweeping new legislation, literally dying at his post the week before it passed. "Komatsu-san did everything," Abe declared; "it was a task he could venture only at the risk of his life."[53]

With the cabinet's commitment to establish a new legal framework, the United States and Japan completed new revised Guidelines for Japan-U.S. Defense Cooperation on April 27, 2015, outlining plans to strengthen cooperation on cybersecurity and space, the defense of Japan's outer islands, sea-lane protection, and coalition operations outside the region. The new defense guidelines also established an Alliance Coordination Mechanism (ACM) to replicate some of the advantages of the joint and combined command relationships and mutual collective self-defense rights that the United States enjoyed with NATO and South Korea.[54] Two days later, on April 29, a triumphant Prime Minister Abe received a standing ovation in the first ever address by a Japanese prime minister to a joint session of the U.S. Congress.[55]

THE LEGISLATIVE BATTLE AND THE CONTINUING UNDERTOW OF ANTI-MILITARISM

But Abe still had to deliver the legislation. His speech to Congress was intended—and granted—to create a strong political tailwind in Tokyo and not just to declare victory. On May 15 the cabinet formally submitted a comprehensive package of "Legislation for Peace and Security." There were ten bills in all. Whereas every previous Japanese government had chosen incremental legislative changes to address security upgrades— passing at most one or two of these types of bills at a time—Abe chose to clean up every remaining uncertainty about Japan's ability to be a proactive security actor in one grand move.[56]

Abe and his allies relished the coming Diet debate. He had near total unity within the ruling LDP, and his pacifist-leaning coalition partners in the Kōmeitō Party had been convinced to support the legislation by the government's decision to use a "positive list" of measures that would be allowed under collective self-defense rather than the more permissive "negative list" of what would explicitly *not* be allowed that was preferred by Pentagon planners and Japan's more conservative security experts.[57] Kōmeitō also needed a label for the new policy that would indicate to its political base (particularly the *Sōka Gakkai* religious organization's activist women's and youth divisions) that it remained committed to the peaceful intent of Article Nine of the constitution. The Abe government had chosen for that purpose the term "a proactive contribution to peace" (*sekkyokuteki heiwashugi*), which had been used by officials as early as 1977 to connote continuity in Article Nine when embarking on new defense policies and was resurrected by Abe's team in 2013. As Aki-yama Daisuke observes in his probing study of the doctrinal roots of the security legislation, the Japanese government had essentially stolen the "proactive contribution to peace" concept from European peace studies and then diluted the pacifist intent, to the enormous ire of the devotees of peace studies in Japan.[58] But those esoteric scholars enjoyed only a narrow audience in the opposition parties, which were themselves weak and divided after Abe's 2012 election. The left-leaning members of the former DPJ now in the new Constitutional Democratic Party and their allies in the smaller Communist and Social Democratic Parties accused Abe of tabling unconstitutional "war legislation" and pointed to *Asahi Shimbun* polls showing that a majority of the public opposed collective self-defense. But other polls in the conservative *Sankei Shimbun* showed the opposite, that a majority supported the government's position. LDP politicians reported from across the country that their rank-and-file members were confident and enthusiastic about the coming fight.[59]

Yet the headwinds of pacifism and the complexity of navigating Diet deliberations proved far more challenging than Abe and his allies had anticipated. The government chose to show what was permissible for the Self-Defense Forces by using fifteen concrete examples (eight dealt directly with collective self-defense) that had been tortuously negotiated with coalition partner Kōmeitō.[60] Abe's proxies in the media and com-mentariat found that they had difficulty following the logic negotiated by the lawyers and politicians and consequently spread contradictory and damaging interpretations of what was actually allowed in op-eds and TV news programs. Knowing that the majority of Japan's consti-tutional scholars were on the left and opposed collective self-defense, the government tried to find independent constitutional scholars for the Diet deliberations who could explain Komatsu's logic, but those wit-nesses also became confused by the political and operational aspects of the fifteen examples, and in one case government witness Hasebe Yasuo confessed to the Diet that the package of security bills may have actually been on shaky legal ground because terms such as "act of aggression" were being used in new ways by the government.[61] Some scholars, like diplomatic historian and Yoshida scholar Sakamoto Kazuya, made articulate and compelling arguments to the public that the law was necessary to save the constitution in the context of a changing security environment, as Japan's Yoshida himself would have recognized.[62] But many other scholars and pundits who supported the legislation applied their own spin or inserted old ideological pet peeves that muddied the government's arguments.

Abe himself was skillful in handling the opposition's assaults on the legislation in the Diet. He focused on three main examples to illustrate when collective defense would be justified: to respond to a blockade in the Straits of Hormuz, to come to the aid of American ships with Japanese citizens on board, and to help defend a U.S. Aegis cruiser on patrol in the western Pacific. When told by the opposition that Japan would not have to operate with the United States in the government's example of the Straits of Hormuz being shut down since there would be alternate pipelines for oil, Abe rebutted that the worldwide demand to use those pipelines would constrict supply and therefore meet the threshold of threatening Japan's survival and leaving no other means but collective self-defense.[63] The opposition had even less luck convincing the public that it should not assist American ships if Japanese on board were under threat, since Abe pointed out that this would represent the very definition of defending those citizens' "life and liberty."[64] And when the opposition challenged his assertion that Japan could legally provide defense for U.S. Aegis cruisers patrolling against enemy missile attacks, Abe explained that Japan alone would not have the capability to defend against the full range of attacks and the loss of the U.S. ship would therefore threaten the Japanese peoples' own "right to life, liberty and pursuit of happiness."[65]

Abe returned from the daily debates to his office energized, but the rest of his government was exhausted by the four months of political debate it took to get the legislation through. And despite Abe's performance, the government's message remained confusing, since the fifteen case studies left room for opponents to find multiple angles to assert that the scenarios would not have to involve collective self-defense if they were only modified slightly to fit the rules for individual self-defense.[66] Ministers and politicians less deft than Abe had difficulty with this thrust and parry. Meanwhile, the much smaller but more focused Communist and Social Democratic Parties came out with a simple and gripping message in their national campaign: "Your children will be conscripted for war."[67] Polls that summer showed that 81 percent of the public found the government's explanation "insufficient," and the centrist *Nihon Keizai Shimbun* cautioned that while the government had convincingly explained the need to strengthen deterrence, it had not fully made the case that it had to be done with collective self-defense.[68]

It would be wrong to assert, as critics in Japan tried, that Abe eventually rammed the legislation through without thorough debate. In all, Abe and the cabinet participated in over one hundred hours of public deliberations in the Diet.[69] If anything, it was the most transparent debate about Japan's right of collective self-defense in postwar history, since the earlier deliberations had largely been held behind closed doors in the CLB. The legislation eventually passed the Lower House on July 16 as crowds protested outside, and then passed both houses successfully on September 19 despite filibustering by opposition leaders.[70] Support for Abe's government dipped single digits to 41 percent, but unlike his grandfather after passage of the 1960 security treaty, Abe recovered to remain in power for years to come.[71]

In the end, the government prevailed by convincing the public and the media that the constraints would be adequate to prevent militarization. Komatsu's "basic logic" worked. The limitation of collective self-defense to minimal force and only in circumstances where Japan's "national survival" left no other options (called the "three conditions") proved politically sufficient, even though those judgment calls would logically reside with the prime minister and the cabinet in a crisis, barring a Supreme Court decision or no-confidence resolution in the Diet against the government.[72] As the *Nihon Keizai Shimbun* put it in a supportive editorial, the new legislation would allow the easy dispatch of the Self-Defense Forces but would also come with a "high level of accountability" for any government.[73] The legal restrictions were eased to strengthen deterrence, but the antiwar sentiment of the Japanese public remained little moved.

As careful Japan scholars like Jeffrey Hornung, Adam Liff, and Mike Mochizuki have each observed, the new legislation represented both more and less change than met the eye.[74] Japan was still not a "normal" ally capable of doing what Australia, Britain, or even Korea could in military affairs. Yet one veteran Ministry of Defense official captured the historic significance of what had happened when he told me that "for the first time in my career, our forces can prepare to fight alongside the United States." *Nihon Keizai Shimbun* called it "an incredibly significant turning point for Japan's security policy."[75] Importantly, the one opposition argument that failed to stick was the claim that Japan did not need to strengthen deterrence alongside the United States in the increasingly dangerous external security environment—a point that even Abe's nemesis, the left-leaning *Asahi Shimbun*, conceded.[76] And in the Diet interpolations the government gave the example of Australia, a nontreaty ally that might also be able to operate with Japan's forces under collective self-defense. That example elicited no significant opposition, and editorials in *Nihon Keizai Shimbun* and elsewhere welcomed the collective self-defense right as an opportunity for "US allies and friends (such as Japan, South Korea, Australia, India, and Southeast Asia) to work together to create the security cooperative network to confront China."[77] Nor was there notable opposition from abroad. Forty-four nations expressed some form of official support for the legislation, with Indonesia, Vietnam, and the Philippines most forward-leaning in East Asia. The South Korea government, troubled by political disputes with Japan over history but cognizant of the need for an effective U.S.-Japan alliance for security on the peninsula, asked only for adherence to the Peace Constitution. Only China expressed concern, though North Korea engaged in predictable hyperbole about Japanese militarism.[78]

NO ESCAPE FROM THUCYDIDES

Politically bruised but alive, Abe had successfully shored up the operational and political credibility of the U.S.-Japan alliance as a counterbalance to China and a pillar of stability in Asia. Beijing's efforts to promote the international isolation of Abe in op-eds and propaganda around the world the year before had completely failed, as we saw in the last chapter and as Beijing must have realized when Abe received a rousing welcome in the U.S. Congress in April 2015. Americans' trust in Japan, already the highest of any ally other than Britain, Canada, and Germany, went even higher in polls taken by the Chicago Council on Global Affairs in 2015.[79] Bipartisan support for the alliance in the U.S. Congress had never been stronger.

Yet Thucydides's ghost still hovered over the Prime Minister's Office. The Japanese public strongly supported the alliance, but in polls they began expressing concern about whether they could trust the United States now that it was apparent that dependence would deepen for common security. Abe had first encountered this same uncertainty about the American commitment at the end of the George W. Bush administration, when North Korea negotiator, Ambassador Christopher Hill, had convinced the State Department in 2008 to reverse earlier commitments not to lift terrorism sanctions on North Korea until progress was made on accounting for Japanese citizens abducted by the North. Abe argued in the Oval Office that this gesture to Pyongyang would undercut Japan's position in Asia but failed to reverse the U.S. policy shift.[80] President Barack Obama tried to reassure the Japanese public during an April 2014 visit to Tokyo by meeting with the families of the abductees and reaffirming his personal commitment that Article V of the U.S.-Japan Security Treaty would apply to the defense of the Japanese-administered Senkaku Islands.[81] However, senior members of the Obama administration created new uncertainty when they ignored Japanese official entreaties and welcomed China's proposal for establishment of a "New Model of Great Power Relations" between Washington and Beijing aimed at establishing a bipolar condominium that Beijing designed to deliberately marginalize Japan and other U.S. allies in regional diplomacy.[82] Even Obama's April 2014 reiteration of U.S. support on the Senkakus struck the Japanese media as being overly guarded in order to avoid offending Beijing.[83]

THE TRUMP SHOCK

All of these doubts about the Bush and Obama administrations would then pale in comparison with the shock Tokyo received in 2016 with the election of a U.S. presidential candidate who had run against the free trade, multilateralism, and strong alliances that were central to Japan's expectations of American leadership in the world. In 2015 Pew polling, 66 percent of Japanese respondents had expressed confidence in President Obama to "do the right thing in world affairs," despite misgivings about his administration's readiness to stand up to China. The percentage of Japanese expressing confidence in President Trump in 2017 was a mere 24 percent.[84] So important was the alliance and a personal relationship with the American president that Abe had broken all protocol and precedent to visit with Democratic candidate Hillary Clinton in New York in September 2016.[85] When Trump surprised Abe and the world with an upset victory on November 8, 2016, Abe used his congratulatory call to propose departing from his planned visit to Latin America the next week to convene an early meeting with President-Elect Trump in New York.[86] The two leaders struck up what was probably the warmest relationship Donald Trump developed with any allied leader, and Abe used multiple summits and rounds of golf with the president to reinforce the importance of the alliance, explain the China challenge, urge a firm stand on North Korea, and jump-start a bilateral U.S.-Japan trade agreement to keep open the prospect that a future administration might return to the Trans-Pacific Partnership. In contrast to his European or Canadian counterparts, Abe never once criticized Trump or his policies, even after Japan was slapped with steel tariffs and Trump ignored Abe's advice and told North Korean leader Kim Jong Il that he wanted to withdraw U.S. troops from Korea someday.[87]

Abe's efforts were aided by a national security establishment under Trump that held far more traditional Republican views on alliances and defense policy than the president himself. The drafters of the 2017 U.S. National Security Strategy clearly premised their commitment to strategic competition with China on deeper defense cooperation with Japan.[88]

The architects of the State Department's Free and Open Indo-Pacific Strategy took their cues from Japan's own earlier policy-planning document by the same name.[89] Indeed, the overall U.S. strategy reflected the same maritime strategic perspective behind Abe's worldview and thus an explicit rejection of the bipolar condominium implicit in China's proposed New Model of Great Power Relations. Meanwhile, the new U.S. International Development Finance Corporation was clearly modeled on Japan's Bank for International Cooperation (JBIC) and immediately established a close strategic partnership with JBIC to counter China's ambitious Belt and Road Initiative. And the NSC staff in both countries worked closely to try to craft summits that would convince Trump to follow Abe's advice on strategy, with which Trump's NSC staff largely concurred.

The Japanese public appeared to understand this, with 67 percent expressing confidence in 2017 Pew polls that the United States would defend Japan if attacked—a 7-point increase from the Obama years.[90] An anonymous senior foreign ministry official created trouble with the campaign of Democratic presidential candidate Joe Biden by writing in *The American Interest* in 2020 that Abe's foreign policy team worked better with the Trump team on security issues than they had with Obama's team (others in the foreign ministry disputed that author's thesis and authenticity, and a 2020 Center for Strategic and International Studies [CSIS] poll of foreign policy experts in Japan found that a majority preferred Joe Biden to Trump).[91]

Yet despite some alignment with the national security professionals in Washington, the repeated shock waves from Trump himself appear to have compounded the Japanese public's angst at dependence on the United States despite the more muscular defense posture in Washington. A shocking 62 percent of Japanese respondents to the 2017 Pew poll said that U.S. power was a threat to Japan's interests, a sharp uptick from the Obama years, and in a December 2018 Yomiuri/Gallup poll, only 30 percent of Japanese responded that they trusted the United States.[92] The Yomiuri/Gallup poll found that majorities in both the United States and Japan thought the alliance was important for regional security (64 percent in Japan and 70 percent in the United States)—which was consistent with other polling—and 75 percent of the Japanese respondents considered China a military threat. So the structural underpinnings of the alliance were still strong, but the Japanese public clearly felt the acuteness of Thucydides's dilemma. As one of Abe's intellectual allies, Keio University professor Hosoya Yūichi, put it to the *Nikkei Shimbun* in July 2020, reflecting on the apogee of Trumpism in the weak U.S. leadership role on display during the COVID-19 pandemic, "Japan will have to rethink its dependence on the United States for defense."[93] One of the principal architects of Abe's grand strategy, former deputy national security advisor Kanehara Nobukatsu, was even more blunt when he told an audience in Washington the next month that America's "vacancy of leadership is hurting our unity" in dealing with China.[94]

A MORE EVEN KEEL?

In 2021 the incoming Biden administration was well aware of this damage but also surprisingly objective about the strengths of the previous administration's connection with Japan. Biden chose as the first ever White House senior coordinator on the Indo-Pacific the veteran alliance-builder Kurt Campbell, who had led the strengthening of the U.S.-Japan alliance in the Pentagon in the mid-1990s and then subtly pushed back against the Obama administration's early flirtation with respecting China's "core interests" when he was assistant secretary of state for East Asia and the Pacific from 2009 to 2013.[95] Biden's embrace of Abe's Quad (the Japan-U.S.-Australia-India partnership) and the Free and Open Indo-Pacific framework and an invitation to Prime Minister Suga for the president's first in-person summit in Washington in April 2021 played well in Japan, but it was also hard to undo all the uncertainty caused by American vacillation over the previous fifteen years.

Nevertheless, for Japan, the alliance with the United States is now undeniably more important than it has been in decades. Abe's acceptance and even embrace of entrapment risks with the 2015 defense guidelines and related security legislation were a necessary step to ensure that Japan would not be abandoned by Washington, and subsequent polls in both countries demonstrated that the publics believed he had succeeded insofar as deterrence against China was concerned. Greater jointness with the United States also gave Japan more tools to shape American decision making and manage the risks of entrapment. The U.S. side now has more latitude to plan Japan "in" for contingencies in the western Pacific, and this reality will result in corresponding dependence on Japan for logistical support, intelligence, maritime security, and other critical operations in a contingency. As one senior U.S. military officer told me, the United States and Japan were moving from "interoperability to interdependence."[96] In theory, entrapment now runs both ways.

Abe did not want the alibi his predecessors had long used of telling the Japanese public that they had not known before that force was used or telling the Americans that Japan could not act. Abe was prepared to risk the political consequences necessary to demonstrate that Japan was a proactive and not reactive partner, as he did when publicly expressing support for the option of military options in the Trump administration's confrontation with North Korea in 2017 while simultaneously insisting on prior consultation in any use of force by Washington.[97] For Abe that was a matter of deep personal conviction. For future Japanese prime ministers, it will be an inescapable matter of national security law and public expectations.

The new security legislation and defense guidelines were aimed at strengthening deterrence and dissuasion. It was the first and most critical aspect of Abe's external balancing strategy vis-à-vis a more assertive and coercive China. But the line of advantage in strategic competition with China was already playing out on a much broader chessboard in Asia that required much more than just military tools. Japan also needed a strategy—preferably with the United States—to shape regional order in terms of diplomacy, trade, infrastructure, and the democratic values that would distinguish Japan's leadership from China's.

4

THE INDO-PACIFIC

*It is high time for Japan to pursue its divine mission and
liberate Asia.*
—ŌKAWA SHŪMEI, 1922

Japan has become the leader of the liberal order in Asia.
—THE LOWY INSTITUTE ASIA POWER INDEX, 2019

While the two most important pieces in Japan's new strategy are China and the United States, the chessboard upon which the game is being played is the Indo-Pacific. In fact, the history of Japanese strategy since the Meiji era is in many ways a history of different paths taken to define an Asian regional order that would maximize Japan's prosperity, autonomy, and legitimacy vis-à-vis threatening hegemonic powers. In the 1890s, Japan chose a path that led to collision with China over the definition of modernization on the Korean peninsula. In the 1930s and 1940s, Japan pushed for autarkic control over East Asia and ended in a bloody clash with China and the maritime democracies. At the end of the Cold War, Japan struggled to define regional norms and rules in a way that would limit unipolar U.S.

pressure on Japan's own political economy while keeping the United States in Asia as a pillar of stability. Today Japan has chosen the path of close alignment with the United States and other maritime powers based on commonly shared democratic norms and a definition of the region that has been expanded to an "Indo-Pacific" concept that increases the partnerships needed to maintain a favorable equilibrium vis-à-vis China—now the great challenge to a regional order that favors Japan.

Yet within the boundaries of what Abe defined as the new Japan-U.S.-Australia-India "Quad" lies a patchwork of states in Southeast Asia with widely different political systems—some as threatened by democracy as by China's authoritarianism. In that space Japan's most important instruments are not balance of power or democratic norms per se, but infrastructure financing, capacity building, multilateral diplomacy, rulemaking, and soft power. Japan has wielded these eclectic tools with far more nuance and skill than either Washington or Beijing, as evidenced by the huge lead Japan enjoys over these larger powers on questions of trust in public and elite surveys everywhere in South and Southeast Asia.

Whether Japan's regional strategy ultimately succeeds will depend on how successfully Tokyo can marry geopolitical alignment of the major maritime powers with direct engagement of the smaller states at risk of falling under China's sway, and whether that creates a new equilibrium that entices China to participate in regional integration without demanding hegemonic control over the smaller powers. Japanese thinking on this question is well ahead of the other members of Abe's "security diamond," in large part because there has been a strategic consensus about the China challenge in Tokyo longer than there has been in Canberra, Washington, or Delhi. But Japanese policymakers have also struggled to manage the inherent contradictions that come with their eclectic approach. Geopolitical alignment is critical, but how can Japan maintain an inclusive vision for the region while reinforcing ties with the other major powers to stop Chinese hegemony? Winning the values debate with China is part of the larger contest for regional leadership, but how can Japan apply that principle vis-à-vis the nondemocratic behavior of Cambodia, Myanmar, or the Philippines without pushing them to China? Japan is an attractive economic partner for all these countries, but does Japan have enough heft to continue insisting that they follow Tokyo's model of modernization or definition of the rules for trade and investment? And finally, can Japan keep regional institution building tethered to global rules at a time when global governance is coming apart?

Though Japan has chosen radically different paths in its search for an advantageous regional order over the past 150 years, these are not entirely new questions. Very similar questions about the right balance of power, ideational framing, economic development model, and multilateral institutional architecture have animated Japanese debates about regional order since the Meiji era—even if Japan's answers today have defined the country as a net exporter of security and prosperity in Asia rather than the revisionist power it once was.

This chapter begins by tracing the roots of Japanese strategies to define Asian order vis-à-vis previous hegemonic threats and then turns to the mix of balance-of-power, ideational, economic, and institution-building tools that make up Japan's Free and Open Indo-Pacific strategy today.

PAN-ASIANISM AND HEGEMONIC COMPETITION BEFORE 1945

Awakened by the Anglo-French defeat of China in the Opium Wars, Tokugawa Japan was forced to consider the vulnerabilities posed by the weak and porous regional order that stood between the home islands and the rapacious European imperial powers. From the beginning, the discourse split between those like the drunken gentleman of Western learning in Nakae Chōmin's parable who sought benign patronage of fellow Asian states in pursuit of Western concepts of modernization and those like the red-faced samurai in Nakae's book or Yoshida Shōin in the 1850s who sought security through preemptive conquest of Asia based on an anti-Western ideology.[1] These two competing visions for Japan's regional role defined the debate over the tools Japan would use over the next eighty years to maximize autonomy and prestige.

As historian Frederick Dickinson has noted, after the First World War the contradiction between the two distinct visions for Japan's diplomacy and national mission began to intensify: one liberal, maritime, and pro-British and the other anti-liberal, Asianist, and pro-German.[2] The result was Japan's rejection of the maritime democracies and global order and its preference for the autarkic authoritarian spheres of influence of the 1940 Axis pact with fascist Germany and Italy. Yet scholars have been too quick to dismiss the rise of anti-Western pan-Asianism as cynical realpolitik or to argue that Japanese statesmen can be expected to eschew the kind of transcendental moral purposes in foreign policy that characterize the American way of statecraft.[3] While Japan's foreign policy may show less of what historian Ken Pyle calls "moralizing, sentimentalizing or emotionalism,"[4] the fact is that Japanese statesmen have long found that geopolitical competition also requires deliberate ideational competition.

In this context, the historian Cemil Aydin finds that the useful comparison for Japan's experimentation with ideology as a foreign policy tool is not maritime Britain, but rather Turkey. Pan-Asian and pan-Islamic ideas emerged almost simultaneously in Japan and Turkey in the late nineteenth and early twentieth centuries around the search for an anti-Western frame to reconceptualize modernity and the international order. Both Turkish and Japanese intellectuals sought to learn from Western modernization but also criticized the European and Atlantic powers for violating their own professed standards for civilization, claiming instead for themselves the mantle of legitimate civilizing power in their own regional contexts.[5] The Japanese seemed to give proof of this concept to the admiring Turks with the first modern victory by an Asian over a European power in the 1904–1905 Russo-Japanese War.

Pan-Asianism in Japan, like pan-Islamism in Turkey, had many strains that are relevant to our understanding of Japanese foreign policy, not only in the twentieth century but also today. Hotta Eri describes three dominant strains of pan-Asianism that emerged in the first part of the twentieth century in Japan. The first and most benign was advanced by art scholar Okakura Kakuzō (also known as Tenshin) at the turn of the century as a vision of common Asian spiritualism to counter the pernicious effects of Western materialism. In his famous *Book of Tea* (1906), Okakura presented pan-Asian spiritual and aesthetic values not as inimical to Western values, but rather as a compatible corrective to industrialization and materialism. In Okakura's version of pan-Asianism, Japan would take its rightful place as the synthesis of Asian cultures: "the museum of Asiatic civilization: and yet more than a museum because the singular genius of the race leads it to dwell on all phrases of the ideals of the past, and in that spirit of living Advaitism which welcomes the new without losing the old."[6] The second strain was Sinic pan-Asianism, which held that Japan, China, and Korea would form a common alliance based on shared Confucian values and national commitments to self-strengthening. While Japanese intellectuals held that their own country was furthest along in this process of self-improvement, the premise was that all Sinic cultures would become natural allies in the formation of a new Asian order by and for Asians. While strongest in Japan, both of these pan-Asian visions had adherents across the continent of Asia.

The most remembered form of pan-Asianism in the West is represented by the aggressive nationalism that emerged with the third of Hotta's three strains: *Meishuron*. Proponents of *Meishuron* viewed China's weakness as a threat to the very survival of Japan. Like Uchida Ryōhei and Tōyama Mitsuru, founders of the ultranationalist Dark Ocean Society (*Genyōkai*) and Black Dragon Society (*Kokuryūkai*), they advocated a militarist crusade to conquer China in order to defend Asia and Japan. The most consequential holder of this view was probably Ishiwara Kanji, the architect of Japan's wars with China in the 1930s.[7] Ishiwara proselytized an apocalyptic vision—particularly in the imperial Japanese army—that a massive civilizational war between East and West was inevitable and that Japan's only hope for survival was to prepare for total war by placing Manchuria, China, and Korea under an East Asian League reverent to the Japanese emperor.[8] Tragically, his messianic version of pan-Asianism came to dominate Japanese strategy in the lead-up to the Second World War.

Yet there was nothing inherent in the first two strands of pan-Asianism that made Ishiwara's dark vision inevitable. My first boss and mentor in the Japanese Diet, LDP representative Shiina Motoo, would often describe how growing up in the Japanese puppet state of Manchukuo in the 1930s his father's colleagues from the Japanese Ministry of Commerce and Industry would gather for drinks at his house "full of energy and hope": "They would talk about building industry . . . about building the country. Their idea was for the five races—Manchus, Chinese, Mongolians, Koreans and Japanese to live and work together . . . in harmony."[9]

Racism at the hands of the West contributed to this idealistic vision of Sinic pan-Asian solidarity. The pride the Japanese had once felt with the establishment of the Anglo-Japanese alliance gave way to one of shame when the Anglo-American powers rejected Japan's proposal for an antiracism clause in the League of Nations charter negotiations in 1919. In response to this offense, Japanese newspapers proclaimed that Japan's national responsibility was to "insist on the equal international treatment of all races. . . . No other question is so inseparably and materially interwoven with the permanency of the world's peace as that of unfair and unjust treatment of a large majority of the world's population."[10] Ōkawa Shūmei introduced a new way to think about Japan's leadership in the region when he argued in his influential 1922 book, *Fukkō Ajia no Shomondai* (Problems of a resurgent Asia), that it was now high time for Japan to pursue its "divine mission and liberate Asia."[11]

When war broke out with the Anglo-American powers in December 1941, American diplomats and intelligence officers reported with surprise from across Southeast Asia that Japan's brand of pan-Asian "liberation" from Western imperialism was working against the U.S. war effort because the United States was allied with Southeast Asians' former British, French, and Dutch imperial masters.[12] As Jeremy Yellen notes in his recent history of the Greater East Asia Co-Prosperity Sphere, elites in the subjugated former European colonies tried to use Japan's new pan-Asianism to achieve state building not possible under the Europeans.[13] But Japan insisted on its own racial and national strata within the sphere based on an elaborate doctrine centered on the Japanese people as the "leading race" (*shidō minzoku*) and the purity of the Japanese spirit (*Yamato Damashii*).[14] With the demands of total war, the militarists became ever more desperate and brutal. As Dower notes in his seminal study *War Without Mercy*, "In the end, their own oppressive behavior toward other Asians earned the Japanese more hatred than support."[15]

ASIAN MODELS OF ECONOMIC MODERNIZATION

Crucial to both the Sinic and *Meishuron* strains of pan-Asianism was advancing an Asian model of economic modernization. Japan's own example of indigenizing critical industries such as steel, chemical engineering, and shipbuilding under the Meiji slogan "Rich Nation/Strong Army" (*Fukoku Kyōhei*) established an inspiring example for modernization and anti-imperialism to many in Manchuria, North China, and Korea—and also provided a justification for Japan to place these rich regions under Japanese imperial tutelage.

Japan learned from the other imperial powers that infrastructure development was particularly important to spheres of influence. Britain's empire in Asia was reinforced by the Suez Canal, France's by the Banque de L'Indochine and the Port of Saigon, and Russia's by the Trans-Siberian Railroad. In the first decades of the twentieth century, railroads became the locus of geopolitical competition in north China and Manchuria because the unequal treaties granted extraterritoriality to the owners on either side of the track. Japan's own bureaucratic, intelligence, and military expansion followed closely the laying of new track by the Japanese-run South Manchuria Railway (*Mantetsu*).[16] Beyond the pronounced competition for imperial influence through railroads, imperial Japan also expanded its reach through telecommunications investments, banking, and technical training for local officials.[17] As historian Peter Duus has noted, imperial Japan learned and then demonstrated in Northeast Asia that "since the onset of the industrial revolution, the ability of one country to dominate another is often a function of greater economic development rather than sheer military strength, and the boundaries of empire do not always align themselves with where the map is painted red. Imperialist expansion can, and often does, take less visible and less direct forms than territorial conquest."[18]

While the *Meishuron* strategy of harnessing economic empire for total war against the West ended in flames in 1945, Japanese leaders returned to this broader focus on leadership in infrastructure and economic development to prevent hostile hegemons from dominating Asia—and would come to recognize in China's Belt and Road Initiative the same economic tools of imperialism Japan itself had once harnessed.

THE ROLE OF REGIONAL INSTITUTIONS

Finally, Japan's prewar efforts at shaping regional order depended on institution building. While Japan's pursuit of an autarkic regional bloc under the Greater East Asia Co-Prosperity Sphere stands as a parable on the necessity of effective global economic connectivity and governance, Japanese leaders in the prewar era at one point did approach the nascent multilateralism of the 1920s with enthusiasm. As Dickinson explains in *World War I and the Triumph of a New Japan*, "World War I gave Japan the opportunity to become an integral player in a remarkable transformation of world politics."[19] Whereas the Anglo-Japanese alliance had been greeted by paintings depicting the Emperor Meiji and King Edward of equal stature in 1902, Japan's anticipated influence in the post-war order was depicted in fictitious paintings of the Emperor Taishō sitting tall next to King George V and Tsar Nicholas II.[20] Nor was that diplomacy marked by failure on the whole. Japan's introduction of the antiracism clause in the Paris peace negotiations crumbled in the face of American, Canadian, and Australian anti-immigrant sentiment, but Japanese diplomats did win important geopolitical gains in China and the South Pacific at Versailles. Three years later in the Washington Naval Treaty negotiations, the United States and Britain yielded to Japanese demands for a ban on fortifications in exchange for naval armaments limitations on the imperial Japanese navy. International agreements served Japan in other sectors as well. By the end of the 1920s, the visionary banker Inoue Junnosuke was aligning the yen with the global gold standard to enhance Japan's international economic influence and Japan's business *zaibatsu* leaders were hobnobbing with representatives of J. P. Morgan and Barclays Bank.[21] Japan at the end of the First World War was emerging as what we would later call a "responsible stakeholder" in the new regional and global order because that stance served Japanese interests and prestige as one of the victors in the war.

The underlying structure of international politics would rapidly change in the coming decade, however, as the underpinnings of European power, American internationalism, global trade, and the gold standard all collapsed. The West had turned protectionist and inward-looking in its economic distress, and by 1932 a "new consensus" had taken hold in Japan against the earlier alignment with international treaties and norms.[22] The "anti-treaty" faction opposed to the Washington Treaty limitations on shipbuilding rose to prominence in the navy; the foreign ministry developed what became the "Amau doctrine" advocating Japanese hegemonic control over Asia; and Finance Minister Inoue was assassinated by right-wing military officers in February 1932 as a lesson to all others who would put Japan's fate in the hands of Western financiers. It was time, Ishiwara Kanji declared after Japan quit the League of Nations in 1933, to create a new "East Asian League" opposed to the West.[23] The institutions of regional order Japan forced on Asia were now designed to create autarky and separation from the global rules and norms that mainstream Japanese diplomats had championed only a decade earlier.

Yet the question remains whether Japan's brief enthusiasm for internationalism in the Taishō era was the aberration or whether the turn toward militarism was. After the war Japanese political leaders and diplomats embraced regional and global multilateralism not as a rejection of the entire prewar period, but as a return to the path not taken after the 1920s—one that postwar statesmen like Shidehara and Yoshida had experienced themselves. As they did so, the earlier tensions between intra-Asian solidarity and global governance would once again resurface.

REGIONALISM AND INSTITUTION BUILDING
DURING THE COLD WAR

In his vision for postwar international relations, Yoshida aimed to harness and then manage American power while gradually reconstituting Japan's economic power and acceptance in Asia. Fortunately for Yoshida, the American architects of containment strategy came to pursue essentially the same goals, as was noted in the last chapter. In the early postwar years, the vacuum left by the collapse of Japan's empire was filled with nationalist and communist rebellions from Malaya to Korea. It was clear that overstretched European troops in Southeast Asia and unprepared U.S. troops in South Korea would only be able to briefly stem the tide without a longer-term path to economic growth and stability in the region. In 1947 the U.S. State-War-Navy Coordinating Committee (SWNCC) recommended the revival of Japan as the engine of growth for Asia, and in 1948 President Truman approved a $1.3 billion aid package to Tokyo aimed at recentralizing more of the region's trade through Japan to shore up "the border area in the worldwide clash between communism and democracy."[24] By 1965, the year Tokyo graduated from receiving World Bank loans, the Japanese economy was fueling growth in Malaysia and Thailand and reinforcing the region against the further spread of communism from Indochina. That same year Japan signed a normalization treaty with Korea backed by $800 million in aid.[25]

Driven by American strategies of containment, Japan's partial return to the center of Asian economic order opened the way for thinking in Tokyo about an ideational frame to restore legitimacy and influence. Here again, the useful comparison is with Turkey. Postwar Japanese and Turkish strategic decisions on regional policy were increasingly informed by inherited perceptions of self that were derived from each country's respective imperial past.[26] For Japan, the clearest line from prewar to postwar pan-Asianism was embodied in Professor Akamatsu Kaname's "flying geese model" of economic development. Like other leading Japanese scholars in the 1930s, Akamatsu was influenced by the national identity philosophy and Hegelian dialectical logic of the German historical school, which he harnessed to argue that Japan offered a superior historical model for rapid development by other developing Asian nations. Akamatsu's theory fit well within Hotta's example of Sinic pan-Asianism even at a time when *Meishuron* was emerging as the dominant strain within prewar Japan.[27] As the Ministry of International Trade and Industry (MITI) began withdrawing support for uncompetitive "sunset" industries and encouraging them to move to less developed Asian countries in the 1950s and early 1960s, Akamatsu revived his theory in a seminal publication in the *Journal of Developing Economies* in 1962.[28] Whereas MITI was seeking to shield Japanese corporate losers from destructive capitalism, Akamatsu argued that what was good for Japan was also good for Asia, pointing to a benign leadership role for Tokyo linked to a state-led model of capitalism distinct from the West. Japan would be the "flying goose" at the head of the "V" formation, he wrote, pulling the region toward its own successful industrialization.

By the 1970s the specter of American retreat from Asia after the Vietnam War gave further space for the development of new pan-Asian theories for restored Japanese leadership in the region. When Prime Minister Tanaka Kakuei traveled to Indonesia and Thailand in 1974, he expected to wallow in the region's enthusiasm for Japanese economic leadership, but his motorcade was instead stoned by protestors still harboring anti-Japanese sentiments from the war. Three years later, Prime Minister Fukuda Takeo made another attempt to cement ties on the tenth anniversary of the establishment of the Association of Southeast Asian Nations (ASEAN). His three-part "Fukuda Initiative" emphasized that Japan no longer had militaristic or hegemonic aspirations for the region, would focus on "heart-to-heart" communications, and would treat ASEAN as an equal partner in regional development.[29] The "heart-to-heart" diplomacy was backed by a very large check of $1.5 billion in aid.[30] Fukuda also diverged from U.S. policy by actively promoting Vietnam's membership in ASEAN, the first independent and proactive Japanese diplomatic initiative in the region since 1945.[31] (His son Yasuo attempted a similar gentle approach to the region as prime minister in 2007–2008.)

On the centennial of the Meiji Restoration, confidence grew in Tokyo that Japan could resume a more benign leadership role in the region, shorn of the hierarchical and exploitative aspects of prewar pan-Asianism and more empathetic than the American approach yet not to the point of risking American protection. Emboldened by the positive response from within ASEAN and the continued churn and uncertainty in American policy toward Southeast Asia, Foreign Minister Ōkita Saburō, in a major speech in Seoul in April 1985, used Akamatsu's flying geese theory as the centerpiece of his vision for a more proactive Japan in Asia.[32]

JAPAN'S BUBBLE ECONOMY AND THE RETURN OF ASIANISM

However, the year 1985 would become historically significant in Japan's relationship with Asia and the United States for a more important reason. In September of that year the finance ministers of the G-7 countries met at the Plaza Hotel in New York City and, bending to domestic political pressure over Japan's massive trade surpluses, agreed to depreciate the U.S. dollar in relation to the Japanese yen and the German Deutsch mark. Though few recognized it at the time, this strong yen was the driver of Japan's asset-driven "bubble economy." By 1987 the dollar had lost over half of its value vis-à-vis the yen and Japanese manufacturers were scrambling to relocate production to North America, but also to take advantage of the now far cheaper relative costs of establishing supply chains in Southeast Asia. The Plaza Accord caused more American anxiety about Japan rather than less, as cash-rich Japanese firms began purchasing trophy assets like Rockefeller Plaza and Pebble Beach and journalists began writing bestsellers like *Buying into America* (this was also when a brash real estate mogul in New York named Donald Trump began taking out advertisements in newspapers attacking Japan).[33] U.S.-Japan trade negotiations became more acrimonious and more focused on structural differences in Japan's economy rather than just sectoral issues. The U.S. trade representative shifted in 1989 from "Market-Oriented-Sector-Specific" (MOSS) talks to the sweeping "Structural Impediments Initiative" (SII). Japan's entire economic model and legitimacy as the lead flying goose in Asia was under political and ideational assault by the world's leading power. Yet this was also precisely the time when Asian leaders like Mohammed Mahathir of Malaysia began championing an East Asia Economic Caucus to compete with Europe and North America and Lee Kwan Yew of Singapore began proclaiming a neo-Confucian pan-Asianist theory of his own.[34]

This debate with the United States over "Asian values" escalated between 1985 and the 1997–1998 financial crisis as Japanese thought leaders sought a defensive argument against American pressure (*gaiatsu*) and a mantle for benign leadership in Asia. Within the LDP and the foreign, trade, and finance ministries, prominent "Asianists" rose to senior positions—motivated by their experiences fighting with American trade negotiators one day and then bonding with Asian counterparts who sought Japanese aid and investment the next. One prominent "Asianist," Deputy Foreign Minister Ogura Kazuo, wrote in 1993 that Western-style capitalism had reached a dead end and proposed that Japan and Asia join hands to advance a new "Asian Theory of Capitalism."[35] His finance ministry counterpart, Sakakibara Eisuke, argued in *Beyond Capitalism: The Japanese Model of Market Economics* (1993) that Japan's economic model valued people and social harmony, in contrast to the brutal Anglo-American free-market model of economic development, and was therefore more suitable for Asian development.[36] Sakakibara's finance ministry then funded a controversial study of the "Asian Miracle" at the World Bank to try to prove the assertion.[37] The Japanese foreign policy intellectuals' zeitgeist was captured by Funabashi Yōichi's article "The Asianization of Asia" in the winter 1993 issue of *Foreign Affairs*, in which he wrote that "Asia will no longer put up with being treated simply as a card; it will now demand respect as a player. Its success stories are likely to inspire and provide voice for original, distinctly Asian ideas on a host of issues."[38]

This was a very different pan-Asianism from the prewar variant, to be sure. Sakakibara and Ogura were seeking Asian solidarity as evidence of Japan's new leadership and for leverage over the United States rather than autarky. They were themselves internationalists and sometimes far-sighted reformers within their respective ministries. Funabashi became bureau chief for *Asahi Shimbun* in Washington in the early 1990s and encouraged younger Japan hands like myself to contribute to a stronger U.S.-Japan alliance. Yet at the same time, as Dower demonstrated in his shocking comparison of prewar and postwar images in U.S.-Japan relations in 1993, anger and racially tinged images crept into other intellectuals' commentary about divergent values on both sides of the Pacific.[39] Japanese journalists, scholars, and politicians promoted a new *Nihonjinron* that sought to explain the uniqueness of Japanese ideas and even the physiology of the Japanese brain.[40] In the U.S.-Japan trade wars of the period, leading political figures argued that Japanese intestines were too long to handle American beef imports and Japanese snow was too delicate for handling Western skis.[41] Americans shot back, with Texas senator Phil Graham said to have told a visiting Japanese delegation, "Well our cowboy hats won't fit in your little cars!!!" Though few Japanese intellectuals claimed that Japan was destined to be the "leading race" of Asia as their prewar predecessors had, many advocates of the new pan-Asianism in the 1980s and early 1990s did express Japanese uniqueness in terms of culture, physiology, and pacifism.[42] Others, like nationalistic politician Ishihara Shintarō, evoked earlier visions of *Mieshuron* pan-Asianism with his bestseller *The Japan That Can Say No* and then his coauthored book with Mahathir, *The Asia That Can Say No.*[43]

These narratives about Asian integration and solidarity were backed by real structural changes to the political economy of the region that occurred at the same time. On the back of massive capital investment following the 1985 appreciation of the yen, Japanese companies began supplanting their American counterparts as the main source of new technology for countries like Malaysia and Thailand, while Japanese suppliers followed the large companies to set up supply chains linking them to Japan. Scholars like Kozo Yamamura and Walter Hatch warned of the "keiretsu-ization" of Asia, in reference to Japan's closed and quasi-monopolistic postwar industrial groupings at home.[44] Neoclassical economists argued that macroeconomic structural changes alone were sufficient to explain this phenomenon without the need to find particular agency, but MITI anticipated and lubricated the shift in production to Asia with the 1987 New Asian Industries Development Plan and parallel foreign aid strategies. As Ken Pyle noted in 1996, "These various policies seek a Japanese-style economic leadership that advances the cause of Japan's domestic restructuring and improves its trade imbalance with the US at the same time that it lays the basis for a soft, region-wide integration of economies under Japanese leadership."[45] The U.S. government worried in particular that Japan was providing development assistance and investments in critical infrastructure that would permanently freeze out U.S. firms in Southeast Asia. In an echo of railroad competition in north China and a foreshadowing of the wars over 5G with China three decades later, the George H. W. Bush administration clashed with Japan in Indonesia over electronics giant NEC's bid to rebuild that country's telecommunication infrastructure at the expense of AT&T.[46]

Plans for regional institutions flowed in parallel with the emerging Asianist identity formation and Japanese-led growth of intraregional trade. Geopolitics had been unforgiving of Asian-only multilateralism during the Cold War (except for ASEAN), since these proposals were recognized in both Washington and Tokyo as abetting Soviet efforts to weaken the U.S. network of bilateral alliances in the region.[47] Indeed, in 1986 Soviet leader Mikhail Gorbachev responded to the strengthening of the U.S.-Japan alliance under Nakasone and Reagan with a major speech calling for Asian-only multilateral institutions to replace bilateral alliances.[48] As the threat from Moscow subsided, however, Japanese statesmen responded to growing sentiments in the region for an Asian-led, and therefore implicitly Japanese-centered, framework for economic integration. Japan and Australia hosted the first Pacific Economic Cooperation Council (PECC) summit of business leaders in 1980, and Tokyo then supported Australian prime minister Bob Hawke's proposal for an East Asian free-trade organization focused on "open regionalism"—but pointedly without mentioning the United States as a member.[49] When Australia and Japan began working on a regionwide trade ministerial in 1989—motivated in part to form a counterweight to the new North American Free Trade Agreement (NAFTA)—U.S. secretary of state James Baker leaned into the Japanese bureaucratic establishment to ensure that the North Americanists prevailed over the Asianists and included the United States as a founding member of what became the Asia-Pacific Economic Cooperation (APEC) forum.[50]

Internally divided over how uniquely Asian regional institutions should be, the foreign ministry North Americanists drove the initial script for APEC, with Foreign Minister Hata Tsutomu emphasizing before the first summit inclusive of the United States in 1993 that the forum should align with global-level agreements like the new World Trade Organization (WTO) and stay focused on process rather than outcomes.[51] But the need for a pan-Asian counterbalance to American unipolarity reemerged with the 1997–1998 Asian Financial Crisis as the Japanese delegation to APEC (joined by dozens of protectionist LDP agricultural caucus members) organized an East Asian front to defeat a U.S. proposal to climb out of the crisis through early voluntary sectoral liberalization (EVSL) commitments.[52] That same year the finance ministry's Sakakibara tried unsuccessfully to promote his idea for a separate Asian Monetary Fund at the Hong Kong meeting of the World Bank and the International Monetary Fund (IMF). As Japan scholar Glenn Hook notes, "The demands placed on the affected economies by the International Monetary Fund (IMF) in the wake of the crises—namely, trade liberalization, deregulation, privatization and the general shrinking of the role of the state in the national economy—was part of a political project to promote a neo-liberal system of governance in East Asia" that threatened Japan's leadership and own economic model.[53] While Japanese leaders no longer claimed to be the leading race in Asia as they had before the war, they did increasingly argue that they had a responsibility as the leading economy to stand up for more state-centered forms of economic development.

THE DEMISE OF ASIANISM

Yet the year 1998 was probably the high-water mark of Japanese enthusiasm for East Asian groupings designed to compete with or counterbalance the West. As chapter 2 emphasized, Japan-China relations were now entering a new and far more competitive phase, and Asian-only group-ings increasingly advantaged Beijing over Tokyo. Regional institutions also became less important in managing U.S. unipolar influence with the establishment of the WTO and the subsequent sheathing (until Donald Trump) of unilateralist American tariffs as a weapon against Japan. In addition, the structural shifts with the appreciation of the yen in 1985 changed by the late 1990s. While intraregional trade rose above 50 per-cent of all trade, international financial flows remained overwhelmingly global in nature, and Japan's own economy benefited from increasing openness to foreign direct investment, which rose dramatically in 1998 from 0.062 percent to 0.324 percent of GDP—still low by Organisation for Economic Co-operation and Development (OECD) standards but a new historic high for a country devoid of natural resources and depen-dent on exports.[54]

The philosophical debate over Asian values also began to ebb by the end of the 1990s. Despite the impact of Samuel Huntington's "Clash of Civilizations?" article in Foreign Affairs in 1993, scholars like William Theodore de Bary, David Hitchcock, and Inoguchi Takashi began to push back against the idea that Confucianism somehow provided a com-mon ideational glue in Asia, drawing on surveys and historical data to demonstrate the growing desire for more accountable democratic gover-nance across the region.[55] The debate over Asian values also diminished as the United States became more "Japanese" in its own approach to the region, agreeing to collaborate with Japan's 1998 $30 billion Miyazawa Initiative and to institute reforms within the World Bank to reflect the lessons of the Asian Financial Crisis.[56] The ideational clash between Washington and Tokyo was soothed by convergence around a common agenda—and by both allies' belated recognition that they could not have handled the crisis without the other. And, of course, the sheen came off of Japan's own seemingly unstoppable economic model as growth slowed dramatically in the "lost decade" of the 1990s after Japan's asset bubble burst in 1990.

Ultimately, the search for a unique Asian identity for Japanese for-eign policy strategy in the 1990s produced a legacy that was helpful for the region. Japan played an important bridging role with Hun Sen's government in the Cambodian peace settlement of the mid-1990s, for example, and brought heft to the establishment of the ASEAN Regional Forum in 1993—the first regionwide meetings to discuss security issues.[57] Though often caught between Washington and ASEAN on issues ranging from the financial crisis response to the international community's isolation of Burma, Japan developed through trial and error a fine-tuned appreciation of the worldview within ASEAN. Japan was the first G-7 country to urge support for the countries struck by the financial crisis, and ASEAN member states would not forget.[58] But at the same time, Japanese diplomats learned that trust alone was insufficient to stop Chinese coercion and co-option within ASEAN—a lesson reinforced when ASEAN refused Japanese requests for endorsement of Tokyo's bid for a permanent UN Security Council seat in 2005 and when ASEAN remained silent in the Senkaku crises with China in 2010 and 2012.[59] Recognition grew in Tokyo that Japan's window into ASEAN development and security concerns was now actionable only in concert with the other great maritime democracies, particularly the United States.

The anti-Western version of the East Asia Community idea reappeared from the dead briefly one last time with Hatoyama's term as DPJ prime minister in 2009–2010. Hatoyama had been particularly taken in the 1990s by the sentiment of "datsu-bei/nyū-A" ("separate from the United States and join Asia"—a reversal of Fukuzawa's famous "datsu-A" or "leave Asia" formula in the Meiji period). Hatoyama saw pan-Asianist interruption of Japan's postwar alliance-centered strategy as fulfillment of his grandfather's anti-Yoshida legacy. When the DPJ came to office, the real power behind Hatoyama—Tanaka Kakuei's former protégé Ozawa Ichirō—embraced the same vision as an internal political hammer to beat down the pillars of long-term LDP rule, including the powerful business federation Keidanren, the North Americanists in the foreign ministry, and the U.S.-Japan alliance itself. Yet these were also some of the most important pillars of Japan's national strength in Asia.[60] The DPJ leadership's myopic campaign to restructure domestic political institutions sowed uncertainty in Asia about Japan's commitment to the alliance and opened a vacuum that China exploited. No serious contender in the post-Abe era seems likely to resuscitate the East Asia Community idea to battle the United States anytime soon. Hatoyama thought he would kill the Yoshida doctrine with his grandfather's vision from the 1950s, but all he killed was his own grandfather's residual legacy. Instead, the honor of ending the Yoshida doctrine would fall to the grandson of Hatoyama's rival—Abe Shinzō—who would not only change Japan's foreign policy strategy but also how the rest of the region defined "Asia."

A Free and Open Indo-Pacific

The core Japanese concept of what defines "Asia" underwent a profound change in the first decades of the twenty-first century. The change reflected the geopolitical challenge of an ambitious and resurgent China and Japan's need to protect the rules and influence that had given Tokyo a privileged position at the end of the previous century. Once again, a geopolitical rivalry would shape how Japan sought to define norms and institutions in the region.

The first pronounced change came with a new conceptual map of Asia. The geographic concept of a distinct Asian region was originally European, since sinocentrism had for millennia anchored whatever sense of common destiny there was in the Celestial Court's Mandate of Heaven rather than in clear geographic boundaries of the kind that marked the Roman or Ottoman Empires. Japan had seized on the Western definition of Asia with the establishment of the Greater East Asia Co-Prosperity Sphere, which simultaneously replaced Western imperialism and discredited sinocentric definitions of regional order. In the 1980s and 1990s, Asianists in Japan seized on the newer East Asia Community concept to capture the footprint of Japanese investment and economic development models. Notably, this map of Asia did not initially include India, which had been an object of Japanese conquest during the war but never part of the Japanese empire or postwar economic investment footprint in the region.

With the resurgence of Chinese power at the end of the twentieth century, however, the narrow East Asian map once championed by Japan became Beijing's preferred framework. Australians were stunned, for example, to find that when China launched the Boao Forum in early

2001 as a competitor to the Davos Forum in Switzerland, the meeting's logo was changed to remove Australia and New Zealand from Asia, leaving a large blank space on the map south of Indonesia.[61] More pernicious examples followed, in particular Beijing's proposal through proxy members of ASEAN that an early East Asia Summit be held in Beijing with the host to determine the agenda and no participation from the United States.[62]

Hashimoto Ryūtarō first attempted to broaden Japan's regional partnerships as part of external balancing against China in the late 1990s with the Russia card and his "New Eurasia" diplomacy.[63] Prime Minister Mori Yoshirō then made a brief attempt at outreach to India with a visit in the summer of 2000 to Delhi, where the former rugby player was mocked for his sweat-drenched visit to the Taj Mahal. But ultimately it was the iconoclastic Koizumi who threw out the old formulations for Japan's relationship with the rest of Asia and introduced an entirely new ideational and geographical vision for the region.

Since 1957 every new prime minister had confirmed in his first Diet address that Japan's international role would be based on three pillars: the United Nations system (Japan was admitted to the UN in 1956), the U.S.-Japan Security Treaty, and relations with Asia. In his first speech to the Diet as prime minister in May 2001, Koizumi ended that tradition, declaring that Japan would henceforth play a global role based on *two* pillars: (1) the Japan-U.S. relationship, which would be the "foundation to maintain and enhance Japan's friendly relations with its neighbors," and (2) Japan's "leadership in enhancing the international system appropriate for the twenty-first century."[64] Gone was any of the previous vision of autonomy created by the juxtaposition of Japan's Asian and Western identities. Koizumi's Japan stood as a global norm-setter positioned in Asia. Why Koizumi and not Hashimoto or Mori? Because Koizumi intended to change Japan's economic model as well.

The next January in Singapore, Koizumi gave a speech proposing a new "Initiative for Development in East Asia" (IDEA). The acronym "IDEA" was not a coincidence. Koizumi argued in his speech that since the success of the 1977 Fukuda doctrine and heart-to-heart exchange with ASEAN, Japan had failed to reform its own economy and had left the region weaker for that. His implicit criticism of Japan's enabling role in the crony capitalism that contributed to the 1997–1998 Financial Crisis was followed by a pledge that Japan would now be a leader on reform and would also assist ASEAN states with their own reforms and modernization. This pledge extended to "accelerating democratization in Myanmar." The core "idea" Japan offered would not be the defense of a uniquely Japanese and Asian "anthropocentric" model of capitalism, but instead Japanese leadership toward the future based on the observation that "all of the ASEAN countries increasingly share the basic values of democracy and market economy." "China will surely make an enormous contribution to regional development," he added, but the message he sent was that Japan would be the nation with the right idea for development in the region. And to be certain this focus on democracy and free markets had full support in the future of East Asian integration, Koizumi urged the inclusion of Australia and New Zealand as core members.[65]

Seasoned Asia scholar Soeya Yoshihide of Keio University observed that with the inclusion of Australia and New Zealand and the emphasis on "modern" values, Koizumi's 2001 speech "ignited a process of conceptual competition between China and Japan."[66] While closely aligned with U.S. policy goals and framing of issues in Asia, the speech was actually not coordinated with Washington ahead of time and was crafted by one of the foreign ministry's strongest advocates of a more independent Japanese foreign policy in the region and a nemesis of Abe Shinzō's, the stubborn and iconoclastic Tanaka Hitoshi, who proudly bore the nickname "Mr. Kokueki" ("Mr. National Interest").[67] Cut from similar cloth as Sakakibara and Ogura during an early period of Japanese economic and diplomatic statecraft, Tanaka's definition of an independent Japanese foreign policy drove him to an emphasis on global norms and balance of power in conjunction with the United States and its closest maritime allies.[68] Tanaka clashed with his American counterparts almost as much as Sakakibara and Ogura had, but he worked in Asia to advance democratic values that Japan shared with the United States rather than using relations with Asia to counter Washington.

Australia, which featured prominently in Koizumi's IDEA speech, was a critical partner as Japan worked to define the new power map of

Asia. Australia had worked with Japan to launch APEC in the late 1980s and shared with Tokyo an interest in developing both intra-Asian and trans-Pacific economic frameworks at the same time. In 2001 Australia's Japanese-speaking secretary of foreign affairs, Ashton Calvert, proposed a regular "Trilateral Security Dialogue" (TSD) among Washington, Tokyo, and Canberra that Deputy Secretary of State Richard Armitage and Vice Foreign Minister Takeuchi Yukio enthusiastically joined the month after Koizumi's IDEA speech. Though China was constantly in the background, the TSD focused on ways to shore up regional architecture and was used by Tokyo and Canberra to press the new Bush administration to be a steady participant in forums such as APEC (the message was heard and George W. Bush became the only U.S. president to make every APEC summit).[69] In 2005 the Japan-Australia strategic relationship took another important step forward when Australian troops were dispatched to operate with Japan's Self-Defense Forces ground contingent in southern Iraq.[70]

India was next to be welcomed into Japan's expanding definition of what was still being called an East Asia Community. The right wing of the LDP had long harbored close ties with the anti-China hawks of the Indian conservative parties, such as Defense Minister George Fernandes, and had admired Indian justice Radhabinod Pal, who alone had argued that Japan was not guilty of aggressive war at the Tokyo War Crimes Tribunal in 1948. However, the mainstream of the Japanese business community and LDP found India too exotic and the association with Judge Pal (who is still honored at the Yasukuni Shrine) too controversial. China was by far the more important market and multiplier of Japan's influence during the late Cold War. The India card might have been attractive as Japan-China competition intensified in the late 1990s, but India's 1998 nuclear test repelled a Japanese public still angry at China's own nuclear testing earlier in the decade.

Koizumi's 2001 victory broke some of these constraints, but it was three developments in 2004–2005 that ultimately propelled India-Japan alignment forward. The first was the rapid and effective response of the ad hoc Quad task force led by the United States, Japan, Australia, and India to provide humanitarian and disaster relief in the immediate aftermath of the massive December 2004 Asian tsunami. The ease with which these four democratic maritime states mustered the willpower and resources to provide public goods to the region—and the gratitude of states like Indonesia on the receiving end—were an important revelation.[71] The second action-forcing event was China's bid for control over the new East Asia Summit in 2004–2005, which prompted coordination between Japan and Singapore to add India to the list of members on top of Australia and New Zealand as a counterweight to Beijing. And the third action-forcing event was the announcement by U.S. president George W. Bush and Indian prime minister Manmohan Singh in July 2005 that the United States and India would pursue a peaceful nuclear cooperation agreement to bring India back into the nonproliferation world if not the 1968 Treaty on the Non-Proliferation of Nuclear Weapons itself. The effort would require Indian membership in the Nuclear Suppliers Group (NSG), and one of the most important votes would be nonproliferation stalwart Japan. The Bush administration quietly urged Tokyo to support India's membership, and a 1.5-track trilateral dialogue was established by the Center for Strategic and International Studies (CSIS), the Japan Institute of International Affairs (JIIA), and the Confederation of Indian Industry (CII) with leading corporate and foreign affairs figures, including Abe's ally Chairman Kasai of Central Japan Railway, to build support across the LDP and Keidanren.[72] India's attraction grew as a geopolitical counterweight to China and a destination for Japanese infrastructure investment and connectivity across the southern flank of the Eurasian continent.

ABE'S FIRST ATTEMPT AT A NEW ASIAN ALIGNMENT

As Abe prepared to assume leadership of the LDP and Japan from Koizumi in 2006, he signaled an intention to solidify the new alignment with Asia's maritime democracies. In his manifesto, *Utsukushii Kuni e* (Toward a beautiful country), he proposed to elevate the informal Japan-U.S.-Australia-India "Quad" task force to a formal leaders' summit.[73] India was particularly important to Abe's vision. Under Abe,

India rose to become the top recipient for official development assistance (ODA) as the two countries launched the massive Delhi-Mumbai Industrial Corridor Project.[74] In 2006 Japan also joined India's annual Malabar naval exercises for the first time (eventually becoming a permanent member in 2015).[75] Abe now regularly anchored Japan's definition of the region on India, emphasizing in a speech in Delhi in August 2007: "Now, as this new 'broader Asia' takes shape at the confluence of the two seas of the Indian and Pacific Oceans, I feel that it is imperative that the democratic nations located at opposite edges of these seas deepen the friendship among their citizens at every possible level. . . . Moreover, this is not only an investment for the two countries but also for the future of this new 'broader Asia.'"[76]

The Australia leg also continued moving forward at a brisk clip. In March 2007 Australian prime minister John Howard and Abe issued a "Japan-Australia Joint Declaration on Security Cooperation"—Japan's first bilateral security agreement with any country other than the United States since the war (the declaration was a comprehensive work plan for defense cooperation rather than a treaty with an explicit security guarantee like Article V in the 1960 U.S.-Japan Security Treaty).[77] The next October, Foreign Minister Asō Tarō signed a similar agreement with India.[78]

In parallel with the Quad proposal and strengthened Japan-India and Japan-Australia ties, the Japanese foreign ministry put forward a broader concept to guide Japan's Asia strategy around the same principles of universal values, economic connectivity, and maritime security. In a speech at JIIA in November 2006, Foreign Minister Asō Tarō introduced his "Arc of Freedom and Prosperity"—a vision of diplomatic partnerships and logistical connectivity from the Russian Far East around the periphery of China as far as Europe.[79] Evocative of Nicholas Spykman's "Rimland Theory" of geopolitics, which had shaped early American strategies of containment, the Arc appeared to many to be a transparent zero-sum strategy for limiting China's influence.[80] The branding was also somewhat complicated by the inclusion of Russia, Myanmar, and other still less-than-democratic governments in the mix of "freedom and prosperity." Despite these flaws, the Arc of Freedom and Prosperity represented a first if ultimately unsuccessful effort to incorporate the multiple diverse states not in the Quad that were at risk of falling under Chinese influence but not ready or able to join Abe's vision of a great-power collective.[81]

The Quad and the Arc proved short-lived, however. Skeptical bureaucrats in all four countries' foreign ministries convened an initial Quad meeting with the aim of slow-rolling it. Officials in the National Security Council (NSC) or prime ministerial offices in all four capitals were more enthusiastic, but Australia, Japan, and the United States were all on the verge of leadership transitions toward the center or center-left, where there was no enthusiasm for "neocon" strategies, particularly as the Iraq War grew unpopular. When Fukuda Yasuo came to office as prime minister in September 2007, he championed his father's softer "heart-to-heart" approach to Asia and quietly set aside both the Quad and the Arc of Freedom and Prosperity. The new Australian government under Labor Party leader and prime minister Kevin Rudd then made a more deliberate and public declaration of the Quad's demise upon taking power in 2007—to Tokyo's consternation, since there was still support for a softer version of maritime alignment if not Abe's original summit construct.[82] Japan and Asia were simply not ready for divisive external balancing or redrawing of the Asia map. But Asia—and Abe—would change.

ABE 2.0: FOIP AND THE RETURN OF THE QUAD

When Abe returned to power in December 2012, he resurrected his original concepts, pulling the original foreign ministry architects of the Quad and the Arc back from exile and into the center of power in the Prime Minister's Office. Asō, an early supporter of Abe's restoration, became deputy prime minister and finance minister. Yachi Shōtarō, who had coordinated the Arc as vice minister of foreign affairs, came out of retirement to become Abe's national security advisor with diplomat Kanehara Nobukatsu as his deputy on the new NSC staff. Asō's former speechwriter at the foreign ministry, journalist Taniguchi Tomohiko, became Abe's foreign policy speechwriter. The first product of this brain trust was a December 2012 article penned by Abe highlighting the "security diamond" that connected Australia, India, Japan, and Hawaii around common commitments to "safeguard the maritime commons stretching from the Indian Ocean region to the western Pacific" and "democracy, the rule of law, and respect for human rights."[83] Unsure of where the Obama administration or the Julia Gillard government in Canberra would be on the Quad idea, Abe avoided the mistakes of his 2006 Quad rollout by introducing a concept rather than a concrete diplomatic proposal that would force governments to take a position.

Meanwhile, the epicenter of geopolitical competition with China—and Beijing's effort to isolate Abe early in his term—shifted to Southeast Asia. Abe followed his "security diamond" article with a visit to every ASEAN country in his first year in office.[84] His ground game proved effective in terms of blunting Chinese efforts to isolate him in Asia, but the Japanese government still lacked a framework that would envelop the entire region in a more coherent and inviting formulation than the earlier Arc of Freedom and Prosperity and the newly restored Quad concept. Where the Arc had drawn lines around the Eurasian Rimland—creating a Spykman-like mental map of forward littoral containment against China, Abe returned instead to the core geographic features that connected the Quad countries and formed a benign and protective blanket around Southeast Asia—the Pacific and Indian Oceans.[85] First introduced in his 2007 speech in India, Abe revived the two ocean theme in speeches in Jakarta in January 2013 and at CSIS in Washington in February of that year.[86] That March, the Japan Institute for International Affairs (JIIA) completed a study for the Ministry of Foreign Affairs on how to operationalize this emerging Indo-Pacific concept in foreign, defense, and economic development policies.[87] The JIIA study pointed to Australian, American, and Indian scholars like Rory Medcalf, Andrew Shearer, and C. Rajamohan who had begun emphasizing the strategic centrality of the Indian Ocean several years earlier. The report argued that the Indo-Pacific concept could link Japan with key allies and partners and prevent a "vacuum" in the confluence of the Indian and Pacific Oceans that China was trying to fill.[88] Further evidence of the strategic logic of this geographic construct was provided by a 2014

CSIS survey of strategic elites in Asia that showed broad acceptance of the term "Indo-Pacific" in the maritime democracies and a concomitant and revealing disdain for the term among Chinese foreign policy intellectuals.[89]

In August 2016 Abe used the Tokyo International Conference on African Development (TICAD) summit of African leaders to formally announce a new "Free and Open Indo-Pacific strategy."[90] While the setting was a bit unusual for unveiling a foundational strategy for China's neighborhood, Abe explained that the concept linked the Indian and Pacific Oceans, which were the oceans that in turn connected Japan to Africa. The speech was little noticed in Washington or East Asia, however.

The strategy next appeared in the June 2017 *Kaihatsu Kyōryoku Hakusho* (White paper on development cooperation 2017) as the guiding framework for future economic assistance.[91] But perhaps the most consequential presentation of the Free and Open Indo-Pacific strategy (or FOIP, as it was now being called) was when Deputy Foreign Minister Suzuki Hiroshi presented the concept to his American counterpart in the new Trump administration in the fall of that year. The State Department Policy Planning Office, eager to provide Secretary of State Rex Tillerson with a coherent statement on Asia policy before the secretary's first trip in the region to India, latched on to the concept and even the name. FOIP fit with the new U.S. National Security Strategy's framing of strategic competition with China, and the State Department India Desk knew it would play well in Delhi. At CSIS on October 18, Tillerson declared that "it is vital that the Indo-Pacific . . . remain free and open."[92] The next month in Tokyo, Trump and Abe confirmed their cooperation with any country in the region that shared their vision of a free and open Indo-Pacific and pledged to work together on three pillars: promotion of fundamental values, pursuit of economic prosperity, and peace and stability.[93] Though Trump himself rarely uttered any of those words ever again, his national security establishment was fully on board with the Japanese strategy and issued a detailed progress report on their own Free and Open Indo-Pacific strategy the next November.[94] For a Japanese foreign ministry used to reacting to American policy initiatives toward the region, it was an almost unprecedented role reversal.

FOIP would continue to evolve. ASEAN leaders initially expressed uncertainty about a strategy that was not based on ASEAN centrality (embedding regional multilateralism in ASEAN capitals), and so Tokyo began speaking of a Free and Open Indo-Pacific "vision" instead of "strategy" that would be more inclusive and flexible.[95] ASEAN then produced its own *ASEAN Outlook on the Indo-Pacific* in June 2019—one that reasserted the organization's emphasis on ASEAN centrality, internal connectivity, and consensus-based approaches inclusive of China. The ASEAN *Outlook* was not an endorsement of FOIP, but it was clearly much closer to Japan's formulation than to China's new One Belt One Road Initiative (later changed in the English rendering to the "Belt and Road Initiative") or Xi Jinping's calls for a "community of common destiny."[96] Indonesia, which was asserting its position as a "global maritime fulcrum" at the middle of the Indo-Pacific, was a key driver behind the ASEAN outlook.[97] In Europe, maritime powers Britain, France, and the Netherlands each also announced Indo-Pacific strategies, with others to follow.[98]

Central to Japan's development of FOIP has been a focus on capacity building within the Indo-Pacific. Japan officially began capacity-building programs for Southeast Asian militaries in 2012 (mostly with training programs) and then in April 2014 issued a cabinet decree relaxing the so-called Three Principles on arms exports, which opened the way for joint development of weapons systems with the United States but also sales and leases to other like-minded states of Japan's own equipment.[99] China's construction of artificial islands in 2015 and categorical rejection of the United Nations Convention on the Law of the Sea (UNCLOS) Tribunal ruling in favor of the Philippines in 2016 accelerated Tokyo's efforts. In 2017 Japan transferred five fixed-wing TC-90 aircraft to the Philippines and upgraded the armed forces of the Philippines Bell UH-1 "Huey" helicopters the next year, with more assistance, including the sale of maritime radars, to follow.[100] The effort continued under the Suga administration as the new prime minister inked an agreement in Hanoi in October 2020 to increase Japan's export of patrol boats and other equipment to Vietnam.[101] Japan also provided legal, diplomatic, and technical assistance for Southeast Asian claimants battling Beijing's expansive definition of China's "nine-dash line" boundary in the South

China Sea.[102] No one in the region was surprised when a 2020 survey by the Singapore-based Yusof Ishak Institute of Southeast Asian Studies of professionals across the region chose Japan as the strategic partner of choice to help hedge against China-U.S. strategic competition.[103]

This was not the exact playbook Abe had in mind with his original proposals for the Arc of Freedom and Prosperity in 2007, but the new version did reflect a constant calibration in Japan's effort to prevent Chinese hegemony over the rest of Asia. Effective strategy requires contextual intelligence—the ability to adjust when things do not work—and in his second term Abe and his senior advisors demonstrated just that. The influential international relations scholar Tanaka Akihiko reflected mainstream views in Abe's circles when he wrote in 2018 that FOIP was now "Japan's grand strategy." However, when the Japanese government was told by Southeast Asian officials that Tokyo would do better to suggest a "vision" for the entire region rather than extension of a strategy designed to enhance Japan's security and prosperity, Tokyo adjusted course. The next year Tanaka's colleague from Tokyo University, Kitaoka Shinichi, explained that what Japan was offering the region was now "a vision . . . not a strategy."[104] Ultimately FOIP was a strategic *framework* that enhanced Japan's influence, increased alignment among the major maritime powers around China, and imposed discipline and priorities on Japan's foreign, defense, and aid policies. It focused on empowering developing Asia through development and infrastructure and attracting those countries to the rules-based order that Japan favored.

The Quad also made a comeback over the course of Abe's second term, offering the external balance-of-power construct needed to reinforce FOIP from the outside—like the flying buttresses that hold up European cathedrals without changing the elegant design the parishioners see from within the nave. Working-level talks resumed in Manila on the margins of an ASEAN meeting in November 2017, where the four countries agreed to meet biannually to promote a "free and open and inclusive Indo-Pacific" based on the four countries' commitment to a "rules-based order."[105] The India-Australia leg continued to lag—in part because of lingering Indian suspicions of the Rudd government's opposition to the Quad and halting of uranium sales to India—but also because Delhi needed Australia as a scapegoat to demonstrate its caution to Beijing. Over the next two years, however, China's expanding military footprint in the Indian Ocean and the Himalayas spurred Delhi to begin strengthening that fourth leg. Most notable was India's decision to reinvite the Royal Australian Navy back into the Malabar exercises in 2020.[106] Then on October 6, 2020, reflecting Indian alarm at Chinese use of force in the border dispute between the two countries, the four foreign ministers met in Tokyo for the first fully dedicated Quad session (previous meetings had always been on the margins of other multilateral settings).[107]

FOIP and the Quad were particularly influential in the Trump administration's military-heavy national security establishment because the proposals evoked foundational concepts in the American tradition of maritime strategy. Commodore Matthew Perry, whose Black Ships had opened Japan in 1853, had predicted that someday the navies of the United States, Britain, and Japan would safeguard the Pacific Ocean, an idea echoed four decades later by the preeminent American thinker on sea power, Alfred Thayer Mahan.[108] With Australia and India as the twenty-first-century representatives of British sea power in the Indo-Pacific, Abe had replicated the proposals of the most influential strategic thinkers on Asia in American history. The American and Japanese maritime traditions and external balancing strategies were converging.

When Joe Biden defeated Trump for the presidency in 2020, many Japanese observers feared that there would be a return to the Obama administration's more restrained view of competition with China and skepticism about the Quad. The Cassandras in Tokyo could not have been more wrong. Biden continued referring to the "Free and Open Indo-Pacific," despite the preference among his political advisors for a framework different from Trump's. Then he hosted the first Quad summit in March 2021 (by video conference because of the pandemic) with Prime Minister Suga and their Indian and Australian counterparts, announcing major deliverables, including a plan to provide 1 billion doses of COVID-19 vaccine for developing Asia and new coordination on rare earth metals.[109] Abe's original proposal for a Quad summit not only made a comeback but was now suddenly a centerpiece of the variable geometry of Asia's complex diplomacy.[110] Significantly, the Biden playbook, led by veteran alliance manager Kurt Campbell from the White House, had taken a page from Japan's own approach to shaping regional order. The focus was not on containing or even countering China, but rather on helping Asia. Beijing objected strongly to the Quad in subsequent bilateral meetings with the United States in Alaska on March 18–19 and rushed frenetically to signal closer cooperation with Moscow, Pyongyang, and Tehran—but the desperation in China's response only revealed how effective the Quad meeting had been, since the response from Southeast Asia was overwhelmingly enthusiastic. Seeing this reaction, other U.S. allies in Europe and the Pacific Rim began joining military exercises or considering participation in the Quad in some form.[111]

As an example of external balancing, Abe had scored an enormous success with FOIP and the Quad. However, the longer-term durability of that strategic framework would still rest on the credibility of the democratic norms at its core, the ability of Japan to compete with China on economic infrastructure and rulemaking, and the future regional institutions needed to ultimately bridge the divide with China over the longer term.

IDEATIONAL COMPETITION

The ideational glue behind the Quad, the Arc, and FOIP—and the target of greatest cynicism in each case—was the argument that Japan could be a champion of democracy, rulemaking, and human rights in a complicated Asian patchwork of different political regime types. In fact, there is ample evidence that elites in Asian states are far more attracted to norms of good governance, democracy, and rule of law than any competing vision of authoritarian capitalism emanating from Beijing.[112] But Japan's own brand and effectiveness at advancing these norms continue to be a subject of scholarly and political debate.

The emergence of democracy as a major theme in Japan's foreign policy did not begin with Koizumi or Abe, but instead with an earlier iconoclast from outside the LDP mainstream. When Hosokawa Morihiro cobbled together a multiparty coalition to briefly knock the LDP from power for the first time in 1993, he emphasized the importance of Japan's democratic identity in his first speech to the Diet as prime minister.[113] His point was that his new anti-LDP coalition had greater legitimacy because the peaceful revolution in Japan was part of a larger wave of post–Cold War democratization then under way in Central and Eastern Europe—indeed, the LDP that Hosokawa had knocked out of power was itself a product of the Cold War. Hosokawa's government did not last long, but democracy returned as a major theme in the reaffirmation of the U.S.-Japan alliance in Clinton and LDP prime minister Hashimoto's April 1996 Joint Declaration on Security, which reaffirmed the two leaders' "commitment to the profound common values that guide our national policies: the maintenance of freedom, the pursuit of democracy, and respect for human rights."[114] Much of the drafting of that declaration was led by "Mr. National Interest"—Tanaka Hitoshi—then deputy director general of the North American Affairs Bureau.

However, in other statements being drafted at the time by Tanaka's foreign ministry colleagues that were related to Asia and regional initiatives, like Hashimoto's "New Eurasia" diplomacy, democratic values remained more muted. Hashimoto's balance-of-power diplomacy at this point was testing realpolitik rather than ideational competition. Indeed, much of Japan's ideational competition was still aimed across the Pacific at that point. Hashimoto was himself a veteran of tough trade fights with the Clinton administration in 1993 and 1994 in his post as MITI minister, and the trade and finance ministry officials were still engaged in hot arguments with the Clinton administration about the legitimacy of Asian economic development models. Thus, in introducing his "New Eurasia" diplomacy initiative in August 1997, Hashimoto noted Japan's attachment to liberal democracy as one value system, but asked rhetorically, "To what degree can we demand others' acceptance of this value system as one superior to other value systems?" It was better, he joked, to address these issues quietly over prodigious amounts of alcohol with

Chinese counterparts, as he had done immediately after the Tiananmen incident in 1989.[115]

This background explains why Koizumi's emphasis on market-oriented reforms and democracy in Singapore in January 2002 was such a turning point. Like Hosokawa, Koizumi was a reformer trying to break the LDP's closed power structures—only this time from inside the party. Changes in Japanese politics introduced by Hosokawa in 1993 had not given way to a competitive two-party system, as many political commentators had hoped, but the new electoral system he introduced did succeed in breaking the old faction's control over LDP decision making and led eventually to the broader enfranchisement of grass-roots party members in the selection of party leader.[116] Like other great reformers, Koizumi went over the heads of the faction bosses and built his campaign around populism and a commitment to decisive reform that appealed to the local party members and the public. He vowed to "change the LDP and if it doesn't change to destroy it."[117] His new "idea" in Singapore was that democratic reforms in Japan would serve as a model not only for the future of Japan but also for the region as a whole.[118] As Asō put it at the time, Japan would use its experiences to be a "thought leader" in Asia.[119]

When Abe made what politicians were by now calling "values-oriented diplomacy" a central theme in his first term as prime minister in 2006–2007, old guards in the LDP initially mobilized to block him.[120] In a split evocative of the 1960s-era pro-Taiwan and pro-Beijing "Asian Problems Study Group" and "Asian-African Problems Study Group," three LDP elders—Yamazaki Taku, Kato Kōichi, and Koga Makoto—formed what the media called the YKK Group to sustain their overall influence and to prevent further erosion of the party's older ideology-free approach to Beijing. In response to YKK, a much larger group of younger LDP Diet members formed a new parliamentary league to advance "values diplomacy."[121] The liberal *Asahi Shimbun* editorialized that these "Abe cheerleaders" were unwise to create an "us-versus-them" split in Asia between China and the democracies.[122] The time was not ripe for values-oriented diplomacy, which was being equated with the Bush administration's increasingly unpopular Iraq War by liberal institutionalists in both the

United States and Japan. Abe probably also hampered acceptance of the normative construct by wielding values as an ideological cudgel against the old guard of the LDP and the *Asahi Shimbun* the way Koizumi had used economic reform to beat them down—the difference was that people understood how they benefited from economic reform but not from the ideological fights. Just as Fukuda quietly shelved the Quad and the Arc of Freedom and Prosperity when he replaced Abe in 2007, he also replaced "values-oriented diplomacy" with what he now called "synergy diplomacy" between Japan's alliance with the United States and its relationship with Asia in pursuit of an open regional order.[123]

By the time Abe made his political comeback in 2012, however, the appetite for emphasizing democratic norms in Japanese foreign policy had clearly grown. As Kanehara explained in an article penned in 2011, countries always have three national interests in their foreign policy—security, prosperity, and values—and so should Japan.[124] Abe's 2013 *National Security Strategy* listed "universal values" no less than ten times as the core of Japanese national interests across a wide range of issue areas.[125]

But was it real? Critics emphasized that Japan's newfound enthusiasm for advancing democratic norms was not matched by equal enthusiasm for addressing Japan's past aggression in Asia.[126] Many of the conservatives behind Abe's values diplomacy, including Abe himself, had long harbored resentment that the language of "universal norms" was used by Beijing, *Asahi Shimbun*, and others on the left to perpetuate Japan's guilty status after the war and to handicap Japan as a great power. Abe was earlier on the record criticizing the Tokyo War Crimes Tribunal as victors' justice and had once opposed the official 1993 statement by Chief Cabinet Secretary Kōno Yōhei accepting Japanese culpability for the wholesale coercion of the euphemistically named "comfort women" forced into sexual servitude for the imperial Japanese army.[127] Abe and his allies were also associated with efforts to produce more nationalist textbooks in the 1990s that minimized Japan's culpability for war and destruction in Asia.[128] Some of Abe's strongest supporters from his time in the political wilderness continued attacking Korea and urging greater patriotic education and rejection of war guilt through publications from

Sakurai Yoshiko's Japan Institute for National Fundamentals—which many journalists assumed reflected Abe's own true feelings.[129] In the most extreme cases, violently pornographic nationalist *manga* by Kobayashi Yoshinori expressed pure hatred of Abe's critics and urged unapologetic rejection of war guilt (I was featured as a stooge of *Asahi Shimbun* in one Kobayashi cartoon after urging greater efforts at understanding with South Korea in 2007).[130]

On the other hand, as Ken Pyle has noted, Abe's "Heisei" generation of political leaders "constitute the first generation whose entire schooling has been under democratic principles mandated by the Fundamental Law of Education of 1947, which the Occupation drafted. During their life span, there has been a growing understanding and acceptance of the fundamental notions of democratic government, albeit in a distinctly Japanese form. Postwar high-school textbooks at first explained democratic values in a way that blurred respect for hierarchy and individualism, but more recently they have been clearer in explaining the concepts of democracy and human rights."[131]

Linguist Kevin Doak has noted that the discourse of leaders like Abe is markedly different from that of earlier generations of conservatives. Whereas right-wing discourse before and after the war gravitated to the language of "ethnic" (*minzoku*) nationalism, evident in narratives about the superiority (or after the war, the uniqueness) of the Japanese race, Abe's generation of conservatives has turned instead to the use of "civic" (*shimin*) nationalism, which values the democratic rights of citizenship regardless of race.[132] It was these modern democratic values that defined Japan for Abe, rather than the attributes of the Japanese race that animated nationalists of earlier generations.

Officials and journalists in Abe's office joked that in his first year back in power the prime minister would follow the universalist values diplomacy of Yachi and Kanehara during the week but then play golf with his right-wing political friends on the weekend, forcing his staff to pull him back toward the center again every Monday. The test of which "Abe" would prevail was clear to all—the seventieth anniversary of the end of World War II on August 15, 2015.

CONFRONTING HISTORY

The seventieth anniversary statement marking the end of the Second World War, scheduled for August 15, 2015, was recognized as a momentous test of Abe's political acumen. With a more centralized leadership system, Abe would be able to determine the contents of the statement with greater latitude than his predecessors, who had been forced to arbitrate the content with multiple faction bosses across the political spectrum. Abe was determined to make this the *final* statement—to remove August 15 as an annual occasion for China (and to some extent South Korea) to demand concessions of Japan and remind the world of Japan's moral inadequacies as a major power. Making this the final authoritative word on the war would also satisfy Abe's political supporters. However, for the statement to be credible, he needed polls to reflect *majority* support from the public. The next target in his concentric ring of support would have to be the members of the Quad, and particularly the United States. Washington's judgment of the statement would depend on how well it was received in Southeast Asia and South Korea. Abe could be fairly confident about Southeast Asian support, given his intensive personal diplomacy and the fact that all polls in the region were highly favorable to Japan. Korea would be harder—though Seoul had only so much latitude to either accept or reject the statement because of polarized domestic politics and pressure from the United States for solidarity among allies. It was assumed that China would be the most negative, but the whole point was to isolate Beijing and remove the history card as a weapon to be used against Japan—so Beijing's response would not be the pacesetter. This was the political geometry that would guide drafting of the statement.

If this was to be the penultimate statement on the war, the philosophy of the statement also needed to go well beyond the myopic debates about whether to include specific words such as "remorse" (*owabi*) or "reflection" (*hansei*) that had consumed politicians with previous apologies. Recognizing this fact, historian Haneda Masashi of Tokyo University recommended that the government borrow from new trends in the scholarship of global history to go big—to provide the larger context that explained Japan's history in three parts: the competitive imperial world order into which Japan modernized, Japan's descent into militarism as that world order collapsed, and Japan's postwar role in building a more peaceful and prosperous world order.[133] That much broader global and historical context—focusing on one hundred years instead of twenty, and the entire world instead of just East Asia—would allow greater candor about the specific damage and suffering that Japan had caused during the war but would absolve Japan of the permanent enemy status enshrined in the UN Charter and wielded repeatedly by Beijing.

Abe announced in his New Year's press conference in January 2015 that he would "consolidate wisdom when considering what the Abe administration can send out as a message to the world concerning Japan's remorse over World War II, the path we have walked since the war as a peace-loving nation, and how Japan will contribute further to benefit the Asia-Pacific region and the world."[134]

The next month a special Advisory Panel on the History of the Twentieth Century convened the first of seven meetings under the president and CEO of Japan Post, Nishimuro Taizō, to examine the history of Japan's path to war in the context of the twentieth century and to consider previous efforts at reconciliation and the lessons Japan should learn in defining its future role. The members of the panel were almost entirely center or center-right thinkers, including thought leaders like Iizuka Keiko of the *Yomiuri Shimbun* and former diplomat Okamoto Yukio. Not included were pundits further on the right who were previously associated with Abe, such as Sakurai Yoshiko. Meanwhile, right-wing members of the LDP demanded establishment of a special committee on "restoring Japan's honor" to push for rejection of previous apologies just as Abe was formulating the seventieth anniversary statement. Abe and his allies skillfully put the committee under centrists like former foreign minister Nakasone Hirofumi and ex-diplomat Inoguchi Kuniko to allow internal venting but contain the rebellion on the right.[135]

When Abe issued his statement, it was by far the longest ever read by a Japanese prime minister on the war and contained the most detailed acknowledgment of the damage and suffering Japan had caused. In the statement, Abe argued that Japan had modernized rapidly in a sense of

crisis to maintain its own independence in the face of "waves of colonial rule" but with the Manchurian crisis in 1931 became a "challenger to
the international order," "took the wrong course and advanced along the
road to war." Then

> countless lives were lost among young people with promising futures.
> In China, Southeast Asia, the Pacific islands and elsewhere that became
> the battlefields, numerous innocent citizens suffered and fell victim to
> battles as well as hardships such as severe deprivation of food. We must
> never forget that there were women behind the battlefields whose hon-
> our and dignity were severely injured.
>
> We will engrave in our hearts the past, when the dignity and hon-
> our of many women were severely injured during wars in the twentieth
> century. Upon this reflection, Japan wishes to be a country always at the
> side of such women's injured hearts. Japan will lead the world in making
> the twenty-first century an era in which women's human rights are not
> infringed upon.[136]

While it was less than could have been said about the suffering Japan
caused, it was far more than the Japanese public had ever heard their
prime ministers say before (at 1,673 words in the English translation,
it was almost three times longer than devout pacifist Social Democrat
Murayama Tomiichi's statement on the fiftieth anniversary in 1995).[137]

The public split at first. *Kyodo News* found that 44 percent viewed
the statement favorably, slightly more than those who viewed it nega-
tively.[138] But that support grew after the Kōmeitō Party leader praised
Abe's words.[139] The Obama administration, which had been urging Abe
to be forward leaning, immediately offered a positive assessment, with
the U.S. NSC spokesman welcoming Abe's "expression of deep remorse
for the suffering caused by Japan during the World War II era, as well
as his commitment to uphold past Japanese government statements on
history"—a point emphasized because Abe had questioned earlier government positions on the comfort women issue.[140] Korea, as hoped, sent
a response somewhere between ambivalent and supportive, with President Park Geun-hye telling the public that even though parts were not

satisfactory, Abe made it clear that the views shown by past Japanese cabinets are unwavering.[141] The only negative response other than North Korea, as expected, was China, though the Chinese spokesman chose to attack Japan's "wars of aggression" rather than critique the statement per se.[142] On the whole, Abe had hit the targets he wanted. There was no significant pressure at home or abroad for new statements of remorse when subsequent August 15 anniversaries came, and no government in South or Southeast Asia—or the West—would challenge Japan's inherent right to advance a vision based on Japan's own example of democracy and rule of law and proactive contribution to international peace. History would come back to complicate Japan-Korea relations, but that friction now proved the exception rather than the rule.

CHAMPIONING DEMOCRACY IN PRACTICE

Yet if Japan established credibility on the normative framing of the Free and Open Indo-Pacific vision, questions remain about whether Japan is actually doing enough to advance democratic governance in the region. Understanding early on that Japan needed to put its money where its mouth was, Abe as chief cabinet secretary in 2005 had personally led a Commission on Overseas Economic Cooperation with the aim of mainstreaming democratic values in Japan's ODA policies. The commission draft report the next year stated that Japan's assistance abroad should contribute to a prosperous and stable world order "based on liberty, democracy and the rule of law," but specific proposals were then blocked by JICA (Japan International Cooperation Agency) and foreign ministry development assistance experts who were wedded to the apolitical "human security" priorities of the revered former UN high commissioner on refugees, Ogata Sadako. The proposal for values-oriented development assistance went the way of other such initiatives when Fukuda came into office in 2007.[143]

Returned to power, Abe resumed his earlier efforts, and in 2015 his government produced a new Official Development Assistance Charter that included democracy promotion as a priority.[144] From a low of around $5 million per year in the 1990s, Japan's democracy assistance increased under Abe to over $300 million per year at a time when the overall ODA budget was stagnant (the initial upward trajectory began under the DPJ-led Noda government). By comparison, however, Japan still lags behind other donors such as Australia, Canada, the United States, or the Scandinavian countries in the proportion of aid dedicated to governance and democracy, with over 98 percent of Japanese aid still going to governments rather than directly to civil society groups and most of that amount focused on technical assistance.[145] A survey of Japanese Diet members in 2020 showed strong support for increasing aid, though civil society support still ranked well below health and education as a priority.[146]

At the same time, a multiparty Japan Center for International Exchange (JCIE) study group on the future of democracy led by former ambassador Takasu Yukio continued mobilizing support to expand governance and democracy support, including expanding grant aid directly to nongovernment sectors.[147] Meanwhile, in the Diet, Amari Akira made democracy and governance ancillary themes in his "Parliamentary Group on Rule-Making" in 2020 as his group examined ways to protect the international liberal order against mercantilism and authoritarianism.[148]

Japanese attitudes on international human rights violations are also undergoing transition. One striking example was the result of a 2020 CSIS global survey on China policy in the United States, Europe, and Asia in which Japanese foreign policy thought leaders were found to be the *most* willing to pressure China on human rights related to Hong Kong.[149] Traditionally, the Japanese foreign ministry has been far more hesitant to criticize human rights violations than its counterparts in the West. That began to change in the 2000s as the Japanese public learned shocking details of how North Korea had abducted scores of Japanese citizens in the 1970s and 1980s and used them to train spies. Bipartisan leagues formed in the Diet to demand the abductees' return, and the foreign ministry has cosponsored UN resolutions on North Korean human rights every year since 2008 (with one exception).[150] The Japanese government has also become more outspoken on human rights violations in China, reflecting shifting attitudes revealed in the 2020 CSIS survey. In response to Beijing's 2020 Hong Kong National Security Law, for example, Japan opted not to join the U.S.-led statement along with the United Kingdom, Canada, and Australia, but did issue a statement expressing "serious concern"—the most robust of any East Asian neighbor of China.[151] And in March 2021 a new intraparty caucus on human rights was established by former defense minister Nakatani Gen, with participation across all of Japan's political parties, including the Communist Party. The group promised to increase interparliamentary cooperation with Europe, Asia, and North America to address growing human rights violations in Xinjiang and Hong Kong.[152] The preliminary focus on China was predictable in the context of growing competition with Beijing across a range of issues.

Japan's approach to Southeast Asia—the object of competition for influence with China—has traditionally been more circumspect, with a preference for quiet pressure on human rights violations rather than overt criticism vis-à-vis important strategic partners in the region like the Philippines or Vietnam. However, the instances of overt criticism and direct pressure have been on the increase. DPJ foreign minister Okada Katsuya sent his Burmese counterpart storming from the room when he criticized the junta's treatment of Aung San Suu Kyi in 2010, and later in 2017 Japan and the United States issued a joint statement in New York at the UN General Assembly expressing concern over the Rohinge refugee crisis in Myanmar, this time criticizing Suu Kyi's government.[153] Senior U.S. officials reported that interactions with Tokyo in the wake of the 2021 coup and violence in Myanmar had none of the "Asian values" defensiveness of previous interactions between U.S. and Japanese officials trying to address crises in that country.[154] Seeing China's direct technical and political support for the junta's roundup of protestors, Japanese officials concluded that targeted counterpressures were required and then closely coordinated measures with the United States and other members of the Quad, as well as with Indonesia within ASEAN. Still, Japan has yet to impose large-scale sanctions against countries in Southeast Asia that violate human rights, as the U.S. Congress or administrations have on multiple occasions. To the extent that sticks are discussed in Tokyo, it is in the context of denying carrots—of limiting economic assistance to countries that violate human rights and therefore create an uncertain investment environment. Having advanced values as a central organizing theme in foreign policy strategy, the Japanese government will continue facing hard choices about how to address human rights violations when economic and diplomatic trade-offs are required.

On the whole, however, values diplomacy took root in the second Abe government in ways that few would have anticipated when he first proposed the theme in 2006. China's increased pressure on the neoliberal order was clearly a factor, which also explains why Australian, European, and other advanced democracies began emphasizing democratic norms more in their foreign policies in the same period.[155] In addition, by 2020 the broad assault on international rulemaking was translating into direct images of citizens in Hong Kong struggling to protect their democratic rights—middle-class cosmopolitan citizens with whom the Japanese public could easily relate. Abe and his allies also used values-oriented diplomacy as a unifying theme in his second term rather than as a wedge against the left as he had in his first term, as the composition of the Advisory Panel on the History of the Twentieth Century suggests. The discourse on democracy promotion in foreign aid broadened to include bipartisan committees made up of LDP and DPJ members and advocates of human security like Ogata protégé and career diplomat Takasu. Just as CSIS surveys of foreign policy elites in Asia found growing Japanese enthusiasm for the Indo-Pacific as a geopolitical construct, these surveys also demonstrated that Japanese thought leaders had become second to none in the region in prioritizing the importance of free and fair elections, good governance, human rights, and women's empowerment to the future of the Asian order and in rejecting "non-interference in internal affairs" as a principle that should be maintained.

Indeed, Chinese thought leaders are now most committed to the themes of sovereignty and noninterference among regional experts, and Chinese diplomats are now the ones waving those banners in regional conferences.[156] Centrists and liberal internationalists like former *Asahi Shimbun* editor Funabashi Yōichi now regularly employ language describing Japan's mission as the builder of a new order "that forms free and democratic countries and values rule of law."[157] In Washington in 2013 Abe had declared that Japan would never be a tier two country. To do that he needed to make democratic norms a unifying theme rather than a weapon against the left—and he largely succeeded.

THE GEOPOLITICS OF ASIAN ECONOMIC CONNECTIVITY

Japan's shifting normative agenda in the region under Abe followed a combination of external and internal changes, and so did Japan's regional economic agenda. As political economist Katada Saori notes in *Japan's New Regional Reality*, "The Japanese government has, for the two decades since the 1990s, shifted its regional geoeconomic strategy from one based on neomercantalism (promoting the country's industries) to a more liberal one that aims to set rules and establish institutions for the region's public good." Japan, Katada concludes, has become "much more supportive of U.S.-led neoliberal policies," with the goal of "obtaining a strategic upper hand against its rival, China."[158] Steve Vogel and other scholars of the Japanese economy have charted how increased overseas investment and changes in corporate governance have made "Japan, Inc." far less adamant about protection at home and far more committed to protection of global rules abroad.[159] These changes began well before Abe came to power because of Koizumi's breaking of the bureaucracy-LDP nexus through the partial privatization of the postal savings system, the placement of new limits on bureaucrats' "descent from heaven" (*amakudari*) into the private sector, and the introduction of competitive metrics on stock valuation in the Tokyo Stock Exchange. From 1980 to 2004 corporate profits in Japan had been lower than government revenue, but after 2004 they were higher.[160] What was good for competitive Japanese multinationals in Asia was now far more important to Japan's success than what was good for protected sectors within Japan. Japan's status as a leading creditor nation further reinforced the

important of global economic rulemaking at a time of Chinese revisionism and uncertainty in geopolitics.

The competition for economic rulemaking vis-à-vis China would
primarily be regional, however, and not global. Repeating the competitive dynamics from a century earlier, the focus would be on infrastructure. When Xi Jinping announced China's One Belt One Road Initiative
in Jakarta in October 2013 as a centerpiece of the "China-ASEAN Community of Common Destiny," Japanese officials suspected that Beijing
was throwing money at ASEAN to overwhelm the open democratic
"two oceans" vision Abe had offered in his own speech in Jakarta the
previous January.[161] When Xi followed up with a new proposal for a
Chinese-led Asia Infrastructure Investment Bank (AIIB) in June 2014,
Abe's government and the United States refused to join. Japanese officials argued that the fund would undermine the transparency and
accountability of the IMF and the Asian Development Bank (ADB)—a
noteworthy role reversal from Japan's position on the Asian Monetary
Fund fifteen years earlier.[162]

By the time of Xi's AIIB announcement, the Japan Bank for International Cooperation (JBIC) had already been distributing about half
of its loans for infrastructure finance for years and had far more experience than China. Speaking to a Japan-Asia conference in Tokyo in
May 2015, Abe urged his Asian counterparts not to be "pound wise and
penny foolish" when it came to borrowing for infrastructure. Japan was
committed to innovative economic integration based not on "quality
over quantity" but "quality *and* quantity." Abe was not saying that governments in the region should refuse China's largesse—his government
was sufficiently attuned to ASEAN sentiments to know that it would be
foolish to demand they choose between Japan and China—but rather
that the region should see Japan as a *high-quality* alternative to China's
nontransparent financing. To that end, he pledged a new Partnership for
Quality Infrastructure under which Japan would work with the ADB
to provide Asian economies with innovative infrastructure financing
at a scale of $110 billion over five years.[163] The Ministry of Economy,
Trade and Industry (METI) elaborated that this new partnership would
involve four pillars:

1. expansion and acceleration of assistance through the full mobilization of Japan's economic cooperation tools;

2. collaboration between Japan and the ADB;

3. measures to double the supply of funding for projects with relatively high risk profiles by such means as the enhancement of the function of the JBIC; and

4. promotion of "quality infrastructure investment" as an international standard.

In briefings across the region and to other donor countries, Japanese officials emphasized that the life-cycle costs would be lower for Japanese than Chinese projects and that Japan had a history of avoiding "debt traps" that would force developing countries into a new-imperialist dependency on China.[164] It was well known that even though Japan's pledge rivaled China's in total dollars, there would still not be enough financing to meet the region's demand for infrastructure. The goal was not to drive out China, but rather to give developing countries options and leverage to change Chinese behavior and push Beijing toward adoption of global standards and less mercantilist and predatory policies.

The urgency of organizing a strategy to compete with what China was now calling the BRI (Belt and Road Initiative) became apparent in early 2015 when Indonesia suddenly chose China's relatively untested high-speed rail system over the more established Japanese bullet train, which Tokyo had been preparing to build for the Indonesians since 2008.[165] The circumstances around Jakarta's sudden shift to China were criticized by Chief Cabinet Secretary Suga Yoshihide as suspiciously "lacking in transparency," and scholars subsequently concluded that China had accepted terms that Japan would not, such as zero fiscal spending by Indonesia and demands for completion of the high-speed rails in parts of Java that lacked sufficient economic activity to sustain the project without massive debt.[166] These shortcomings would become evident to the Indonesians later, but in 2015 Tokyo faced an unexpected crisis in its effort to be Southeast Asia's infrastructure partner of choice.

To stay competitive, Japan's new infrastructure strategy would require agility and more external partners. The former was achieved with changes in the JBIC charter in 2016 that gave the bank more latitude to make strategic investments that might involve higher levels of risk.[167] JBIC was also now led by one of the most strategic thinkers in Tokyo, Maeda Tadashi, whose resume over three decades working at the bank included senior advisory roles for both LDP and DPJ governments and an unparalleled personal network in the global worlds of finance and investment.

The external partners for infrastructure investment would come from the Quad—or at least two other members. The Obama administration had opposed the AIIB in 2014 but was handicapped by insurgent Republicans in the House of Representatives who were threatening to defund JBIC's smaller U.S. counterpart, the Overseas Private Investment Corporation (OPIC).[168] When the Trump administration announced strategic competition with China and the Free and Open Indo-Pacific in 2017, however, the Congress came around on a bipartisan basis and offered some of the tools necessary by replacing OPIC with the new Development Finance Corporation (DFC) through the BUILD Act of October 2018.[169] Though many of the mechanics would remain unique to U.S. policy, DFC was largely modeled on JBIC, with expanded lending authority (most importantly the ability to take equity positions) and authorization to extend $60 billion, or more than double OPIC's earlier cap.[170] In July the United States, Japan, and Australia announced a "Trilateral Partnership for Infrastructure Investment in the Indo-Pacific" and signed a memorandum of understanding (MOU) implementing the partnership in November with the new U.S. DFC, with initial projects focused on Indonesia and a critical undersea telecommunications cable link in the South Pacific.[171]

While the United States remained skeptical of cooperation with China's BRI—sending only a senior U.S. NSC official to Beijing's first Belt and Road Forum in May 2017, Japan's goal was now to shape rather than ostracize.[172] JBIC governor Maeda accompanied Abe on his October 2018 visit to Beijing, where he and his counterpart at the China Development Bank agreed to explore cooperation between FOIP and BRI. Remarkably, the Chinese side signed up to all the principles Maeda demanded with respect to debt sustainability and transparency.[173] The

Chinese bankers, being bankers, were eager to improve sustainability and accountability as stewards of Chinese national funds and to avoid the moral hazard that would confront China if Beijing stood alone trying to recover unpaid debts. Warnings from the IMF about debt traps with BRI no doubt reinforced the sense of international isolation among the executives of the China Development Bank.[174] The promise of joint Sino-Japanese work went largely unfulfilled, however. The problem was not just geopolitics. Japanese officials found that the China Development Bank was not yet technically proficient enough to manage complicated public-private partnerships (PPPs) in a global market or politically empowered enough by the many officials around Xi Jinping claiming ownership of BRI to align with Japan on specific projects.[175] Still, Tokyo did not give up the goal of eventually bending China's approach toward Japan's—just as Japan itself had abandoned its own Asian Monetary Fund scheme and aligned with global norms in the region's debt crises two decades earlier.

SEEKING TO BEND—NOT BREAK—BRI

Japan's quality infrastructure strategy was in many ways a response to China's own ambitions, yet on balance it continues to shape China's approach to lending more than Beijing has shaped Tokyo's. Beijing even co-opted the Japanese term "quality infrastructure" in branding its second annual Belt and Road Forum (BARF II) in April 2019.[176] The strategic focus in Tokyo and the harnessing of global and regional governments and lending organizations, as well as the "quality" branding, have all been largely successful. Yet as China expands BRI to the even more expansive "Digital Silk Road" and the "Ice Road" to the Arctic, it remains an open question whether Japan's strategy will ultimately bend Chinese ambitions in a more benign direction.

That said, Japan had fought China at least to a draw in the infrastructure race in Southeast Asia by 2020. While Beijing won the high-speed rail competition in Indonesia and took one of the two bullet train lines in Thailand, Japan won the bullet train concession from Vietnam and beat out China on conventional rail and mass-transit systems across the region. By 2020 Japan had secured 240 infrastructure projects overall in Southeast Asia, compared with 210 for China.[177] Japan's projects in the six largest ASEAN countries had risen to $367 billion, against China's $255 billion.[178] Japan also clearly surpassed China in terms of customer satisfaction in the recipient states, with its focus on quality infrastructure and investment in human capital in the region, including commitments in 2018 to groom over 18,000 manufacturing and digital industry specialists in ASEAN.[179] And over that same period Japan became the lead coordinator for other democracies that were also entering the infrastructure fray—beginning with the United States and Australia, and increasingly with European donors.

By the summer of 2020, Beijing was acknowledging the fine print from its earlier victory over Japan in the competition for Indonesia's high-speed rail link, conceding that the project would be delayed due to unforeseen (or unrevealed) cost overruns. Amazingly, the Chinese authorities proposed that Japan come in to complete the project and finish it on time—a proposal Tokyo rejected because of the lack of transparency in China's overall effort.[180] While Japan made some adjustments to compete with China, Beijing continued looking more likely to gravitate to Japan's FOIP standards than the other way around. As a strategy to force China to compete on fair terms and perhaps eventually change its own nontransparent and debt-heavy approach, Japan had put the right pieces in place by empowering recipient states and engaging in collective balancing with other lenders.

THE LONG-TERM PLAY: REGIONAL AND GLOBAL RULEMAKING

Japan's early post–Cold War foreign policy vision had been animated by the belief that an East Asia Community comparable to European and North American integration was possible in Japan's own neighborhood. Japan had tried to be a leader in regional multilateralism, beginning with the 1991 Nakayama proposal to institutionalize the ASEAN foreign ministers' meetings with the rest of Asia, and it continued championing similar ideas throughout the decade.[181] But with Beijing's growing revisionism Tokyo found itself increasingly playing defense—arranging the geometry of multilateral meetings in order to blunt Chinese ambitions to dominate the new intraregional architecture. This competition ground down community building. The inclusion of Australia, New Zealand, India, and ultimately the United States (after 2009) in the new East Asia Summit had more than blunted China's initial efforts to dominate that forum, but in exchange Beijing was able to include Russia, which weighed down the summit to the point that it had little agenda-shaping power. In response to China's coercive expansion in the South China Sea, Japan joined with the United States and other U.S. allies in the ASEAN Regional Forum (ARF) to muscle through language insisting that China negotiate with ASEAN on a code of conduct over maritime disputes rather than pick off the smaller states one by one.[182] However, that effort faltered in July 2016 when Beijing bribed ASEAN's rotating chair Cambodia with $600 million to block a statement from the association calling on China to abide by the ruling of the UNCLOS Tribunal that China's expansive definition of maritime claims was contrary to international law and precedent.[183] Competition with China and ASEAN's insistence on consensus-based decision making combined to neuter the ASEAN-based institution building at the center of Nakayama's original 1991 proposal.

Throughout this period CSIS surveys of regional strategic thinkers showed a marked decline in Japanese optimism about regionwide multilateralism, with fewer than 5 percent of Japanese experts saying in 2014 that they thought a new East Asia community might be constructed in the coming decade—the most pessimistic view of any of the ten countries surveyed.[184] By 2021 the new energy in Japanese diplomacy was shifting toward the external balancing of the Quad. But none of this means that Japanese diplomats are retreating from regionwide multilateralism—far from it. Participation in ASEAN-centered multilateral architecture like the ARF and the East Asian Summit (so-called ASEAN centrality) had been a core reason for Japan's high level of trust within the region. Competition for influence in Southeast Asia meant that Japan had to play better than China—which Japan was—even if the results continued to fall short of the earlier optimism about East Asia community building.

LEADING ON REGIONAL TRADE NEGOTIATIONS

Japan has had more success building regional agreements around trade that might shape Chinese economic behavior, though not without considerable setbacks and frustrations here as well. Under Abe, Japan focused on a two-track approach. One track was pursuit of an intra-regional agreement centered on ASEAN but including Japan, Korea, China, Australia, New Zealand, and India—the Regional Comprehensive Economic Partnership (RCEP). Negotiations began in earnest in 2013 after several years of preparatory discussions on the margins of ASEAN summits. The other track was the U.S.-centered Trans-Pacific Partnership (TPP), which Abe formally asked to join in 2012, transforming the pact into a powerhouse of Pacific Rim countries anchored on the first and third largest economies in the world. In the 2014 CSIS surveys, Japanese thought leaders identified TPP as by far the more important of the two agreements (92 percent chose TPP as the top priority compared with 68 percent who chose RCEP). The logic was clear: TPP standards were higher, and the agreement was expected to give Japan and other participants significant leverage in tough negotiations with China under RCEP.[185] This symbiotic relationship between the trans-Pacific and intraregional agreements was important, since Japan had agreed with the United States, China, and the other participants in the 2007 Sydney APEC summit that both agreements should someday converge in a comprehensive Free Trade Area of the Asia Pacific (FTAAP).[186]

However, both TPP and RCEP suffered major setbacks in 2016 when the Trump administration announced it would withdraw from the newly completed TPP pact and the Modhi government in India began obstructing liberalization efforts in RCEP. Rather than faltering, however, Abe's government pushed forward with both TPP and RCEP. So crucial was the trans-Pacific leg to regional rulemaking that Abe prevailed upon the other TPP parties to both sign the newly named Comprehensive and Progressive Agreement for Trans-Pacific Partnership (CPTPP) in March 2018 and to keep open a seat for the United States to eventually rejoin.[187] His government then reluctantly agreed to let India drop out of RCEP in 2019 so that the intraregional leg of trade liberalization could be completed in a signing ceremony in November 2020.[188] While RCEP had begun as the less important of the two agreements to Tokyo, the Japanese government now concluded that RCEP offered the greater prospect for promoting Japanese economic growth: a 2.7 percent increase in real GDP.[189] Though the agreement fell well short of CPTPP standards in the areas of labor rights, digital trade, the environment, trade in services, and disciplines of the huge state-owned enterprises supported by China, RCEP did harmonize rules of origin and reduce tariffs in ways that incentivized all the economies to maintain significant supply chains with one another, particularly between Japan and China, which had no trade agreements in place before RCEP.[190]

This was an economic success for Japan, but not yet a strategic success. For without the U.S. presence in rulemaking in the region, Japan would not have the heft to change China's increasingly predatory economic policies. Abe and Suga continued pressing Presidents Trump and then Biden to come back to TPP, knowing that the agreement was supported by U.S. business and even the American public.[191] As of publication of this volume, however, Tokyo had little to show for its entreaties. Small victories were won in a partial renegotiation of TPP bilaterally with the Trump administration that was ratified by the Japanese Diet in December 2019 and concluded as an executive agreement by the Trump administration.[192] However, this bilateral mini-TPP essentially represented a cease-fire agreement after the Trump administration's unilateral tariffs on Japan over steel led to Japanese retaliation on agriculture, which compounded the losses of U.S. cattlemen and farmers already facing stiffer competition from Australian and Canadian ranchers, who were now inside CPTPP. The bilateral U.S.-Japan agreement did contain one promising new element, though: a digital trade chapter that experts in both countries thought might be expanded as an interim sectoral deal on hi-tech trade.[193] In terms of pressuring China to follow global rules on behind-the border issues like state-owned enterprises and intellectual property rights, however, the 2019 U.S.-Japan agreement paled in comparison with TPP. And to make the geopolitics even more complicated for Tokyo, China informed New Zealand in September 2021 of its intention to formally seek membership in CPTPP. Japan and Australia would hold off Beijing and wait for Washington…but for how long was not clear.[194]

Despite these setbacks, the period from 2012 to 2020 represented a profound transformation in Japan's strategy for regional economics. A once reluctant Japan had now come to embrace and even lead free-trade agreements—beginning with modest pacts signed with Singapore in 2002 and then Mexico and Australia—and now with the throttle fully opened. Before Abe came to power in 2012, only 16 percent of Japan's trade was covered by liberalizing agreements with other countries—well below the level set by other advanced economies in Asia, like Korea at 36 percent or Singapore and Australia, which were even more open.[195] Keidanren had lamented in 2011 that Japan's lack of free-trade agreements was handicapping the country compared with Korea's earlier expansion of deals with the United States and Europe.[196] Abe heard the Japanese business community and pushed through agreements that surpassed Korea's efforts, including TPP, RCEP, and a bilateral economic partnership agreement (EPA) with the European Union that entered into force in January 2019.[197] By the time Abe resigned in 2020, the amount of Japanese trade covered by free-trade agreements (FTAs) and EPAs had more than quadrupled to over 80 percent.[198]

Two decades after the United States and Japan had clashed over the need for global norms in Asian economic agenda setting, the two countries had done a nearly total role reversal. As Abe explained in an address to the seventy-third session of the United Nations General Assembly in September 25, 2018, "The free trade system enabled the countries of Asia, one after the other, to achieve take-off and fostered the middle class in each of these countries."[199]

Japan may not have had the economic heft to replace the United States as the pillar of trans-Pacific economic integration, but it is positioned to hold the line on the original U.S. agenda for liberalization until American politics settle.[200]

TRYING TO RESCUE THE DEMOCRACIES' LEAD ON GLOBAL GOVERNANCE

While the focus of this chapter has primarily been on Japan's strategy to compete with China by shaping a more favorable regional order in Asia, that effort cannot be separated from the competition to define global governance—a contest in which Japan has also been fully engaged. As Donald Trump began attacking and retreating from traditional postwar American leadership in the G-7, UN, and Bretton Woods systems, Xi Jinping declared in 2017 that China would henceforth champion "the evolution of the global governance system" as part of China's push "for the great success of socialism with Chinese characteristics."[201] The extent to which China truly seeks revisionism or just defense advantage in global governance continues to occupy scholars' attention in the United States, but for Japan that competition at the global level is already palpable.[202] The challenge for Japan during the Trump period was that in the meetings of the WTO or other multilateral organizations, Japanese officials had only limited ability to forestall Chinese and sometimes Russian efforts to push their own agenda—even when Japanese officials worked in concert with Canada, Australia, or other like-minded democracies. For many in Tokyo, the reassertion of the democracies' leadership on the global governance agenda had to begin where Japan was most privileged of all the Asian democracies—the G-7.

With the exception of maverick leaders like Nakasone or Koizumi, Japan's prime ministers were often passive and defensive in the annual G-7 summits of the leading democracies, usually appearing off to the side in the leaders' group photos. The tall and handsome Nakasone was the first to make a point of moving toward the center of the group for the cameras, while Koizumi used his intimate knowledge of baseball to ensure that he was always seen sharing intense discussions with George W. Bush during the photo (about fastballs and not global economics, as it turned out). Abe was cut from the same mold, but he was thrust into the role of actually having to lead on consensus building within the group, particularly as the trans-Atlantic rift grew with Trump. As host of the 2016 Ise-Shima Summit, Abe reached agreement from the other leaders on the importance of "quality infrastructure," turning the global summit of democracies to Japan's agenda in Asia, among other topics.[203] The next year Donald Trump almost exploded his first G-7 summit in Italy, and the following year in Canada Trump stormed off without agreeing to the traditional joint communiqué.[204] Rather than join in the condemnation of the volatile American president, Abe privately scolded his counterparts for embarrassing Trump, reminding the Canadians and Germans that like Japan they were not permanent members of the UN Security Council and needed the G-7 to function for their own purposes regardless of how maddening Trump was.[205] Abe's desperation to save the forum was captured in an iconic photo of the session released to the press by the Canadians that showed the other leaders lecturing a sullen Trump, sitting with his arms stubbornly folded, while Abe stands between the conflicting factions looking concerned and seeking to reconcile them.[206]

Japan also delivered at the broader G-20 summit the next year, forging agreement on the principles for Data Free Flow with Trust that notionally would prevent data localization by countries like China.[207] The fact that China signed on to the statement had relatively little significance, however, since Beijing only ignored it afterwards. It was the G-7 that was the real conning tower for global governance for Japan, and Tokyo has resisted any and all efforts to either broaden or dilute its role, particularly as competition with China has intensified.

The diplomatic historian Frederick Dickinson described Japanese enthusiasm for participating in the burgeoning multilateralism of the post–World War I era as part of building a "new Japan." By the 1930s Japan was instead pushing for an autarkic regional order. Today Japan's strategies for regional and global governance are once again inseparable. As China's revisionism spreads from regional to global issues, Japan will likely continue its own expansive strategy to preserve and strengthen the rules-based order and to unite Europe and the United States in forums like the G-7 as an extension of Abe's external balancing strategy—with liberal institutionalist characteristics.

AN ASSESSMENT OF JAPAN'S INDO-PACIFIC STRATEGY

By the time Abe stepped down in 2020, Japan's strategy toward the Indo-Pacific had achieved many of the objectives set forth in the 2013 National Security Strategy. The ideational glue of the Free and Open Indo-Pacific vision reinforced external balancing among the major maritime powers around China without alienating the smaller ASEAN states stuck in the middle. The FOIP quality infrastructure strategy of JBIC created capacity in those states and empowered them vis-à-vis China without forcing a choice that might have driven them away or subjected them to Chinese coercion. Defense ministry capacity building across ASEAN reinforced these efforts. Japan's leadership in sustaining CPTPP helped counteract a vacuum in American-led rulemaking for the region. And Japan did what it could to hold together the trans-Atlantic relationship that was so crucial to Japan's own efforts to maintain a rules-based order in the Indo-Pacific. Table 4.1 illustrates how central Japan has become to the international relations of the Indo-Pacific compared with other powers in the region.

By any metric Japan's strategy from 2012 to Abe's resignation in 2020 was a significant improvement over that of his predecessors and compares favorably with the regional strategies of the United States, Australia, Korea, or India. In its effort to quantify power and influence in the Indo-Pacific, the Australian Lowy Institute determined in 2019 that Japan was now "the leader of the liberal order in Asia," as was noted in the introduction.[208] Japan did more with less, Lowy concluded, as "a quintessential smart power, making efficient use of limited resources to wield broad-based diplomatic, economic and cultural influence in the region."[209] Other Lowy polls found that Australians actually had more confidence in Abe than in their own prime minister in 2018, and far

TABLE 4.1 Relative strengths of Japan and other powers in Southeast Asia

	Major military exercises		FDI/trade in 2019	Diplomatic relations
	Bilateral	Multilateral		
United States	• ASEAN • Brunei • Indonesia • Malaysia • Singapore • Thailand	• RIMPAC[a] • SEACAT[b] • Cobra Gold • Pacific Partnership • Pitch Black • Cope Tiger • Komodo	**FDI**: 24,079.62 (millions of dollars) **Trade:** 2$94,793,331,219	• Majority trust U.S. as strategic partner and security provider over China • Most would opt for alignment with U.S. over China if forced to choose
China	• Cambodia (Golden Dragon) • Malaysia • Singapore • Thailand (Blue Strike)	• Falcon Strike and Strike	**FDI**: 8,895.94 **Trade:** 305,413,238,926	• Most influential economic power • Most influential on political and strategic issues
Japan	• Indonesia • Philippines • Singapore • Thailand	• RIMPAC[a] • SEACAT[b] • Cobra Gold • Pacific Partnership • Komodo • Japan-Australia-Brunei-Singapore	**FDI**: 20,635.62 **Trade:** 116,118,692,488	• Most trusted by wide margin • Most reliable if U.S. becomes unreliable • Not seen as capable of leadership on its own
EU	Individual states join exercises	Individual states join exercises	**FDI**: 15,405.54 **Trade:** 126,710,707,113	• Seen as hedge against U.S.-China competition • Most trusted leader to promote a rules-based order

Note: Military exercises are compiled from national defense ministry publications. Trade and FDI figures are from ASEAN official statistics: "Trade in Goods (IMTS), Annually, HS 2-Digit Up to 8-Digit (AHTN), in US$," International Merchandise Trade Statistics, ASEANStats, https://data.aseanstats.org/trade-annually; "Flows of Inward Foreign Direct Investment (FDI) into ASEAN by Source Country (in million US$)," Foreign Direct Investment Statistics, ASEANStats, https://data.aseanstats.org/fdi-by-hosts-and-sources. Diplomatic relations assessments are drawn from the 2021 ISEAS survey: Sharon Seah, Hoang Thi Ha, Melinda Martinus, and Pham Thi Phuong Thao, *The State of Southeast Asia: 2021 Survey Report*, ISEAS Yusof Ishak Institute, February 10, 2021, https://www.iseas.edu.sg/wp-content/uploads/2021/01/The-State-of-SEA-2021-v2.pdf.

[a] Rim of the Pacific Exercise.
[b] Southeast Asia Cooperation and Training.

more than in Xi Jinping.[210] Polling by Japan's foreign ministry found in 2020 that 93 percent of Southeast Asians found Japan to be a "reliable partner"—far more than said the same about China.[211] When the ISEAS Yusof Ishak Institute in Singapore surveyed Southeast Asian elites on their strategic preferences in early 2021, Japan stood out as most trusted, the best alternative should U.S. leadership falter, and a close second to the European Union as most likely to uphold a rules-based order and international law.[212] Korea's Samsung Economic Research Institute national brand survey has also consistently listed Japan's as the best national "brand" from Asia in terms of substance and image and the top brand globally in terms of image.[213]

But these surveys also had a warning for Tokyo. Abe's Free and Open Indo-Pacific vision found strong support at home and in the United States, Europe, and the region. But Abe had only mixed success in restoring a favorable equilibrium vis-à-vis China. Only 3 percent of respondents to the ISEAS survey thought Japan had the most influence in Southeast Asia, compared with half who chose China. Despite praise for "smart power," the Lowy Institute ranked Japan in second place behind China for aggregate leadership influence in Asia and warned that Japan was still perilously close to "middle power" status.[214] In the constant calibration to maintain a favorable regional order, Japan will likely have to do even more external balancing. And one missing element in Japanese statecraft toward the region has clearly been Tokyo's dysfunctional relationship with South Korea.

5

KOREA

*The Korean peninsula is a dagger aimed at the heart of
Japan.*

—JAPANESE MILITARY ADVISOR KLEMENS WILHELM
JAKOB MECKEL, 1885

*We want South Korea to behave as a country should—to
reflect seriously, keep its international promises, and respect
international law.*

—SANKEI SHIMBUN, JANUARY 2021

P olling of strategic elites in Asia by the Center for Strategic and
International Studies (CSIS) in 2014 and 2020 showed that no
other country more closely aligned with Japanese norms with
respect to future regional order than the Republic of Korea (ROK)—
and that includes fellow Quad members India, Australia, and the United
States.[1] No country other than Japan places higher priority on U.S. forward presence in Asia than Korea. Historically, no geographic point on
the continent has held more importance to Japanese interests than the
peninsula that formed the "dagger aimed at the heart of Japan."[2] From the

perspective of geopolitical and normative alignment, no country should have been more front and center in Japan's Free and Open Indo-Pacific (FOIP) vision than Korea.

And yet no other democratic nation has seen its relationship with Japan slide into such an intractable impasse in recent years. Over the last decade, Japan and the Republic of Korea have suspended direct intelligence cooperation for long periods; clashed in the United Nations over heritage sites and nonproliferation; actively lobbied against each other's diplomatic proposals in Washington; eschewed direct bilateral summit meetings at international gatherings; sanctioned each other over history and technology concerns; downgraded each other's rankings in official diplomatic reports; and failed to coordinate responses when China declared an air defense identification zone (ADIZ) over both countries' separate territorial claims in maritime Northeast Asia. The persistent and recurring friction between these two democratic allies of the United States represents one of the most vexing foreign policy problems faced by Washington, and perhaps the greatest weakness in Japan's own grand strategy.

It is tempting to dismiss the Japan-Korea problem as a function of Abe and Moon Jae-in's particular political ideologies, since Abe is on the right and Moon is on the left. Leadership has been an important intervening variable, to be sure, but there are deeper structural and ideational factors that threaten to continue damaging bilateral relations beyond the Abe-Moon era. At a systemic level Japan and Korea are diverging in their respective strategies for managing China, even as they continue to embrace a U.S.-led order in Asia. And while both countries advance democratic norms, Japan is using those universal norms in an attempt to shape regional order while Korean political leaders are seizing democratization as a reason to renegotiate earlier agreements with Japan over historical grievances.

After examining these geopolitical and ideational disconnects in Japan's relations with Korea, this chapter will return once again to the role of leaders in inflaming—but perhaps solving—the confrontations across what one side calls the Sea of Japan and the other adamantly maintains must be called the East Sea.[3]

THE GEOPOLITICAL DISCONNECT

As counterintuitive and counterproductive as Japan's strategic approach to Korea may seem in terms of balance-of-power logic (a point American observers repeatedly make to Tokyo), an explanation for this anomaly can be found in the longer history of Japan's relationship with China. Hans Morgenthau, the father of postwar realist theory, explained the phenomenon in *Politics Among Nations*, noting that Japan's activism on the Korean peninsula since the first century BC has largely been a function of whether China was weak or powerful.[4] Hideyoshi's invasions at the end of the sixteenth century had many purposes, from demonstrating Japanese martial prowess to forestalling conquest by the newly arriving Spanish and Portuguese, but the major draw was the weakness of the Ming Empire and Hideyoshi's vision of toppling that empire to assert Japanese hegemony in Asia.[5] Tokugawa Japan retreated during the Qing Empire's period of hegemonic control over the continent, but Meiji Japan returned to the great game on the peninsula at the end of the nineteenth century precisely when the decline of the Manchus' empire opened a vacuum for Russian expansion through the peninsula toward Japan. It is therefore significant that Japan's current relationship with Korea is evolving in the context of Chinese expansion and Japan's reinforcement of an offshore maritime strategy.

Korea, meanwhile, is returning to a historic pattern of cautious risk mitigation vis-à-vis a rising China. As Korea's leading Japan scholar, Park Cheol Hee, observes, Japan is mustering its strength to compete with China at a systemic level while South Korea is stuck in a position of "strategic ambiguity," seeking to retain a U.S. defense commitment on the peninsula without antagonizing Beijing in a way that would undermine Seoul's leverage toward North Korea or bring Chinese punishment down on Korea's more heavily exposed companies in the Chinese economy.[6] Historical precedent also causes diverging priorities: while Japan has spent centuries developing strategies to shape the broader regional order in Asia, Korea has remained tightly focused on security and stability on the peninsula itself.

Victor Cha observed in *Alignment Despite Antagonism*, his authoritative study of U.S.-Japan-Korea trilateral relations, that Korean "internal vacillation, coupled with the peninsula's geostrategic location, made
Korea a coveted prize in the Sino-Japanese competition for regional
hegemony."[7] From Tokyo's perspective, Korean failure to counterbalance
China today is evidence of just such vacillation. In 2005, for example,
President Roh Moo Hyun proposed that South Korea would serve as
a "balancer" in Northeast Asia, allied with the United States but subtly
shaping regional power competition by maneuvering between Japan and
China.[8] When Abe first proposed the U.S.-Japan-Australia-India Quad
in 2006, it was Korea and not China that most actively lobbied against
the proposal in Washington.

When Xi Jinping began advancing his proposal for a "New Model
of Great Power Relations" in 2013, many Korean scholars concluded
that Asia would fall under a new U.S.-China bipolar condominium
with Japan relegated to tier two status.[9] Park Geun-hye's newly elected
government picked up this theme when her foreign minister reported
to the National Assembly that Park's foreign policy would prioritize
relationships with the United States and China followed by Japan and
Russia at the next tier (precisely the tier two level Abe declared that
same year that Japan would never join).[10] The Korean Ministry of Foreign Affairs later scrambled to explain that there was no intention to
downgrade Japan, but Park seemed to confirm the demotion by proposing a trilateral U.S.-China-Korea diplomatic framework to manage
security issues in Northeast Asia, notably without Japan at the table.
Abe dispatched Vice Foreign Minister Saeki Akitaka to Washington
to lobby against the trilateral proposal, just as Korea's foreign ministry had lobbied against Abe's Quad in 2006.[11] Caught in the middle,
the U.S. State Department honored Korea's request but appeased Japan
by counterproposing a more modest 1.5-track U.S.-China-Korea academic trilateral led by myself and Victor Cha of CSIS.[12] In the Japanese
foreign ministry's next annual *Diplomatic Bluebook* in 2015, Tokyo
appeared to downgrade Korea in retaliation, dropping previous references to shared "fundamental values such as freedom, democracy and
respect for basic human rights" and stating only that the two countries

needed a "good relationship" (reference to "strategic interests" was restored in 2018).[13]

From Japan's perspective, Korea is also undermining efforts to secure the maritime domain against Chinese expansion. When Beijing declared an expanded ADIZ over both the Senkakus and Korea's Iodo (Socotra Rock) in 2013, the Korean government unsuccessfully went on its own to Beijing asking for an adjustment, while Japan coordinated on a military and diplomatic response with Washington and explicitly ordered national airlines *not* to comply with China's demands.[14] Korea's dispute with Japan over the Korean-occupied Liancourt Rocks (Dokdo/Takeshima) loomed much larger for Seoul than China's imposition of an ADIZ over the submerged Iodo rock. When Koreans and Japanese explained why their two countries have bad relations in public opinion polls in 2019, half of Koreans pointed to the Dokdo/Takeshima dispute as the cause, compared with only one-quarter of Japanese.[15] To the extent that Korea has a maritime dimension to its strategic culture, in other words, Japan looms as the more revisionist power rather than China, even though Japan is far less likely to resort to actual force. To the extent that Japan is trying to prevent China's dominance of the maritime domain, Korea is seen as a liability.

One of Japan's most observant and sympathetic scholars on Korea, Michishita Narushige, has argued that ultimately South Korean thought leaders are motivated by a " 'discount Japan' movement aimed at advancing Korean prestige and influence by casting aspersions on Japan."[16] Korea, Michishita concludes, has a choice like Japan of "balancing" China together with the United States, but instead appears to have chosen "bandwagoning" with China.[17] Elite and public opinion polling in Korea actually suggests the opposite—that the United States is trusted two to three times more than China and that Koreans see a U.S.-led order as far preferable to Chinese hegemony.[18] Few Americans who understand the depth of the U.S.-ROK joint and combined military relationship or the U.S.-ROK academic, business, and cultural ties would argue that Korea is dealigning. Nor do non-Japanese scholars of Korean strategic culture anticipate bandwagoning by this fiercely proud nation.[19] But at the same time, there is no doubt that Korean foreign policy decisions have undermined Japan's own strategy and—from Tokyo's perspective—aided and abetted Chinese hegemonic ambitions in Asia. As a result, the best and brightest in Japan's foreign ministry are choosing postings in the United States, India, Indonesia, or other growth partners for the FOIP strategy. One experienced Japanese diplomat lamented to me that he spent over 85 percent of his time in a multilateral post in 2017–2018 countering Korean diplomatic attacks on Japan. Frustrated Korean diplomats privately acknowledge the same phenomenon. A small handful of Korea/Japan hands in the two foreign ministries struggle to find traction but spend most of their time putting out fires to prevent further deterioration of relations.

THE NORTH KOREA FACTOR

To the extent that the Venn diagrams of geopolitics and threat perception have directly overlapped for Seoul and Tokyo, it is around the North Korean military threat. Pyongyang's development of dozens of nuclear weapons and many hundreds of ballistic missiles capable of striking Japan has put Japanese forces in the front lines of deterring North Korea in a way not seen since the Korean War (when imperial Japanese navy sailors were remobilized for mine clearing around the peninsula). Recognizing that U.S.-ROK military planning relies heavily on Japan's ability to secure a "rear area" to reinforce the peninsula, the South Korean defense ministry cautiously welcomed the 1997 revised U.S.-Japan defense guidelines and agreed to join a new U.S.-Japan-ROK trilateral defense policy forum that same year.[20] Japan and Korea tightened defense cooperation again in 2010 when North Korea sank the ROK Navy corvette *Cheonan* and killed two civilians in the shelling of Yeonpyeong Island that November. In response to the North Korean attacks, Secretary of State Hillary Clinton and Foreign Ministers Maehara Seiji and Kim Sung-hwan issued a joint statement in Washington on December 6 pledging to "build on mutual bilateral responsibilities to deal effectively with common security threats."[21] Before Seoul balked at the very last minute, the working draft had included language much closer to a collective security reference stating that an attack on any one of the three would be seen as a threat to all.[22] Had that final element been included, the agreement would have been one of the most consequential in the recent diplomacy of Northeast Asia.

However, as Brad Glosserman and Scott Snyder observe in their study of Japan-Korea relations, bilateral alignment and coordination on North Korea often dissipate within months of Pyongyang's provocations.[23] The 2010 North Korean attacks propelled forward the completion of a bilateral Japan-Korea intelligence-sharing agreement that would be considered fairly standard among and between U.S. allies. This General Security of Military Information Agreement (GSOMIA) is a technical commitment rather than a treaty per se, but hours before the signing ceremony in Seoul, the Blue House was forced to withdraw because influential political leaders insisted at the last minute that the agreement be brought before the National Assembly like a treaty.[24] I happened to be entering the Blue House on that day to visit with Korean NSC staff, just as an extremely agitated and irate Japanese delegation was exiting through the same door, having just been told the news. The respected and influential deputy national security advisor in Seoul responsible for the negotiation—whom I was going to see that day—was forced to resign and was later subjected to an official investigation. This was a cautionary tale for future Korean officials who would try to advance relations with Japan.[25]

Japan and Korea have also struggled to remain in sync not only on defense but also with respect to diplomacy toward North Korea. The disconnect began in 1990 when Japanese political strongman Kanemaru Shin rushed to meet with Kim Il-sung to negotiate normalization without consulting with Seoul first.[26] Japan and Korea coordinated diplomacy better at the end of the decade after U.S. special envoy William Perry established the U.S.-Japan-ROK Trilateral Coordination and Oversight Group (TCOG) in 1999.[27] In the 2000s, however, Japanese and Korean views on North Korea began to diverge again as both countries' politics shifted right and left, respectively. Abe rose to political prominence from the position of deputy chief cabinet secretary because he served as a visible brake on "Mr. National Interest"—the energetic Tanaka

Hitoshi—who in this case had secretly brokered a summit between Prime Minister Koizumi and North Korean leader Kim Jong-il in September 2002.[28] Abe accompanied Koizumi and Tanaka to Pyongyang, insisting that the delegation bring their own bento lunch boxes rather than rely on North Korean hospitality and avoid any smiles or bonhomie in front of the press. When Tanaka orchestrated the *faux* "discovery" of half a dozen Japanese abducted by North Korea for Koizumi to bring home from Pyongyang to meet with their families, an outraged Abe successfully convinced Koizumi to let them remain in Japan despite Tanaka's commitments to the North Korean side that they would be sent back.[29] In the final blow, Abe marginalized Tanaka in the foreign ministry and arranged for the promotion of Yachi in his stead to be vice minister in 2004.

This history is well known to Korean political and diplomatic observers, of course. Moon's progressive government was particularly alarmed at what it saw as Abe's encouragement of Donald Trump's threat to use force against the North after Pyongyang's nuclear and intercontinental missile tests in 2017.[30] In fact, Abe was aligning with Trump for broader geopolitical purposes, and the Japanese foreign ministry was quietly trying to slow down U.S. military strikes behind the scenes, but Japan-Korea coordination was so broken that Seoul did not fully appreciate the actual alignment of its own interests with Japan in Washington. When Moon helped to broker Trump's summit with Kim Jong-un in Singapore in June 2018, it was Tokyo's turn to worry that the left-leaning Moon was encouraging Trump to sell out Japan for a cheap deal with the North.[31] These fears were confirmed in part—despite repeated efforts by Abe to pull back Trump in private—when the American president announced after meeting with Kim that he would end "war games" with Korea and Japan around the peninsula and that he hoped also to withdraw U.S. troops from the Korean peninsula in the future.[32]

Neither Japan, nor Korea, nor even the Pentagon was consulted beforehand on these announcements regarding the alliances—which Trump reportedly discussed only with Putin and Kim Jong-un.[33] The damage to Japanese interests was compounded when Trump and Secretary of State Mike Pompeo stated that they were only interested in a deal with Pyongyang that addressed the intercontinental ballistic missiles (ICBMs) targeting the United States and not the growing number of intermediate-range missiles aimed at Japan that Abe had urged be addressed as well.[34] Fifteen years earlier Japanese and Korean diplomats would have come together in the TCOG process to shape American views together (which they did in my experience during the Six-Party Talks), but Trump's disruptive showmanship and years of mutual mistrust between Seoul and Tokyo left the two U.S. allies each struggling on their own to manage Washington.

Recognizing that the winds had shifted from war to high-level diplomacy after Trump's meeting with Kim, Abe announced in a speech at the United Nations General Assembly in September 2018 that he too was "ready to break the shell of mutual distrust with North Korea, get off to a new start, and meet face-to-face with Chairman Kim Jong-Un."[35] The North Koreans—in hot pursuit of a grand bargain with the American president—ignored Abe's overture and subsequently announced an end to all cooperation with South Korea as well, blowing up the glitzy inter-Korean liaison office built by the Moon government in Kaesong on the North Korean side of the Demilitarized Zone (DMZ).[36] As both Abe's and Moon's appeals for an unconditional summit with Kim Jong-un were being rebuffed by Pyongyang, the two leaders were unable to agree on terms for their own bilateral meeting in June 2020 at the G-20 Osaka summit because of an ongoing dispute over historical grievances, described later in this chapter. In fact, Moon was the only leader invited to Osaka with whom Abe did not meet bilaterally.[37] Both Abe and Moon could agree to meet with the murderous Kim Jong-un unconditionally, it seemed, but not with each other.

The threat from North Korea to Japan hardly abated, of course. Japanese officials and intelligence officers understood that North Korean missile and nuclear weapons capabilities continued to expand during this period, despite the lack of a visible North Korean resumption of nuclear tests that prompted Donald Trump to repeatedly congratulate himself.[38] Perhaps because the threat is less visible, Japan's threat perception has also shifted in ways that would make close coordination with Seoul less urgent. In 2012, the year Abe returned to power, Japanese government polling indicated that the public considered North Korea the top threat to Japan, followed by China's military buildup.[39] By 2015 China was eclipsing North Korea in assessments of military threats in the *Defense of Japan*.[40] And on the China front, Korea was now seen in Tokyo as a liability, despite the far more dangerous and immediate military threat emanating toward both countries from North Korea.

The Ideational Disconnect

These disconnects between Japanese and Korean strategic priorities and threat definitions only begin to explain the dysfunctional relationship between Seoul and Tokyo. Equally important are diverging national narratives and identity politics. At a time when Japan is emphasizing democratic norms as the legitimizing framework for ideational competition with China—democratic norms that polls show Koreans overwhelmingly support—progressive Korean political leaders are claiming that rule of law and respect for human rights require renegotiation of diplomatic settlements with Japan over historical grievances that were negotiated by less democratic Korean governments, thus ironically reinforcing Beijing's narrative that Japan should perpetually be disqualified as a norm-setter in Asia.

The restructuring of domestic politics in both countries has exacerbated this ideational disconnect. Before democratization in Korea in the late 1980s and Japan's political revolution in the early 1990s, the Korean government spoke with a more unified position on Japan while the Japanese government had to contend with deep ideological divisions with the ruling LDP on issues related to history. Now the two countries have reversed positions: Japanese politics are far less polarized on issues of foreign affairs and history, while the underlying polarization in Korean politics has emerged unchecked with the end of authoritarianism.[41] As a result, Korean political leaders have far less maneuverability on Japan than before, while Japanese leaders face far fewer repercussions domestically when they antagonize Korea. With the ascent of Moon Jae-in, even scholars (including progressives) have also noted the increasing use of authoritarian tools by the left in Korea to stifle dissent on the right, tools that include investigations of conservative policymakers, judges, scholars, and media and industry leaders—often for actions taken to improve relations with Japan.[42] This antidemocratic trend was the backdrop for the Japanese foreign ministry's downgrading of "shared values" with Korea in the 2015 *Diplomatic Bluebook*. While Korea is not alone among advanced democracies in witnessing creeping authoritarianism in the second half of the twenty-first century, the antidemocratic attacks on conservatives who are more inclined to cooperate with Japan has been a major cause of distrust in Tokyo. Meanwhile, unregulated social media in both countries has added tension with increased use of terms such as "anti-Japan" on popular Korean platforms and terms such as "Ilbe" and "hate Korea" on Japan's 2channel.[43]

Finally, diverging scholarly and media narratives about Japan's security policies have reinforced a sense of incompatible values between the two countries. Japanese scholars, journalists, and policymakers hear high praise from their North American, South Asian, and Southeast Asian counterparts for Abe's proactive regional security policies. Even Chinese scholars have become more circumspect in their criticism as they have sought common ground with Japan in the context of intensifying U.S.-China friction. In contrast, Korean scholars and journalists rarely point to the objective security conditions that drive Japan's proactive security policies, invariably framing the changes under Abe as entirely endogenous in origin. Korean journalism and scholarship are the *most* critical of Japan's security policies in the region today (with the important if predictable exceptions of China and North Korea). As a result, many Japanese scholars, journalists, and policymakers have become dismissive and desensitized to Korean concerns even when they are completely legitimate.

REOPENING OLD WOUNDS AND OLD AGREEMENTS

With these growing ideational problems, it would not have taken much to set Japan-Korea relations back. The proximate cause of the current political confrontation over history was the reopening of earlier bilateral agreements intended to settle the question of reparations related to Japan's wartime forced recruitment of laborers for Japanese munition factories and comfort women for military brothels. After World War II the major Allied powers all waived such reparations in the San Francisco peace treaties in 1951, but the two Koreas, China, and Russia were not invited because of the ongoing Korean War. President Park Chunghee's government then followed the Western camp's example and permanently waived all Korean claims in exchange for the $800 million in Japanese aid that accompanied the two countries' treaty on normalization of relations in 1965.[44] That bilateral agreement did not satisfy everyone, however, as surviving comfort women in Korea began telling their stories and mobilized for redress while scholars and journalists in Japan began uncovering archival evidence of the Japanese government's direct involvement in the repression of these women. These discoveries prompted an official Japanese government study in the early 1990s that found that Japan had, in fact, engaged in "large scale coercion" of Korean women to serve in military brothels.[45] In August 1993 Chief Cabinet Secretary Kono Yohei responded to those findings with an official expression of remorse and established an indirect compensation fund for the victims, though virtually no payments were ever accepted by the Korean side.[46]

Abe is partly to blame for the current dispute because as prime minister he stated to the press on March 1, 2007, that there actually was "no evidence to prove there was large scale coercion of the Comfort Women."[47] Koreans were outraged, and Abe knew he had overstepped by indulging in old political battles at home without thinking about the diplomatic repercussions abroad. The issue had always been a bitter pill for Abe, who had been elected just before Kono's 1993 statement alongside other young conservatives campaigning on a pledge to end Japan's apology-driven diplomacy and passivity in world affairs. Ignored by Kono and lame-duck prime minister Miyazawa Kiichi, Abe and his cohort of backbenchers were even further incensed by world media reports comparing Japan's wartime behavior to horrific contemporaneous reports of Serb soldiers using rape as a weapon of war in the Bosnia conflict.[48] His feelings on the subject were strong, but not his diplomatic judgment in March 2007.

The predictable result of Abe's 2007 statement was that not a single government or serious historian abroad came to Japan's defense. When the U.S. Congress introduced legislation to compel Japan to apologize after Abe's lack of remorse, Secretary of State Condoleeza Rice pointedly refused Japanese requests for help lobbying the Hill, even though the State Department was actively working to defeat parallel legislation on Turkey's Armenian genocide.[49] The anti-Japan bill was later defeated, but only through the Japanese embassy's direct lobbying and with little help from the U.S. government or even Japanese Americans, who refused to come to the embassy's aid. A week after publicly questioning the Kono statement, Abe took to the airwaves on *NHK* to explain that he had misspoken. Undeterred, his supporters on the far right were furious and continued making their case.[50] In 2015, for example, a group of Japanese historians produced a lengthy study detailing technical flaws in the Japanese government's 1993 report and arguing that other countries had also used brothels at the time, but that exercise did more harm for their cause than good.[51] When a Harvard law professor caused a firestorm by regurgitating these arguments in a 2021 paper focusing on the comfort women's "contractual" obligations, only a fraction of the Japanese historians who had signed the 2015 article thought it was a good idea to come to his defense.[52]

Abe was therefore much more circumspect about the comfort women when he returned to power in 2012. However, events in Korea were already careening out of control with a series of rulings by the Korean constitutional and supreme courts that reopened the question of reparations more broadly. In August 2011 the Constitutional Court of Korea ruled that it would be a violation of the victims' rights under Korea's constitution for the Korean government not to secure compensation from Japan.[53] At the time, Prime Minister Noda and President Lee Myung-bak agreed in a bilateral meeting to have their vice foreign ministers address the issue, and the next March Japanese vice minister Sasae Kenichiro proposed to his counterpart a formula that would have provided a new apology and compensation scheme but would still not have accepted legal liability or the prioritizing of the Korean court's decision over an international treaty.[54] The Korean vice minister offered counterproposals that would have allowed Seoul to argue that Japan had accepted a kind of legal culpability in acknowledging the Korean court decision, but the language proved unacceptable to Tokyo.

Abe tried to calm things after returning to power by sending a positive signal to his new counterpart, Park Geun-hye, but with little success. During his CSIS speech in February 2013, for example, Abe praised Park and noted that his grandfather was very close to her father Park Chung-hee, whom Kishi considered *very friendly* to Japan—hardly the kind of endorsement that would help Park resolve debate over the issue at home, even if well intentioned.[55]

Eventually Park and Abe reached a political settlement on the comfort women issue in December 2015, on the fiftieth anniversary of Japan-ROK normalization, that approximated Japan's last proposal. Abe issued an apology, said Japan would establish a new fund, agreed that the issue was finally and irreversibly solved, and agreed to refrain from accusing or criticizing Korea on this issue in the international community. The Japanese government's understanding was that Park had agreed that the settlement was final and irreversible, acknowledged Japan's concerns about the comfort women statue in front of its embassy in Seoul, and also committed not to accuse or criticize Japan on this issue in the international community.[56] However, the immediate response from the Korean public proved devastating for Park. Gallup polls in January 2016 found that only 26 percent of Koreans supported the agreement, while surviving comfort women openly opposed it. The Japanese press reported that these survivors were in some cases being staffed by radical pro–North Korean nongovernmental organizations (NGOs), which only reinforced the Japanese public's impression of Korean fecklessness rather than the human dimension of the victim's suffering.[57] Park and her party then collapsed politically over a corruption scandal, losing April National Assembly elections and falling into disarray with her impeachment and arrest in December 2016 and the election of the progressive Moon Jae-in in May 2017.

Moon—who had campaigned in part on criticism of Park's 2015 agreement on the comfort women—was then paralyzed himself by a new round of Supreme Court decisions. The most significant came in

October 2018 when the court ruled that Japan's Nippon Steel and Sumitomo Metal Corporation was liable for damages demanded by a former victim of forced labor, ninety-four-year-old Lee Chun-sik.[58] Other cases proceeded against different Japanese corporations. Abe called the rulings "impossible in the light of international law," and Foreign Minister Kono Taro declared that the October decision "completely overthrows the legal foundation of the friendly and cooperative relationship that Japan and the Republic of Korea have developed since the normalization of diplomatic relations in 1965."[59]

Moon's new government stumbled for a year, trapped by public opinion, Moon's own campaign pledges, and the prosecution of Park and the former Supreme Court chief justice on charges of colluding to ensure that earlier rulings did not damage diplomatic relations with Japan.[60] In the summer of 2019 the Korean side offered to help the Japanese government pay the compensation, but Tokyo was unwilling to stray from the final settlement of claims in the 1965 treaty or to risk encouraging other claimants around the world to try for the same deal.[61] Japan counterdemanded that the issue be put to arbitration as stipulated in the 1965 treaty, but that was refused by Seoul. When the Korean Supreme Court ordered the distribution of Japanese corporate assets to the victims, the Japanese government responded by rejecting Korean corporations' requests for export licenses of sensitive technologies.[62]

The Korean side then refused to engage in scheduled technical talks on export controls, where the specific violations cited by Japan's government might have been addressed. Efforts by conservative Korean lawmakers to establish a private fund paid for by both countries' corporations—who shared alarm at the impact of the court decision on their businesses—were roundly defeated in the National Assembly in late 2019.[63] Privately, Japanese CEOs I spoke with expressed skepticism about whether the scheme would have survived politics in Tokyo had it even passed in Seoul. As of 2020, the most draconian steps by each government were averted and a lower Korean district court showed a possible way out of the crisis when it threw out the case against Japanese companies, but the legal issue remained unresolved and the political impasse continued.[64]

THE U.S. FACTOR

Genron NPO surveys in Japan and Korea in 2019 indicated that large majorities of Japanese and Koreans could agree on one thing—that relations were bad.[65] As to why they were bad, Japanese by a wide margin answered, "because Korea continues to criticize Japan on history issues," while Koreans answered that relations were bad because of territorial disputes and Japan's "refusal to address history issues." The fact that Korea was an outlier in confronting Japan on history only reinforced Japanese impressions that Seoul was leaning toward China's vision of regional order. The Japanese government faced no pressure at home or from key allies and partners to pay reparations. In 2007 Korea had held the high ground on the comfort women issue internationally because Japan had threatened to revoke the forward-looking Kono statement. In 2020 it was Korea that stood alone diplomatically because its government was refusing to abide by the terms of an international treaty. Yet the Korean government also feared the domestic backlash if it defied the popular will by failing to implement the Supreme Court ruling. Japanese political leaders saw little advantage in taking steps to transform the political atmosphere until Korea dropped its demands. When Suga replaced Abe in September 2020, his first move vis-à-vis Seoul was to announce that he would not participate in a planned China-Japan-ROK summit with Moon Jae-in until the threat to seize Japanese corporate assets was removed, though he did engage in a positive meeting with South Korea's visiting intelligence chief in Tokyo that November.[66]

In previous cases the U.S. government would have quietly weighed in to help Seoul and Tokyo overcome domestic opposition to resolving disputes, as the Obama administration quietly did in the lead-up to the Abe-Park December 2015 agreement. However, President Trump undercut his own officials when he bemoaned requests that he bring Moon and Abe closer together, whining to the press in July 2019, "How many things do I have to get involved in?"[67] Behind the scenes Pentagon officials prevailed upon the Moon government not to suspend the intelligence-sharing GSOMIA agreement with Japan, which Park's government had brought back into effect in 2016. At higher political levels,

however, Trump did little to repair relations among America's two closest allies in Northeast Asia the way Bush or Obama had before him.[68]
Instead he continued his effusive praise of Kim Jong-un and his criticism
of allies ripping off the United States until he left office. When President
Joe Biden tried to improve Japan-Korea relations in his initial discussions with Suga and Moon in 2021, he could at least be confident that the
divisions between Seoul and Tokyo were not about shared interests with
the United States, but he had a lot of lost ground to make up.

THE POLITICAL LEADERSHIP VARIABLE

While the geopolitical and ideational divergence between Japan and
Korea has created a major structural impediment to improving bilateral relations, agency still matters. It is worth nothing that Abe endured
Donald Trump's repeated insults, unreasonable demands for host nation
support, requests for the Nobel Peace Prize nomination, and erratic
positions on critical issues like North Korea and the Trans-Pacific Partnership (TPP). Abe did so because the U.S.-Japan alliance was so central to Japanese strategy and regional stability. Abe was also prepared to
meet unconditionally with Kim Jong-un despite the improbability that
Kim would have returned any further abducted citizens, let alone abandoned his nuclear weapons.

Abe also cashed in his credibility with the right for a major diplomatic initiative to resolve the long-standing Northern Territories issue
with Russia. Seeking only the return of two of the four island groups
occupied by the Kremlin since the Second World War (Habomai and
Shikotan), he visited Moscow in 2013 and Vladivostok in 2018.[69] In
May 2016 his government proposed a major "Eight-Point Cooperation
Plan" on economic issues despite lukewarm backing in Japan's business
community and zero progress on the territorial issue.[70] Indeed, the geopolitical impediments to a breakthrough with Moscow were far more
significant than those confounding Japan's relations with Korea. Putin
was fundamentally opposed to the U.S. alliance system in Asia, whereas

Korea, like Japan, depended on that system for national survival. As Abe engaged in his diplomatic overture to Moscow, the Russian Air Force returned to Cold War levels of intrusion into Japanese airspace and the Russian Army began deploying advanced rocket systems and unmanned aerial vehicles (UAVs) on the Northern Territories.[71] The Korean Navy provocatively named their new large-deck amphibious ship *Tokdo*, but the Korean military never posed an actual threat to Japan's Self-Defense Forces. And while Putin undermined democracies and watched as his political opponents were assassinated overseas, Korea was expanding its overseas assistance for women's empowerment and democracy in Asia.[72]

Abe's attempt to use the "Russia card" was doomed to fail because Putin was not prepared to reinforce Japanese power and influence if it strengthened the United States' global position—which was central to Abe's strategy. Put another way, the United States was far more important than Russia to Abe's strategy of countering China, while China was far more important than Japan to Putin's strategy of countering the United States. In contrast, a thaw with Seoul would have been far more effective in blocking Chinese hegemonic ambitions because improved relations might have moved U.S. bilateral alliances in Northeast Asia toward a de facto collective security arrangement. In geopolitical terms, Korea would have been the much smarter play in terms of both outcome and feasibility (even if there is some merit to Japan in longer-term engagement with Russia).

The mirror image of all these strategic points applies to Korean political leadership as well. Moon Jae-in might have taken a page from another progressive leader, Kim Dae Jung, who defied political headwinds to issue a joint statement with Prime Minister Obuchi Keizo in 1998 that opened full cultural relations for the first time, addressed history by welcoming a leading role for Japan in Asia, and gave both countries greater credibility vis-a-vis North Korea, China, and the United States.[73] Instead, Moon fueled populism during the election and used antidemocratic tools against his opponents after the election, was paralyzed by the Supreme Court decision, and failed to build alliances within Japan for realistic solutions. Neither Moon nor Abe came into office intending for relations to become more confrontational, but neither used his political capital in creative ways to prevent that confrontation.

One recurring problem has been that each government has been tempted to hope that leadership changes on the other side would lead to improved relations without any particular effort needed on its own part. Abe's government hoped that Park would make necessary changes in Korea's position because of her father's strong ties to Japan, often failing to realize that this history was more of a liability for her government than an advantage and rarely thinking of a strategy toward Seoul beyond a few rhetorical gestures. Koreans in turn hoped that leaders after Abe would be able to accept reparations claims, failing to realize the strong public and political consensus in Japan that the government should do no such thing. The two governments also suffered from a predisposition to assume the worst of counterparts who come from the opposite ideological perspective. In Korea, 80 percent of the public had a negative image of Abe in 2019 polls. This was more negative than their image of Kim Jong-un—but also the exact opposite of Abe's positive image among all other democratic states around the world and especially in Asia.[74] Over half of Japanese had developed a negative image of Moon—not as bad as Abe's image in Korea, but an impediment to mutual trust and worse than the Japanese public's impression of every other world leader other than Xi Jinping and Kim Jong-un.[75] The most common refrain of Japanese diplomats that I heard was that things will improve when Moon is gone. While assessment of leadership should be a major consideration in diplomacy, it had become an alibi for inaction.

Future Japanese leaders may or may not have sufficient agency to resolve the underlying legal and diplomatic disagreements with Seoul. If Seoul retains its insistence on reparations or fails to find a way around the Supreme Court decision, then a transformational breakthrough will prove challenging. However, there should be no doubt that Japanese leaders do have sufficient agency to change Korean impressions of Japan. If Abe had put in the same amount of effort with Moon that he did with Putin, or had offered the same openness to summits that he proposed to Kim Jong-un, the political atmosphere between Japan and Korea might have been quite different. Successful statecraft is often a matter of parking contentious issues in a process that calms the public's ire while focusing leaders on more pressing areas of common interest. Statecraft is also about the use of creative symbolism. Telephone calls with the Korean president during moments of tension with North Korea, summits at historic locations like the Japanese resort of Atami where Korea's "Amelia Earhart" crashed and Kim Dae Jung laid a marker with Japanese prime minister Mori in 2000, and impromptu drop-ins on visiting Korean delegations—these are all the kinds of tools leaders use to change dynamics with other countries. These are still tools available to Abe's successors to address the critical unfinished piece of the FOIP strategy.

6

INTERNAL BALANCING

With Japan you quickly go from grand strategy to
fruit puree.

—GEORGE SCHULTZ, 1993

Henceforth, the government will conduct unified manage-
ment of information relating to diplomacy and national
security and make important policy decisions promptly
under the leadership of the prime minister.

—CABINET INFORMATION OFFICE, 2014

As Kenneth Waltz explains in his *Theory of International Pol-*
itics, states have two basic means of achieving a favorable
balance of power: external and internal efforts.[1] Thus far this
book has focused on Japan's external balancing strategies, but over the
past decade Japan has intensified internal balancing as well. For the most
part this effort has involved *qualitative* changes—specifically, the consolidation and centralization of crisis management and national security
decision making to reduce inefficiencies, harness domestic sources of
power, and sharpen external impact. As the Lowy Institute's 2019 index

of national power astutely observed, Japan has become "a quintessential smart power," making efficient use of limited resources to wield broad-based influence.[2]

This decisive nation-state was not the postwar Japan that most scholars and diplomats confronted in the late twentieth century. In the 1980s Japan scholar Kent Calder labeled Japan "the reactive state," and the Dutch journalist Karel van Wolferen famously described Japan as a headless polity in which competing bureaucracies and corporate groupings secretly checkmated one another and foreign powers.[3] As Japanese bureaucrats used to quip about this stovepiping: "ka ga atte, kyoku ga nai, kyoku ga atte, shō ga nai . . ." ("you have a division but no bureau, a bureau but no ministry"), with the words "no ministry"—shō ga nai— being a pun in Japanese for "no hope".

The Cold War structure of international politics reinforced this frag-mented decision-making process in what many scholars assumed was an immutable feature of Japanese political culture. Since Japan's greatest source of autonomy and legitimacy was its economic performance, there was a logic to maintaining low-risk political leadership and sustaining stovepipes that protected the distribution of wealth to key constituencies behind the ruling Liberal Democratic Party (LDP) while proving conve-niently impenetrable to outsiders. Japan thrived with first-rate compa-nies and bureaucrats and third-rate political leaders, as many observers put it at the time. But with the collapse of the Japanese economic bubble and with it the old distributive "1955 system" of Japanese politics in the 1990s, the Japanese people grew tired of their country's persistence as a "reactive state" in international affairs. A new generation of leaders emerged looking to restructure government to achieve more decisive outcomes, particularly with respect to national security. Abe among them pulled together all these strands to consolidate Japan's first modern national security establishment.

It is appropriate to end this book with a focus on this institutional transformation within Japan because it will influence the trajectory of Japanese grand strategy going forward. Just as the U.S. National Security Act of 1947 still governs the formulation of U.S. strategy (a copy was hung prominently outside the Situation Room of the White House when

I worked there), so too Abe's institutional reforms have established a dramatically new framework for decision making in Japan. How effectively future prime ministers use these tools is one area of uncertainty, of course. As Peter Rodman observed in *Presidential Command*, his history of variations in National Security Council (NSC) functionality in the United States, the commander in chief gets the NSC he deserves.[4] However, Japanese leaders will henceforth ignore these new tools at their peril. When the public was asked by *Yomiuri Shimbun* what qualities they wanted in Abe's replacement in September 2020, the highest priority, with 92 percent of respondents, was "crisis management skills"— beating out "leadership," "experience," and "economic management."[5]

The chapter begins with a history of Japan's past internal balancing strategies to demonstrate how external crises and shifting international power dynamics have repeatedly led to major institutional reforms at home. The chapter then explains how Abe realigned Japanese national security institutions and strengthened the power of the Prime Minister's Office to ensure that Japan's statecraft in a newly competitive environment is faithful to the original ancient Greek concept of *strategos*— meaning "from the commander." The chapter concludes by examining how this qualitative internal balancing has begun to unleash new *quantitative* power with respect to military capabilities and economic growth. Thus far this quantitative side of Abe's internal balancing strategy has been more of a mixed success, though—a reminder that when it comes to power, even "quintessential smart powers" need capacity. But that part of the story is not complete, and more dynamism may yet be unleashed from within. That certainly has been the pattern of Japanese history.

PRECURSORS TO JAPAN'S NEW NATIONAL SECURITY ESTABLISHMENT

When Japan emerged from isolation in the nineteenth century and began constructing its own nation-state, there were many models from which to choose. American observers like Commodore Matthew Perry hoped Japan would eventually choose to become a republic and align with the

United States. The British saw natural affinity around the new maritime aspects of Japan's emerging international consciousness. But it was the Prussians who had most recently built a centralized national security apparatus and a new national identity from the top down—and that was the example that had the most profound impact on the Meiji leaders' vision for their own internal state formation. In the decades before the 1889 Meiji constitution, Chancellor Otto von Bismarck had defeated Germany's rival France, marginalized the numerous German dukes and princes to centralize power under the kaiser, built a national education system to solidify a common identity, and established a national conscript army and general staff.[6] To Japanese leaders, the Prussian idea advanced by Leopold von Ranke in the 1830s of building a nation-state around *der Primat der Aussenpolitick* ("primacy of foreign policy") was the essence of what was needed to catch up and survive in a competitive international system.[7] Japanese delegations flocked to Berlin, including the principal drafter of the Meiji constitution, Itō Hirobumi. As historian Bernd Martin notes:

Conditions in Germany clearly made the Japanese guests feel more at home. From the outset the powerful German state based on military victories, the patriotic feeling of national unity that seemed to characterise the relationship between the people and their leaders, and, last but not least, the powerful influence of the state bureaucracy in all fields, including economic issues, held a strong fascination for the traditional Japanese elite who were trying to stabilise their own social position by means of a programme resting on ideological restoration and, at the same time, technological modernisation.[8]

Where the Tokugawa Shogunate had been satisfied to rule through loyal but decentralized *daimyō* (lords), the Meiji leaders now required a national education system, a tax policy, a conscript military, a railway network, and a bureaucracy like Germany's to compete and survive. Emulating Bismarck's preferences for the Prussian Junker class in Germany, the Meiji leaders also ensured that the samurai class would be privileged in Japan.[9] Economic modernization was fused with military power, as captured in the four-character slogan "Rich Nation/Strong Army."[10]

This drive for modernization under the ruling samurai class contained within it the seeds of militarization, conflict, and ruin for Japan—just as it did for Germany. The Meiji oligarchs established a popularly elected National Assembly "primarily in order to create a sense of national unity and to convince the West of Japan's 'enlightenment,'" as political historian Peter Duus notes.[11] Meanwhile, the military was able to bypass the civilian leadership and even to bring down cabinets by threatening to resign as ministers of the army and navy.[12] By the 1930s political parties grew weak as education, election, and "peace preservation" laws prevented independent inquiry, social mobilization, or any effective checks or balances on the government. Rather than producing a dictator as in Germany, however, these authoritarian trends only reinforced the earlier fierce rivalries between the Satsuma and Chōshū Clans—now manifest between the imperial army and imperial Japanese navy. Internal contestation was exported rather than resolved. The conflicts at the top led to decisions that were enormously risky for Japan—invading China and attacking the United States, for example—but made perfect sense in terms of preserving the respective bureaucratic positions of the army and navy. This inability to manage internal bureaucratic competition proved as tragic a factor for Japan as militarism or racism.[13]

Yet one important feature of the rush to modernization would not be forgotten. Japan became a major world power in this period by doing more with less. The fact is that as Japan rose to tier one status and brief domination of East Asia between 1860 and 1938, the actual Japanese share of global GDP grew from only 2.6 percent to 3.8 percent. As historians from Beasley to Pyle have emphasized, it was ultimately organizational focus and determination that led to Japan's ability to challenge China and the West.[14]

POSTWAR BUREAUCRATIC POLITICS

Postwar reforms under the U.S. occupation were intended to bring full democracy to Japan by creating the checks and balances that had been missing in the Meiji constitution. Ironically, the resulting power vacuum probably made Yoshida Shigeru one of the most powerful Japanese prime ministers of the postwar era, as he manipulated the occupation general headquarters (GHQ) and bent still reconstituting bureaucracies to his will.[15] With time, however, the bureaucracies that survived the occupation, like the powerful Ministry of Finance, increasingly came to dominate the policy process. Prime ministers were further boxed in by the rival faction leaders who came to control various cabinet portfolios assigned to them.[16] For decades the top bureaucrats in each ministry—the administrative vice ministers (*jimujikan*)—held the greatest influence over decision making while the small Prime Minister's Office (*Kantei*) was run by seconded officials from those same ministries whose future and greatest allegiance would always be tied back to the vice ministers.[17] The policy process was one of constant arbitration among bureaucratic actors, with only the most skilled prime ministers able to actually assert control.

In fits and starts, though, a series of Japanese prime ministers did make efforts to centralize more authority in the *Kantei*. Change sometimes came from strong-willed leaders who bucked the consensus-oriented factional system. Sometimes it came because scandals or crises highlighted the need for decisive leadership and crisis management functions.[18] The weakening of factions after 1993 electoral reforms also gave prime ministers more room for maneuvering.

The first after Yoshida to make a bid for more centralized decision making in the *Kantei* was Ōhira Masayoshi, who became prime minister on December 7, 1978. Ōhira's biographers and advisors described him as wanting to "clear away the vestiges of a cloudy era, to shed light on what society should look like in the future, and to construct specific methods by which Japan might attain these goals."[19] Ōhira organized the first substantive interagency process in the *Kantei* by establishing study groups of officials, business leaders, and scholars to recommend medium- to long-term strategy on key challenges facing Japan in the 1980s, particularly as they related to fiscal pressures, the environment, and energy. While Ōhira's most important policy legacy was in the area of tax reform, his study groups also touched on foreign affairs in response to rising international expectations that Japan would give more back to the international community after decades of stunning high-speed economic growth. One of Ōhira's study groups advanced the concept of "comprehensive security policy" (*Sōgō Anzen Hoshō Seisaku*) as a way for Japan to play more of a leading role in the world by harnessing its diplomatic, development, and energy policies rather than turning to military instruments of power.[20] Though somewhat toothless, Ōhira's Comprehensive Security Strategy stands as the first national strategy from the *Kantei* aimed at shaping Japan's external environment after the war.

A more deliberate effort to establish a national security policy apparatus in the *Kantei* came a few years later under Nakasone Yasuhiro, who served in the top post from 1982 to 1987. Nakasone was Abe before Abe. A product of the anti-mainstream factions and a persistent critic of Yoshida's passivity on the world stage, Nakasone had worn a black armband during the U.S. occupation in "mourning" for Japan's lost sovereignty and in 1970 tried unsuccessfully to use his position as defense agency director general to propose a massive expansion of Japanese defense spending and the introduction of new offensive weapons systems.[21] As Shinoda Tomohito notes in one of his detailed studies of Japanese leadership politics, Nakasone came to the premiership determined to "exercise top-down leadership in governing as a president-like national leader by avoiding the traditional way of the prime minister influenced by the old customs under the prewar constitution."[22]

Nakasone built on Ōhira's precedent—and used some of his same brain trust—to create official and unofficial advisory councils that would bypass bureaucratic channels. He also promised a "handcrafted diplomacy" (*tezukuri gaikō*): for example, by deploying Itochu Corporation chairman Sejima Ryūzō as a personal envoy to coordinate policy with President Chun Doo-hwan in Korea.[23] With *der Primat der Aussenpolitick* in mind, Nakasone stopped the constant rotation of cabinet members and put Abe's father, Abe Shintarō, in charge of the foreign ministry for an unprecedented four-year term, empowering him vis-à-vis the bureaucrats and international counterparts. Nakasone's own tenure corresponded with Ronald Reagan's, with whom he developed a close partnership backed by well-developed ties between the White House

National Security Council staff and Nakasone's own staff in the *Kantei*, further enhancing his own role in foreign affairs.

Nakasone presided over a *Kantei* that was still institutionally weak, but he compensated for that institutional weakness with high-quality personnel choices. Critical to his success was the chief cabinet secretary, Gotōda Masaharu, who began transforming that job from one of arbitrating policies among ministers to one of providing more policy direction to the cabinet. The LDP factions and the bureaucracy fought back, but Gotōda pointed to Japan's poor coordination in response to the 1983 Soviet downing of Korea Air Flight 007 as evidence that Japan needed a professional crisis management system directly under the prime minister.[24] Gotōda reinforced his staff by appointing National Police Agency official Sassa Atsuyuki to lead a new crisis management office within the *Kantei*. The debonair cognac-drinking Sassa, who had once commanded the police unit defending the Diet during the antigovernment protests against Kishi in 1960, held detailed dossiers that kept many of the bureaucrats who were in Gotōda's way quiescent.[25] Gotōda's next step was to change the Cabinet Law to vest his office with formal power to direct policy, but here he was checkmated by the bureaucracies and other faction bosses. Nevertheless, he was able to leave a legacy of important organizational changes within the *Kantei*, including the establishment of a Cabinet Office for External Affairs (staffed by the foreign ministry diplomats), a Cabinet Office on Security Affairs (staffed by the defense agency), an autonomous Public Relations Office, and an autonomous Cabinet Information and Research Office.[26]

While Nakasone made full use of these bureaucratic resources, however, the future of the system depended heavily on politics and personalities. Nakasone had enjoyed a stable long-term government with the backing of his old nemeses in the mainstream Tanaka Faction, who were generally satisfied to let him play in foreign policy as long as they could harness his national popularity to retain control of the economic levers of government. This cynical arrangement sometimes earned the prime minister the nickname "Tanakasone" from the press, but it gave him the power to pursue more deliberate and strategic foreign and security policies. When Nakasone's successors after 1987 proved far less interested in international affairs and less capable of maintaining power, the system Gotōda built for Nakasone atrophied.

A series of crises in the first half of the 1990s then brought back the importance of establishing a crisis management function in the *Kantei*. After the August 1990 Iraqi invasion of Kuwait, Prime Minister Kaifu Toshiki followed the advice of the old-school vice minister of foreign affairs Kuriyama Takakazu and decided to keep Japan's response within traditional diplomatic channels instead of using Gotōda's structure to coordinate decision making under the *Kantei*. The result was a disaster for Japan's international image as Tokyo stumbled in multiple attempts to send noncombatant personnel and reluctantly provided $14 billion to the U.S.-led coalition, having earlier declared that it would only be providing $1 billion "and not a dollar more!"[27] Then in January 1995 over 5,000 people died in the massive Hanshin Earthquake in Kobe as the government fumbled the emergency response and left-leaning local officials obstructed the deployment of Self-Defense Forces for emergency relief operations. Three months later an apocalyptic cult called Aum Shinrikyo released deadly sarin gas into the Tokyo subway system, paralyzing the government once again as twelve Japanese succumbed to the fumes and many thousands were injured.[28] At the end of 1996, revolutionaries in Peru seized the Japanese ambassador and many of his staff during the emperor's birthday celebration, and the Japanese government sat frozen until Peruvian special forces raided the residence five months later in an attack marred by noncoordination with Tokyo and the summary execution of captured terrorists.

The political and bureaucratic worlds were stirred to action by these humiliating failures. Within the LDP, Ozawa Ichirō led a study of Japan's failings in the Gulf War in 1992 that he later revised and published as *Blueprint for a New Japan*, in which he lamented that Japan was like a lumbering dinosaur: the hands and feet of the political structure were created, but the "brain" to govern them was not.[29] Meanwhile, the foreign ministry moved to correct the organizational shortcomings laid bare in the Gulf War by establishing a new Comprehensive Foreign Policy Bureau (*Sōgō Gaikō Seisaku Kyoku*) in 1993 to combine the policy-planning and crisis response functions that had been lacking.[30] This new NSC-like organization within the ministry soon attracted the best and brightest midlevel officials and began steadily transforming the culture of diplomacy in Japan.

Then in 1995 LDP secretary general Hashimoto Ryutaro commissioned a series of studies on crisis management to position himself as successor to the affable but incapable socialist prime minister Murayama Tomiichi, who had presided during the Hanshin Earthquake and Aum Shinrikyo disasters. When he assumed the premiership the next year, Hashimoto returned to the kind of decisive national security leadership that had characterized Nakasone's tenure. On the international scene, he agreed to revise defense guidelines with the United States to cover regional contingencies (as noted in chapter 3) and sought a new external balancing in Asia through outreach to Russia (as noted in chapter 4). At home he chaired a new Council on Administrative Reform that recommended measures to strengthen the role of the Chief Cabinet Secretariat and to create the post of deputy chief cabinet secretary for crisis management[31] In 1999 the Diet passed these reforms into law, finally establishing the authorities Gotōda had sought fifteen years earlier. Hereafter Japanese law would state that "the Cabinet Secretariat is the highest and final organ for policy coordination under the Cabinet" and responsible "to present policy direction for the government as a whole, and to coordinate policy strategically and proactively."[32] Going forward, the most important post that future prime ministers would assign—and the one often least understood by foreign governments—would be that of chief cabinet secretary.

Hashimoto had used the Japanese government's failed crisis management as the anvil on which to forge new authorities for the *Kantei*, but structural changes in Japanese domestic politics and the international system contributed as well. As was noted, the 1993 changes to Japan's election system had weakened the factions in the LDP and broadened the mandate for party members outside of Tokyo, reducing the dependence of LDP prime ministers on retaining balance and consensus across all the factions.[33] After a decade of political, economic, and psychological stagnation, Japanese political leaders could no longer aspire to the top post by virtue of their skills at distributing wealth from Japan's economic growth or backroom deals with other faction leaders. As Hashimoto vied for the presidency of the LDP in 1995, he and his rivals started a new tradition by publishing books to appeal to the public with self-proclaimed bold leadership visions.[34] The Japanese public's changing expectations of their leaders were even more evident when the controversial nationalist Ishihara Shintarō was elected governor of Tokyo in 1999—not because of his policy positions, but based on the voters' view expressed in exit polls that he had the greatest *ketsudanryoku* ("decisiveness").[35]

THE KOIZUMI REVOLUTION AND THE DPJ DEVOLUTION

No leader up to that point did more to seize upon that expectation of decisiveness than Koizumi Junichiro, who took advantage of the weakened factions and broader enfranchisement of party members to win the LDP presidency in April 2001. Koizumi's popularity rested on his clarity of communication and unrelenting determination to see through his promises. In that sense he was the most disciplined prime minister Japan had seen in at least a generation. However, the structure of his *Kantei* was still largely ad hoc and riven with internal divisions. On foreign policy, his moderate chief cabinet secretary Fukuda Yasuo diverged from his more hawkish deputy chief cabinet secretary Abe Shinzō on issues ranging from North Korea negotiations to Yasukuni Shrine, foreshadowing their own respective governments' later differences on issues related to values diplomacy and the Quad.[36] Koizumi also broke the policymaking process in the foreign ministry by inviting the gruff populist daughter of Tanaka Kakuei, Tanaka Makiko, to join his cabinet as foreign minister. The foul-mouthed and uncouth Tanaka promptly began tormenting senior diplomats, mocking American officials, and adlibbing diplomatic positions.[37]

Yet in the end, Koizumi's own disciplined vision and message control lent a strategic direction to his foreign policy that surpassed both Nakasone's and Hashimoto's. Within an hour of the 9/11 attack, for example, Koizumi declared the event a "significant contingency" and established a liaison office at the Situation Center of the cabinet (later upgraded to the Emergency Anti-Terrorism Headquarters). This was a deliberate

departure from how Kaifu had responded to the Gulf crisis by outsourc-
ing policy management to the foreign ministry. Days later Koizumi called
the first cabinet-level meeting of the NSC since 1998, reinforcing to the
cabinet that *his* office would manage Japan's response.[38] Ironically, the
chaos sown by Tanaka at the foreign ministry meant that senior foreign
ministry officials began taking policy coordination on counterterrorism
and other security issues directly to Chief Cabinet Secretary Fukuda at
the *Kantei*, reinforcing a de facto NSC staff system directly under Koizumi. Koizumi also acted on 9/11 to introduce legislation passed in the
Diet in 2003 that strengthened the authority of the prime minister to
direct the Self-Defense Forces and even limited certain individual rights
in times of national emergency.[39] These powers were still well below those
of a British prime minister or American president, but they were unprecedented for Japan in the postwar era. Indeed, for decades a small group
of conservatives within the LDP had been blocked from even introducing such *Yuji Hosei* ("emergency situation legislation") to the floor of the
Diet, but Koizumi's government passed the bill with 90 percent support
from members present.[40] Decisiveness had a power all its own.

George W. Bush administration officials—many of whom had lived
through the travails of the Kaifu administration while working for his
father during the 1990–1991 Gulf War—were relieved to find veterans of
that same experience on the Japanese side advising Koizumi. In fact, Bush
entered office intent on building a relationship with Japan that might
approach the historic "special relationship" between the United States and
Britain.[41] To that end, deliberate steps were taken by Washington to reinforce the "presidential" style of leadership Koizumi intended to exhibit,
including the installation of direct secure telephone links between the
Kantei and the White House for the first time; joint U.S.-style intelligence
briefings for the two leaders; and unprecedented levels of prior consultation on a range of U.S. diplomatic and defense measures taken after 9/11.

Breaking down the internal Japanese and bilateral U.S.-Japan stovepipes on intelligence was of particular importance to both Tokyo and
Washington. After 9/11 Koizumi empowered senior National Police
Agency official and University of Virginia graduate Kanemoto Toshinori to establish Japan's first Joint Intelligence Council (*Gōdō Jōhō Kaigi*)

based on a new government-wide clearance system in the *Kantei* to ensure rapid dissemination of intelligence across ministries and to the prime minister for the first time in Japan's postwar history.[42] With a strong demand-side pull for a unified intelligence picture from the *Kantei*, intelligence officials overcame many of their own long-standing bureaucratic rivalries to support the most powerful prime minister in their lifetimes. One of these officials described to me how profound it was to see all the cabinet members of Japan's NSC stand to attention for the first time when Koizumi entered the room in September 2005— something common in the White House Situation Room when the president enters, but a scene no one had ever seen in the *Kantei*.[43]

When Abe succeeded Koizumi in 2006, he attempted to institutionalize a national security structure that would go beyond crisis management to ensure that the *Kantei* also had the authority and capacity to conduct strategic planning and to direct all relevant ministries and military services toward a common national purpose. To this end, Abe established and personally chaired the Council on the Strengthening of the Functions of the Prime Minister's Office Regarding National Security (*Kokka Anzen Hoshō ni Kansuru Kantei Kinō Kyōka Kaigi*).[44] In the meantime, he asked future Tokyo governor Koike Yuriko to be Japan's first national security advisor. The English- and Arabic-speaking Koike was an independent thinker and a careful student of Koizumi's populist leadership style, which she would later use to great effect to tame the LDP members in the city assembly as governor of Tokyo. As national security advisor she had no new statutory authority per se, but she gathered around her a group of energetic younger officials seconded from the ministries of foreign affairs, trade, and defense to design an NSC system that could be established with amendments to the Cabinet Law.[45]

While Abe laid careful plans for establishing an NSC system, however, he made fatal mistakes in managing the *Kantei* overall. Learning the wrong lessons from his experience under Koizumi, he concluded that it would be best to surround himself with ideologically like-minded policy advisors and avoid the debates and tensions he had seen serving as chief cabinet secretary for Koizumi. As Uesugi Takashi notes in his probing postmortem on Abe's first term, "everyone was friends and they did not have tense relations which once existed in Koizumi's cabinet," but they also vied to tell the prime minister what they thought he wanted to hear rather than what he needed to hear.[46] Instead of a deliberative and strategic organization, Abe presided over an overly ideological team that failed to prepare him for the economic and political crises that would exacerbate his illness and poleaxe his administration before an actual NSC system could be established. In retrospect, Koizumi's popular mandate and political power had been as important as the institutional structures he established. Abe had failed massively on that front. His successor, Fukuda Yasuo, put plans for an NSC on the back shelf along with Abe's vision for the Quad and values diplomacy.

For the Democratic Party of Japan (DPJ) that took power in 2009, wresting policy authority from the bureaucracies was even more important than it had been for the LDP. Ozawa Ichirō, the strongman behind the DPJ government of Hatoyama Yukio, had himself been deputy chief cabinet secretary during Japan's disastrous Gulf War response and later chaired the 1992 study group within the LDP that reflected on that experience to recommend more decisive and presidential-style leadership in Japan. As the shadow warrior behind the Hatoyama government in 2009, however, Ozawa primarily aimed to destroy the power structures of the LDP from which he had defected rather than introduce effective crisis management and strategic planning functions. Instead of bringing cohesion to strategy and crisis response, Ozawa served as a wrecking ball behind the scenes. Badly divided ideologically, the DPJ government agreed to introduce a UK-style policy unit to coordinate on economic issues, but national security problems proved too divisive for top-down *Kantei* coordination.[47]

These modest institutional reforms in the *Kantei* received some press attention, but the main political thrust of the Hatoyama and Kan governments was populist bashing of the bureaucrats. Under what bruised senior officials referred to in disgust as "Jacobin show trials," the once powerful vice ministers were dragged in front of the cameras to defend their ministries' budgets under the hostile cross-examination of TV-announcer-turned-populist-politician Renhō.[48] Back home in their ministries, they were forced to take a back seat to young and inexperienced parliamentary vice ministers from the party whom they were told should be treated like powerful political appointees in the U.S. system. One sullen senior official at the time told me that if the monkeys wanted to try to fly the plane, it was fine with him—let them crash!

The public enjoyed the spectacle at first, but then crises struck again in rapid succession with the 2010 Senkaku crisis (when the Chinese fishing boat rammed a Japanese Coast Guard cutter) and then the massive March 2011 Great Tohoku Earthquake, tsunami, and Fukushima nuclear disaster. Chaos was no longer the DPJ's political ally. Numerous postmortem analyses of the government's response to "3/11" pointed to haphazard coordination across ministries, confused lines of authority, and contradictory messages to the public and allies in the midst of the disaster.[49] While some younger political figures, like Kan's minister of state for nuclear power policy, Hosono Gōshi, distinguished themselves in the heat of the crises, the DPJ as a whole paid a heavy political cost for years of attacking the bureaucracy.

Nevertheless, the consensus that Japan needed an NSC system continued to grow even during the DPJ years. The defense ministry's 2010 National Defense Program Guidelines included a provision to study the establishment of "a body in the Prime Minister's Office which will be responsible for national security policy coordination among relevant ministers and for providing advice to the Prime Minister."[50] Acting on that proposal, Noda assigned Nagishima Akihisa as his national security advisor in anticipation of strengthening the NSC function within the *Kantei*. As with Noda's other national security policies, however, it would be left to Abe to pick up the baton after the DPJ's stunning electoral defeat in December 2012.

ABE AND JAPAN'S NEW NATIONAL SECURITY ESTABLISHMENT

When Abe returned to power in late 2012, he did more than just dust off his original plans for an NSC system. The original intent was still there: to move from crisis management to the effective integration of crisis response *and* longer-term strategic planning. But the DPJ government's flailing responses to crises in the intervening years had lent additional urgency and illuminated two additional requirements. First, confused messaging during the Senkaku and Tōhoku crises had undermined Japan's position with both the United States and China, reinforcing the need for what an independent task force on the establishment of a new NSC under Funabashi Yoichi called "credibility, predictability, and continuity" in Japanese security policy.[51] Second, Chinese maritime and mercantile coercion in the 2010 and 2012 Senkaku crises had elevated the importance of central coordination across civil and military agencies to manage "grey zone" tactics targeting the seams between peacetime and wartime operations. It was clear that Japan needed a new concept and toolkit to shape the external environment consistently across times of calm or crisis—and one that integrated military, economic, and diplomatic instruments so that adversaries could not exploit those seams. A debate about restructuring the *Kantei* to avoid embarrassing failures in crisis response had matured to a focus on the institutional restructuring needed to ensure maximum alignment of diplomatic, military, and other tools to compete with a more revisionist China. Indeed, this mission had become the entire predicate of Abe's political resurrection within the LDP.

Within months of returning to power, Abe organized a new expert panel (now called the Advisory Council on the Establishment of a National Security Council—*Kokka Anzen hoshō Kaigi no Sōsetsu ni kan suru Yūshikisha Kaigi*) to prepare the outlines of legislation establishing an NSC system. That legislation passed in the Diet on November 27 by wide margins, and in December 2013 the NSC and National Security Staff were formally inaugurated.[52] The Cabinet Information Office explained that the new NSC would "serve as the command center for the country's diplomatic and security policies: henceforth, the government will conduct unified management of information relating to diplomacy and national security and make important policy decisions promptly under the leadership of the prime minister. . . . The NSC will overcome the sectionalism among ministries and agencies to conduct policymaking in a strategic and flexible manner."[53]

That same month the *Kantei* issued Japan's first National Security Strategy (NSS) document, which would thereafter supersede the previous policy documents emanating separately from the ministries of defense and foreign affairs and would serve as the basis for all international security policy planning and pronouncements by the bureaucracy.[54] In theory the U.S. policy process is also supposed to flow from the White House National Security Strategy to the separate Pentagon and State Department strategic reports, but with changes in the cabinet and unforeseen political developments, this sequencing is often interrupted or ignored in Washington (as I know from having participated in the drafting of several myself). Under Abe, it was not. The 2013 *Kantei* strategy served as the enduring framework for the entirety of Abe's next seven years in office—an impressive feat for any democratic government.

The new NSS staff were themselves drawn primarily from the ministries of foreign affairs and defense and the Self-Defense Forces, but not the Ministry of Economy, Trade and Industry (METI), as Koike had proposed in the first Abe government. Plans were also initially drawn up for outside scholars to serve on the National Security Staff as occurs in the U.S. system, though none were actually recruited during Abe's tenure. The NSC began meeting weekly and sometimes daily, bringing together the prime minister, foreign minister, chief cabinet secretary, and defense minister for the purpose not of consultation, but of actually determining strategy and policy and providing guidance to the ministries. Instead of being briefed by bureaucrats on their respective policies, the four ministers were given decision documents requiring their guidance. No national security official in Japan had ever seen anything like it before.[55]

Much of the success of Japan's NSC hinged on the lessons Abe had learned from his earlier failed tenure as prime minister. This time he appointed experienced and influential officials and politicians to the key posts overseeing the new national security establishment rather than just his friends and ideological allies. His chief cabinet secretary, Suga Yoshihide, disciplined the bureaucracies by exerting unprecedented control over personnel appointments through the establishment in May 2014 of a Cabinet Bureau of Personnel Affairs.[56] Many of the best and brightest officials now sought appointments on the National

Security Staff to advance their careers. The administrative vice ministers back in the ministries had lost one of their most important tools for defying the prime minister—control over his and their own staff. Abe's first national security advisor (officially the "secretary general of the NSC"), Yachi Shōtaro, had himself been administrative vice minister at the foreign ministry in the first Abe government and understood these bureaucratic dynamics well. Yachi was also a veteran of secret negotiations with both Beijing and Seoul and understood how critical it was for Japan to maintain a disciplined long-term strategy in order to regain the initiative toward those two countries after years of reactive and confused diplomacy. Yachi's patient chess-like focus on strategy earned him the moniker "Japan's Henry Kissinger" from impressed observers.[57] Critical to Yachi's success internally and vis-à-vis China was also what Japan scholar Giulio Pugliese calls the "hybrid model" of leadership connecting the *Kantei* with both the Japanese bureaucracy and counterparts on the U.S. NSC staff.[58] The role of the White House in reinforcing the power and influence of the *Kantei* had earlier been evident in the ad hoc relationships established under Nakasone and Koizumi, and this was now being institutionalized under Yachi, who made regular trips to meet his counterparts in Washington.[59]

Traditionalist critics, like former prime minister Fukuda, warned that this new system would politicize the bureaucracy and "ruin the state."[60] It would be more accurate to say that under Abe the NSC system provided the "credibility, predictability, and continuity" in national security policymaking that Japan had lacked under the earlier LDP and especially DPJ governments. The success of the new NSC system was most evident in Japan's shaping of U.S. strategy toward Asia—a core mission for Abe in his second term. Fukuda was not wrong in predicting that the new system weakened the bureaucracies' independence—a weakness that a demagogic leader could theoretically exploit in future. But while Abe's *Kantei* disciplined the bureaucracy, it did not punish it as the DPJ had. If anything, the mainstream officials within the ministries—particularly foreign affairs and defense—were well aligned with Abe's strategy.

A more astute criticism would be that the new NSC excluded economic experts. It mattered that the architects of the NSC in the second term were primarily diplomats rather than politicians like Koike, who had chosen to include officials from METI on her precursor NSC staff (though not the powerful Ministry of Finance—after a lunch with Koike at the time I witnessed her rebuff the vice minister of finance as he pleaded with her to include someone on the new NSC staff from his once dominant ministry). The national security experts in the foreign ministry had long been aligned with the uniformed military and increasingly with the defense ministry civilian officials on questions of strategy.[61] Relations with METI were somewhat more contentious, however, because of the trade officials' growing ambitions to shape international strategy as their own mission in domestic industrial policy waned.

Abe's powerful chief of staff was himself a METI veteran—the former deputy director general of the Agency for National Resources and Energy (ANRE), Imai Takaya.[62] Imai later publicly acknowledged the bifurcated policy process that sometimes resulted on international economic policy questions. For example, Imai was responsible for Japan's decision to participate in China's Belt and Road Forum in 2018 and to offer major economic packages to Russia as inducement for resolving the Northern Territory issues—both done over the objections of the Ministry of Foreign Affairs (MOFA) and NSS officials worried about divergence from the U.S. strategy on China and Russia.[63] Wary of the growing fissure within the policy process, Suga and Yachi's successor, former police agency official and intelligence chief Kitamura Shigeru, finally established a new economics division within the NSS in 2019.[64] Not only was it better to have METI inside the tent, but the security challenges confronting the NSC were increasingly related to technology competition with China on 5G and the need to better fuse Japan's civilian and military technology innovation. These were issues about which a younger generation of METI officials were as inclined as their foreign and defense ministry counterparts to align with the United States and other like-minded allies to protect Japan against predatory Chinese techno-nationalism. METI officials also recognized that they needed their own access to the U.S. NSC to curb excessive U.S. export control rules that hurt Japanese corporations. Integrating diplomatic, defense, and economic tools under one NSC staff was a critical step in establishing unity of purpose.

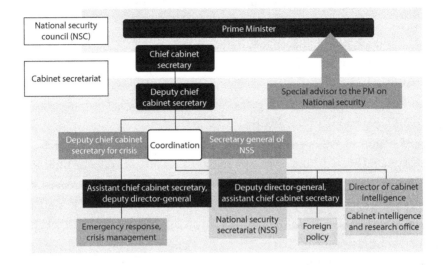

FIGURE 6.1 Organization of Japan's National Security Council

CENTRALIZING INTELLIGENCE FUNCTIONS

In addition to the establishment of the NSC, two other lines of effort defined Abe's centralization of strategic policymaking and crisis management. The first was the strengthening of the intelligence assessment and coordination function within the *Kantei*. As Richard Samuels writes in his sweeping history of Japanese intelligence policy, Abe succeeded in putting in place the "crown jewels" of intelligence reform that had defied LDP conservatives for decades.[65] The quest had begun in 1980 after a Japan Self-Defense Forces (JSDF) brigadier general passed confidential information to Soviet spies. That so-called Miyanaga Incident prompted LDP hawks to begin pushing for legislation to impose Japan's first postwar criminal penalties for espionage. The effort peaked in 1988 when a draft "antispy law" (*supai bōshi hō*) failed to make it out of the LDP's Policy Affairs Research Council (*Jimintō Seichōkai*).[66] Even the centrist *Nihon Keizai Shimbun* had warned at the time that the bill would "endanger fundamental human rights enshrined in the constitution."[67]

When Abe's government introduced a new State Secrecy Law (*Tokutei Himitsu no Hogoni Kansuru Hōritsu [Tokutei Himitsu Hogo Hō]*) in 2014, the politics had changed dramatically. The *Nihon Keizai Shimbun* flagged the importance of ensuring freedom of information for citizens and journalists but did not challenge the constitutionality of the bill as the paper had thirty-six years earlier.[68] Even the left-leaning *Asahi Shimbun* generally followed that line, urging measures to avoid over-application of the law and criticizing the vague definition of "specially designated secrets," but not challenging the fundamental constitutionality of secrecy legislation. Meanwhile, the conservative papers like *Yomiuri* expressed support as long as freedom of information was guaranteed.[69] Opposition to the bill was further muted by the fact that the DPJ administration of Kan Naoto had actually begun drafting the legislation itself after embarrassing leaks from the Japan Coast Guard during the 2010 Senkaku crisis. With noisy protesters demonstrating outside the National Diet and several opposition parties filibustering inside, the ruling coalition finally suspended debate and pushed through the bill on December 6.[70]

The passage of the State Secrecy Law was a political and ideological victory for Abe and his conservative allies. The introduction of strict penal consequences for officials would now make it possible for different ministries to share intelligence in real time without their earlier fear that bureaucratic rivals would leak that intelligence. Perhaps even more importantly, the new legislation made it possible for the United States to share sensitive intelligence derived from technical means not independently available to Japan. Put another way, the Abe government needed stronger walls around sensitive information at home in order to reduce the walls that existed between Japan and the United States. Internal and external balancing were both at stake.

With the successful passage of the State Secrecy Law, Japanese politicians and policy pundits began calling for Tokyo's elevation to the next level of trust—participation in the highly restricted "Five Eyes" intelligence-sharing arrangement among the United States, United Kingdom, Australia, Canada, and New Zealand. To some extent, these proposals resonated in the United States. U.S. legislation on screening strategic investments from China in 2018 included amendments to share relevant legislation with Five Eyes *and* Japan, for example. Some former U.S. officials openly endorsed the idea of Japan joining Five Eyes more broadly—including in the area of overhead imagery, where Japanese satellite technology, analytical capability, and proximity to threats in Northeast Asia are valued.[71]

That said, Japan's intelligence reforms still fall short of Five Eyes expectations in several respects. To begin with, Japan lacks the procedures to limit and control access to national secrets within the Diet comparable to the Westminster controls and the U.S. "Gang of Eight" system, which allow political oversight in these democracies without the risk of politically motivated leaks. In addition, while Japan's analytical capabilities have become world class in the areas of economic intelligence and overhead imagery analysis, Japan has yet to develop an experienced cadre of all-source intelligence analysts comparable to those in the other Five Eyes countries.[72] Other politically sensitive issues that would align Japanese capabilities with the Five Eyes member states remain unresolved, including whether Japan should develop a clandestine service to collect intelligence overseas or establish covert action authorities to strike a political, technological, or economic blow at adversaries. Nevertheless, the consolidation of intelligence analysis under the *Kantei* represents the most significant intelligence reform in Japan's postwar history—providing the NSC with timely information for decision making and steadier coordination with close allies and partners, particularly the United States. One could even argue that the reforms are the most significant in Japan's history, considering the refusal of the imperial army and navy to share intelligence with each other in the 1930s and 1940s.

TOWARD A JOINT FORCE

The second line of effort under the new national security establishment was the introduction of greater consolidation and jointness among the three military services and between civilian and uniformed authorities. Achieving jointness among rival military services has proven a political and bureaucratic challenge for every nation. The United States only established unified civilian oversight of the military when the 1947 National Security Act replaced the separate departments of war and navy with the Department of Defense. Congress imposed more disciplines with the 1986 Goldwater-Nichols Act after the lack of jointness among the U.S. services was tragically laid bare in the failed 1980 hostage rescue in Iran. Three decades later, experts are still lamenting the difficulty of achieving unity of effort among the services.[73]

In Japan's case, jointness among the three services has long taken a back seat to interoperability between the Japan Maritime Self-Defense Forces (JMSDF) and the U.S. Navy. Even Japan's ground and air self-defense forces have historically enjoyed greater interoperability with their American counterparts than with each other. In the past, the U.S. command-and-control setup in Japan has often reinforced this stovepiping. The U.S. Air Force three-star general commanding U.S. Forces Japan (USFJ) historically spent most of his time managing political issues while wearing the operational hat as commander of the Fifth Air Force, based in Yokota. USFJ were never established as an independent joint task force, meaning that they lacked the staff, planning, and authority to command the component army, navy, air force, and marine units ostensibly under their aegis in wartime. Meanwhile, requirements, military exercises, staff exchanges, and even intelligence sharing have more often been determined by the component commanders for the separate U.S. Navy and Marine Corps units based in Yokosuka and Okinawa. Since the U.S. commanders' goal was to confirm combat service support for U.S. units operating in the Far East—and Japan traditionally faced relatively few direct threats in the Sea of Japan—this arrangement sufficed. Put another way, USFJ were a force provider while Japan's three services historically supplemented their counterparts, particularly at sea.

With the evolution of a joint culture in the United States after Goldwater-Nichols and the increasing Chinese and North Korean military threats in the 1990s, Japan began slowly moving in the same direction as the United States, now urged on by USFJ. The 1995 Mid-Term Defense Buildup Plan was the first to emphasize jointness and interoperability as major objectives.[74] In 2006 the defense ministry upgraded the previous Joint Staff Council from a consultative body to a new Joint Staff Office with more extensive staffing and resources and the authority to be a "force user" with the separate services now the "force providers."[75] During the DPJ years the Self-Defense Forces operated jointly in real-world contingencies for the first time—conducting counterpiracy operations based out of Djibouti in the Gulf of Aden beginning in 2009 and monitoring North Korean missile tests in 2012.[76] Further reforms were announced by the Ministry of Defense in 2013 after Abe returned to office, specifying plans to remove the barriers between civilian officials and uniformed personnel, to emphasize capabilities based on total optimization and joint operations, and to strengthen joint operational planning.[77] Abe's comprehensive security legislation in 2015 also included legislation that rolled back decades of civilian primacy over the uniformed military, establishing the authority of the JSDF to give military advice without receiving civilian clearance first.[78] Another wave of reforms in 2017 established a strategic planning division and abolished the operations bureau in the Ministry of Defense, which had the effect of placing more operational command-and-control responsibilities with the uniformed military.[79]

The services also realigned themselves to provide more flexible and joint capability. The Ground Self-Defense Forces (GSDF) activated its first amphibious brigade and first Ground Component Command (following the establishment of air and maritime component commands), both in 2018.[80] The three services simultaneously began conducting joint amphibious exercises with the help of the U.S. Marine Corps.[81] The Japan Coast Guard also began realigning more closely with the Japan Maritime Self-Defense Forces (JMSDF) as Tokyo sought to manage Chinese grey zone incursions that struck at the seam between law enforcement and military operations—notably in response to People's Liberation Army (PLA) navy grey hull warships operating just over the horizon as China's own Coast Guard tested Japanese administrative control over the Senkaku Islands.[82] In 2013 the commandant of the Coast Guard was appointed from among the uniformed ranks for the first time (rather than imposed from the civilian transport ministry bureaucracy), providing further evidence that capabilities and performance now mattered more than bureaucratic equities.[83] Beginning in 2015, the Coast Guard also began regular exercises with its old bureaucratic rivals in the JMSDF.[84]

The integration of the uniformed military with the new NSC was particularly significant. As with other areas of personnel in the cabinet office, Abe chose the most outstanding military officer to chair the joint staff regardless of bureaucratic equities or interservice balance—giving Admiral Kawano Katsutoshi an unprecedented three terms (2014–2019) in the top military post as well as unprecedented access to the *Kantei*.[85] The self-effacing Kawano was in fact a risk-taker after Abe's own mold. In the days after the 9/11 terrorist attack, then Captain Kawano had authorized the dispatch of two JMSDF destroyers to escort the carrier USS *Kitty Hawk* out of Tokyo Bay—a powerful image that made the front page across the United States and almost cost Kawano his job as operations director on the maritime staff. As chairman, Kawano pushed jointness and interoperability and championed joint capabilities in cyber, surveillance, and space. He also pushed—unsuccessfully in the end—for appointment of a joint operational commander to serve under him with responsibility for directing operations in contingencies when he as chairman would likely be working political and strategic issues with the prime minister and the cabinet.[86]

This centralization, authorization, and alignment of the uniformed military behind national strategy conform exactly with Barry Posen's foundational theory of military organizational dynamics. As he put it in his seminal work, *The Sources of Military Doctrine*, "Balance of power theory suggests that states respond to potentially dangerous increases in the power of their putative adversaries. . . . Balancing behavior is both qualitative and quantitative. States not only seek allies and build up their military power, they audit their military doctrines. Such audits mitigate the tendency toward stagnation predicted by organization theory."[87]

None of these reforms in Japan would have been possible without a transformation in the Japanese public's view of their own military—which in turn resulted from the exogenous security pressures flagged by Posen, but also generational change and the heroic performance of the JSDF in responding to the March 2011 Great East Japan Earthquake. In 1988 public opinion polls, the Japanese public expressed a low estimation of the JSDF and a majority questioned whether they would even fight to defend Japan from attack.[88] In 2018 the JSDF were listed as the institution the Japanese public trusted *the most*—ahead of educators, religious leaders, and government officials.[89] It mattered that not just Abe, but also the Japanese public, were proud to see senior officers in uniform advising their prime minister. Or as Keio University professor Hosoya Yūichi puts it in his 2019 book, *Gunji to Seiji: Nihon no Sentaku* (Military and politics: Japan's choices), the government's mission is no longer to protect civilians *from* the military, but rather for the citizens to decide how the government should employ the military to protect them from external threats.[90] Unity of purpose across military organizations, alongside national political leaders and the public at large, is the essence of successful qualitative internal balancing.

As with the formation of the NSC, however, in some areas Japan's defense reforms have fallen short. Longevity—of Abe and Kawano both—was an important factor, and it is unlikely that bureaucratic or Diet politics will yield such an enduring combination again soon. The failure to establish a joint operational command will leave an undue burden on Kawano's successors should a major contingency require simultaneous direction of the Self-Defense Forces and coordination with the prime minister and the cabinet. Joint capabilities are still largely dependent on marrying together separate platforms, with only a few examples of truly joint assets, such as the Global Hawk unmanned surveillance drones, a program that has been under perpetual political pressure because it has no service home.[91] Finally, while the establishment of a new Acquisition, Technology and Logistics Agency (ATLA) in 2015 significantly improved project management, the agency remains torn between delivering capabilities and nursing Japan's highly domesticated defense industrial base.[92] At a time when the PLA Air Force was deploying more fifth-generation fighters than Japan could put up in a fight, for example, ATLA was still debating whether to pursue an indigenously designed fighter that would take longer to develop and cost more than coproduction or direct commercial purchase from the United States.[93] It is politically understandable that ATLA would come under pressure from the Diet to reduce dependence on U.S. imports for the most advanced equipment, since foreign military sales (purchases through the U.S. government) increased in Japan more than tenfold in less than a decade, from $390 million to a record high of $4.4 billion in FY 2016.[94] The cost of improved military capabilities is less control of systems integration for Japanese companies, a bitter pill for a country that was debating technological independence from the United States only two decades ago.[95]

These shortcomings notwithstanding, Japan's defense reorganization represents one of the most significant in modern East Asian history. Japan is no longer alone in that effort, however, for Beijing announced in 2016 its own major reforms to make the PLA more joint, interoperable, and effective in wartime.[96] The contest continues, and Japan will not be able to rest on its laurels.

QUANTITATIVE INTERNAL BALANCING

The transformational reorganization of Japan's national security institutions just described represents a successful example of qualitative internal balancing. Put another way, Abe significantly improved the ways that Japan employed its means in international security affairs. However, *quantitative* internal balancing will also remain crucial to Japanese strategy in the years ahead. Where would Japan derive more endogenous material power? This chapter concludes with a brief examination of two areas where Japan has struggled with mixed success to increase opportunities for quantitative improvements in national power: military capabilities and economic performance.

MILITARY CAPABILITIES

In terms of rapid quantitative improvements in military power—as opposed to qualitative organizational changes that allow the more effective employment of such capabilities—structural realists would likely consider nuclear weapons to be the quickest power correction available to Japan. Reflecting offensive realism theory, political scientists from Herman Kahn to Henry Kissinger speculated during the Cold War that Japan could and probably would develop its own nuclear deterrent to match its rising economic power.[97] For some experts, the same logic would seem to apply to a Japan facing declining relative power after the Cold War.[98] Certainly Japan has the nuclear, missile, telemetry, and satellite technologies needed to piece together a deliverable nuclear weapon and deliverable system in shorter time than almost any other non-nuclear state.[99]

But that is in theory. In reality, Japan is a status quo power intent on preserving the neoliberal order that has benefited the country since 1945 and not a rogue state like North Korea or Iran that could pursue nuclear weapons without existential costs to its economic and political connectivity with the rest of the world. Here cultural norms are also a massive impediment for Japan, with public opinion polls consistently demonstrating that over 80 percent of respondents would oppose possession of nuclear weapons under any circumstances.[100] These antinuclear norms are institutionalized in Japan's "Three Non-Nuclear Principles"—a cabinet decree banning the possession, stationing, or transit of nuclear weapons in Japan. The Japanese nuclear physics community, which would presumably be responsible for developing such capabilities, is particularly opposed to nuclear weapons.[101]

This is not to say that Japan would never develop nuclear weapons. Japanese diplomacy for decades has subtly aimed to remind the world that it has that option so that it could maintain leverage vis-à-vis the United States to maintain extended deterrence and to pressure the other nuclear weapons states to advance disarmament and arms control.[102] The Three Non-Nuclear Principles could be changed by the cabinet at any time, and there has been debate in the recent past about relaxing them to allow U.S. deployments of tactical nuclear weapons to deter North Korea.[103] However, the barriers to development and possession of nuclear weapons in Japan go well beyond cultural and political norms to also include the logic of deterrence. As a practical matter, the pursuit of autarkic nuclear weapons would undermine the credibility of the U.S. extended deterrent and leave Japan with less aggregate capability vis-à-vis China, Russia, or North Korea. Thus, even those few experts in Japan who advocate nuclear weapons ultimately conclude that the only effective option would be to deploy "dual-keyed" weapons systems with the United States or mutually agreed-upon independent weapons to supplement rather than replace U.S. extended deterrence.[104] In other words, Japan will do everything to maintain the credibility of U.S. extended deterrence before actively considering independent nuclear weapons. And while candidate Donald Trump said he did not care if Japan developed nuclear weapons, there is little indication that the U.S. government is inclined to let the credibility of the U.S. nuclear guarantee lapse or to change its strategy to include Japanese nuclear weapons in the overall U.S. deterrence formula.[105]

Conventional military capabilities are another matter. After a decade of declining defense spending, Abe inaugurated steady increases in Japan's defense budget beginning in 2014, raising the amount to $48.7 billion with small increases each subsequent year throughout his time in office.[106] However, Japan still spends less than 1 percent of GDP on defense and ranks thirty-second in per capita defense spending, below Barbados and Bermuda—and Northeast Asia is hardly as placid as the Caribbean.[107] In nominal terms, Japan's 2018 budget was comparable to the 1997 budget, so the modest increases under Abe were hardly radical.[108]

More significant are the specific conventional military capabilities Japan is beginning to consider, develop, or deploy. For over a decade the JSDF have been shifting to the southwest—away from the Cold War concentration against potential Soviet attacks around Hokkaido. The JSDF are attempting to counter China's A2/AD (anti-access/area denial) capabilities with their own Japanese version of A2/AD southwest of Okinawa, backed by Type 88 anti-ship missile batteries; anti-aircraft batteries; new F-15 fighter squadrons in Okinawa; establishment of an amphibious brigade; new Coast Guard headquarters and ship upgrades based in Okinawa; commissioning of twenty-two attack submarines, including the new *Taigei* class ("Giant Whale"); and the commissioning of the JS *Kaga* and JS *Izumo* helicopter carrier/destroyers—de facto light aircraft carriers with hardened decks capable of carrying the F-35B STOL (short takeoff and landing) fighters.[109]

Within this capability set, the most significant development since Abe returned to office has been the unprecedented focus on offensive strike capabilities. Since the early 1980s, the United States and Japan have divided roles, missions, and capabilities between the American "spear" and the Japanese "shield," but that division has been under steady revision for a decade. The Japan Air Self-Defense Forces (JASDF) has begun procuring long-range anti-ship missiles (LRASMs) (air-to-ground anti-ship missiles) and joint air-to-surface standoff missiles–extended range (JASSM-ER) (air-to-ground missiles).[110] More dramatic have been leaks that the Japan Ministry of Defense is examining options to procure longer-range Tomahawk cruise missiles that would be capable of striking targets within China or North Korea. These procurements follow in the wake of a larger national debate about Japan's requirement for "enemy base counterstrike" (*teki kichi kôgekinôryoku*), which the Cabinet Legal Office determined in 1956 would theoretically fall within the scope of self-defense allowed by the constitution and which the ruling LDP called for studying in a 2017 report—a proposal endorsed by Prime Minister Abe at the time and then again in July 2020 by Defense Minister Kōno Tarō.[111]

As of 2021 the scope of that new capability was still being debated: should Japan's forces have missiles capable of hitting enemy forces in the First Island Chain for deterrence by denial, or longer-range weapons capable of hitting Chinese or North Korean bases and infrastructure for deterrence by punishment? The former would have support within the United States, for example, while the latter would raise the specter that the United States could be entrapped in a conflict escalated by Japan absent more integrated bilateral joint and combined command and control over the weapons. Increasingly, though, Japan's national security scholars are arguing for the latter—deep-strike capability—because of the deterioration in Japan's relative combat power vis-à-vis China.[112]

After the PLA conducted a successful anti-satellite test in 2007, Japan also introduced a series of major reforms to its space policy to maintain interoperability with the United States, deter Chinese aggression in outer space, and develop new indigenous capabilities. In 2008 the Diet passed the Basic Space Law to allow utilization of space for defense purposes for the first time.[113] The Japan Ministry of Defense launched its first command-and-control satellite in 2017, the *Kirameki-2*, and in one of his last meetings in the *Kantei* in the summer of 2020, Abe told the Space Council that Japan must "deepen our cooperation, beginning with the field of space, to boost our deterrence and response capabilities," ordering greater alignment between Japan's new Space Operations Squadron of the JASDF and the new U.S. Space Force.[114] Beginning from a paltry cybersecurity community of fewer than one hundred people in 2008, Japan also rapidly ramped up its cybersecurity capabilities, passing a Basic Act on Cyber Security in November 2014 and standing up a Cyber Security Strategic Headquarters and a National Center of Incident Readiness and Strategy for Cybersecurity (NISC) in the *Kantei* and a Cyber Defense Group under the JSDF.[115] By 2019 regional commands within Japan were forming cyberspace defense units, beginning with the GSDF Southwest Command covering the Senkakus.[116]

Any veteran of the U.S.-Japan alliance in uniform on the U.S. side can attest to the fact that in both qualitative and quantitative terms the JSDF are a far more capable—and lethal—fighting force today than even a decade ago, even if nominal defense spending has not increased significantly. However, candid veterans like Grant Newsham, a fluent Japanese-speaking former U.S. marine colonel with decades of experience liaising with the JSDF, will also point to the remaining deficiencies: weakness in joint operations and communications, logistics, timelines and sequences for mobilization, war stocks (ammunition and materiel), manpower and recruitment, casualty replacement planning, and realistic war-fighting training and exercises.[117] A 2020 RAND Corporation study concluded that while Japan had made significant improvements in defense capabilities and posture, including sea-lane defense and improved mobility for the ground forces, there were significant shortcomings with respect to logistics, jointness, and modernization of key platforms.[118] That many of these problems also plague U.S. allies and partners from NATO to Taiwan puts the shortcomings in context but removes none of the urgency of addressing them.

Japan's struggle to restore economic growth and productivity since the "lost decades" of the 1990s could fill a large tome in itself, but economic output may ultimately be the most important source of longer-term internal balancing available to Japan. Studies by the Japan Center for Economic Research (JCER) shortly after Abe came back to power suggested that the right combination of structural reforms could deliver a sustained annual growth rate of over 2 percent for Japan—providing more resources for infrastructure financing, diplomacy, and closing of military capability shortfalls.[119] Abe's own recognition of this fact was clear when he told me over lunch in the *Kantei* in July 2013 that as a matter of national security he intended to spend 70 percent of his time focused on the economy.

Abe's strategy for unleashing greater economic growth—the cleverly named "Abenomics"—cannot be compared with the wholesale liberalization efforts undertaken by Margaret Thatcher in the United Kingdom in the 1970s or Ronald Reagan in the United States in the 1980s to unleash economic vitality in the Cold War struggle against communism. Abe's political premise was that he would not gore the sacred cows of any major LDP constituency the way Koizumi had gone after the postal savings system. Instead, Abe won broad political support to target "three arrows" under the January 2013 cabinet decision on Emergency Economic Measures for the Revitalization of the Japanese Economy.[120] The first arrow was aggressive monetary policy through quantitative and qualitative monetary easing to free Japan from the deflation trap that had held down investment and growth for two decades.[121] The goal here was a target inflation rate of 2 percent that would incentivize consumption. The second arrow was fiscal stimulus, initially through a December 2014 package of ¥3.5 trillion and subsequent packages timed to offset the impact of consumption tax increases necessitated by Japan's aging society.[122] The third arrow was structural reform, with the most important changes applied in labor law; new rules for the Tokyo Stock Exchange to spur investment and return on investment; and an immigration law to provide more short-term laborers and ease restrictions on tourism. Perhaps the most ambitious reform was Abe's personal championing of "womenomics" to increase productivity through raising women's participation rate in the workforce to the levels of the United States or Western Europe.[123]

Did it work? Under Abenomics Japan sustained its longest growth streak since World War II; exporters posted windfall profits from the weaker yen that resulted from monetary easing, causing share prices to hit a twenty-seven-year high; tourism in Japan tripled with immigration reforms; and women's participation rate in the workforce actually surpassed the U.S. level.[124] On the other hand, the average annual growth rate in Japan amounted to only 1.1 percent per annum under Abe—not the 2+ percent rate economists thought possible; Japan's share of global forex (foreign exchange) transactions fell below where it was when Abenomics was launched in 2013, dropping Japan behind Singapore and Hong Kong in Asia; the inflation target of 2 percent was never met; the contribution of productivity gains to Japanese economic growth fell in relative terms; and womenomics reached diminishing returns as the large influx of women in the workforce collided with residual discrimination in promotion and the logistical challenges of long commutes and insufficient daycare.[125]

To some extent, the declining impact of Abenomics can be blamed on seismic exogenous shocks to the global economy, particularly the 2020 coronavirus pandemic, which caused Japanese exports to drop a shocking 54 percent and Japanese private consumption to fall by 29 percent.[126] Neoclassical economists also concluded that Abenomics had relied too much on reversing deflation and fueling the Tokyo Stock Market rather than achieving structural market-based reforms in the economy that would lead to sustained growth.[127] Other economists argued that the biggest problem was Abe's support for budget deficit hawks in the finance ministry who insisted on introducing consumption tax hikes that sapped consumer spending.[128] Few observers were prepared to call Abenomics a failure overall, but most agreed that the promised structural reform proved insufficient to sustain growth at Japan's real potential.

Yet just as the reforms associated with qualitative internal balancing are not over, the search for further sources of quantifiable power also continues. Previously unshakable norms are being broken in this scramble to find resources to compete. One noteworthy example is the composition of the military, traditionally the most male-dominated of

Japanese institutions. Simply put: Japan's demographic decline means that the JSDF will not have enough personnel to "man" the force without increasing the number of female recruits for all military occupations, including frontline combat roles. In 2019 women accounted for only 6.5 percent of all service members, but the defense ministry has set a target of 10 percent by 2030 (compared with about 16 percent in the U.S. and Australian militaries). Japanese women have now completed paratrooper training and fighter school and have taken command of Japan's advanced Aegis destroyers. Changes in combat roles for women in the U.S. military took decades of effort and the empaneling of a special advisory board to press the services from the outside, but Japan in only a few years has opened up almost every military occupation specialization to women, with the defense ministry pushing for further changes in recruitment, retention, and logistics to achieve its gender diversity goal.[129] The Japanese bureaucracy is also changing the future of diplomacy and security, with entering classes that are 54 percent female for the foreign ministry, 62 percent for the justice ministry, and a historic high of 37 percent across the government overall.[130]

Other supposedly unshakable cultural norms are also changing under the pressure of demographics and geopolitics. Immigration legislation in Japan has fallen well short of establishing a rapid pathway to citizenship, with the clear preference for temporary work permits to fill understaffed parts of the service economy, but Japan is now the fourth highest recipient of foreign workers in the world (the number doubled in Abe's first five years).[131] As one longtime Japanese scholar of immigration noted, "Abe's government introduced these reforms not to change Japanese society, but to sustain Japanese society," setting the stage for more open immigration as the country integrates foreign labor into the economy and society over the coming years. It is prominent conservative politicians in the LDP who are now pushing for more open immigration policies—in contrast to the trend in conservative politics in the United States, Germany, or other G-7 countries, where conservative parties are unifying against open borders. And in Japan's case the arguments for openness are often made on the grounds of national security and economic performance.[132]

Other areas are emerging as targets of Japanese growth strategy, including Suga Yoshihide's focus on the digital economy as a central policy pillar after Abe.[133] Japan is still far below the United States or China in "unicorns"—hi-tech start-ups that eventually reach a market capitalization of over $1 billion—but the numbers are starting to steadily increase.[134] Meanwhile, indexes on Japan's commitment to governance and reform showed a marked increase in confidence from global experts and investors as Suga took the helm.[135] In short, the internal balancing story is not yet complete.

STRATEGIC COMPETITION AND INSTITUTIONAL REALIGNMENT

The main focus of this book has been Japanese grand strategy and therefore the ways that national means are employed, rather than a detailed assessment of Japanese material capabilities per se. Yet because the purpose of Japanese strategic thinking in the Abe era has been to maximize influence at a time of declining relative power, the internal balancing component of strategy has also been critically important to our understanding of the sustainability of the new grand strategy. Abe's biggest gains in this respect were primarily in qualitative organizational reforms; while these are easier to achieve than immediate quantitative gains, they can also be the precursors to larger changes in the economic and military output of nations.

As we have seen, these institutional changes within Japan are the culmination of decades of momentum rather than an aberration or sudden departure under Abe. As historian Carol Gluck explains, "The problem faced by any conception of Japanese history is to explain the lastingness, the conspicuous durability, of Japan's institutional structures, often to the point that they seem to violate historical common sense."[136] It took over three decades from the arrival of Commodore Perry's Black Ships in 1853 to the 1889 Meiji constitution and the establishment of a modern Japanese state, for example. From the collapse of the Cold War to Abe's

consolidation of a new national security establishment was a comparable twenty-five years.

Future prime ministers of Japan will now have at their disposal the
powerful instruments left by Abe—and in many respects they will be
bound by them. There will be no excuse for passivity, no alibi in times
of crisis, no tolerance from the public for reacting to rather than shaping regional developments. The external balancing strategies explored in
chapters 2 through 5 necessitated the organizational changes introduced
by Abe and will in many respects be sustained by this new institutional
realignment and the Japanese peoples' growing sensitivity to the external security environment.

Indeed, the broad consensus and momentum behind the strategies
described in this volume point to one of Japan's most significant sources
of internal power. As the Brookings Institution's Mireya Solís has noted,
the Japanese people are embracing globalism and international trade at
a time when the rest of the G-7 countries are polarized around issues
of trade, immigration, and regionalism. In part, as she explains, Japan
has weathered offshoring and economic integration with China without massive displacement in the labor market.[137] Under Abe's tenure the
number of Japanese who said they were happy with life hit 73.9 percent, the highest ever since the government began asking the question
in 1963.[138] This unity stands in contrast to the polarized politics of neighboring Korea and of Japan's closest ally, the United States. Any assessment of national power must include not only military forces, economic
strength, and alliances—but also internal unity of purpose. This is not to
say that democratic Japan is lacking in rich debate about politics, security, society, and economics—one need only tune in to the late-night
roundtable shows on Japanese television for evidence of that vibrancy.
But the strategic trajectory of Japan is fueled by internal consensus as
much as the external challenges that helped to forge it. And that trajectory has bought the United States time to deal with its own internal fis-
sures and strategic adjustments in a competition with China that Japan's
leaders recognized long ago.

CONCLUSION

The End of the Yoshida Doctrine

Throughout the postwar era, Japanese leaders could not escape the Yoshida doctrine. Most prime ministers hailed from the mainstream factions and embraced the irascible Yoshida's vision of minimizing geopolitical risk and focusing on economic growth under the benevolent but carefully circumscribed security relationship with the United States. Some, like Abe's grandfather Kishi Nobusuke or Nakasone Yasuhiro, explicitly challenged the premise of Yoshida's grand strategy but did so in a careful balancing act that depended on the mainstream factions for political support and that rarely lasted. With the collapse of the Cold War and Japan's old model for economic development and then the rise of a revisionist China, the pillars of the Yoshida doctrine crumbled and collapsed. I described the beginning of that transition in *Japan's Reluctant Realism* in 2001, but that earlier book reached the conclusion that Japan was still searching for a strategy. Under Abe Shinzō Japan found it. For a generation, political leaders in Japan will be following the trajectory set by Abe—who unlike Yoshida chose to codify in clear national security documents, speeches, and laws many of the specifics of his own doctrine. There will undoubtedly be contestation, debate, and unresolved tensions over human rights or trade with China, for example—Japan is a democracy, of course—and the tough choices involved in economic relations with China and security dependence on the United

States will not become easier in the coming decade. There will also be wide variation in the effectiveness of Japanese leaders and perhaps even reason to expect a series of relative weak leaders after Abe, as occurred in the wake of the strong-willed Nakasone and Koizumi governments. There will be leaders who push back from the right or left against the new grand strategy, as Kishi once did against Yoshida's from the right and Miki Takeo and others did from the left.

However, a generation of political leaders in Japan will now likely base their foreign policies on the coordinates set during Abe's tenure as prime minister. Indeed, Abe's influence on succeeding prime ministers may prove even greater than Yoshida's. Certainly, the other factions within the Liberal Democratic Party (LDP) are more closely aligned with Abe's strategy than many were with Yoshida's vision during the Cold War. Japan's main opposition parties are also much closer to the government's foreign policy line than the Socialist Party was to the LDP during the Cold War. In part that is due to the Democratic Party of Japan's (DPJ's) brief experience governing from 2009 to 2012—which ultimately changed the party more than it changed Japan. I remember meetings in 2005 at the White House, where I urged then opposition DPJ leader Okada Katsuya to help Japan establish the kind of bipartisanship around our alliance that we enjoyed with Australia and Britain. Okada was receptive but at the time faced opposition from Ozawa Ichirō and other deconstructionists in the party. Later as foreign minister under the DPJ government, Okada helped to ensure that his party established its bona fides as a more credible manager of the alliance. The bizarre rhetoric of DPJ prime minister Hatoyama Yukio in 2009 about countering the United States with an East Asia Community with China is now met with embarrassed murmurs by his former colleagues, who recognize how self-defeating that stance was for Japan.

The Constitutional Democratic Party (CDP), which is made up of the more progressive members of the former DPJ, had 57 out of 465 seats in the Lower House in 2021 and was critical of the ruling coalition's security policies—including recognition of the right of collective self-defense—but supports the alliance and competition with China overall. The next largest opposition party on the left is the Japan Communist Party (JCP), which had 12 seats in the Lower House in 2021. The JCP's platform is critical of the U.S.-Japan alliance but has muted the call for its abrogation, while the party revised its platform for the first time in 2020 to attack the Chinese Communist Party (CCP) for human rights violations, prompting a harsh rebuke from Beijing.[1]

As the table C.1 indicates, those leading political figures vying for the premiership in Japan from across the LDP and the opposition vary on tactics but not core elements of the new grand strategy consummated under Abe. On the left, Edano Yukio of the CDP favors more multilateralism and relatively less defense spending, for example, but would not reverse any other aspects of Abe's legacy on internal and external balancing, promising a more robust stand on human rights and maritime security vis-à-vis China. Within the LDP, former defense minister Ishiba Shigeru has emerged as the most outspoken challenger to Abe's legacy, yet his differences are also about process—for example, asking the United States to review bilateral agreements on defense to give Japan greater "equality"—but otherwise little different from Abe's strategy, which Ishiba himself helped to build as former defense minister. At the time of publication of this volume, neither Ishiba nor Edano seemed well positioned to succeed Abe's chosen successor, Suga Yoshihide. The more likely candidates—Kono Taro, Kishida Fumio, or further down the road, Koike Yuriko—were all key partners to Abe as he consolidated his strategy. The four contenders to replace Suga after his poor political performance in the face of the COVID crisis in September 2021 all premised their strategies—like Abe—on strategic competition with China but not catastrophe with China. To the exent domestic politics present a major uncertainty going forward, it will be a problem of execution should the country enter another extended period of rapid turn-over in leadership.

IF NOT FOR ABE?

As I was finishing this book, one former student now engaged in her own dissertation work at MIT, Mina Pollmann, asked me an intriguing retrospective question. What if there had been no Abe? What if he had

TABLE C.1 Post-Abe political leaders' views on national security strategy

	Kono Taro	Ishiba Shigeru	Kishida Fumio	Koike Yuriko	Edano Yukio
U.S.-Japan Alliance	Important not just for Japan, but also for peace and stability in the region.	Should be more "symmetrical."- Japan should review the security treaty and the status of forces agreement.	The cornerstone of Japan's diplomacy. Japan must maintain the alliance and strengthen it further.	The foundation of Japan's diplomacy. Japan will work to further strengthen the alliance.	Should strive for a "healthy" (kenzen) alliance with no "sontaku." Work to avoid base relocation to Henoko.
China	China must pay a "cost" when it violates international rules and norms. But it makes sense to cooperate where possible.	Need to build a trustful relationship with China but avoid overreliance. An Asian NATO could deter Chinese maritime aggression.	Improving Japan-China relations will benefit the international community. Japan must cooperate while ensuring that China plays by the rules.	Close to Secretary-General Nikai, who is pro-China. But past statements point to concerns about China's increasing military power.	Japan should strive to deepen understanding and mutual trust, while taking a stronger stance on human rights violations and maritime assertiveness.
Free and Open Indo-Pacific (FOIP)	Japan and other like-minded nations must cooperate to maintain an international order based on common values.	Follow Abe's FOIP strategy and develop it. Create a collective security system based on international law that can partially include China.	Universal values such as democracy, freedom, and the rule of law are essential for the stability and prosperity of the Indo-Pacific.	The Asia-Pacific and Indian Ocean are important.	Multilateral cooperation among Asia-Pacific nations and Japan's neighbors, such as China and South Korea, is valuable.
Korea	Korea must not unilaterally overturn the resolved historical issues, but the Japan–Republic of Korea relationship is "indispensable."	Japan must keep working to repair the relationship and understand Korea's perspective. Abe and other lawmakers are correct that Korea must compromise on historical issues.	Japan should work to improve relations but cannot compromise on historical issues that have been resolved in accordance with international law.	Policies relating to North Korea should be hawkish. Abductee issue should be at the forefront. Japan can improve messaging on historical issues.	Though Japan is not in the wrong on historical issues, the Abe government did not try to understand and improve relations with South Korea.

(continued)

TABLE C.1 *(continued)*

Internal balancing	Executive power should be centralized with the *Kantei* through mechanisms like the National Security Council (NSC). "Small government" and developing the defense industry are important.	It is important to support the NSC, protect state secrets, and establish a National Economic Council. Defense spending could be increased above 1 percent cap, and a basic law on security should be drafted.	Enhancing defense capabilities is important, but they should be more efficient. Japan needs a "digital garden city national initiative" to make use of the latest technology to improve the economy.	The NSC is important, and the Diet should be reformed into a unicameral system. "Yurinomics," which relies less on fiscal and monetary policy, should be an alternative to "Abenomics."	Executive function should be stronger, but organizations should be "weak but firmly independent." Endlessly increasing the defense budget and raising the consumption tax should be discouraged.

not recovered physically or politically to retake the helm in 2012? These kinds of "what if" questions about leaders are challenging for political scientists and usually asked by historians. But they offer an important opportunity to think about the role of agency. The story of Abe's new grand strategy is that it is not entirely new because of the enduring geographical features of Asia and shifts in the structure of international politics that began when Abe was only a backbencher in the LDP. But Abe's leadership was catalytic. My answer to Mina was the best I could offer and may have to suffice for now. Without Abe, Japan would likely have continued moving forward with a contested "metaprocess" toward consolidation of a new grand strategy, but in the absence of Abe's sweeping legislative and institutional changes, that process would have taken longer and been much less effective.

Then there is the question of whether more profound or unexpected shifts in the structure of international politics might yet change the strategic framework bequeathed by Abe. The answer is yes, of course, since shifts in the balance of power helped to produce his strategy in the first place. Intensifying U.S.-China strategic competition was largely anticipated in Abe's approach, and so it would not be as disruptive to the new

grand strategy as one might expect. What would cause more disconti-
nuity would be U.S. retrenchment from Asia. Japanese strategists have
never completely discounted the possibility of American withdrawal
and will not easily do so after the experience of Donald Trump. When I
ask the most sophisticated Japanese strategic thinkers I know what they
would do in such a scenario, however, their answer is "more with Australia and India"—which would basically be an intensification of Abe's
external balancing strategy. Nuclear weapons or other major changes in
internal balancing strategy might also surface in Japan's national debate
in such an extreme scenario, but the scenario would indeed be extreme
and contrary to over two centuries of American history with Asia.[2]

An alternative scenario would be Chinese reform and opening and an
end to the era of coercion, authoritarianism, and strategic competition that
Xi Jinping has wrought. Japanese strategic thinkers have not discounted
this possibility either. Indeed, the Free and Open Indo-Pacific (FOIP)
vision aims to bend the arc of history in that more benign direction. In
that happier scenario, Japan's new grand strategy would be relaxed, but
there would still likely be strong elements of internal and external balancing as a hedge. My dissertation and first book, *Arming Japan*, examined
the intense techno-nationalist tensions that emerged in U.S.-Japan relations at the end of the Cold War and used case studies to demonstrate
how resilient the alliance was even in the absence of a unifying external
threat. The book was published in 1995—after the Soviet Union collapsed
but before the Taiwan Straits crisis awoke Tokyo and Washington to the
next geopolitical challenge from China. As long as the United States has
some leading role in underpinning regional and international order, Japan
will be highly incentivized to continue using the alliance and doing what it
can—as Abe did—to shape Washington's choices.

AMERICA AND JAPAN: THE NEW SPECIAL RELATIONSHIP

When Harold Macmillan was serving as liaison to General Dwight D.
Eisenhower in the Mediterranean in 1942, he famously observed to his
British colleague: "We, my dear Crossman, are Greeks in this American

empire. You will find the Americans much as the Greeks found the Romans—great big vulgar, bustling people, more vigorous than we are and also more idle, with more unspoiled virtues, but also more corrupt. We must run A.F.H.Q.[Allied Forces headquarters] as the Greeks ran the operations of the Emperor Claudius."[3] The description might resonate with Japanese officials trying to manage their deepened security relationship with the United States today. Macmillan's quote about the Americans is often cited in histories of what subsequently unfolded between Washington and London: development of the U.S.-UK "special relationship" that steered the West through the Cold War and the collapse of the Soviet Empire. As historians know, that relationship was special in both its closeness and its contentiousness. British and American officials clashed over nuclear weapons, fighter jet development, the 1957 Suez crisis, the Vietnam War, and China. Yet maintaining this closest of bilateral relations received consistent bipartisan support on both sides of the Atlantic, and a high price was paid politically and geostrategically by either ally when it moved on an international issue *without* support from the other.[4]

If there is a new "special relationship" in the unfolding strategic competition with China in the twenty-first century, it is between the United States and Japan. The differences between Japan and the United Kingdom are considerable, of course. Unlike Britain, Japan has no nuclear weapons or reciprocal obligations to defend the United States if it comes under attack. It was Britain and Australia that invoked Article V of their treaties to come to the defense of the United States after 9/11, not Japan. Moreover, as was noted in chapter 6, there are still multiple hurdles to Japan having the special "Five Eyes" intelligence-sharing relationship enjoyed by the United States and the United Kingdom. Furthermore, Britain is a permanent UN Security Council member, and Japan appears unlikely to become one, despite U.S. support. Perhaps no relationship can easily supplant a partnership forged in blood from the Battle of the Atlantic in World War II to the Korean War and Afghanistan. There are probably more British soldiers on duty in the United States today— often commanding Americans—than at any point since the War of 1812 (and thankfully, on our side this time). As of this book's publication, there are no similar arrangements for Japanese officers with the U.S. military.

Yet the strategic relationship between the United States and Japan has a uniqueness all its own in the twenty-first century. Whether Japanese officials see themselves as the Greeks to our Romans, there is no doubt that, of America's allies, Japan has emerged as the most important *thought leader* on China strategy. As was noted at the outset of this volume, Japan is the only U.S. ally that is fully engaged on all aspects of strategic competition with China, and the impact on U.S. policy has been evident. To reiterate: the American strategic framework for Asia is essentially based on the Japanese foreign ministry's FOIP vision; the U.S. International Development Finance Corporation and the U.S. strategy to counter China's Belt and Road Initiative are modeled on and depend on the Japan Bank for International Cooperation; the American strategy for blocking predatory Chinese firms from the 5G market was started in Japan by Japan's Ministry of Economy, Trade and Industry; and the Quad summit was originally Abe's proposal. Where the United States has turned away from its own strategic initiatives—with the Trans-Pacific Partnership (TPP) or the World Trade Organization (WTO), for example—Japan has stepped in to keep those multilateral pillars of regional and global order standing upright until the United States can reengage. The 2020 CSIS survey of thought leaders around the world on China strategy revealed not only that Japanese thinking aligned closely with thought leaders in the United States and Western Europe, but also that no two countries were more closely aligned on everything from deterrence to technology to human rights issues with respect to China as Japan and the United States.[5]

Japan also occupies a position of major influence on Asian regional integration that contrasts with Britain's retreat from Europe after Brexit. While relations with Korea and China are significant impediments, Japan nevertheless enjoys a position as thought leader in Asia that is now as indispensable as Britain's role once was in steering trans-Atlantic interests during Europe's postwar regional integration. Moreover, Japan's thought leadership is now almost entirely aimed at reinforcing the kind of open regional order that American strategists have sought for decades.

When Prime Minister Suga traveled first to Vietnam and Indonesia in October 2020 rather than to the United States, no American commentator fretted about Japan's return to anti-American proposals of the 1990s for "datsu-Bei/Nyu-A" ("separating from America and going into Asia"). Indeed, in an increasingly multipolar Asian order, Japan has emerged as a critical hub among like-minded states in the region. At the end of the Cold War, Secretary of State James Baker called for maintenance of the "hubs and spokes" arrangement of bilateral alliances tied to the United States rather than a new multilateralism to replace those alliances—but Japan is now helping to forge a future of "hubs" and spokes among U.S. allies and partners. This networking of alliances and strategic partnerships reinforces the U.S.-led open regional order even when the United States is not itself the hub in every case.

THE ONLY AMERICANS WE HAVE

As Abe clearly recognized, Japan's strategic success rests heavily on the United States. Macmillan's colleagues reminded him in 1942 that the Greeks who advised the Roman proconsuls were slaves and not masters of their own fate. Macmillan and his colleagues were not slaves, of course, but Britain had no choice but to excel at shaping American strategic decision making in the twentieth century, since a world without American leadership would have been simply untenable for London. As one British foreign secretary is rumored to have said to his European counterparts after hearing their complaints about Washington during the Cold War, "Yes . . . what you say is all true, but they're the only Americans we have." Abe's grand strategy is most impressive for its success in influencing the most important single variable in Japanese foreign policy—the United States of America. Americans should feel no more resentment at this than they would toward Britain, since the objectives of Abe's strategy were largely aligned with the interests of the American people and the price of admission was for Japan to increase its own risk and contribution within the alliance. Hence the observation of one senior U.S. military officer in the Indo-Pacific to me in October 2020 that the United States and Japan have moved from "interoperability to interdependence." Nor should Americans necessarily fear Japanese hedging—aside from the fact that it serves as a warning that the U.S. strategy is itself falling short—since hedging strategies in Japan have been most noteworthy for their emphasis on cooperation with Europe and other U.S. allies in Asia to compensate for American shortcomings.[6] The fact is that this networking of trans-Atlantic and Pacific alliances is also a long-standing objective of U.S. strategy.

Polls cited throughout this volume indicate that Americans increasingly understand the importance of Japan and the alignment of Japanese and American interests. It is less clear whether American foreign policy leaders fully understand the success of Japan's new strategy or its lessons and significance for U.S. strategic competition with China. Most of the foreign policy experts at senior levels of the incoming Biden administration in 2020, while accomplished and experienced, would have been considered Atlanticists earlier in their careers. Many came of age in the Democratic Party during earlier periods of trade friction with Japan. They came back into office in 2021 much more pro-Japan (*shin-nichi*) but not necessarily more knowledgeable about Japan (*chi-nichi*).

There is reason for confidence in the next generation of American foreign policy thought leaders on Asia, who came to professional prominence in think tanks, universities, and government during the decade of Abe's consolidation of Japan's grand strategy. Those who regularly traveled to Southeast Asia or examined regional debates over diplomacy, development, and security will not have missed the impact of Japan in the increasingly competitive environment in the Indo-Pacific. The U.S. military is also finally undergoing its own correction. After years of senior officers being promoted to command for combat experience in the Middle East, leaders of the military services are now increasingly likely to be veterans of the Indo-Pacific theater, where interoperability with Japan would be a high priority. Meanwhile, a new generation of foreign policy leaders in Congress, like Senator Dan Sullivan of Alaska or Representatives Mike Gallagher of Wisconsin or Stephanie Murphy of Florida, are focusing on Japan and other U.S. allies as they prepare for a career that will be consumed by competition with China. In the

American business community there are also experienced veterans of joint ventures with Japanese counterparts at home and abroad. Still, many of the American participants in the U.S.-Japan Business Council are primarily from companies looking at growth in Japan rather than those looking for opportunities for coordinating strategies on China. When briefing the leaders of a major technology-focused business association in 2020, I was surprised to find that none of the participants had engaged in any discussion with their Japanese counterparts about Huawei or predatory Chinese technology policies.

An effective U.S. strategy on China—for businesses, the Pentagon, or the State Department—will depend on working with Japan and knowing Japan's own strategic thinking and impact. Hopefully, this book will help.

As this book was going to print in 2021, the Japanese government was beginning work on a new National Security Strategy (NSS) document to supplant the original 2013 strategy published by Abe at the outset of his term. The new NSS was expected to build on Abe's framework while focusing on shortcomings revealed over the previous eight years in areas such as cybersecurity, defense capabilities, technology competition, and rulemaking. Japan's success in these endeavors will be important not only in competing with China over the medium term, but also in reinforcing the rules and alignments that could possibly bend the region back toward the trajectory of integration, cooperation, and prosperity that initially characterized the twenty-first century. There will be numerous potential obstacles, from demographics to Chinese military expansion, in the way—but there should be no doubt that the world will be safer and more prosperous to the extent that Japan *does* succeed.

NOTES

ACKNOWLEDGMENTS

1. Michael J. Green, *By More than Providence: Grand Strategy and American Power in the Asia Pacific Since 1783* (New York: Columbia University Press, 2017).

INTRODUCTION

1. A survey of Nikkei readers in April 2010 found that 84.7 percent agreed with this criticism of Hatoyama. The corresponding analysis piece by Hiroyuki Akita states that U.S. officials called Hatoyama "untrustworthy." See Hiroyuki Akita, "Bei Seifu ga Kōgen Shinai Hatoyama Shushō e no 'Honne'" [What the U.S. government really thinks of Prime Minister Hatoyama], *Nihon Keizai Shimbun*, April 21, 2010.
2. Richard L. Armitage and Joseph S. Nye, *The U.S.-Japan Alliance: Anchoring Stability in Asia*, Center for Strategic and International Studies, August 2012, https://csis-website -prod.s3.amazonaws.com/s3fs-public/legacy_files/files/publication/120810_Armitage _USJapanAlliance_Web.pdf.
3. Shinzō Abe, "Japan Is Back: By Shinzo Abe, Prime Minister of Japan, February 22, 2013, at CSIS," Ministry of Foreign Affairs of Japan, February 22, 2013, https://www.mofa.go .jp/announce/pm/abe/us_20130222en.html.
4. Dean Acheson, *Present at the Creation: My Years in the State Department* (New York: Norton, 1969).
5. In 2012, Japanese views of China hit an all-time low, with unfavorability up to 84.3 percent from 78.3 percent the previous year; see "Genron NPO Dai Hachi-kai Nitchū Kyodō Yoron Chōsa no Kekka Kōhyō" [Genron NPO announces the results of the eighth Japan-China joint public opinion survey], *Genron NPO*, June 20, 2012, https:// www.genron-npo.net/press/2012/06/npo-10.html.

6. Kenneth N. Waltz, *Theory of International Politics* (Reading, MA: Addison-Wesley, 1979), 168–70.

7. Rex Tillerson, "Defining Our Relationship with India for the Next Century: An Address by U.S. Secretary of State Rex Tillerson" (speech, Center for Strategic and International Studies, Washington, DC, October 18, 2017), https://www.csis.org/analysis/defining -our-relationship-india-next-century-address-us-secretary-state-rex-tillerson; Ankit Panda, "US, Japan, India, and Australia Hold Working-Level Quadrilateral Meeting on Regional Cooperation," *The Diplomat*, November 13, 2017, https://thediplomat.com/2017/11/us -japan-india-and-australia-hold-working-level-quadrilateral-meeting-on-regional -cooperation/.

8. Denghua Zhang, "The Concept of 'Community of Common Destiny' in China's Diplo-macy: Meaning, Motives and Implications," *Asia and the Pacific Policy Studies* 5, no. 2 (May 2018): 196–207.

9. *Asia Power Index 2019: Key Findings*, Lowy Institute, https://power.lowyinstitute.org /downloads/Lowy-Institute-Asia-Power-Index-2019-Key-Findings.pdf.

10. The White House, *National Security Strategy of the United States of America (NSS)* (Washington, DC: White House, 2017), 2–3, https://www.whitehouse.gov/wp-content /uploads/2017/12/NSS-Final-12-18-2017-0905.pdf; Japan Kantei [Prime Minister's Office], *National Security Strategy*, December 17, 2013, http://japan.kantei.go.jp/96_abe/documents /2013/__icsFiles/afieldfile/2013/12/17/NSS.pdf.

11. The phrase is borrowed from Kurt M. Campbell and Jake Sullivan, "Competition With-out Catastrophe: How America Can Both Challenge and Coexist with China," *Foreign Affairs* 98, no. 5 (September/October 2019).

12. Zack Cooper and Hal Brands, "It Is Time to Transform the US-Japan Alliance," *Nikkei Asia*, October 25, 2020, https://asia.nikkei.com/Opinion/It-is-time-to-transform-the -US-Japan-alliance.

13. Mireya Solís, "The Underappreciated Power: Japan After Abe," *Foreign Affairs* 99, no. 6 (November/December 2020): 123–32.

14. Masataka Nakagawa, "Japan Is Aging Faster Than We Think," *East Asia Forum*, Octo-ber 17, 2019, https://www.eastasiaforum.org/2019/10/17/japan-is-aging-faster-than-we -think/; *Annual Report on the Ageing Society [Summary] FY 2019*, Cabinet Office Japan, June 2019, https://www8.cao.go.jp/kourei/english/annualreport/2019/pdf/2019.pdf.

15. "Annual Report on the Labour Force Survey 2018," Statistics Bureau of Japan, http:// www.stat.go.jp/english/data/roudou/report/2018/index.html; "White Paper on Inter-national Economy and Trade 2013," Ministry of Economy, Trade and Industry, updated June 18, 2014, https://www.meti.go.jp/english/report/data/gIT2013maine.html; *Nichi EU EPA ni Tsuite* [About Japan-EU EPA], Ministry of Foreign Affairs of Japan, https:// www.meti.go.jp/policy/trade_policy/epa/epa/eu/pdf/eu_epa_201901.pdf; *Defense White Paper 2018*, Ministry of Defense of Japan, 495.

16. Michael J. Green, *By More than Providence: Grand Strategy and American Power in the Asia Pacific Since 1783* (New York: Columbia University Press, 2017), 2–5.

17. Michael Blaker's classic study of prewar decision making in Japan was replicated in postwar essays by Karel van Wolferen and other critics of Japanese obfuscation. See

Michael Blaker, *Japanese International Negotiating Style* (New York: Columbia University Press, 1977); Karel van Wolferen, *The Enigma of Japanese Power: People and Power in a Stateless Nation* (New York: Vintage, 1989).

18. Quoted in Green, *By More than Providence*, 403.

19. Richard Samuels, *Rich Nation, Strong Army* (Ithaca, NY: Cornell University Press, 1996); Eric Heginbotham and Richard Samuels, "Mercantile Realism and Japanese Foreign Policy," *International Security* 22, no. 4 (Spring 1998): 171–203; Wayne Sandholtz et al., *The Highest Stakes: The Economic Foundations of the Next Security System* (Oxford: Oxford University Press, 1993).

20. See Michael J. Green, *Japan's Reluctant Realism: Foreign Policy Challenges in an Era of Uncertain Power* (New York: Palgrave Macmillan, 2001). The emphasis on Japanese attention to rank and prestige is explained as enduring aspects of Japanese strategic culture in Kenneth Pyle, *Japan Rising* (New York: Public Affairs, 2008), and *The Japanese Question: Power and Purpose in a New Era* (Washington, DC: AEI Press, 1996).

21. Richard K. Betts, "Is Strategy an Illusion?" *International Security* 25, no. 2 (Autumn 2000): 22.

22. Since the publication of *Reluctant Realism*, a number of scholars have presented authoritative accounts of the contestation in Japan over national security ideas and policies, noting the growing impact of external factors on Japanese decision making and institutional change, though not the increasing consensus and coherence in Japanese strategy that emerged in the era of Abe Shinzō. See, for example, Richard J. Samuels, *Securing Japan: Tokyo's Grand Strategy and the Future of East Asia* (Ithaca, NY: Cornell University Press, 2007); Andrew L. Oros, *Japan's Security Renaissance: New Policies and Politics for the Twenty-First Century* (New York: Columbia University Press, 2017); and Sheila A. Smith, *Japan Rearmed: The Politics of Military Power* (Cambridge, MA: Harvard University Press, 2019).

23. The classic illustration of these bureaucratic frictions despite geopolitical alignment remains Richard Neustadt, *Alliance Politics* (New York: Columbia University Press, 1970).

24. The most detailed account of Abe's personal and political journey in English to date is Tobias S. Harris, *The Iconoclast: Shinzo Abe and the New Japan* (London: C. Hurst, 2020).

25. "Abe Seiken wo Hyoka 71 percent" [71 percent positive on Abe's administration], *Asahi Shimbun*, September 24, 2020, https://www.asahi.com/articles/DA3S14609608.html.

26. Bonnie Bley, "Size vs Statecraft: How Japan and India Play the Major Power Game," Lowy Institute, January 6, 2019, https://www.lowyinstitute.org/publications/size-vs-statecraft-how-india-and-japan-play-major-power-game.

27. "Japan's Suga Is Voters' Favorite as Opposition Picks New Leader," Reuters, September 9, 2020, https://www.usnews.com/news/world/articles/2020-09-09/japans-suga-is-voters-favourite-to-succeed-pm-abe-poll.

28. There is still some debate among historians about whether Yamagata conceived of the "line of advantage" himself or borrowed the label somewhat retroactively after hearing the term from Austrian scholar and strategist Lorenz von Stein, who had tutored Meiji

leaders like Yamagata and Ito Hirobumi during their study tours of Europe in the late 1880s. Either way, the concept of shaping the external environment to prevent threats to Japan remained the same—until distorted by militarists and imperial army officers invested in expanding their initial continental toehold in Korea and by Yamagata himself, who decided in 1895 after the defeat of China that Japan would have to "extend" the line of advantage prepare for "leadership in Asia." See Jitsuo Tsuchiyama, "The Balance of Power in Korea, and Japan," *Japan Review* 2, no. 4 (Spring 2019): 29–33; Tomoyuki Muranaka, *Meijiki Nippon ni Okeru Kokubou Senryaku Tenkan no Haikei—Chousen wo 'Riekisen' to Suruni Itaru Made* [The background of the national defense strategy conversion in Japan of the Meiji era—until it comes to make Korea into an "interest line"], *Nihon University Graduate School of Social and Cultural Studies Bulletin*, No. 5 (2004): 100–11, https://atlantic2.gssc.nihon-u.ac.jp/kiyou/pdfo5/5-100-111-muranaka. pdf; Roger F. Hackett, "The Meiji Leaders and Modernization: The Case of Yamagata Aritomo," in *Changing Japanese Attitudes Toward Modernization*, ed. Marius B. Jensen, Robert N. Bellah, et al. (Princeton, NJ: Princeton University Press, 1965), 249.

29. Kitaoka Shinichi, "The Strategy of the Maritime Nation Japan: From Fukuzawa Yukichi to Yoshida Shigeru," in *Conflicting Currents: Japan and the United States in the Pacific*, ed. Williamson Murray and Tomoyuki Ishizu, 39–50 (Santa Barbara, CA: Praeger, 2010).

30. "Japan's Proactive Contribution to Peace," Cabinet Public Relations Office, Government of Japan, Spring 2014, https://www.japan.go.jp/tomodachi/2014/spring2014/japans _proactive_contribution_to_peace.html.

31. The most important explanations of the impact of pacifist norms on Japan's international role are Peter J. Katzenstein and Yukio Okawara, "Japan's National Security: Structures, Norms and Policies," *International Security* 17, no. 4 (Spring 1993): 84–118; Thomas U. Berger, "From Sword to Chrysanthemum: Japan's Culture of Anti-militarism," *International Security* 17, no. 4 (Spring 1993): 119–50; and Andrew L. Oros, *Normalizing Japan: Politics, Identity, and the Evolution of Security Practice* (Stanford, CA: Stanford University Press, 2008).

32. See, for example, Alexis Dudden, "Bullying and History Don't Mix: *Ijime to Rekishi wa Aiirenai*," *Asia-Pacific Journal* 10, no. 54 (December 2012), https://apjjf.org/-Alexis -Dudden/4752/article.html; Linda Sieg, "Japan's Shinzo Abe: Comeback Kid with Conservative Agenda," Reuters, December 16, 2012, https://www.reuters.com/article/us -japan-election-abe/japans-shinzo-abe-comeback-kid-with-conservative-agenda -idUSBRE8BF08A20121216; Shinya Oba, "Abe Seiken: Nagasaki Shichōga Keikaikan, Hikaku Heiwa Kokkawo" [Abe government: Nagasaki mayor shows concern: "Non- nuclear and peaceful country"], *Mainichi Shimbun*, December 19, 2012; "Abe Seiken ni Kyokuu Seijika Fujin Kankoku Medhia ga Kenen" [Ultra-right-wing politicians join Abe government: South Korean government's concern], *Chuo Nippo*, December 12, 2012, https://s.japanese.joins.com/JArticle/165606?sectcode=A10&servcode=A00; "Japan Must Face Up to History in Abe Era," *People's Daily Online*, January 5, 2013, http://en.people.cn/90777/8078951.html.

33. Sheila Smith, *Intimate Rivals: Japanese Domestic Politics and a Rising China* (New York: Columbia University Press, 2014).

1. THE HISTORIC ROOTS OF MODERN JAPANESE GRAND STRATEGY

1. "Opinion Poll on Japan," Ministry of Foreign Affairs of Japan, March 18, 2020, https://www.mofa.go.jp/press/release/press4e_002784.html.

2. Kent E. Calder, "Japanese Foreign Economic Policy Formation: Explaining the Reactive State," *World Politics* 40, no. 4 (July 1988): 517–41.

3. Kanehara Nobukatsu, *Rekishi no Kyōkun: Shippai no Honshitsu to Kokka Senryaku* [The lessons of history: Reasons for defeat and national strategy] (Tokyo: Shinchōsha, 2020); for an English summation, see " 'Rekishi no Kyokun' Author Talk with Prof. Nobukatsu Kanehara," Sasakawa Peace Foundation USA, August 26, 2020, https://spfusa.org/event/rekishi-no-kyokun-author-talk-with-prof-nobukatsu-kanehara/.

4. Sato W., *Nihon no Suigunshi* (Maritime military history of Japan) (Tokyo: Hara Shobo, 1985), 19–20.

5. As late as the 1980s, leading Japanese political scientists continued to argue that Japan's political democracy had to be understood as a modern institution overlaid on a millennia-old feudalistic political culture born of geography. For example, see Junichi Kyōgoku, *Nihon no Seiji* (also translated by Nobutaka Ike as *Political Dynamics of Japan*) (Tokyo: University of Tokyo Press, 1983).

6. William Theodore de Bary, *Nobility and Civility: Asian Ideals of Leadership and the Common Good* (Cambridge, MA: Harvard University Press, 2004), 72.

7. James L. Huffman, *Japan in World History* (New York: Oxford University Press, 2010), 146; Masao Kikuchi and Yujiro Hayami, "Agricultural Growth Against a Land Resource Constraint: A Comparative History of Japan, Taiwan, Korea, and the Philippines," *Journal of Economic History* 38, no. 4 (December 1978): 839–64; Yoshi S. Kuno (Yoshi Saburo), *Japanese Expansion on the Asiatic Continent; A Study in the History of Japan, with Special Reference to Her International Relations with China, Korea, and Russia* (Berkeley: University of California Press, 1937), 9.

8. The Tokugawa shogun cut Japan off from outside commerce to prevent interference in Japan's internal politics; Tokugawa Ieyasu did authorize limited construction of European ships of sail and even an expedition across the Pacific before his successors banned any further oceangoing shipbuilding starting in 1640.

9. Stuart D. B. Picken, *Historical Dictionary of Shinto* (Blue Ridge Summit, PA: Scarecrow, 2010); *Nihonshoki/Kojiki* citations from John Brownlee, *Political Thought in Japanese Historical Writing: From Kojiki (712) to Tokushi Yoron (1712)* (Waterloo, ON: Wilfrid Laurier University Press, 1991), 10; Donald L. Philippi, trans., *Kojiki* (Tokyo: University of Tokyo Press, 1968), 257–58.

10. Citation is from Ihara Takushū, "Chūgoku to Nihon no Kokkōjuritsuno Kigen: Kenzuishi Onono Imoko" [Origin of diplomatic relations between China and Japan: Japan's mission to Sui Onono Imoko], *Ajia Gakka Nenpō* 6 (2012): 27–35; Delmer M. Brown, ed., *The Cambridge History of Japan* (Cambridge: Cambridge University Press, 1993), 182.

11. Watanabe Hiroshi, *A History of Japanese Political Thought, 1600–1901* (Tokyo: International House of Japan, 2012), 288.

12. Watanabe, *A History of Japanese Political Thought*, 283.

13.   Watanabe, *A History of Japanese Political Thought*, 289.

14.   Brendan Simms, *Three Victories and a Defeat: The Rise and Fall of the First British Empire* (New York: Basic Books, 2007), loc. 1236 of 3362 on iPad.

15.   Michael J. Green, *Japan's Reluctant Realism: Foreign Policy Challenges in an Era of Uncertain Power* (New York: Palgrave Macmillan, 2001), 113; Christopher Harding, "Self-Defence and Self-Cultivation in the Genesis of Japanese Imperialism," in *Echoes of Empire: Memory, Identity and Colonial Legacies*, ed. Kalypso Nicolaïdis, Berny Sèbe, and Gabrielle Maas (London: I. B. Tauris, 2015), 175.

16.   Joshua A. Fogel, *The Edwin O. Reischauer Lectures: Articulating the Sinosphere: Sino-Japanese Relations in Space and Time* (Cambridge, MA: Harvard University Press, 2009), 15–16; Brown, *The Cambridge History of Japan*, 206–8.

17.   The Korean peninsula was not only an object of Sino-Japanese competition but also the closest conduit for culture and technology to move from China and even India into Japan. The record of Japan importing learning through Korea goes back to the fourth century. Tumult, war, and Japanese invasions in the fourth to seventh centuries uprooted Korean populations, which intermingled with Japan and brought Buddhism, which had spread to the Baekje from India along the Silk Road.

18.   Nishikawa Joken, *Nihon Suidoku*; cited in Watanabe, *A History of Japanese Political Thought*, 290.

19.   *Kaikoku-Heidan* [Discussion concerning military matters of a maritime nation], (1791; Toyko: Tonansha, 1923), 1:2.

20.   W. G. Beasley, *Japanese Imperialism, 1894–1945* (Oxford: Clarendon, 1987), 28.

21.   Watanabe, *A History of Japanese Political Thought*, 291.

22.   "Hotta Masayoshi's Memorandum on Foreign Policy" [undated, probably late December 1857], in *Select Documents on Japanese Foreign Policy: 1853–1868*, ed. and trans. W. G. Beasley (London: Oxford University Press, 1967), 165–68.

23.   See section titled "Kaigun Kakuchō no Hitsuyō" [The need to expand the navy], in Fukuzawa Yukichi, *Fukuzawa Yukichi Zenshū* [Collected works of Fukuzawa Yukichi], vol.16 (Tokyo: Iwanami, 1971).

24.   See Watanabe, *A History of Japanese Political Thought*, 285.

25.   For instance, Ienaga Saburō criticizes him by pointing out similarities between Nobuhiro's concept and the Greater East Asia Co-Prosperity Sphere; see Saburō Ienaga, *The Pacific War: World War II and the Japanese, 1931–1945* (New York: Pantheon, 1978), 5.

26.   Yoshida Shōin, "Letter to Yamada Uemon," in *Yoshida Shōin Zenshū* [Collection of Yoshida Shōin's work] (Tokyo: Iwanami Shoten, 1940), 284.

27.   Nakae Chōmin, *A Discourse by Three Drunkards on Government*, trans. Nobuko Tsukui (1887; Trumbull, CT: Weatherhill, 1984), 99–100.

28.   Marius Jansen, *Sakamoto Ryoma and the Meiji Restoration* (New York: Columbia University Press, 1964).

29.   John Moore, "The 'Nobody' Who Changed Japan," *Japan Times*, June 8, 1999, https://www.japantimes.co.jp/culture/1999/06/08/books/book-reviews/the-nobody-who-changed-japan; Jun Hongo, "Sakamoto, the Man and the Myth," *Japan Times*, April 27, 2010, https://www.japantimes.co.jp/news/2010/04/27/reference/sakamoto-the-man-and-the-myth.

In a survey conducted by Lifenet Insurance Company in January 2010, 14.2 percent of the 1,000 people polled said Sakamoto Ryōma was most fit to be described as "Japan's version of Barack Obama" because he was innovative and displayed strong leadership that changed the country.

30. Andrew Gordon, *A Modern History of Japan from Tokugawa Times to the Present* (New York: Oxford University Press, 2003), 18, 57.

31. Kaishū Katsu, *Kaishū Sensei Hikawa Seiwa* [The idyllic story of Mr. Kaishū] (Tokyo: Tekka Shoin, 1898).

32. Michael J. Green, *By More than Providence: Grand Strategy and American Power in the Asia Pacific Since 1783* (New York: Columbia University Press, 2017), 70–73.

33. Green, *By More than Providence*, 97.

34. S. C. M. Paine, *The Japanese Empire: Grand Strategy from the Meiji Restoration to the Pacific War* (Cambridge: Cambridge University Press, 2017), 178.

35. Satō Tetsutarō, *Teikoku Kokuboshiron* [On the history of imperial defense] (Tokyo: Tokyo Insatsu Kabushiki Kaisha, 1908).

36. George Alexander Ballard, *The Influence of the Sea on the Political History of Japan* (New York: Dutton, 1921), 295.

37. Akira Iriye, *After Imperialism: The Search for a New Order in the Far East, 1921–1931* (Cambridge, MA: Harvard University Press, 1965), 4, 278, 284; William Wirt Lockwood, *The Economic Development of Japan: Growth and Structural Change* (Princeton, NJ: Princeton University Press, 1954), 63–70.

38. Beasley, *Japanese Imperialism*, 36–37. Charles Schencking also makes a compelling argument that historians make a mistake by lumping the navy in with militarists in opposition to the supposedly liberal political parties. See J. Charles Schencking, *Making Waves: Politics, Propaganda, and the Emergence of the Imperial Japanese Navy, 1868–1922* (Stanford, CA: Stanford University Press, 2005), 77.

39. Hiroyuki Agawa, *The Reluctant Admiral: Yamamoto and the Imperial Navy* (Tokyo: Kodansha International, 1979), 285–86.

40. Ballard, *The Influence of the Sea*, 296.

41. Iokibe Makoto, ed., *The Diplomatic History of Postwar Japan* (New York: Routledge, 2011). Japan's maritime and continental debates over grand strategy also echo those in Britain and the United States. British strategists for centuries debated whether the security of the realm rested on the "wooden walls" of the Royal Navy or on more direct military and diplomatic intervention on the continent of Europe (see Simms, *Three Victories and a Defeat*, 53. U.S. grand strategy toward the Pacific has also been shaped by the tensions between those who argue for an offshore maritime strategy centered on Japan and the first island chain and those who advocate a position secured with China on the continent—a debate that began in 1853 as Commodore Matthew Perry denied the U.S. commissioner in China's request to use his fleet to show the flag and open China during the Taiping Rebellion (Perry instead went to Japan, of course) and one replayed most recently as the Obama administration debated whether to accept Beijing's proposal for a "new model of great power relations" at Japan's expense. The British and American maritime arguments had a pronounced influence on Japan's own

debate, but Japan's late arrival to maritime thinking and the dominance of earlier geographic insularity and emphasis on the sword resulted in a very different outcome.

42. Richard J. Samuels, *Securing Japan: Tokyo's Grand Strategy and the Future of East Asia* (Ithaca, NY: Cornell University Press, 2008), 32.

43. Samuels, *Securing Japan*, 30.

44. See Green, *Japan's Reluctant Realism*, 15–16; John W. Dower, *Empire and Aftermath: Yoshida Shigeru and the Japanese Experience, 1878–1954* (Cambridge, MA: Council on East Asian Studies, Harvard University, 1988), 375, 380, 386, 424–25.

45. For more, see Nathaniel Bowman Thayer, *How the Conservatives Rule Japan* (Princeton, NJ: Princeton University Pres, 1969), 12–13.

46. Hara Yoshihisa, *Kishi Nobusuke—Kensei no Seijika* (Kishi Nobusuke: Power politician), (Tokyo: Iwanami Shoten, 1995), 22, 28–29, 459.

47. Karl Gustafsson, Linus Hagström, and Ulv Hanssen, "Japan's Pacifism Is Dead," *Survival: Global Politics and Strategy* 60, no. 6 (2018): 142. There were important exceptions, including anti-mainstream leader Miki Takeo, who pushed for a more pacifist set of controls on Japanese arms exports and nuclear weapons in the mid-1970s. At times, Japan's choices were debated in the ruling party in ways more evocative of Nakae Chōmin's three drunkards. As the Cold War polarized politics around the world, the LDP also split into warring "study groups" on the future of Japan's foreign policy. In 1964 a group of ninety-eight Diet members formed the Asian Problems Study Group (*Asia Kenkyūkai*) to advocate stronger Japanese support for Taiwan and opposition to the People's Republic of China (PRC). The members of this "A-ken" were opposed by sixty-eight members who formed the Asian-African Problems Study Group ("AA-ken" or *Asia-Africa Mondai Kenkyūkai*) to advocate closer ties to China and the nonaligned world. When Richard Nixon initiated U.S.-China rapprochement in 1971 and Japan rushed the next year to normalize relations with the PRC before the United States did, the distinctions between the two groups became confused. Japan's economy now grew in tandem with China's opening but with Japan seemingly the senior partner—allied with the United States but speaking for Asia—the perfect settlement of the debate that animated Nakae Chōmin's three drunkards.

48. Matake Kamiya, "Nihonteki Genjitsushugisha no Nationalism Kan" [Japanese-style realists' perspective on nationalism), Kokusai Seiji [International politics] 170 (October 2012): 15; Matake Kamiya, "Nihonteki Genjitsushugisha no Kokusai Kikōkan" [The international context of Japanese-style realism] (presentation to Osaka University, December 12, 2016).

49. The author interviewed the younger Kōsaka as a student in the 1980s and heard this refrain, usually as he expressed delight at the opportunity to speak in English about the U.S.-Japan alliance.

50. Kōsaka Masataka, Kaiyokokka Nihon no Kosō [The concept of Japan as a maritime nation] (Tokyo: Chūō Kōron Shinsha, 2008), 175; Inazō Nitobe, Bushido: The Soul of Japan (Philadelphia: Leeds and Biddle, 1900).

51. See, for example, Maruyama Masao, " 'Genjitsu'-shugi no Kansei: Aru HenshŪsha he no Tegami" [The pitfalls of realism: A letter to certain editors], Sekai 77 (May 1952): 122–30.

52. Sakamoto Yoshikazu, "Chūritsu Nihon no Bōei Kōsō" [Defense concept of a neutral Japan], in *Sengo Gaikō no Genten* [The roots of postwar foreign policy], 98–129 (Tokyo: Iwanami Shoten, 2004).

53. Thomas U. Berger, "From Sword to Chrysanthemum: Japan's Culture of Anti-militarism," *International Security* 17, no. 4 (1993): 119–50, https://doi.org/10.2307/2539024.

54. Kamiya Fuji, "Heiwa Kyōzon Tagenka Kokuren" [Peaceful interdependence, diversification, and the United Nations], *Gendai no Me* 5, no. 4 (June 1964); Kamiya Fuji, *Gendai Kokusai Seiji no Shikaku* [Perspectives of contemporary international politics] (Tokyo: Yuhikaku, 1966).

55. Masamichi Inoki, Kōsaka Masataka, and Kazuki Kasuya, *Inoki Masamichi Chosakushū* [The Inoki Masamichi collection] (Tokyo: Rikitomi Shobō, 1985).

56. Kōsaka Masataka, "Genjitsushugisha no Heiwaron" [A realist's views on peace], *Chuo Koron* 78, no. 1 (January 1963): 38–49.

57. See chapter 3 titled "Kokusai Kikō to Heiwa" [International organizations and peace], in Kōsaka Masataka, *Kokusai Seiji* [International politics] (Tokyo: Chūkō Shinsho, 1966).

58. Kōsaka Masataka, *Kaiyō Kokka Nihon no Kōsō* [The concept of Japan as a maritime nation] (Tokyo: Chuô Kôron, 1965), 244–50.

59. Kōsaka *Kaiyō Kokka Nihon no Kōsō*, 354–55.

60. *Sōgō Anzen Hoshō Kenkyū Gurūpu Hōkokusho* [Comprehensive National Security Group Report], July 2, 1980; Sado Akihiro, "Anzen Hoshō Seisaku no Tenkai ni miru Nihon Gaikō no Kisō" [Base layer of Japan's diplomacy through the evolution of national security policy], *Kokusai Mondai* 578 (January/February 2009).

61. I was invited to speak to Okazaki's study group for Japan and also happened to be in Tokyo when Okazaki passed away. His memorial service was a stunning tribute to his influence, with dozens of prominent conservative politicians, intellectuals, business leaders, and Asian diplomats arriving to pay their respects. Sadly, I was the only representative from the United States, despite his enormous influence on the alliance. For more on Okazaki's influence, see Hidekazu Sakai, "Return to Geopolitics: The Changes in Japanese Strategic Narratives," *Asian Perspective* 43, no. 2 (2019): 297–322, https://doi.org /10.1353/apr.2019.0012.

62. For details and an explanation of the Reagan administration's maritime strategy, see Green, *By More than Providence*, 400–8.

63. For more on this period, see Eric Heginbotham and Richard J. Samuels, "Mercantile Realism and Japanese Foreign Policy," *International Security* 22, no. 4 (Spring 1998): 171–203; Wayne Sandholtz, Michale Borrus, et al., *The Highest Stakes: The Economic Foundations of the Next Security System* (Oxford: Oxford University Press, 1992); Green, *Japan's Reluctant Realism*, 1.

64. Cited with permission of Aso Taro, April 8, 2021.

65. Kōsaka's proteges who then advised Abe include: Nakanishi Teramasu of Kyoto University, Tadokoro Masayuki of Keio University, Sakamoto Kazuya of Osaka University, and Nakanishi Hiroshi of Kyoto University.

66. Prominent liberal internationalists in this vein would include Funabashi Yōichi, Inoguchi Takashi, and Fujiwara Kiichi. See Funabashi Yōichi, Michel Oksenberg, and

Heinrich Weiss, *An Emerging China in a World of Interdependence: A Report to the Trilateral Commission* (New York: Trilateral Commission, 1994); Takashi Inoguchi, "Conclusion: A Peace-and-Security Taxonomy," in *North-East Asian Regional Security: The Role of International Institutions*, ed. Takashi Inoguchi and Grant B. Stillman, 181–205 (Tokyo: United Nations University Press, 1997).

67. Uesugi Takashi, *Kantei Hōkai* [Collapse of Prime Minister's Office] (Tokyo: Shinchō-sha, 2007), 19–20.

68. Abe Shinzō, lunch with the author, the Prime Minister's Office (*Kantei*), July 22, 2013.

69. Prominent among these associations were conservative commentators like Sakurai Yoshiko and politicians like Etō Shinichi who pushed within the LDP and directly with Abe for rejection of criticism of Japan's past. See Justin McCurry, "With Friends like These . . . Shinzo Abe's Tactless Colleagues Cause Consternation," *The Guardian*, February 21, 2014, https://www.theguardian.com/world/2014/feb/21/shinzo-abe-tactless-colleagues-japan-prime-minister. In 2015 the U.S. Congressional Research Service also highlighted Abe's association "with groups arguing that Japan has been unjustly criticized for its behavior as a colonial and wartime power. Among the positions advocated by these groups, such as *Nippon Kaigi Kyokai*, are that Japan should be applauded for liberating much of East Asia from Western colonial powers, that the 1946–1948 Tokyo War Crimes tribunals were illegitimate, and that the killings by Imperial Japanese troops during the 1937 'Nanjing massacre' were exaggerated or fabricated." See Congressional Research Service, CRS Report No. RL33436, September 29, 2015, https://crsreports.congress.gov/product/pdf/RL/RL33436/91.

70. Bastian Harth, "Interview–Tomohiko Taniguchi," *E-International Relations*, April 29, 2019, https://www.e-ir.info/2019/04/29/interview-tomohiko-taniguchi/.

71. Kantei National Security Council, *National Security Strategy*, December 17, 2013, http://japan.kantei.go.jp/96_abe/documents/2013/__icsFiles/afieldfile/2013/12/17/NSS.pdf.

72. "A New Vision from a New Japan, World Economic Forum 2014 Annual Meeting, Speech by Prime Minister Abe," *Kantei*, January 22, 2014. http://japan.kantei.go.jp/96_abe/statement/201401/22speech_e.html. What was at stake for Japan as a maritime state mattered for the entire world. As one of his closest thinkers, Kanehara Nobukatsu, put it before returning to the Kantei as deputy national security advisor: "Japan needed to maintain access to international markets via its alignment with the U.S.-led postwar liberal order, a dependable supply of energy, and protected maritime lanes to import and export goods. Japan's status as an island-nation means that the country is vulnerable to any disruptions of the sea lanes around the country, as most of its imports will come via maritime commerce. Japan's concern with China's militarization of the South China Sea reflects Tokyo's concern regarding this vulnerability." See Nobukatsu Kanehara, "Kokka Kokueki Kachito Gaikô Anzenhoshô" [Nation, national interest, value, diplomacy, and national security], in *Ronshû Nihon no Gaikô to Sôgôteki Anzenhoshô* [Collection of essays: Japanese diplomacy and comprehensive national security], ed. Shotaro Yachi, 17–56 (Tokyo: Wedge, 2011).

2. CHINA

Yoshida's line, cited in the epigraph to this chapter, in Japanese was "kimitachi wa kore-kara wa chuugoku wo yoku minasai," and it was his message to the entering Ministry of Foreign Affairs (MOFA) class of 1961, conveyed to me by Katō Ryōzō, MOFA class of 1965, who heard it repeatedly from his seniors. With permission from Ambassador Katō on April 9, 2021.

1. "End Drift to War in the East China Sea," *Financial Times*, January 23, 2014, https://www.ft.com/content/7d713b60-8425-11e3-b72e-00144feab7de.

2. M. Taylor Fravel, "International Relations Theory and China's Rise: Assessing China's Potential for Territorial Expansion," *International Studies Review* 12, no. 4 (December 2010): 505; see also Steven E. Miller, "Introduction: The Sarajevo Centenary—1914 and the Rise of China," in *The Next Great War? The Roots of World War I and the Risk of U.S.-China Conflict*, ed. Richard N. Rosecrance and Steven E. Miller (Cambridge, MA: MIT Press, 2014).

3. "Why the China-US-Japan Balance of Power Is So Vital," *Straits Times*, September 13, 1997; see also "How US, Japan Can Help Integrate China into the World Community," *Straits Times*, November 20, 1996.

4. Quoted in Henry A. Kissinger, *A World Restored: Metternich, Castlereagh, and the Problems of Peace* (Boston: Houghton Mifflin, 1973), 33. Originally from Viscount Castlereagh, *Correspondence, Dispatches, and Other Papers*, ed. Marquess of Londonderry, 12 vols. (London, 1848–52) 9:474, April 19, 1814.

5. Yuichi Hosoya, *Kokusai Chitsujo* [The international order] (Tokyo: Chuko Shinsyo, 2013), 139.

6. Quoted in Kenneth Bourne, *The Foreign Policy of Victorian England, 1830–1902* (Oxford: Oxford University Press, 1970), 388. The original text is from Derby's Ministerial Statement in the House of Lords, July 9, 1866.

7. Hosoya, *Kokusai Chitsujo*, 178.

8. Yukiko Koshiro, *Imperial Eclipse: Japan's Strategic Thinking About Continental Asia Before August 1945* (Ithaca, NY: Cornell University Press, 2013), 39.

9. Quoted in Ian H. Nish, *The Anglo-Japanese Alliance: The Diplomacy of Two Island Empires, 1894–1907* (London: Bloomsbury Academic, 1985), 378.

10. John W. Dower, *Empire and Aftermath: Yoshida Shigeru and the Japanese Experience, 1878–1954* (Cambridge, MA: Harvard University Press, 1979), 37.

11. On Yoshida and Europe, see Valdo Ferretti, "In the Shadow of the San Francisco Settlement: Yoshida Shigeru's Perception of Communist China and Anglo-Japanese Relations," *Japan Forum* 15, no. 3 (2003): 425–34. President Dwight D. Eisenhower and his vice president, Richard M. Nixon, decided to give Kishi some leeway to establish informal trade with China in the late 1950s because they trusted the Japanese leader's anticommunist credentials. Nancy Bernkopf Tucker, *The China Threat: Memories, Myths, and Realities in the 1950s* (New York: Columbia University Press, 2012), 136–37.

12. Michael J. Green, *By More than Providence: Grand Strategy and American Power in the Asia Pacific Since 1783* (New York: Columbia University Press, 2017), 371.

13. Michael J. Green, *Japan's Reluctant Realism: Foreign Policy Challenges in an Era of Uncertain Power* (New York: Palgrave Macmillan, 2001), 79–81.

14. Examples of the collapse theory include Toshiya Tsugami, *Chūgoku Taitōno Shūen* [End of China's rise] (Tokyo: Nikkei, 2013) (written by a former Ministry of Economy, Trade and Industry [METI] official); Naoki Tanaka, *Chūgoku Daiteitai* [China, the great stagnation] (Tokyo: Nikkei, 2016) (written by a head of the Center for International Public Policy Studies (CIPPS), an independent think tank).

15. "Tanaka Moto Shushō, Kangeki no Namida—Kō Sōshoki ga Hōmon 'Taisetsuna Furuki Yūjin'" [Former prime minister Tanaka moved to tears—General Secretary Jiang visits "an important, old friend"], *Nihon Keizai Shimbun*, April 8, 1992.

16. Green, *Japan's Reluctant Realism*, 96–98.

17. For coverage of Koizumi's Marco Polo Bridge visit on October 9, see "Hōchuno Koizumi Shushō Rokokyōde Aitōnoi, Shinryakuno Giseishani Owabi" [Prime Minister Koizumi expressing his condolences and apology toward victims of Japan's aggression at Marco Polo Bridge during his China visit], *Mainichi Shimbun*, October 9, 2001.

For coverage of Koizumi's Yasukuni visit on August 14, see "Koizumi Shushō Yasukuni wo Maedaoshi Sampai" [Prime Minister Koizumi visited Yasukuni ahead of schedule], *Asahi Shimbun*, August 14, 2001; "Dakyō no Sue no Yasukuni Jinja '13-nichi Sampai'" [Yasukuni Shrine visit on the 13th, after a compromise], *Nihon Keizai Shimbun*, August 14, 2001; "Koizumi Shushō ga Yasukuni Jinja Sampai '15-nichi' Sake Maedaoshi" [Ahead of schedule Prime Minister Koizumi visited Yasukuni Shrine, avoiding "the 15th"], *Yomiuri Shimbun*, August 14, 2001.

18. James Manicom, *Bridging Troubled Waters: China, Japan, and Maritime Order in the East China Sea* (Washington, DC: Georgetown University Press, 2014), 92.

19. Sheila Smith, *Intimate Rivals: Japanese Domestic Politics and a Rising China* (New York: Columbia University Press, 2015), 101, 118.

20. "Joint Statement Between the Government of Japan and the Government of the People's Republic of China on Comprehensive Promotion of a 'Mutually Beneficial Relationship Based on Common Strategic Interests,'" Ministry of Foreign Affairs of Japan, May 7, 2008, https://www.mofa.go.jp/region/asia-paci/china/joint0805.html.

21. Nicholas Szechenyi, "China and Japan: A Resource Showdown in the East China Sea?" *National Interest*, August 10, 2015, https://nationalinterest.org/blog/the-buzz/china-japan-resource-showdown-the-east-china-sea-13540; *Japan-China Joint Press Statement: Cooperation Between Japan and China in the East China Sea*, Ministry of Foreign Affairs, June 18, 2008, https://www.mofa.go.jp/files/000091726.pdf; *The Current Status of Chinese Unilateral Development of Natural Resources in the East China Sea*, Ministry of Foreign Affairs, March 21, 2020, https://www.mofa.go.jp/files/000091726.pdf.

22. *Asahi Shimbun*'s poll the day after the 2009 election showed that 81 percent of voters thought the DPJ won because people wanted a change of government, while only 38 percent responded that the DPJ victory was due to its policy. For further details, see Michael J. Green, "Japan's Confused Revolution," *Washington Quarterly* 33, no. 1 (January 2010): 3–19; Michael J. Green, "The Democratic Party of Japan and the Future of the U.S.-Japan Alliance," *Journal of Japanese Studies* 37, no. 1 (January 1, 2011): 91–116.

23. Shingo Ito, "Japan's New PM Proposes East Asian Community to China," *Taiwan News*, September 23, 2009.

24. On China's response, see "Chinese Premier Urges Japan to Release Chinese Skipper Immediately, Unconditionally," *Xinhua*, September 22, 2010; Sachiko Sakamaki, "Four Japanese Held in China as Boat Tensions Escalate," *Bloomberg Business*, September 23, 2010; Keith Bradsher, "Amid Tensions, China Blocks Vital Exports to Japan," *New York Times*, September 22, 2010; "U.S. Says China Must Clarify Rare Earth Exports," *USA Today*, October 28, 2010.

   On Japan's response, see Ministry of Foreign Affairs of Japan, "Recent Developments in Japan-China Relations: Basic Facts on the Senkaku Islands and the Recent Incident" (slides, October 2010); Krisanne Johnson, "Q&A: Japanese Foreign Minister Seiji Maehara on China, the Yen," *Wall Street Journal*, September 25, 2010.

   On the release of the Chinese captain, see Martin Fackler and Ian Johnson, "Japan Retreats with Release of Chinese Boat Captain," *New York Times*, September 24, 2010; Ayai Tomisawa and Jeremy Page, "Japan-China Tensions Enter New Phase," *Wall Street Journal*, September 26, 2010; "Kan Rejects Beijing's Demand for Apology," *Japan Times*, September 27, 2010.

   For further details on the 2010 Senkaku incident, see Manicom, *Bridging Troubled Waters*; Michael Green, Kathleen Hicks, Zack Cooper, John Schaus, and Jake Douglas, *Countering Coercion in Maritime Asia* (Washington, DC: Center for Strategic and International Studies, 2017), 66–94.

25. "Tokyo to Buy Disputed Islands, Says Governor Ishihara," *BBC News*, April 17, 2012, https://www.bbc.com/news/world-asia-17747934; "Senkaku 3-tōwo Kokuyūka" [Government to nationalize three Senkaku Islands], *Nihon Keizai Shimbun*, September 11, 2012; Tsuyoshi Sunohara, *Antō Senkaku Kokuyūka* [Secret feud: The national purchase of the Senkakus] (Tokyo: Shinchōsha, 2013).

   On China's response, see *Defense of Japan 2013* (Tokyo: Japan Ministry of Defense, 2013), 172–73; "Chūgokukini Kinkyū Hasshin Saita Kūji, 12gatsu madeni 160kai" [Most aircraft scrambles against China by the Japanese Air Self-Defense Forces, 160 times by December], *Asahi Shimbun*, January 25, 2013.

26. Green, *By More than Providence*, 477; Nicholas Kristof, "Treaty Commitments; Would You Fight for These Islands?" *New York Times*, October 20, 1996; Larry A. Niksch, "Senkaku (Diaoyu) Islands Dispute: The U.S. Legal Relationship and Obligations," EveryCRSReport.com (website), September 30, 1996.

27. "Biden Affirms Security Treaty Applies to Senkaku Islands in Suga Call," *Nikkei Asia*, November 12, 2020, https://asia.nikkei.com/Politics/International-relations/Indo-Pacific/Biden-affirms-security-treaty-applies-to-Senkaku-Islands-in-Suga-call.

28. For Japanese perspectives on China's grey zone and salami slicing tactics, see Tetsuo Kotani, "The Senkaku Islands and the U.S.-Japan Alliance: Future Implications for the Asia-Pacific," Project 2049 Institute, March 14, 2013, https://project2049.net/2013/03/14/the-senkaku-islands-and-the-u-s-japan-alliance-future-implications-for-the-asia-pacific/; Satoru Mori, "Countering Beijing's Unilateral Revisionist Actions in the East China Sea: The Case for a Restraint Compellence Approach," in *East China*

Sea Tensions: Perspectives and Implications, ed. Richard Pearson (Washington, DC: The Maureen and Mike Mansfield Foundation, 2014), 51–58; Jesse Johnson, "Chinese Senkaku Swarm Tactic Spells Trouble for Japan," *Japan Times*, August 7, 2016, https://www .japantimes.co.jp/news/2016/08/07/national/politics-diplomacy/senkaku-swarm-tactic -spells-trouble-tokyo/#.Xy1rvUkpDso; Lyle J. Morris, Michael J. Mazarr, Jeffrey W. Hornung, Stephanie Pezard, Anika Binnendijk, and Marta Kepe, *Gaining Competitive Advantage in the Gray Zone: Response Options for Coercive Aggression Below the Threshold of Major War* (Santa Monica, CA: RAND Corporation, 2019), https://www.rand .org/pubs/research_reports/RR2942.html.

29.   Shinzo Abe, *A New Era Requires New Political Will: An Address by the Honorable Shinzo Abe, Former Prime Minister of Japan*, Brookings Institution, April 17, 2009, 7, https:// www.brookings.edu/wp-content/uploads/2012/04/20090417_abe.pdf.

30.   *Remarks by Former Japanese Prime Minister Shinzō Abe*, The Hudson Institute, October 15, 2010, 5, https://www.hudson.org/content/researchattachments/attachment/824 /abe_final.pdf.

31.   On public polls: The 2010 Pew survey showed that 69 percent of Japanese respondents had unfavorable views of China. For further details, see *Obama More Popular Abroad Than at Home, Global Image of U.S. Continues to Benefit*, Pew Research Center, June 17, 2010, 51, https://www.pewresearch.org/wp-content/uploads/sites/2/2010/06/Pew-Global-Attitudes -Spring-2010-Report-June-17-11AM-EDT.pdf.

On elites: The 2009 CSIS survey of elites showed that 51 percent of Japanese respondents viewed China as a threat to peace and stability in the next ten years. For further details, see Bates Gill, Michael Green, Kiyoto Tsuji, and William Watts, *Strategic Views on Asian Regionalism: Survey Results and Analysis*, Center for Strategic and International Studies, February 2009, 7, https://www.csis.org/analysis/strategic -views-asian-regionalism.

32.   *National Security Strategy, Kantei*, December 17, 2013, 12, https://www.cas.go.jp/jp/siryou /131217anzenhoshou/nss-e.pdf.

33.   *Defense of Japan 2015* (Tokyo: Japan Ministry of Defense, 2015), 43–45, https://www.mod .go.jp/e/publ/w_paper/pdf/2015/DOJ2015_1-1-3_web.pdf; Smith, *Intimate Rivals*, 232–33.

34.   Itsunori Onodera, "On the Publication of *Defense of Japan 2018*," in *Defense of Japan 2018* (Tokyo: Japan Ministry of Defense, 2018), https://www.mod.go.jp/e/publ/w_paper /pdf/2018/DOJ2018_Full_1130.pdf.

35.   *Defense of Japan 2018*, 3, 106–7.

36.   *Nippon no Boei 2019* [Defense of Japan 2019] (Tokyo: Japan Ministry of Defense, 2019), 274. Some experts note that Japan is more likely than other countries to scramble when intruders approach, but even allowing for that higher state of readiness, the increase was noteworthy and corresponded with independent assessments by the RAND Corporation and others. See, for example, Edmund J. Burke, Timothy R. Heath, Jeffrey W. Hornung, Logan Ma, Lyle J. Morris, and Michael S. Chase, *China's Military Activities in the East China Sea: Implications for Japan's Air Self-Defense Forces* (Santa Monica, CA: RAND Corporation, 2018), https://www.rand.org/pubs/research_reports/RR2574 .html.

37. "Remote Control: Japan's Evolving Senkakus Strategy," Asia Maritime Transparency Initiative (AMTI), Center for Strategic and International Studies, July 29, 2020, https://amti.csis.org/remote-control-japans-evolving-senkakus-strategy/.

38. Hideshi Tokuchi, "Will Japan Fight in a Taiwan Contingency: An Analysis of the 2021 Defense White Paper of Japan," The Prospect Foundation, August 20, 2021, https://www.pf.org.tw/article-pfen-2089-7283.

39. Cited with permission of Katō Ryōzō, April 9, 2021.

40. Green, *Japan's Reluctant Realism*, 80–82; "Taichū Enshakkan Hōshiki Minaoshi" [Reviewing the yen loan process], *Nihon Keizai Shimbun*, January 1, 1995; "Kaku Jikken Mondai" [The nuclear test problem], *Asahi Shimbun*, May 20, 1995.

41. "Chūgoku Shushō Senkaku 'Nihonga Nusunda' Potsudamu de Enzetsu" [Chinese premier: "Japan stole" Senkaku, during the speech in Potsdam], *Nihon Keizai Shimbun*, May 27, 2013; Kimie Hara, "The Post-War Japanese Peace Treaties and the China's Ocean Frontier Problems," *American Journal of Chinese Studies* 11, no. 1 (April 2004): 1–24.

42. Green, *Japan's Reluctant Realism*, 229–69.

43. William W. Grimes, "The Asian Monetary Fund Reborn? Implications of Chiang Mai Initiative Multilateralization," *Asia Policy*, no. 11 (January 2011): 79–104; C. Randall Henning, "The Future of the Chiang Mai Initiative: An Asian Monetary Fund?" Peterson Institute for International Economics, Policy Brief 09–5, February 2009.

44. The agreement was reached at the twelfth ASEAN+3 Finance Ministers' Meeting in Bali, Indonesia, on May 3, 2009. For more information, see "The Joint Media Statement of the 12th ASEAN Plus Three Finance Ministers' Meeting Bali, Indonesia, 3 May 2009," Association of Southeast Asian Nations, October 10, 2012, https://asean.org/?static_post=the-joint-media-statement-of-the-12th-asean-plus-three-finance-ministers-meeting-bali-indonesia-3-may-2009-2; Chalongphob Sussangkarn, *The Chiang Mai Initiative Multilateralization: Origin, Development and Outlook*, ADBI Working Paper 230, Asian Development Bank Institute, July 2010, 9, https://www.adb.org/sites/default/files/publication/156085/adbi-wp230.pdf.

45. "ASEAN wa kikini kessokuwo" [ASEAN should unite in times of crisis], *Nikkei Shimbun*, April 9, 2020.

46. Kitaoka Shinichi, "Kokuren Taishi Gemba Karano Teigen: Joninrijikokuiriwa Nihonga Hatasubeki Sekinindearu" [UN ambassador's recommendation from the field: Joining the permanent members is a responsibility Japan should fulfill], Japan Ministry of Foreign Affairs, January 2005, https://www.mofa.go.jp/mofaj/press/iken/05/0501.html; "Ampori Kaikakuwa Shushō Sentōni: Kikokushita Kitaoka Shin'ichi Kokuren Jiseki Taishi" [UN Security Council reform should be headed by PM: by Shin'ichi Kitaoka, who returned from deputy permanent representative of Japan to the UN], *Asahi Shimbun*, September 12, 2006.

47. On the East Asia Vision Group, see "Ajia Tsūka Dekiruka? ASEAN+3 de Shikisha ga Miraizu" [Is "the Asian currency" possible? Experts at ASEAN+3 mapping the future], *Asahi Shimbun*, November 6, 2001; Japan Ministry of Foreign Affairs, *Towards an East Asian Community: Region of Peace, Prosperity and Progress*, East Asia Vision Group

Report 2001, https://www.mofa.go.jp/region/asia-paci/report2001.pdf; on the East Asian Community, see Hisatsugu Nagao, "East Asian Community Closer to Reality," *Nikkei Weekly*, July 12, 2004.

48. Green, *By More than Providence*, 512.

49. Green, *By More than Providence*, 511.

50. For the 2009 survey, see Gill et al., *Strategic Views on Asian Regionalism*, 8; for the 2015 survey, see Michael J. Green and Nicholas Szechenyi, *Power and Order in Asia: A Survey of Regional Expectations* (Washington, DC: Center for Strategic and International Studies, July 2014), https://csis-prod.s3.amazonaws.com/s3fs-public/legacy_files/files/publication/140605_Green_PowerandOrder_WEB.pdf.

51. Liu Xiaoming, "China and Britain Won the War Together," *The Telegraph*, January 1, 2014, https://www.telegraph.co.uk/comment/10546442/Liu-Xiaoming-China-and-Britain-won-the-war-together.html.

52. "Abe Shushō Rekishi Ninshikide Murayama Danwa Keishō" [Prime Minister Abe to follow "Murayama Statement" on history], *Yomiuri Shimbun*, October 3, 2006.

    After the trip, Abe at the press conference said that "Japan . . . in the past has caused tremendous damage and suffering to the people of the Asian countries, and left scars in those people. This feeling is shared by the people who have lived these 60 years and is a feeling that I also share." "Press Conference by Prime Minister Shinzo Abe Following His Visit to China," *Kantei*, October 8, 2006, https://japan.kantei.go.jp/abespeech/2006/10/08chinapress_e.html.

53. In a July 2013 interview, then special advisor to the cabinet Yachi Shotaro said Abe was interested in resuming dialogues with China. "Chikyūwo Fukansuru Abe Gaikō Yachi Shōtarō Naikaku Sambō Intabyū" [Abe diplomacy that takes a panoramic perspective of the world map: Interview with Yachi Shotaro, the special advisor to the cabinet], *nippon.com*, July 5, 2013, https://www.nippon.com/ja/currents/d00089/.

    In April 2014, Prime Minister Abe met with a son of Hu Yaobang at Kantei, and in September 2014 he said he wanted to improve Sino-Japanese relations. "Shushō Ko Ko Yoho Chōnanto Yōkani Kidan" [Prime minister met with a son of late Hu Yaobang on the 8th], *Nihon Keizai Shimbun*, April 16, 2014; "Shushō Nicchū Kankei 'Kaizen Shitai' " [Prime minister: "Want to improve" Japan-China relations], *Kyodo News*, September 23, 2014.

    In July 2014 former prime minister Fukuda privately met with Xi Jinping in China to discuss improving Sino-Japanese relations. "Fukuda Motoshushōto Shūshuseki Kaidan" [Former prime minister Fukuda meeting with President Xi], *Asahi Shimbun*, August 3, 2014; Fukuda again met with Xi in October 2014 to lay the foundation for the November summit: "Fukudashi Shū Kinpeito Kaidan" [Fukuda meeting with Xi Jinping], *Asahi Shimbun*, October 30, 2014.

54. The Pew Research Center poll conducted in Spring 2014 showed that in India, the United States, Vietnam, Malaysia, Indonesia, the Philippines, and Thailand, the number of people who responded that they had confidence in Abe to do the right thing regarding world affairs was higher than the number who had confidence in Xi Jinping. Notably, in the United States, while 28 percent responded that they had confidence in

Xi Jinping, 49 percent responded that they had confidence in Abe Shinzō. For further details, see *Global Opposition to U.S. Surveillance and Drones, but Limited Harm to America's Image: Many in Asia Worry About Conflict with China*, Pew Research Center, July 14, 2014, https://www.pewresearch.org/global/wp-content/uploads/sites/2/2014/07/2014-07-14_Balance-of-Power.pdf.

55.   "Both sides recognized that they had different views as to the emergence of tense situations in recent years in the waters of the East China Sea, including those around the Senkaku Islands, and shared the view that, through dialogue and consultation, they would prevent the deterioration of the situation, establish a crisis management mechanism and avert the rise of unforeseen circumstances." See "Regarding Discussions Toward Improving Japan-China Relations," Ministry of Foreign Affairs of Japan, November 7, 2014, https://www.mofa.go.jp/a_o/c_m1/cn/page4e_000150.html.

56.   Green, *Japan's Reluctant Realism*, 101.

57.   According to Japan External Trade Organization (JETRO) statistics, the total amount of Japan's outward foreign direct investment (FDI) from 1987 to 2004 was $29.73 billion. "Japan's Outward and Inward Foreign Direct Investment," Japan External Trade Organization, https://www.jetro.go.jp/en/reports/statistics.html.

58.   In a typical experience, sake makers from Tohoku began major exports to China because of its growing middle class. "Michinoku Kuramoto no Chōsen Sake Urikome Kokunai Teimei Beidewa Shinchō" [A quest of Tohoku sake breweries: Promoting "SAKE" as the domestic market stagnates and the U.S. market grows], *Nihon Keizai Shimbun*, December 7, 2005. Nissan, Mazda, and Mitsubishi also targeted a growing market for luxury cars; see "Kōkyūshade Nerau Daishijō Juyō Tayōkani Taiō Pekin Mōtāshō" [Beijing auto show targets a growing market through luxury cars, in reaction to the diverse demand], *Asahi Shimbun*, June 10, 2004.

59.   "China Apologizes to Japan After Minister's Car Attacked," Agence France-Presse, August 9, 2004.

60.   "FY 2019 Survey on the International Operations of Japanese Firms," Japan External Trade Organization (JETRO), (slides, February 27, 2020), 15, https://www.jetro.go.jp/ext_images/en/reports/survey/pdf/jafirms2019-rev.pdf; James Brooke, "China's Economic Brawn Unsettles Japanese," *New York Times*, June 27, 2005; Ho Ai Li, "Japanese Investors Pick ASEAN over China," *Straits Times*, October 24, 2012.

61.   Keith Bradsher, "Amid Tension, China Blocks Vital Exports to Japan," *New York Times*, September 22, 2010.
      After China's embargo of rare earth materials in 2010, Japan joined the United States and European Union in launching a WTO dispute settlement case against China in May 2012. For more, see Smith, *Intimate Rivals*, 192, 201–2.

62.   Kiyoyuki Seguchi, "FDI Toward China: Japanese Companies Becoming More Aggressive," Canon Institute for Global Studies, March 11, 2019, https://cigs.canon/en/article/20190311_5631.html.

63.   Japan Bank for International Cooperation, *Survey Report on Overseas Business Operations by Japanese Manufacturing Companies*, November 26, 2018, 8, https://www.jbic.go.jp/en/information/press/press-2018/pdf/1126-011628_2.pdf; Japan External Trade

Organization, *2018 JETRO Survey on Business Conditions of Japanese Companies in Asia and Oceania*, December 20, 2018, 42, https://www.jetro.go.jp/ext_images/en/reports /survey/pdf/rp_firms_asia_oceania2018.pdf.

64. Shino Yuasa, "Chinese Tourists Flock to Japan, Lift Weak Economy," Associated Press, June 29, 2010; Anna Fifield, "In Japan, Chinese Tourists Are a Welcome Boost—If a Loud, Messy One," *Washington Post*, February 19, 2015. According to the 2019 white paper published by the Ministry of Land, Infrastructure, Transport and Tourism, the number of tourists visiting Japan in 2018 was over 30 million, the highest record. In 2018, while those from China consisted of 26.9 percent of total visitors, their spending consisted of 34.2 percent (1.5 trillion yen) of total visitors. For more details, see *Reiwa Gannen Kankō Hakusho* [2019 Tourism white paper], Ministry of Land, Infrastructure, Transport and Tourism, http://www.mlit.go.jp/common/001294465.pdf.

65. Satoshi Sugiyama, "With Xi Visit Now Delayed, Coronavirus Threatens to Spoil Abe's 2020," *Japan Times*, March 6, 2020. https://www.japantimes.co.jp/news/2020/03/06 /national/xis-japan-visit-delayed-coronavirus-ruin-abes-year/#.XqJo5m4pA0o; Daniel Leussink, "Japan Warns of Coronavirus Hit on Tourism but Keeps 40 mln Visitor Target," Reuters, February 19, 2020, https://www.reuters.com/article/us-china-health -japan-tourism/japan-warns-of-coronavirus-hit-on-tourism-but-keeps-40-mln-visitor -target-idUSKBN20D0NR.

66. Green, *Japan's Reluctant Realism*, 97.

67. Tsukasa Hadano, "Japanese Government Split over China Policy," *Nikkei Asia*, July 8, 2017, https://asia.nikkei.com/Politics/Japanese-government-split-over-China-policy; "Nikaishi Dokujino Taichū Gaikō de Sonzaikan, Abeshushō tono Ondosa, Heigaimo" [Nikai's presence through his distinct China diplomacy, difference with PM Abe may cause a negative effect], *Jiji*, April 24, 2019.

68. "Chairman Nakanishi's Statements and Comments at His Press Conference," Keidanren, October 24, 2018, https://www.keidanren.or.jp/en/speech/kaiken/2018/1024.html #p5; "Nicchū Keizai Kyōrokude Kaizen Kyōchō Shūshuseki Rainen Hōnichino Hōkō" [Japan and China emphasize the improved relations through economic cooperation, President Xi to visit Japan next year], *Asahi Shimbun*, October 27, 2018.

69. Seguchi, "FDI Toward China."

70. Martin A. Weiss, *Asian Infrastructure Investment Bank (AIIB)*, Congressional Research Service, February 3, 2017, 1, https://fas.org/sgp/crs/row/R44754.pdf.

71. See Ministry of Foreign Affairs of Japan, "Prime Minister Abe Visits China," October 26, 2018, https://www.mofa.go.jp/a_o/c_m1/cn/page3e_000958.html; Shi Jiangtao, "China-Japan Ties at 'Historic Turning Point' After Shinzo Abe's Visit, but Can the Goodwill Hold?" *South China Morning Post*, October 28, 2018, https://www.scmp .com/news/china/diplomacy/article/2170469/china-japan-ties-historic-turning-point -after-shinzo-abes-visit.

72. "Japan's Infrastructure Development Strategy: Supporting a Free and Open Indo-Pacific," Center for Strategic and International Studies, October 17, 2019. https:// www.csis.org/events/japans-infrastructure-development-strategy-supporting-free -and-open-indo-pacific.

73. Wayne Morrison, *The Made in China 2025 Initiative: Economic Implications for the United States*, Congressional Research Service, updated April 12, 2019; "Chūgoku Shushō 'Seizō Kyōkokue Tenkan'" [Chinese prime minister's "shift to manufacturing powerhouse"], *Nihon Keizai Shimbun*, March 5, 2015.

74. See Ministry of Internal Affairs and Communications, "Dai 5 sedai ido tsushin shisutemu no donyu no tame no tokutei kichikyoku no kaisetsu keikaku ni kakaru nintei shinsei no uketsuke kekka" [Results of acceptance of applications for authorization of establishment plans for specified base stations for diffusion of 5G mobile communications systems], February 26, 2019, http://www.soumu.go.jp/menu_news/s-news /01kiban14_02000375.html; Yomiuri Shimbun, "Japan to Ban Huawei, ZTE from Govt Contracts," Reuters, December 6, 2018, https://www.reuters.com/article/japan-china -huawei/japan-to-ban-huawei-zte-from-govt-contracts-yomiuri-idUSL4N1YB6JJ; Isabel Reynolds and Emi Nobuhiro, "China Says Unfair Treatment of Huawei Could Damage Japan Ties," *Bloomberg*, March 29, 2019, https://www.bloomberg.com/news /articles/2019-03-29/china-says-unfair-treatment-of-huawei-could-damage-japan-ties.

75. Simon Denyer, "Japan Effectively Bans China's Huawei and ZTE from Government Contracts, Joining U.S.," *Washington Post*, December 10, 2018, https://www.washingtonpost .com/world/asia_pacific/japan-effectively-bans-chinas-huawei-zte-from-government -contracts-joining-us/2018/12/10/748fe98a-fc69-11e8-ba87-8c7facdf6739_story.html.

76. "Gaishi Kisei Seifu Kanyo Tsuyomeru Chūgoku Nentō ni Gijutsu Hogo" [Enhanced government involvement in the foreign exchange regulations for protecting technology with China in mind], *Nihon Keizai Shimbun*, October 9, 2019, https://www.mof .go.jp/english/international_policy/fdi/kanrenshiryou_20200325.pdf.

77. Alexandra Yoon-Hendricks, "Congress Strengthens Review of Chinese and Other Investments," *New York Times*, August 1, 2018.

78. "Japan to Pay Firms to Leave China, Relocate Production Elsewhere as Part of Coronavirus Stimulus," *South China Morning Post*, April 8, 2020. Takashi Tsuji and Kazuhiro Furuyama, "Japan Preps First Subsidy to Company Moving Production Out of China," *Nikkei Asia*, April 21, 2020, https://asia.nikkei.com/Spotlight/Coronavirus/Japan-preps -first-subsidy-to-company-moving-production-out-of-China; Japanese Ministry of Economy, Trade, and Industry, "Reiwa Ninendo Hosei Yosanan No Jigyo Gaiyo" [Overview of supplementary budget for FY2020] (slides, April 2020), 24.

79. "Korona de Seisan Kaiki Hojokin Kyōsōritsu 11bai Masuku ya Iyakuhin" [As the coronavirus promotes reshoring of production, applications for the government subsidy swell to 11 times the budget, many in mask and medical equipment producers], *Nihon Keizai Shimbun*, September 8, 2020.

80. Takashi Shiraishi, "Abe Is Redefining Japan's China Policy for a Generation," *Nikkei Asia*, February 12, 2020.

81. River Davis, "U.S. Allies Capture China Tech Business Despite Washington's Curbs: Huawei Procures 5G Telecommunications Gear from Japan as Beijing Pushes for Global Edge," *Wall Street Journal*, June 29, 2020.

82. "Mapping the Future of U.S. China Policy," Center for Strategic and International Studies, 2020, https://chinasurvey.csis.org/.

83. "Beichū Tairitsu Shijō Yurasu Kiokushia Jōjō Enki Yushutsukiseini Kenen Kakkyōno Kabushikikōkaini Kage Haiteku Kabuno Uwane Omoku" [U.S.-China confrontation shakes the market as KIOXIA postponed listing, concerned by the export control, casting a shadow on the booming IPO with heavy high-tech stocks], *Nihon Keizai Shimbun*, September 29, 2020.

84. "Japanese Business Rethinks Hi-Tech Deals with China," *Nikkei Asia*, September 3, 2020, https://asia.nikkei.com/Politics/International-relations/US-China-tensions/Japanese -business-rethinks-high-tech-deals-with-China.

85. Ito Asei, "Japan's Economic Pragmatism: Cooperating and Competing with China," *Strategic Japan 2021: The Future of Japan-China Relations*, Center for Strategic and International Studies, April 5, 2021, https://csis-website-prod.s3.amazonaws.com/s3fs-public/210405_Ito _Economic%20Relations.pdf?XD7Hb3PUQExuZurkTIbdrWmF.ZYVNI6ph.

86. Mayumi Ogawa and Masako Nagashima, "(Jimintō Sōsaisen) Shushō San-sen Shiji e Asou, Nikai Goetsu Dōshū Shijiritsu Kyūraku ni Taikō" [(LDP presidential election) To counter a sharp decline in approval, Aso and Nikai overcome rivalry to endorse Abe's third term], *Sankei Shimbun*, April 11, 2018.

87. Kei Ishinabe, " 'Donna Koto ga Atte mo Nitchū Yūkō wo Daijini': Jimin Nikai Toshihiro Kanjichō Chūgoku no Kokka Kankō Kyokuchō to Kaidan" ["We need to take care of Japan-China relations no matter what happens": LDP secretary-general Toshihiro Nikai meets with China's director of national tourism], *Sankei Shimbun*, May 13, 2017, https://www.sankei.com/world/news/170513/wor1705130023-n1.htmlhttps://www .sankei.com/world/news/170513/wor1705130023-n1.html.

88. Ito, "Japan's Economic Pragmatism."

89. Yuichi Nohira and Natsuki Okamura, "Nikaiha, Kane to Posuto Shōaku Tahabatsu 'Fuman Maguma no yō' " [Nikai Faction controls money and positions: Other factions' dissatisfaction bubbling up like "magma"], *Asahi Shimbun*, October 8, 2020, https:// www.asahi.com/articles/ASNB77J7QNB7UTFK00J.html.

90. Ryo Aihara and Naoki Tsusaka, "Kokudo Kyōjin-ka Gonen Enchō ni Jūgochōen Shushō Shiji, Nikai-shi Kimoiri" [15 Trillion yen over five years for extended disaster resilience strategy: Prime minister's instructions, backed by Mr. Nikai], *Asahi Shimbun*, December 1, 2020, https://www.asahi.com/amp/articles/ASND13HN5ND1UTFK004.html.

91. Ishinabe, " 'Donna Koto ga Atte mo Nitchū Yūkō wo Daijini.' "

92. Ito, "Japan's Economic Pragmatism." See also Central Committee of the Chinese Communist Party, "Proposals of the Central Committee of the Communist Party of China on Formulating the Fourteenth Five-Year Plan for National Economic and Social Development and the Visionary Goals for 2035," November 11, 2020, http://www.gov .cn/zhengce/2020-11/03/content_5556991.htm.

93. "Amari Keizaishō ga Jinin Kensetsu Gaisha kara Kinsen Juju, Hisho Ryūyō de Inseki" [Economic and fiscal policy minister Amari resigns, takes responsibility for secretary who transferred money received from construction company], *Nihon Keizai Shimbun*, January 29, 2016, https://www.nikkei.com/article/DGXKASFS28H6F_Y6A120C1MM8000/.

94. "Keizai Anzen Hoshō Senryaku, Sōki Sakutei wo Nijūninen ni Suishinhō—Jimin Teigen" [LDP proposal calls for early drafting of economic national security

strategy promotion law by 2022], *Jiji*, December 16, 2020, https://www.jiji.com/jc
/article?k=2020121600901&g=eco; "Teigen 'Keizai Anzen Hoshō Senryaku Sakutei'
ni Mukete" [Recommendation: Toward developing an "economic security strategy"],
Liberal Democratic Party of Japan, December 22, 2020, https://www.jimin.jp/news
/policy/201021.html.

95. "Seifu, Kimitsu ya Gijutsu Mamoru Shikaku Sōsetsu e Kotoshi wa Keizai Anpo no Torikumi Honkakuka" [Government to create qualifications to protect confidential information and technology, full-scale economic security efforts this year], *Sankei Shimbun*,
January 5, 2021, https://www.sankei.com/politics/news/210105/plt2101050013-n1.html.

96. "Seifu, Kimitsu ya Gijutsu Mamoru Shikaku Sōsetsu e Kotoshi wa Keizai Anpo no
Torikumi Honkakuka."

97. Akira Amari, "Amari Akira no Kokkai Repōto Sōran" [Amari Akira's Diet Report No.
410 overview], *Amari Akira Official Blog*, August 6, 2020, https://amari-akira.com/01
_parliament/2020/410.html.

98. Ito, "Japan's Economic Pragmatism," 2.

99. *Joint Statement of the Trilateral Meeting of the Trade Ministers of Japan, the United States
and the European Union*, Washington, DC, January, 14, 2020, https://trade.ec.europa
.eu/doclib/docs/2020/january/tradoc_158567.pdf.

100. "Keizai Anpo Senryaku" [Economic security strategy], *Jiji*, December 16, 2020.

101. "In light of the termination of new ODA to China, Prime Minister Abe expressed his
hope to build an era in which the two countries will work side by side to contribute
to regional and global stability and prosperity through dialogue and human resource
exchange in the field of development and cooperation on global issues. In response,
President Xi expressed his high appreciation for Japan's ODA contributions and made
positive remarks about such cooperation." Ministry of Foreign Affairs of Japan, "Prime
Minister Abe's Visit to China: Overall Summary," https://www.mofa.go.jp/mofaj/a_o/c
_m1/cn/page4_004452.html.

102. "Abe and Xi Pledge to Elevate Ties to a New Level," *Japan Times*, December 23, 2019.

103. According to Genron NPO's opinion poll conducted in September 2019, 45.9 percent in
China responded that they have a "favorable" impression of Japan, the highest record
since the survey began in 2005, whereas 15 percent in Japan responded that they have
a "favorable" impression of China, slightly higher than the previous year (13.1 percent).
For further details, see *The 15th Joint Public Opinion Poll: Japan-China Public Opinion Survey 2019* (Tokyo: Genron NPO, October 2019), http://www.genron-npo.net/en
/archives/191024.pdf.

104. "Japan Records Most Negative View of China as Unfavorable Opinions Surge, Survey Finds," *Japan Times*, October 6, 2020, https://www.japantimes.co.jp/news/2020/10
/06/national/japan-most-negative-view-china-survey/. Pew found that 84 percent of Japanese respondents in 2020 had "no confidence in Xi Jinping to do the
right thing" (up from 81 percent in 2019), while 79 percent said that China did "a
bad job dealing with the coronavirus outbreak" (which is the highest among all the
countries surveyed); for details, see Laura Silver, Kat Devlin, and Christine Huang,
"Unfavorable Views of China Reach Historic Highs in Many Countries," Pew

Research Center, October 6, 2020, https://www.pewresearch.org/global/2020/10/06/unfavorable-views-of-china-reach-historic-highs-in-many-countries/.

105. "LDP Policy Group, Not Party, Requests State to Cancel Xi's Visit," *Asahi Shimbun*, July 8, 2020, http://www.asahi.com/ajw/articles/13526200 (site discontinued), archived at https://web.archive.org/web/20200710114435/http://www.asahi.com/ajw/articles/13526200.

106. "Nihon no Jiki Chū Chūgoku Taishi Naitei Hōdōni Pekin ga Zawatsuku Riyū" [Reasons behind the buzz in Beijing regarding the reports on Japan's next ambassador to China], *JBPress*, July 7, 2020.

107. Shiraishi, "Abe Is Redefining Japan's China Policy."

108. Eri Sugiura, "Japan PM Hopeful Kono Calls for Regular Summit with China," *Nikkei Asia*, September 18, 2001, https://asia.nikkei.com/Politics/Japan-PM-hopeful-Kono-calls-for-regular-summit-with-China?

109. Australian scholar and journalist Richard McGregor nicely captures this dynamic in "How Will Japan's New Leader Handle Growing China-US Tensions?" *Nikkei Asia*, September 22, 2020, https://asia.nikkei.com/Opinion/How-will-Japan-s-new-leader-handle-growing-China-US-tensions.

3. THE UNITED STATES

1. Polls noted in Mike M. Mochizuki, "To Change or Contain: Dilemmas of American Policy Toward Japan," in *Eagle in a New World: American Grand Strategy in the Post-Cold War Era*, ed. Kenneth A. Oye, Robert J. Lieber, and Donald Rothchild, 235–60 (New York: HarperCollins, 1996); Patrick E. Tyler, "U.S. Strategy Plan Calls for Insuring No Rivals Develop," *New York Times*, March 7, 1992; George and Meredith Lebard Friedman, *The Coming War with Japan* (New York: St. Martin's Press, 1991).

2. Michael J. Green, *By More than Providence: Grand Strategy and American Power in the Asia Pacific Since 1783* (New York: Columbia University Press, 2017), 468–69.

3. Michael J. Green, *Arming Japan: Defense Production, Alliance Politics, and the Postwar Search for Autonomy* (New York: Columbia University Press, 1995), 3; Glenn H. Snyder, "The Security Dilemma in Alliance Politics," *World Politics* 36, no. 4 (1984): 466, https://doi.org/10.2307/2010183.

4. Tokutomi Iichiro, ed., *Koshaku Yamagata Aritomo den*, vol. 3 (Tokyo, 1933), 494–96, as quoted in Ian H. Nish, *The Anglo-Japanese Alliance: The Diplomacy of Two Island Empires, 1894–1907* (London: Athlone, 1966), 379–80. At the time Yamagata considered Germany a useful third party to the alliance—much as Mahan viewed Germany as a useful adjunct to a U.S.-Japan-Britain alignment around the same time.

5. Nish, *The Anglo-Japanese Alliance*, 13–14.

6. For details, see John W. Dower, *Empire and Aftermath: Yoshida Shigeru and the Japanese Experience, 1878–1954* (Cambridge, MA: Council on East Asian Studies, Harvard University, 1979), 417, 431; Green, *Arming Japan*, 31–52.

7. Dower, *Empire and Aftermath*, 218.

8. Dower, *Empire and Aftermath*, 38.

9. John G. Ikenberry, *Liberal Leviathan: The Origins, Crisis, and Transformation of the American World Order* (Princeton, NJ: Princeton University Press, 2011), 16–17, 21.

10. For more, see Richard J. Samuels, *Securing Japan: Tokyo's Grand Strategy and the Future of East Asia* (Ithaca, NY: Cornell University Press, 2008), 32–33.

11. Professor Oguma Eiji of Keio University told the Diet in 2004 that the excuse of Article Nine was "unfair" but formed the core of Japan's approach to the alliance for decades. See Oguma Eiji, *Dai Kyūjōno Rekishiteki Keii ni Tsuite* [On the historical background of Article Nine], Commission on the Constitution of the House of Representatives, May 12, 2004, http://www.shugiin.go.jp/internet/itdb_kenpou.nsf/html/kenpou/chosa /15905120guma.pdf/$File/15905120guma.pdf. Yoshida calling opponents of Article Nine "fools" is also noted in Kenneth Pyle, *Japan Rising: The Resurgence of Japanese Power and Purpose* (New York: Public Affairs, 2007), 230; and in Kiichi Miyazawa, *Tokyo-Washington no Mitsudan* [Secret talks between Tokyo and Washington] (Tokyo: Jitsugyo no Nihonsha, 1956), 160; "Miyazawa Moto Shushō Kenpō Zenmen Minaoshi 'Hantai Riyū nai'" [Former PM Miyazawa says there is no reason to oppose constitutional amendment], *Nihon Keizai Shimbun*, February 18, 2004; "Miyazawa Kiichi shi Shūdanteki Jieiken 'Bubunteki Kōshimo' Kaishaku Henkōde Taiō Teian" [Mr. Miyazawa Kiichi: Proposing change in interpretation leading to the partial use of collective self-defense], *Asahi Shimbun*, September 7, 2001.

12. Victor D. Cha, *Power Game: The Origins of the American Alliance System in Asia*, (Princeton, NJ: Princeton University Press, 2016), 181–82.

13. Peter J. Katzenstein and Nobuo Okawara, *Japan's National Security: Structures, Norms, and Policy Responses in a Changing World* (Ithaca, NY: East Asia Program, Cornell University, 1993); Thomas U. Berger, "From Sword to Chrysanthemum: Japan's Culture of Anti-militarism," *International Security* 17, no. 4 (1993): 119–50.

14. *Nipponkoku to Amerikagasshūkoku to no aida no anzen hoshōjōyaku* [Security treaty between the United States and Japan], https://www.wikiwand.com/en/Security_Treaty _Between_the_United_States_and_Japan. This was signed in San Francisco on September 8, 1951, and entered into force April 28, 1952. In 1946 under U.S. occupation, Yoshida had renounced even the right of self-defense, but he restored that right with the 1954 law establishing the Self-Defense Forces.

15. Murase Shinya, "Shūdanteki Jieiken wo meguru Kenpō to Kokusaihō" [Collective self-defense in the constitution and international law], in *Kokusai Hō no Jissen* [Practice of international law], ed. Yanai Shunji and Murase Shinya (Tokyo: Shinzansha, 2015), 78–80.

16. "Japan: Article 9 of the Constitution," Law Library of Congress, https://tile.loc.gov /storage-services/service/ll/llglrd/2016295698/2016295698.pdf.

17. *Naikaku hōseikyoku secchi hō shikkō rei* [Enforcement order of CLB establishment law], Order No. 290 of 1952, Art. 8. (fn17, chap. 3), https://elaws.e-gov.go.jp /document?lawid=327CO0000000290.

18. Kiyofuku Chūma, *Saigunbi no Seijigaku* [The politics on rearmament] (Tokyo: Chishikisha, 1985), 129–33.

19. Ministry of Defense (Japan), "Buryoku Kōshi no Ittaika" [Explanation of integration in the use of force], http://www.clearing.mod.go.jp/hakusho_data/2003/2003/html/1521c100.html.

20. Hiroshi Masuda, "Kyū Nichibei Anpo Jōyaku ni iu Kyokutō Jōkō to wa Nanika?" [What is the Far East Clause in the former U.S.-Japan Security Treaty?], in *Nichibei Dōmei Saikō: Shitte Okitai 100 no Ronten* [Rethinking the U.S.-Japan security alliance: 100 issues to know], ed. Nishihara Masashi and Tsuchiyama Jitsuo (Tokyo: Akishobo, 2010), 64–65; see also https://www.mofa.go.jp/mofaj/area/usa/hosho/qa/03_2.html; Article VI of the 1960 treaty states:

> For the purpose of contributing to the security of Japan and the maintenance of international peace and security in the Far East, the United States of America is granted the use by its land, air and naval forces of facilities and areas in Japan. The use of these facilities and areas as well as the status of United States armed forces in Japan shall be governed by a separate agreement, replacing the Administrative Agreement under Article III of the Security Treaty between Japan and the United States of America, signed at Tokyo on February 28, 1952, as amended, and by such other arrangements as may be agreed upon.

21. Ministry of Foreign Affairs of Japan, "Japan-U.S. Joint Declaration on Security—Alliance for the Twenty-First Century," April 17, 1996, https://www.mofa.go.jp/region/n-america/us/security/security.html.

22. Green, *By More than Providence*, 406–8.

23. Green, *By More than Providence*, 406–8.

24. Michael J. Green and Igata Akira, "The Gulf War and Japan's National Security Identity," in *Examining Japan's Lost Decades*, ed. Yōichi Funabashi and Barak Kushner (London: Routledge, 2015). The commander of Operation Desert Storm, Norman Schwartzkopf, was one of the few who said Japan's financial role was crucial, but the image of a passive and frightened economic superpower was indelible.

25. *Kokusai Rengo Heiwa Iji Katsudo to Ni Kansuru Horitsu Shiko Rei* [Act on cooperation with United Nations peacekeeping operations and other operations], Order No. 79 of 1992, https://elaws.e-gov.go.jp/document?lawid=404AC0000000079.

26. *Heisei Jūsan Nen Ku Gatsu Jūichi Nichi No Amerika Gasshū Koku Ni Oite Hassei Shita Terorisuto Ni Yoru Kōgeki To Ni Taiō Shite Okonawareru Kokusai Rengō Kenshō No Mokuteki Tassei No Tameno Shogaikoku No Katsudō Ni Taishite Waga Kuni Ga Jisshi Suru Sochi Oyobi Kanrensuru Kokusai Rengō Ketsugi To Ni Motozuku Jindō Teki Sochi Ni Kansuru Tokubetsu Sochi Hō* [Law regarding special measures concerning measures taken by Japan in support of the activities of foreign countries aiming to achieve the purposes of the Charter of the United Nations in response to the terrorist attacks that took place on 11 September 2001 in the United States of America and subsequent threats as well as concerning humanitarian measures based on relevant resolutions of the United Nations or requests by international bodies], Order No. 113 of 2001; see also Paul Midford, "Japan's Response to Terror: Dispatching the SDF to the Arabian Sea,"

Asian Survey 43, no. 2 (March/April 2003): 333; Larry Wortzel, "Joining Forces Against Terrorism: Japan's New Law Commits More than Words to U.S. Effort," Heritage Foundation, November 5, 2001, https://www.heritage.org/node/19076/print-display; Brad Glosserman, "Mr. Koizumi's Mandate," *Comparative Connections* 5, no. 4 (January 2004), http://cc.pacforum.org/2004/01/mr-koizumis-mandate/.

27. Norimitsu Onishi, "Japan's Troops Proceed in Iraq Without Shot Fired," *New York Times*, October 6, 2004, https://www.nytimes.com/2004/10/06/world/middleeast/japans-troops -proceed-in-iraq-without-shot-fired.html; Japan Ministry of Defense, "JDF: Japan Defense Focus (No. 9)," April 2008, https://www.mod.go.jp/e/jdf/no09/policy.html (site discontinued), archived at https://web.archive.org/web/20130221220840/https:// www.mod.go.jp/e/jdf/no09/policy.html.

28. The threat from China at that point was highlighted in new defense planning guidance and the sudden presence of PLA navy submarines in Japanese straits. See "National Defense Program Guideline, FY 2005," Japan Ministry of Defense, December 10, 2004, https://japan.kantei.go.jp/policy/2004/1210taikou_e.html.

"China Sub Tracked by U.S. Off Guam Before Japan Intrusion," *Japan Times*, November 17, 2004, https://www.japantimes.co.jp/news/2004/11/17/national/china-sub -tracked-by-u-s-off-guam-before-japan-intrusion/; Japan scholar Paul Midford concluded in his research that the George W. Bush administration put far less pressure on Japan during the Global War on Terror than the George H. W. Bush administration had during the first Gulf War. In the White House at the time, that was clearly the American purpose, and Koizumi volunteered to put pressure on Gulf and European allies on behalf of the United States, in a noteworthy role reversal from 1990.

29. A group of former Pentagon officials issued a report in 2009 arguing that Japan's highly symbolic deployments to the Middle East had actually been a distraction from the need to strengthen preparations in the western Pacific; see Michael Finnegan, *Meeting Unmet Expectations in the U.S.-Japan Alliance*, NBR Special Report No. 17, National Bureau of Asian Research, November 2, 2009, https://www.nbr.org/publication/managing-unmet -expectations-in-the-u-s-japan-alliance/.

30. "Japan's PM Rejects 2006 Plan for US Air Base Relocation," *Voice of America*, April 23, 2010, https://www.voanews.com/east-asia/japans-pm-rejects-2006-plan-us-air- base-relocation; Gordon G. Chang, "Will Japan Become a Chinese Colony?" *Forbes*, September 3, 2009, https://www.forbes.com/2009/09/03/japan-china-yukio-hatoyama -opinions-columnists-gordon-chang.html.

31. Joshua Keating, "630 Members of Japan's Ruling Party Headed to China This Week," *Foreign Policy*, December 9, 2009, https://foreignpolicy.com/2009/12/09/630-members -of-japans-ruling-party-headed-to-china-this-week/.

32. For more on the Matsushita Institute, see https://www.mskj.or.jp/en/.

33. Maehara Seiji, "Japan Chair Forum: DPJ's Vision on Domestic and Foreign Policy," Center for Strategic and International Studies, December 8, 2005, https://www.csis .org/events/japan-chair-forum-dpjs-vision-domestic-and-foreign-policy; "Hatoyama Minshu Kanjichō: Bei Tsuijūkara Kokusai Kyōchōe Gaikō Seisaku Tenkan wo Uttae" [DPJ secretary-general Hatoyama: Appealing for shift in foreign policy from obedience

to the U.S. to international cooperation], *Mainichi Shimbun*, February 24, 2009; Kamei Shizuka, "Amerika Tsuijū Ippentō dewa Nihon no Kokueki Sokoneru" [Thorough obedience to the U.S. harms Japan's national interests], July 13, 2006, http://www.kamei -shizuka.net/daily/060713.html.

34. Paul S. Giarra and Akihisa Nagashima, "Managing the New U.S.-Japan Security Alliance: Enhancing Structures and Mechanisms to Address Post-Cold War Requirements," in *The U.S.-Japan Alliance: Past, Present, and Future*, ed. Michael J. Green and Patrick M. Cronin (New York: Council on Foreign Relations Press, 1999).

35. See, for example, Nagashima Akihisa, "Kan Seiken eno Kenpakusho: Kokuekino Hadawo Dōdōto Kakage Senryakuteki Gaikōe Kajiwo Kire!" [Urgent policy recommendation to the Kan administration: Proudly fly the flag of national interest and steer toward strategic diplomacy], https://ameblo.jp/nagashima21/entry-12454916354.html; for English version, see https://ameblo.jp/nagashima21/entry-12454916278.html.

36. *Defense of Japan 2012* (Tokyo: Japan Ministry of Defense, 2012), 115–29, https://www .mod.go.jp/e/publ/w_paper/pdf/2012/21_Part2_Chapter2_Sec2.pdf; *National Defense Program Guidelines for FY 2011 and Beyond*, Japan Ministry of Defense, December 17, 2020, https://www.mod.go.jp/e/d_act/d_policy/pdf/guidelinesFY2011.pdf; "Hikaku Sangensoku Shōraiwa Minaoshi Shin Anpokon Hōkokusho Buki Kinyuwo Kanwa" [A new report by a council on security said three non-nuclear principles to be reviewed in the future, and the banning of weapon exports to be relaxed], *Nihon Keizai Shimbun*, August 28, 2010.

37. I was invited to testify on the subject in the DPJ policy affairs committee on collective self-defense at the time, and the divisions on the subject were patently obvious. "Jieitai Kaigai Haken Minshu Kōkyūhō Seitei Kentō Getsunai Bukai Secchi Shūdanteki Jieiken mo" [Overseas dispatch of Japan Self Defense Forces: DPJ considers establishment of perpetual law along with use of collective self-defense at its subcommittee], *Mainichi Shimbun*, January 4, 2011.

38. Jim McNerney et al., *Partnership for Recovery and a Stronger Future: Standing with Japan After 3-11*, Center for Strategic and International Studies, November 2011, 33, https://csis-website-prod.s3.amazonaws.com/s3fs-public/legacy_files/files/publication /111026_Green_PartnershipforRecovery_Web.pdf.

39. "Shūdanteki Jieiken no Kaishaku Minaoshi Noda Shushō 'Seifu naide Giron'" [PM Noda says the government is considering review of interpretation of collective self-defense], *Asahi Shimbun*, July 10, 2012; "Minshu Kanshi Shushōni 'Hantai' Shūdanteki Jieiken no Kaishaku Minaoshide" [Mr. Kan from DPJ opposes PM's review of interpretation of collective self-defense], *Asahi Shimbun*, October 17, 2012.

40. I was invited to these discussions at one point. Scholars at the Hudson Institute in Washington were particularly close to Abe in his time out of power. For more on the influence of Okazaki and others on Abe, see Hidekazu Sakai, "Return to Geopolitics: The Changes in Japanese Strategic Narratives," *Asian Perspective* 43, no. 2 (2019): 297–322, https://doi.org/10.1353/apr.2019.0012; Tomoko Nagano, " 'Jieitai wa Sensōsuru Guntaini Narimasuyo;' Abe Shushōno Burēn Okazaki Hisahikoshini Kiku Shūdanteki Jieiken" [On the collective self-defense by PM Abe's brain Okazaki Hisahiko: "SDF will

become a military that conducts wars"], *Huffington Post* [Japanese edition], May 19, 2014, https://www.huffingtonpost.jp/tomoko-nagano/okazaki-hisahiko_b_5349355.html.

41. Shinzō Abe, "150 Years ago in a nice hotel near the White House . . ." (Keynote Speech: "An Alliance of Maritime Nations: The United States and Japan," Willard Intercontinental Hotel, Washington, DC, April 17, 2009), http://www.spfusa.org/program/avs /2009/4-17-09abe.pdf (site discontinued), archived at https://web.archive.org/web /20140413184436/http://spfusa.org/program/avs/2009/4-17-09abe.pdf.

42. Tomohiko Taniguchi, "Japan: A Stabilizer for the U.S.-Led System in a New Era," *Asia Policy* 14, no. 1 (January 2019): 172–76, doi:10.1353/asp.2019.0004.

43. Shinzō Abe and Barack Obama, "U.S.-Japan Summit," White House, Washington, DC, February 22, 2013.

44. Phil Stewart, "Gates Pushes Japan on U.S. Troop Shift Plan," Reuters, October 21, 2009, https://www.reuters.com/article/uk-japan-usa-sb/gates-pushes-japan-on-u-s-troop -shift-plan-idUKTRE59K14820091021.

45. "Status of National Security Council," Kantei, http://www.kantei.go.jp/jp/singi/anzen -hosyoukaigi/kaisai.html.

46. "Status of National Security Council." See also Cabinet Secretariat, *Overview of the Act on the Protection of Specially Designated Secrets (SDS)*, https://www.kantei.go.jp /jp/topics/2013/headline/houritu_gaiyou_e.pdf; *National Defense Program Guidelines for FY2014 and Beyond*, Japan Ministry of Defense, December 17, 2013, https://www .mod.go.jp/j/approach/agenda/guideline/2014/pdf/20131217_e2.pdf (site discontinued), archived at https://web.archive.org/web/20140206212736/https://www.mod.go.jp/j /approach/agenda/guideline/2014/pdf/20131217_e2.pdf; "Medium Term Defense Program (FY2014—FY2018)," Japan Ministry of Defense, December 17, 2013, https:// careersdocbox.com/US_Military/75676001-Medium-term-defense-program-fy2014-fy2018 .html; *Building a Dynamic Joint Defense Forces*, Japan Ministry of Defense, https://www .mod.go.jp/e/publ/w_paper/pdf/2016/DOJ2016_2-2-1_web.pdf (site discontinued), archived at https://web.archive.org/web/2017032207065z/https://www.mod.go.jp/e/publ /w_paper/pdf/2016/DOJ2016_2-2-1_web.pdf.

47. For details see Green, *By More than Providence*, 491.

48. "Kai: Inochigake no Shigoto Henshūiin Mochizuki Kōichi" [Explanation by Koichi Mochizuki, senior staff writer: Task one can venture only at the risk of one's life], *Yomiuri Shimbun*, July 24, 2014.

49. For details see *Defense of Japan 2019* (Tokyo: Japan Ministry of Defense, 2019), 199, https://www.mod.go.jp/e/publ/w_paper/wp2019/pdf/DOJ2019_2-1-2.pdf.

50. *Defense of Japan 2019*.

51. "Cabinet Decision on Development of Seamless Security Legislation to Ensure Japan's Survival and Protect Its People," Ministry of Foreign Affairs of Japan, July 1, 2014, https://www.mofa.go.jp/fp/nsp/page23e_000273.html; *Report of the Advisory Panel on Reconstruction of the Legal Basis for Security*, May 15, 2014, http://www.kantei.go.jp /jp/singi/anzenhosyou2/dai7/houkoku_en.pdf; see also "Collective Self-Defense," Sasakawa Peace Foundation USA, October 27, 2015, https://spfusa.org/research/collective -self-defense/.

52. See "Cabinet Decision on Development of Seamless Security Legislation."

53. "Tsuitōshō: Zen Naikaku Hōseikyoku Chōkan Komatsu Ichirōsan" [Obituary: Komatsu Ichirō, former cabinet legislation bureau chief], *Yomiuri Shimbun*, September 27, 2014.

54. "The Guidelines for Japan-U.S. Defense Cooperation," Ministry of Defense of Japan, https://www.mod.go.jp/e/d_act/anpo/; "The U.S.-Japan Alliance," Congressional Research Service, June 13, 2019, https://crsreports.congress.gov/product/pdf/RL/RL33740.

55. "Address by Prime Minister Shinzo Abe to a Joint Meeting of the U.S. Congress: 'Toward an Alliance of Hope,'" Ministry of Foreign Affairs of Japan, April 29, 2015, https://www.mofa.go.jp/na/na1/us/page4e_000241.html.

56. The separate bills—some of which did not deal directly with collective self-defense—were the Self-Defense Forces Law; the International Peace and Cooperation Law; the Law Concerning Measures to Ensure Peace and Security of Japan in Situations in the Areas Surrounding Japan; the Ship Inspection Operations Law; the Law in Response to Armed Attack Situations; the Act on Measures Conducted by the Government in Line with U.S. Military Actions in Armed Attack Situations; the Law Concerning the Use of Specific Public Facilities; the Marine Transport Restriction Act; and the NSC Establishment Act. For details, see "Anpo Kanren Nihōan no Yōshi" [Main points of two security-related bills], *Kyodo News*, May 14, 2015; "Section 2. Outline of the Legislation for Peace and Security," in *Defense of Japan 2016* (Tokyo: Japan Ministry of Defense, 2016), 213, https://www.mod.go.jp/e/publ/w_paper/pdf/2016/DOJ2016_2-3-2_web.pdf; Jeffrey Hornung, "Japan's 2015 Security Legislation: Change Rooted Firmly in Continuity," in *Routledge Handbook of Japanese Foreign Policy*, ed. Mary McCarthy (New York: Routledge, 2018).

57. "Security Legislation Q&A," *Komeito*, July 2016, https://www.komei.or.jp/campaign/sanin2016/topics/heiwaanzenhousei/qa.html.

58. Daisuke Akiyama, *The Abe Doctrine: Japan's Proactive Pacifism and Security Strategy* (New York: Palgrave Macmillan, 2018), 53–133 on Apple ebook.

59. See: https://cdp-japan.jp/policy/constitution; "2016 Sangiingiin Senkyo Kaku Bunya no Seisaku 39 Kenpō" [Policy for each area in the 2016 Upper House election: 39 the constitution], Japanese Communist Party, June 2016, https://www.jcp.or.jp/web_policy/2016/06/2016-sanin-bunya39.html; "Seimei: Aratamete 'Sensōhō' Haishiwo Uttaeru" [Statement: Calling again for the abolition of "war bill"], *Shakaito*, September 19, 2017.

60. "Anpo Hōsei: Yotōkyōgi Teiji sareta 15 jirei Shūdanteki Jieiken ga Kahansū" [Security legislation: Majority of the 15 cases presented by ruling parties are related to collective self-defense], *Mainichi Shimbun*, May 28, 2014; *Report of the Advisory Panel on Reconstruction of the Legal Basis for Security*, June 24, 2008, http://www.kantei.go.jp/jp/singi/anzenhosyou/report.pdf.

61. "Shūin Shinsakai: 'Anpo Hōseiwa Kenpō Ihan' Sankōnin Zenin ga Hihan" [The Commission on the Constitution of the House of Representatives: All unsworn witnesses criticize unconstitutionality of security legislation], *Mainichi Shimbun*, June 5, 2015.

62. Kazuya Sakamoto summary of lecture in *Keidanren*: "Abe Seiken no Gaikō Anzenhoshō Seisaku-Genjō to Kadai" [Diplomatic national security policy of Abe administration:

Status and challenges], *Keidanren Times*, No. 3192, September 18, 2014, https://www
.keidanren.or.jp/journal/times/2014/0918_06.html.

63. "Questions from MP Inada and Response from Prime Minister Abe," Liberal Democratic Party of Japan, updated May 26, 2015, https://www.jimin.jp/news/prioritythemes
/diplomacy/127828.html

64. "Meeting of the Special Committee of the House of Representatives on the Legislation
for Peace and Security of Japan and the International Community," Lower House of
the Japanese Diet, updated July 10, 2015, http://kokkai.ndl.go.jp/SENTAKU/syugiin
/189/0298/main.html.

65. "Meeting of the Special Committee on the Legislation for Peace and Security of Japan
and the International Community," House of the Japanese Diet, updated August 4, 2015,
https://www.sangiin.go.jp/japanese/annai/chousa/rippou_chousa/backnumber
/2015pdf/20151214031.pdf.

66. Seiji Endo, " 'Sekkyokuteki Heiwashugi' o Hihanteki ni Kensho suru" [A critical review
of "proactive contribution to peace"], in *Tettei Kensho: Abe Seiji* [Thorough review of
Abe politics], ed. Nakano Koichi, 116–124; Kyoji Yanagisawa, "Anzenhosho Seisaku:
Sono Engen to Mujun" [The origin and contradiction of the security policy], in *Tettei
Kensho: Abe Seiji* [Thorough review of Abe politics], (Tokyo: Iwanami Shoten, 2016);
148–56; Akira Kato, *Nihon no Anzenhosho* [Security of Japan] (Tokyo: Chikuma Shobo,
2016). These are all cited in Akiyama, *The Abe Doctrine*. For the give and take in the
Diet, see "Meeting of the Special Committee," August 4, 2015; Kazuhito Kusunugi,
"Diet Discussion Surrounding Permission for the Exercise of Collective Self-
Defense," *Legislation and Research Report (Upper House)* 372 (December 2015): 40–44,
https://www.sangiin.go.jp/japanese/annai/chousa/rippou_chousa/backnumber
/2015pdf/20151214031.pdf; "Meeting of the Special Committee," July 10, 2015.

67. "Sanin Shingi Iri Yato Retteru Hari Gekika 'Dokusai no Michi' 'Kūdetā' " [As the Upper
House begins discussing the bill, opposition parties intensify labeling it as "path to
dictatorship" and "coup d'état"], *Sankei Shimbun*, July 28, 2015.

68. "Anpo Hōan Seikei ni Kage Konkokkai Seiritsu 'Sansei' 26 percent Domari 'Seiken
Unei no Shuhō Warui' 38 percent ni (Honsha Yoron Chōsa)" [Security legislation casts
a shadow on the cabinet: Only 26 percent approve its passage during the current Diet
session and 38 percent disapprove the cabinet management] (Nikkei public opinion
poll), *Nihon Keizai Shimbun*, July 27, 2015; "Honne no Anpo Gironde Rikai Fukameru
Doryokuwo" [More effort needed for candor in national security debate to deepen
understanding], *Nihon Keizai Shimbun*, July 17, 2016.

69. Michael Green and Jeffrey W. Hornung, "Ten Myths about Japan's Collective Self
Defense Change," *The Diplomat* July 10, 2014, https://thediplomat.com/2014/ten-myths
-about-japans-collective-self-defense-change/.

70. "Jonathan Soble, "Japan Moves to Allow Military Combat for First Time in 70 Years," *New
York Times*, July 16, 2015, https://www.nytimes.com/2015/07/17/world/asia/japans-lower
-house-passes-bills-giving-military-freer-hand-to-fight.html; Shingo Ito and Daniel Leussink, "Japan Parliament Passes Controversial Security Bills," AFP, September 18, 2015, https://
news.yahoo.com/japan-passes-controversial-security-bills-law-172800247.html.

71. "Naikaku Shiji 41 percent Fushiji 51 percent Futatabi Gyakuten Anpohō 'Setsumei Fujūbun' Honsha Yoron Chōsa" [Approval and disapproval rates reverse once again: Approval for the government proves to be 41 percent while disapproval is 51 percent in Yomiuri public poll—Government explanation of security legislation being insufficient], *Yomiuri Shimbun*, September 21, 2015.

72. "Japan's Security Policy: Development of Security Legislation," Ministry of Foreign Affairs of Japan, updated April 12, 2016, https://www.mofa.go.jp/fp/nsp/page1we _000084.html.

73. "Dō Tsukaukade Kimaru Anpohō no Hyōka" [The assessment of the national security legislation will depend on how it is used], *Nihon Keizai Shimbun*, September 19, 2015.

74. See, for example, Adam Liff, "Japan's Defense Policy: Abe the Evolutionary," *Washington Quarterly* 38, no. 2 (Summer 2015): 79–99; Adam P. Liff, "Policy by Other Means: Collective Self-Defense and the Politics of Japan's Postwar Constitutional Reinterpretations," *Asia Policy* 24, no. 2 (July 2017): 139–72; Jeffrey W. Hornung and Mike M. Mochizuki, "Japan: Still an Exceptional U.S. Ally," *Washington Quarterly* 39, no. 1 (Spring 2016): 95–116.

75. "Dō Tsukaukade Kimaru Anpohō no Hyōka."

76. "Anpo Hōanno Saiketsu Kyōkō Sengono Ayumi Kutsugaesu Bōkyo" [Steamrolling of security legislation: Outrage against Japan's postwar course], *Asahi Shimbun*, July 16, 2015.

77. "Tasukeai de Anzen Hoshōwo Katameru Michie" [Toward a pathway to achieving national security through mutual help], *Nihon Keizai Shimbun*, July 2, 2014.

78. "Anpo Hōan 44kakokuga Shiji Seifu Shiryō Ōbei Ajia Shuyōkokuga Sandō" [Government document shows that 44 states support security legislation, including main European and Asian states], *Sankei News*, August 20, 2015, https://www.sankei.com/politics /news/150820/plt1508200003-n1.html; "Anpohō Seiritsu Sekaino Me wa Kakkoku Seifu no Hannō" [Establishment of security legislation: Responses by foreign governments], *Asahi Shimbun*, September 20, 2015; "Anpohō Sekaiga Kangei Keikai Tōnan A Taichū Yokushiroku ni Kitai" [International community being supportive and wary of security legislation: Southeast Asia expecting deterrence against China], *Nihon Keizai Shimbun*, September 20, 2015.

79. Dina Smeltz et al., *America Divided: Political Partisanship and US Foreign Policy* (2015 Chicago Council survey of American public opinion and U.S. foreign policy) (Chicago: Chicago Council on Global Affairs, 2015), 12, https://www.thechicagocouncil.org/sites /default/files/CCGA_PublicSurvey2015.pdf.

80. "Kakuno Kyōi Rokkakoku Gōi no Uragawa 4: Taikita Yuragu Nichibei Renkei" [Nuclear threat: Behind the scene of 6-country agreement (4): Unstable U.S.-Japan coordination on North Korea policy], *Yomiuri Shimbun*, February 19, 2007. For more context and details, see Green, *By More than Providence*, 507.

81. "Joint Press Conference with President Obama and Prime Minister Abe of Japan," Office of the Press Secretary, White House, April 24, 2014, https://obamawhitehouse .archives.gov/the-press-office/2014/04/24/joint-press-conference-president-obama -and-prime-minister-abe-japan.

82. Susan E. Rice, "Remarks as Prepared for Delivery by National Security Advisor Susan E. Rice" (speech, Georgetown University, November 20, 2013), https://obamawhitehouse .archives.gov/the-press-office/2013/11/21/remarks-prepared-delivery-national-security -advisor-susan-e-rice; Yoji Koda, "Japan's Perspectives on U.S. Policy Toward the South China Sea," in *Perspectives on the South China Sea: Diplomatic, Legal, and Security Dimensions of the Dispute*, ed. Murray Hiebert, Phuong Nguyen, and Gregory B. Polling, 92–95 (Washington, DC: Center for Strategic and International Studies, 2014), https://csis-website-prod.s3.amazonaws.com/s3fs-public/legacy_files/files/publication /140930_Hiebert_PerspectivesSouthChinaSea_Web.pdf.

83. "Shasetsu: Nichibei Shunō Kaidan Ajiano Ishizuee Ippowo" [U.S.-Japan summit meeting: Need to take a step toward Asia's foundation], *Asahi Shimbun*, April 25, 2014.

84. "Japanese Divided on Democracy's Success at Home, but Value Voice of the People," Pew Research Center, October 17, 2017.

85. David Brunnstrom, "Japan PM Stresses Importance of TPP Trade Pact in Clinton Meeting," Reuters, September 19, 2016, https://www.reuters.com/article/us-japan-trade -clinton-idUSKCN11Q0BK.

86. Andy Sharp, "Abe Wooed Trump with Golf, Just Like His Grandfather Did with Eisenhower," *Japan Times*, November 19, 2016, https://www.japantimes.co.jp/news/2016/11/19/national /politics-diplomacy/abe-wooed-trump-golf-just-like-grandfather-eisenhower/#.XxSwLm5Fxyw.

87. Tim Kelly, "Abe Tries to Keep Japan on Trump's Radar Ahead of Singapore Summit," Reuters, June 9, 2018, https://www.reuters.com/article/us-northkorea-usa-japan-analysis /abe-tries-to-keep-japan-on-trumps-radar-ahead-of-singapore-summit-idUSKCN- 1J510H; Brian Murphy and Shibani Mahtani, "With Some Reservations, East Asian Countries Welcome the Trump-Kim Summit," *Washington Post*, June 12, 2018, https://www .washingtonpost.com/news/worldviews/wp/2018/06/12/japan-wanted-kim-jong-un -pledge-to-reopen-issue-of-cold-war-era-abductions-trump-says-they-working-on-that/.

88. Donald J. Trump, *National Security Strategy of the United States of America* (Washington, DC: White House, 2017), 46–47, https://www.whitehouse.gov/wp-content/uploads /2017/12/NSS-Final-12-18-2017-0905.pdf; *Summary of the 2018 National Defense Strategy of the United States of America: Sharpening the American Military's Competitive Edge* (Washington, DC: Department of Defense, 2018), 9, https://dod.defense.gov/Portals /1/Documents/pubs/2018-National-Defense-Strategy-Summary.pdf.

89. U.S. Department of State, *A Free and Open Indo-Pacific: Advancing a Shared Vision*, November 4, 2019, https://www.state.gov/wp-content/uploads/2019/11/Free-and-Open-Indo -Pacific-4Nov2019.pdf. Ministry of Foreign Affairs of Japan, *Free and Open Indo-Pacific*, April 1, 2021, https://www.mofa.go.jp/policy/page25e_000278.html.

90. "Japanese Divided on Democracy's Success at Home."

91. Y.A., "The Virtues of a Confrontational China Strategy," *The American Interest*, April 10, 2020, https://www.the-american-interest.com/2020/04/10/the-virtues-of-a-confrontational -china-strategy/; "Mapping the Future of U.S. China Policy," Center for Strategic and International Studies, https://chinasurvey.csis.org/.

92. "Japanese Divided on Democracy's Success at Home"; "Bōeki Kyōgi Shintende Kaizen Nichibei Yoron Chōsa Sonoichi" [U.S.-Japan joint public poll, Part 1: Improvement

owing to development in trade negotiations], *Yomiuri Shimbun*, December 18, 2019; " 'Nichibei Ryōkō' Nihon Kyūraku 39 percent Honsha Gyarappu Kyōdō Yoron Chōsa" [Yomiuri/Gallup public poll: Views seeing U.S.-Japan relations as good dropped to 39 percent in Japan], *Yomiuri Shimbun*, December 19, 2018; "Nichibei 'Ryōkō' ga Hansū 'Torampu Hikanron' Chinseika Nichibei Kyōdō Yoron Chōsa Sonoichi" [U.S.-Japan joint public poll, Part 1: Half of the respondents think U.S.-Japan relations are good while tragic views on Trump calmed down], *Yomiuri Shimbun*, December 20, 2017.

93. "Keidai Kyōju Hosoya Yūichishi—Anpo Kankyōga Kyūhen Kadono Taibei Izon Dakkyakuwo (Posuto Korona no Nihon Seiji)" [Keio University professor Hosoya Yuichi: Sudden change of security environment requires departure from prior dependence on U.S. (post coronavirus Japanese politics)], *Nihon Keizai Shimbun*, July 7, 2020.

94. " 'Rekishi no Kyokun' Author Talk with Prof. Nobukatsu Kanehara," Sasakawa Peace Foundation USA, August 26, 2020, https://spfusa.org/event/rekishi-no-kyokun-author-talk-with-prof-nobukatsu-kanehara/.

95. For details, see Green, *By More than Providence*, 524–28.

96. David Vergun, "Indo-Pacom Commander Discusses Regional Threats," U.S. Department of Defense, May 23, 2019, https://www.defense.gov/Explore/News/Article/Article/1856670/indo-pacom-commander-discusses-regional-threats/.

97. "Tai Kitachōsen 'Subeteno Sentakushi' Shijie—Shushō Torampushi Rainichide" [PM Abe expresses support in "all options being on the table" during President Trump's visit to Japan], *Kyodo News*, October 29, 2017.

4. THE INDO-PACIFIC

1. M. Earl, *Emperor and Nation in Japan* (Seattle: Washington University of Seattle Press, 1964), 173–74; William G. Beasley, *Japanese Imperialism* (New York: Oxford University Press, 1985), 29.

2. Frederick R. Dickinson, *World War I and the Triumph of a New Japan, 1919–1930* (New York: Cambridge University Press, 2013), xx; Cemil Aydin, "Japan's Pan-Asianism and the Legitimacy of Imperial World Order, 1931–1945," *Asia-Pacific Journal* 6, no. 3 (2008): 1–2, https://apjjf.org/-Cemil-Aydin/2695/article.pdf.

3. Iriye Akira, "Introduction," in *Japan Erupts: The London Naval Conference and the Manchurian Incident, 1928–1932*, ed. James William Morley (New York: Columbia University Press, 1984), 238–39; Kenneth Pyle, *Japan Rising* (New York: Public Affairs, 2008), 68.

4. Pyle, *Japan Rising*, 68.

5. Cemil Aydin, *The Politics of Anti-Westernism in Asia: Visions of World Order in Pan-Islamic and Pan-Asian Thought* (New York: Columbia University Press, 2007), 3, 193, 201.

6. Okakura Tenshin, *The Ideals of the East with Special Reference to the Art of Japan* (London: John Murray, 1903), 5.

7. Eri Hotta, *Pan-Asianism and Japan's War* (New York: Palgrave Macmillan, 2007), 37.

8.   Ishiwara Kanji, *Sensoshi Taikan*, July 4, 1929, reprinted in 2002 by Chuo Koron Shinsha, Tokyo; Ishiwara Kanji, *Manmo Mondai Shiken*, May 22, 1931, in *Ishiwara Kanji Shiro Kokuboronsaku*, ed. Tsunoda Jun (Tokyo: Hara Shobo, 1971), 76–79. See also Peattie Park, *Ishiwara Kanji and Japan's Confrontation with the West* (Princeton, NJ: Princeton University Press, 1975), 178.

9.   As quoted in Martin Weinstein, *The Human Face of Japan's Leadership: Twelve Portraits* (New York: Praeger, 1989), 53.

10.   Marc S. Gallicchio, *The African American Encounter with Japan and China: Black Internationalism in Asia, 1895–1945* (Chapel Hill: University of North Carolina Press, 2000), 20.

11.   Ōkawa Shūmei, *Fukkō Ajia no Shomondai* [Problems of a resurgent Asia] (1922; Tokyo: Chuko Bunko, 1993), 23.

12.   For details of the Joint Chiefs, Department of State, and Office of Strategic Services (OSS) assessments of the initial success of Japanese pan-Asianist propaganda in the war, see Michael J. Green, *By More than Providence: Grand Strategy and American Power in the Asia Pacific Since 1783* (New York: Columbia University Press, 2017), 30–31.

13.   Jeremy A. Yellen, *The Greater East Asia Co-Prosperity Sphere: When Total Empire Met Total War* (New York: Cornell University Press, 2019), loc. 216 of 938, Kindle.

14.   Michael Carr, "Yamato-Damashii 'Japanese Spirit' Definitions," *International Journal of Lexicography* 7, no. 4 (1994): 279–306, 284; Takie Sugiyama Lebra, *Japanese Patterns of Behavior* (Honolulu: University Press of Hawaii, 1976), 163; Daitoa Kensetsu Shingikai, "Daitoa kensetsu shingikai sokai dairokukai giji sokkiroku" [It was stated in the sixth meeting of Daitoa Kensetsu Shingikai in 1942], in *Daitoa kensetsu shingikai kankei shiryo: Sokai bukai sokkiroku* [Documents related to the commission on construction of a Greater East Asian Co-Prosperity Sphere: Records of committee hearings], vol. 1, ed. Kikakuin and Daitoa Kensetsu Shingikai (Tokyo: Ryukei Shosh, 1995).

15.   John Dower, *War Without Mercy: Race and Power in the Pacific War* (New York: Pantheon, 1986), 6.

16.   See, for example, Norton S. Ginsburg, "Manchurian Railroad Development," *Far Eastern Quarterly* 8, no. 4 (August 1949): 398–411.

17.   See, for example, Daqing Yang, *Technology of Empire: Telecommunications and Japanese Expansion in Asia, 1883–1945* (Cambridge, MA: Harvard East Asia Monographs, 2011).

18.   Peter Duus, "Japan's Informal Empire in China, 1895–1937: An Overview," in *The Japanese Informal Empire in China, 1895–1937*, ed. Peter Duus et al., xi–xxx (Princeton, NJ: Princeton University Press, 1989).

19.   Dickinson, *World War I and the Triumph of a New Japan*, 61.

20.   Dickinson, *World War I and the Triumph of a New Japan*, 63.

21.   Mark Metzler, *Lever of Empire: The International Gold Standard and the Crisis of Liberalism in Prewar Japan* (Berkeley: University of California Press, 2006).

22.   Richard J. Samuels, *Securing Japan: Tokyo's Grand Strategy and the Future of East Asia* (Ithaca, NY: Cornell University Press, 2008), 26.

23.   Peattie Park, *Ishiwara Kanji and Japan's Confrontation with the West* (Princeton, NJ: Princeton University Press, 1975), 178.

24. For the 1947 memorandum, see "Memorandum by Mr. John P. Davies, Jr., of the Policy Planning Staff to the Director of the Staff (Kennan)," August 11, 1947, in *Foreign Relations of the United States, 1947*, vol. 6: *The Far East*, Document 393 (Washington, DC: Government Printing Office), 485–86; for quote on aid package to Japan, see Michael Schaller, *The American Occupation of Japan: The Origins of the Cold War in Asia* (New York: Oxford University Press, 1985), 143–44.

25. Victor Cha, *Alignment Despite Antagonism: The US-Korea-Japan Security Triangle* (Stanford, CA: Stanford University Press, 1999), 24.

26. Joshua Walker, *Shadows of Empire: Historical Memory in Post-Imperial Successor States* (Princeton, NJ: Princeton University Press, 2012).

27. Kaname Akamatsu, "Waga Kuni Keizai Hatten no Shuku Gooben Shoohoo" [The synthetic principles of the economic development of our country], in *Shoogyoo Keizai ron* [Theory of commerce and economics], 179–220 (Nagoya, 1932); Terutomo Ozawa, "The Classical Origins of Akamatsu's Flying-Geese Theory: A Note on a Missing Link to David Hume," Working Paper No. 320, Columbia University Center on Japanese Economy and Business, April 10, 2013.

28. Kaname Akamatsu, "A Historical Pattern of Economic Growth in Developing Countries," *Journal of Developing Economies* 1, no. 1 (March/August 1962): 3–25.

29. For details, see Sueo Sudo, *The Fukuda Doctrine and ASEAN: New Dimensions in Japanese Foreign Policy* (Singapore: Institute of Southeast Asian Studies, 1992).

30. Michael J. Green, *Japan's Reluctant Realism: Foreign Policy Challenges in an Era of Uncertain Power* (New York: Palgrave Macmillan, 2001), 170–71.

31. Soeya Yoshihide, "Vietnam in Japan's Regional Policy," in *Vietnam Joins the World: American and Japanese Perspectives*, ed. James W. Morley and Masahi Nishihara (New York: Routledge, 1997).

32. Pekka Korhonen, *Japan and Asia-Pacific Integration: Pacific Romances 1968–1996* (London: Routledge, 1998), 138; Kojima Kiyoshi, "The 'Flying Geese' Model of Asian Economic Development: Origin, Theoretical Extensions, and Regional Policy Implications," *Journal of Asian Economics* 11, no. 4 (2000): 385.

33. Martin Tolchin and Susan J. Tolchin, *Buying into America: How Foreign Money Is Changing the Face of Our Nation* (Washington, DC: Farragut, 1993); Donald J. Trump, "There's Nothing Wrong with America's Foreign Defense Policy That a Little Backbone Can't Cure," *Washington Post*, September 2, 1987.

34. Michael D. Barr, "Lee Kwan Yew and the Asian Values Debate," *Asian Studies Review* 24, no. 3 (September 2000): 309–31.

35. Ogura Kazuo, "Azia no Fukken no Tame ni" [For the restoration of Asia], *Chuo Koron* (July 1993), translated as "Call for a New Concept of Asia" in *Japan Echo* 20, no. 3 (Autumn 1993): 37–44.

36. Sakakibara Eisuke, *Beyond Capitalism: The Japanese Model of Market Economics* (Lanham, MD: University Press of America, 1993).

37. *The East Asian Miracle: Economic Growth and Public Policy* (Washington, DC: World Bank Group, 1993), http://documents.worldbank.org/curated/en/975081468244550798/Main-report. The bank economists eventually conceded some points while retaining their traditional focus on market-based development.

38. Yōichi Funabashi, "The Asianization of Asia," *Foreign Affairs* 72, no. 5 (November/December 1993): 75.

39. John W. Dower, *War Without Mercy: Race and Power in the Pacific War* (New York: Pantheon, 1993), 314–17.

40. Some notable publications on *Nihonjinron* include Takeo Doi, *Amae no Kōzō* [The anatomy of dependence] (New York: Kodansha, 1971); Hiroshi Minami, *Nihonteki Jiga* [Japanese self] (Tokyo: Iwanami Shoten, 1983); Kosaku Yoshino, *Cultural Nationalism in Contemporary Japan: A Sociological Enquiry* (London: Routledge, 1992); Kenzo Tsukishima, 'Nihonjin ron' no Nakano Nihonjin [Japanese within 'Nihonjinron'] (Tokyo: Kodansha, 2000); Masahiko Fujiwara, *Kokka no Hinkaku* [The dignity of the nation] (Tokyo: Shinchosha, 2005).

41. Stuart Auerbach, "Japanese Aide Cites Health, Religious Reasons for Slackening U.S. Beef Imports," *Washington Post*, December 18, 1987.

42. Miwa Kimitada, *Nihon: 1945nen no Shiten* [Japan: Perspectives from 1945] (Tokyo: Tokyo University Publishing, 1986), cited in Sven Saaler and J. Victor Koschmann, eds., *Pan-Asianism in Modern Japanese History: Colonialism, Regionalism and Borders* (London: Routledge, 2007), 32.

43. Shintaro Ishihara and Akio Morita, *"Nō" to Ieru Nihon* [The Japan that can say no] (Tokyo: Kobunsha, 1989); Shintaro Ishihara and Mahathir Mohamad, *"Nō" to Ieru Asjia* [The Asia that can say no] (Tokyo: Kobunsha, 1994).

44. Walter Hatch and Kozo Yamamura, *Asia in Japan's Embrace: Building a Regional Production Alliance* (Cambridge: Cambridge University Press, 1996).

45. Kenneth Pyle, *The Japanese Question: Power and Purpose in a New Era* (Washington, DC: AEI Press, 1996), 133.

46. Kenneth A. Froot and David B. Yoffie, "Trading Blocs and the Incentives to Protect," in *Regionalism and Rivalry: Japan and the United States in Pacific Asia*, ed. Jeffrey Frankel and Miles Kahler, 125–56 (Chicago: University of Chicago Press, 1993), https://www.nber.org/chapters/c7836.pdf.

47. For details, see Green, *By More than Providence*, 411–15.

48. Mikhail Sergeevich Gorbachev, *Speech by Mikhail Gorbachev in Vladivostok, July 28, 1986* (Moscow: Novosti, 1986).

49. Mark T. Berger, "APEC and Its Enemies: The Failure of the New Regionalism in the Asia-Pacific," *Third World Quarterly* 20, no. 5 (October 1999): 1013–30.

50. James Addison Baker and Thomas M. DeFrank, *The Politics of Diplomacy: Revolution, War, and Peace, 1989–1992* (New York: Putnam, 1995), 610–11.

51. Gaimusho (MOFA), *Gaikō Seisho 1993* [Japan Diplomatic Bluebook] (Tokyo: Ministry of Foreign Affairs, 1994), 84.

52. For details, see Green, *Japan's Reluctant Realism*, 211–15.

53. Glenn D. Hook, "Japan's Role in Emerging East Asian Governance," in *Contested Governance in Japan: Sites and Issues*, ed. Glenn D. Hook, Japanese Studies Series, 36 (New York: Routledge, 2008).

54. Data from World Bank: https://data.worldbank.org/indicator/BX.KLT.DINV.WD.GD.ZS?locations=JP.

55. Samuel P. Huntington, "The Clash of Civilizations?" *Foreign Affairs* 72, no. 3 (Summer 1993): 22–49; Takashi Inoguchi and Edward Newman, "Introduction: 'Asian Values'

and Democracy in Asia" (paper in proceedings of a conference held on March 28, 1997, at Hamamatsu, Shizuoka, Japan, as part of the first Shizuoka Asia-Pacific Forum: The Future of the Asia-Pacific Region), http://archive.unu.edu/unupress/asian-values .html#; David Hitchcock, *Asian Values and the United States: How Much Conflict?* (Washington, DC: Center for Strategic and International Studies, 1994); William Theodore de Bary and Weiming Tu, *Confucianism and Human Rights* (New York: Columbia University Press, 1998).

56. William Jefferson Clinton, "Remarks on the Global Economy" (delivered at the Council on Foreign Relations, New York, September 14, 1998); William W. Grimes, *Currency and Contest in East Asia: The Great Power Politics of Financial Regionalism* (Ithaca, NY: Cornell University Press, 2008).

57. Paul Midford, *Overcoming Isolationism: Japan's Leadership in East Asian Security Multilateralism* (Stanford, CA: Stanford University Press, 2020), 105–19.

58. Tadahiro Asami, *Chiang Mai Initiative as the Foundation of Financial Stability in East Asia*, Institute of International Monetary Affairs, March 1, 2005, https://www.asean.org /wp-content/uploads/images/archive/17905.pdf.

59. On Chinese pressure and Japan's failed attempt to gain support from ASEAN: "Kokuren Kaikaku: G4 Ketsugian Nihon ni Kibishii Genjitsu Kyōdō Teian Ajia 3 kakoku dake" [UN reform: G4 resolution, a hard reality for Japan with only three Asian countries as cosponsors], *Mainichi Shimbun*, July 8, 2005. On the 2010 Senkaku issue, at the ASEAN Defense Ministers' Meeting (ADMM-Plus) in October, then defense minister Kitazawa sought to gain support from ASEAN on Japan's territorial claim over the islands, but ASEAN countries, cautious of their relationships with China, avoided explicit endorsement. "ASEAN Kakudai Kokubōshō Kaigi—Nihon Higashi Shinakaini Genkyū" [Japan brought up East China Sea at the ASEAN Defense Ministers' Meeting Plus], *Nihon Keizai Shimbun*, October 13, 2010.

60. Michael J. Green, "Japan's Confused Revolution," *Washington Quarterly* 33, no.1 (January 2010): 3–19; Taro Karasaki and Terashima Jitsuro, "New Asian Focus: China and the Future of the U.S.-Japan Alliance," *Asia-Pacific Journal* 2, no. 6 (June 25, 2004), https:// apjjf.org/-Karasaki-Taro/1632/article.html; Terashima Jitsuro, "Jōshikini Kaeru Ishito Kōsō: Nichibei Dōmeino Saikōchiku ni Mukete" [The will and imagination to return to common sense: Toward a restructuring of the U.S.-Japan alliance], *Asia-Pacific Journal* 8, no. 11 (March 15, 2010), https://apjjf.org/-Jitsuro-Terashima/3321/article.html.

61. Ahmad A. Talib, "New Voice for Asia Gains Momentum with Inaugural Boao Forum," *New Straits Times* [Malaysia], February 27, 2001.

62. For details, see Green, *By More than Providence*, 512–13.

63. On Hashimoto's New Eurasia diplomacy, see Green, *Japan's Reluctant Realism*, 147.

64. Koizumi Junichiro, "Policy Speech by Prime Minister Junichiro Koizumi to the 151st Session of the Diet" (speech, National Diet Building, Tokyo, Japan, May 7, 2001), https://japan.kantei.go.jp/koizumispeech/2001/0507policyspeech_e.html.

65. Koizumi Junichiro, "Speech by Prime Minister of Japan Junichiro Koizumi: Japan and ASEAN in East Asia: A Sincere and Open Partnership" (speech, Singapore, January 14, 2002), https://japan.kantei.go.jp/koizumispeech/2002/01/14speech_e.html.

66. Yoshihide Soeya, "An East Asian Community and Japan-China Relations," *AJISS-Commentary*, April 30, 2010, https://www2.jiia.or.jp/en_commentary/201004/30-1.html.

67. I may have been the first U.S. official to learn about the speech beforehand when I noticed a draft while meeting with a counterpart in the Japanese embassy a week before. This was not a case of the United States somehow pressing Japan to promote democratic or free-market values.

68. Tanaka Hitoshi, *Gaiko no Chikara* [The power of diplomacy] (Tokyo: Nihon Keizai Shimbun, 2009), 152–69.

69. I staffed the first Trilateral Security Dialogue meetings for the NSC.

70. John Hemmings, "What the Bush Era Can Teach Us About Asia," *The National Interest*, April 14, 2016, https://nationalinterest.org/feature/what-the-bush-era-can-teach-us-about-asia-15776; James L. Schoff, "The Evolution of US-Japan-Australia Security Cooperation," in *US-Japan-Australia Security Cooperation: Prospects and Challenges*, ed. Yuki Tatsumi (Stimson Center, April 2015), 39–40, https://www.stimson.org/wp-content/files/file-attachments/US-Japan_Australia-WEB.pdf.

71. Patrick Gerard Buchan and Benjamin Rimland, *Defining the Diamond: The Past, Present, and Future of the Quadrilateral Security Dialogue*, Center for Strategic and International Studies, March 2020, 2, https://csis-website-prod.s3.amazonaws.com/s3fs-public/publication/200312_BuchanRimland_QuadReport_v2%5B6%5D.pdf?fuRA6-mwjWYKqROtSmJD4u5ct.vijdkZv.

72. Office of the Japan Chair, the Japan Institute of International Affairs, and the Confederation of Indian Industry, *The United States, Japan, and India: Toward New Trilateral Cooperation*, U.S.-Japan-India Report, Center for Strategic and International Studies, August 16, 2007, https://csis-website-prod.s3.amazonaws.com/s3fs-public/legacy_files/files/media/csis/pubs/070816_us_j_ireport.pdf.

73. Shinzō Abe, *Utsukushii Kuni e* [Toward a beautiful country] (Tokyo: Bungei Shunju, 2006).

74. Ministry of External Affairs, "Joint Statement Towards India-Japan Strategic and Global Partnership," Government of India, December 15, 2006, https://mea.gov.in/bilateral-documents.htm?dtl/6368/Joint+Statement+Towards+IndiaJapan+Strategic+and+Global+Partnership.

75. https://delhimumbaiindustrialcorridor.com/; Michael J. Green, "Japan, India and the Strategic Triangle with China," in *Strategic Asia 2011–12: Asia Responds to Its Rising Powers*, ed. Ashley J. Tellis, Travis Tanner, and Jessica Keough, 131–59 (Seattle: National Bureau of Asian Research, 2011).

76. Shinzō Abe, " 'Confluence of the Two Seas': Speech by H. E. Mr. Shinzo Abe, Prime Minister of Japan, at the Parliament of the Republic of India," Ministry of Foreign Affairs of Japan, August 2007, https://www.mofa.go.jp/region/asia-paci/pmv0708/speech-2.html.

77. "Japan-Australia Joint Declaration on Security Cooperation," Ministry of Foreign Affairs of Japan, March 13, 2007, https://www.mofa.go.jp/region/asia-paci/australia/joint0703.html; Aurelia George Mulgan, "Breaking the Mould: Japan's Subtle Shift from Exclusive Bilateralism to Modest Minilateralism," *Contemporary Southeast Asia* 30, no. 1 (2008): 52–72.

78.   "Joint Declaration on Security Cooperation Between Japan and India," Ministry of Foreign Affairs of Japan, October 22, 2008, https://www.mofa.go.jp/region/asia-paci/india/pmv0810/joint_d.html; Michael Heazle and Yuki Tatsumi, "Explaining Australia-Japan Security Cooperation and Its Prospects: 'The Interests That Bind?'" *Pacific Review* 31, no. 1 (2018): 38–56, https://www.tandfonline.com/doi/full/10.1080/09512748.2017.1310750.

79.   Aso Taro, "Speech by Mr. Taro Aso, Minister for Foreign Affairs, on the Occasion of the Japan Institute of International Affairs Seminar: 'Arc of Freedom and Prosperity: Japan's Expanding Diplomatic Horizons,'" (speech, Ministry of Foreign Affairs of Japan, Tokyo, November 30, 2006), https://www.mofa.go.jp/announce/fm/aso/speech0611.html.

80.   Green, *By More than Providence*, 209, 225, 277.

81.   Tomohiko Taniguchi, "Beyond the 'Arc of Freedom and Prosperity': Debating Universal Values in Japanese Grand Strategy," German Marshall Fund of the United States, October 26, 2010, https://www.gmfus.org/publications/beyond-arc-freedom-and-prosperity-debating-universal-values-japanese-grand-strategy.

82.   Ramesh Thakur, "Australia and the Quad," *The Strategist*, July 5, 2018, https://www.aspistrategist.org.au/australia-and-the-quad/; Daniel Flitton, "Who Really Killed the Quad 1.0?" *The Interpreter*, June 2, 2020, https://www.lowyinstitute.org/the-interpreter/who-really-killed-quad-10.

83.   Shinzō Abe, "Asia's Democratic Security Diamond," Project Syndicate, December 27, 2012, https://www.project-syndicate.org/onpoint/a-strategic-alliance-for-japan-and-india-by-shinzo-abe?barrier=accesspaylog.

84.   Lavina Lee and John Lee, "Japan-India Cooperation and Abe's Democratic Security Diamond: Possibilities, Limitations and the View from Southeast Asia," *Contemporary Southeast Asia* 38, no. 2 (August 2016): 284–308.

85.   Spykman argued in 1942 that the United States would need alliances and military presence around the "Rimland" of Eurasia to contain the Soviets after the war. The book was highly controversial when it came out, but it informed strategies of containment in the wake of the Korean War. See Nicholas John Spykman, *America's Strategy in World Politics* (New York: Harcourt Brace, 1942).

86.   Shinzō Abe, "The Bounty of the Open Seas: Five New Principles for Japanese Diplomacy," Ministry of Foreign Affairs of Japan, January 18, 2013, https://www.mofa.go.jp/announce/pm/abe/abe_0118e.html.

87.   "Gaimusho HP kara Yomitoku 'Jiyū de Hirekareta Indo Taiheiyō Senryaku' no Rinen to Jissen" [The Free and Open Indo-Pacific (FOIP) concept and process], *From the Oceans*, Sasakawa Heiwa Zaidan (Sasakawa Peace Foundation), April 23, 2018, https://www.spf.org/oceans/analysis_ja02/hpfoip.html#_ftn2.

88.   See, for example, Rory Medcalf, "Pivoting the Map: Australia's Indo-Pacific System," *Centre of Gravity*, Issue 1, Strategic and Defence Studies Centre, ANU College of Asia and the Pacific, Australian National University, November 2012; C. Raja Mohan, *Samudra Manthan: Sino-Indian Rivalry in the Indo-Pacific* (Washington, DC: Carnegie Endowment for International Peace, 2012), introduction, chaps. 6 and 7; Michael Green and Andrew Shearer, "Defining U.S. Indian Ocean Strategy," *Washington Quarterly* 35, no. 2 (Spring 2012): 175–89: all cited in Yoshinobu Yamamoto, "Indo Taihei Yo Gainen

wo Megutte" [Concerning the concept of Indo-Pacific], in *Ajia (Tokuni Minami Shina Kai Indo Yo) ni okeru Anzen Hosho Chitsujo* [Security order in Asia, especially in South China Sea and Indian Ocean], ed. Japan Institute of International Affairs, 5–23, http://www2.jiia.or.jp/pdf/resarch/H24_Asia_Security/introduction.pdf.

89. Michael J. Green and Nicholas Szechenyi, *Power and Order in Asia: A Survey of Regional Expectations*, Center for Strategic and International Studies, July 2014, https://csis-website-prod.s3.amazonaws.com/s3fs-public/legacy_files/files/publication/140605_Green_PowerandOrder_WEB.pdf.

90. *Diplomatic Bluebook 2017*, Chapter 1 Special Feature: "Free and Open Indo-Pacific Strategy," Ministry of Foreign Affairs of Japan, https://www.mofa.go.jp/files/000290287.pdf.

91. *White Paper on Development Cooperation 2017*, Ministry of Foreign Affairs of Japan, https://www.mofa.go.jp/files/000414121.pdf.

92. Rex Tillerson, "Defining Our Relationship with India for the Next Century: An Address by U.S. Secretary of State Rex Tillerson" (speech, Center for Strategic and International Studies, Washington DC, October 18, 2017), https://www.csis.org/analysis/defining-our-relationship-india-next-century-address-us-secretary-state-rex-tillerson.

93. "Japan-U.S. Working Lunch and Japan-U.S. Summit Meeting," Ministry of Foreign Affairs of Japan, November 6, 2017, https://www.mofa.go.jp/na/na1/us/page4e_000699.html.

94. U.S. Department of State, *A Free and Open Indo-Pacific: Advancing a Shared Vision*, November 4, 2019, https://www.state.gov/wp-content/uploads/2019/11/Free-and-Open-Indo-Pacific-4Nov2019.pdf.

95. Shoji Tomotaka, "ASEAN's Ambivalence Toward the Vision of a Free and Open Indo-Pacific: Mixture of Anxiety and Expectation," Sasakawa Peace Foundation, May 10, 2019, https://www.spf.org/iina/en/articles/shoji-southeastasia-foips.html. On ASEAN concerns about FOIP, see William Choong, "The Return of the Indo-Pacific Strategy: An Assessment," *Australian Journal of International Affairs* 73, no. 5 (2019): 415–30.

96. Association of Southeast Asian Nations, *ASEAN Outlook on the Indo-Pacific*, Association of Southeast Asian Nations, June 23, 2019, https://asean.org/storage/2019/06/ASEAN-Outlook-on-the-Indo-Pacific_FINAL_22062019.pdf; Denghua Zhang, "The Concept of 'Community of Common Destiny' in China's Diplomacy: Meaning, Motives and Implications," *Asia and the Pacific Policy Studies* 5, no. 2 (May 2018): 196–207, https://doi.org/10.1002/app5.231.

97. Dewi Fortuna Anwar, "Indonesia and the ASEAN Outlook on the Indo-Pacific," *International Affairs* 96, no. 1 (January 2020): 111–29, https://doi.org/10.1093/ia/iiz223.

98. Her Majesty's Government, United Kingdom, *Global Britain in a Competitive Age: The Integrated Review of Security, Defence, Development and Foreign Policy*, March 2021, https://assets.publishing.service.gov.uk/government/uploads/system/uploads/attachment_data/file/969402/The_Integrated_Review_of_Security__Defence__Development_and_Foreign_Policy.pdf; Ministère des Armées, République Française, *France and Security in the Indo-Pacific*, 2018 (updated May 2019).

99. Mina Pollmann, "The Trouble with Japan's Defense Exports," *The Diplomat*, October 2, 2015, https://thediplomat.com/2015/10/the-truth-about-japans-defense-exports/;

Mitsuko Hayashi, "How Japan Can Forge Resiliency and Defense Capacity Building in the Indo-Pacific in the Era of Covid-19," Center for Strategic and International Studies, July 17, 2020, https://www.csis.org/analysis/how-japan-can-forge-resiliency-and-defense-capacity-building-indo-pacific-era-covid-19.

100. Hayashi, "How Japan Can Forge Resiliency"; Walter Sim, "The Changing Face of Japan-ASEAN Aid: Tokyo Is Moving to Help Countries Build Up Their Military Capacity as Beijing Flexes Its Muscles in the S. China Sea," Straits Times, August 15, 2016, https://www.straitstimes.com/asia/east-asia/the-changing-face-of-japan-asean-aid.

101. "Nichi Betonamu Shunō Kaidan" [Japan-Vietnam heads of state meeting], Ministry of Foreign Affairs of Japan, October 19, 2020, https://www.mofa.go.jp/mofaj/s_sa/sea1/vn/page1_000888.html.

102. "Japan Latest Nation to Contest Beijing's South China Sea Claims," Radio Free Asia, January 23, 2021, https://www.voanews.com/east-asia-pacific/japan-latest-nation-contest-beijings-south-china-sea-claims.

103. Respondents considered Japan the first strategic option (38.2 percent) for hedging against U.S.-China competition, followed by the European Union (31.7 percent) and Australia (8.8 percent); see Tang Siew Mun et al., The State of Southeast Asia: 2020 Survey Report (Singapore: ISEAS Yusof Ishak Institute, 2020), https://www.iseas.edu.sg/images/ pdf/TheStateofSEASurveyReport_2020.pdf.

104. "Indo Taiheiyō no Dōshō Imu: Seisaku Daigakuin Gakuchō Tanaka Akihiko Shi" [Graduate Research Institute for Policy Studies president Tanaka Akihiko on same bed /different dreams in the Indo-Pacific], Nihon Keizai Shimbun, November 20, 2018; Shinichi Kitaoka, "Vision for a Free and Open Indo-Pacific," Asia-Pacific Review 26, no. 1 (2019): 7–17, https://www.tandfonline.com/doi/full/10.1080/13439006.2019.1618592.

105. Ankit Panda, "US, Japan, India, and Australia Hold Working-Level Quadrilateral Meeting on Regional Cooperation," The Diplomat, November 13, 2017, https://thediplomat.com/2017/11/us-japan-india-and-australia-hold-working-level-quadrilateral-meeting-on-regional-cooperation/.

106. Premesha Saha and Harsh V. Pant, "India's Pivot to Australia," Foreign Policy, July 21, 2020, https://foreignpolicy.com/2020/07/21/indias-pivot-to-australia/.

107. "Top Diplomats from 'Quad' Countries to Meet Oct. 6 in Tokyo," Japan Times, September 29, 2020, https://www.japantimes.co.jp/news/2020/09/29/national/japan-us-australia-india-quad-tokyo/#:~:text=The%20talks%20between%20representatives%20of%20the%20democracies%2C%20collectively,on%20the%20sidelines%20of%20the%20U.N.%20General%20Assembly.

108. Green, By More than Providence, 50–51, 79–86.

109. Joe Biden, Narendra Modi, Scott Morrison, and Yoshihide Suga, "Opinion: Our Four Nations Are Committed to a Free, Open, Secure and Prosperous Indo-Pacific Region," Washington Post, March 13, 2021, https://www.washingtonpost.com/opinions/2021/03/13/biden-modi-morrison-suga-quad-nations-indo-pacific/.

110. Colm Quinn, "Biden Attempts to Stretch the Quad," Foreign Policy, March 12, 2021, https://foreignpolicy.com/2021/03/12/quad-summit-japan-india-australia/.

111. Lucy Fisher, "Britain Could Join 'Asian NATO,'" *The Telegraph*, January 21, 2021, https://www.telegraph.co.uk/politics/2021/01/27/britain-could-join-asian-nato-proposal-expand-membership-counter/; Elizabeth Shim, "South Korea Could Work with Quad on Aligned Issues, Report Says," *UPI*, April 6, 2021, https://www.upi.com/Top_News/World-News/2021/04/06/skorea-South-Korea-Quad-policy-aligned/7891617713272/; Anirudh Bhattacharyya, "Canada Joins Quad Joint Naval Exercise in Pacific Ocean," *Hindustan Times*, January 25, 2021, https://www.hindustantimes.com/india-news/canada-to-join-quad-joint-naval-exercise-in-pacific-ocean-101611556512917.html.

112. Michael J. Green, Bates Gill, Kiyoto Tsuji, and William Watts, *Strategic Views on Asian Regionalism: Survey Results and Analysis*, Center for Strategic and International Studies, February 17, 2009, vi, https://www.csis.org/analysis/strategic-views-asian-regionalism; Green and Szechenyi, *Power and Order*, 1, 19; Michael J. Green and Amy K. Lehr, *The Sunnylands Principles on Enhancing Democratic Partnership in the Indo-Pacific Region*, Center for Strategic and International Studies, July 2020, 4, 14, https://csis-website-prod.s3.amazonaws.com/s3fs-public/publication/20710_Green_FullReport_v2_WEB%20FINAL.pdf.

113. Prime Minister Hosokawa Morihiro, *Shoshin Hyomei Enzetsu* [General policy speech], August 23, 1993, https://worldjpn.grips.ac.jp/documents/texts/pm/19930823.SWJ.html.

114. "Japan-U.S. Joint Declaration on Security: Alliance for the 21st Century," Ministry of Foreign Affairs of Japan, April 17, 1996, https://www.mofa.go.jp/region/n-america/us/security/security.html.

115. "Speech by Prime Minister Ryutaro Hashimoto: Seeking a New Foreign Policy Toward China," Ministry of Foreign Affairs of Japan, August 28, 1997, https://www.mofa.go.jp/region/asia-paci/china/seeking.html.

116. Hosokawa's coalition, though short-lived, introduced changes to Japan's electoral laws that included a hybrid regional list system and single-seat districts in the Lower House of the Diet. Since LDP factions had each had representatives in the earlier multiseat district system, the shift watered down politicians' need for factional support and the factions' own influence in Tokyo, opening the way for anti-mainstream populists like Koizumi. Alisa Gaunder, *Japanese Politics and Government* (London: Routledge, 2017), 69–73.

117. Keizo Nabeshima, "Koizumi Takes Aim at Collusion," *Japan Times*, March 25, 2002, https://www.japantimes.co.jp/opinion/2002/03/25/commentary/koizumi-takes-aim-at-collusion/#.XzL7LC2odQI.

118. "Speech by Prime Minister of Japan Junichiro Koizumi: Japan and ASEAN in East Asia: A Sincere and Open Partnership," Cabinet Office of the Prime Minister of Japan, Singapore, January 14, 2002, http:// www.kantei.go.jp/foreign/koizumispeech/2002/01/14speech_e.html.

119. "Asian Strategy as I See It: Japan as the 'Thought Leader' of Asia" (speech by Minister of Foreign Affairs Taro Aso at the Foreign Correspondents' Club of Japan), Ministry of Foreign Affairs of Japan, December 7, 2005, https://www.mofa.go.jp/announce/fm/aso/speech0512.html.

120. "Ronten: Ajia Gaikō Nihon no Eikyōryoku wa Bei no Kokueki Maikeru Guriin (Kikō)" [Michael Green: Japan's influence in its diplomacy within Asia is a U.S. national interest], *Yomiuri Shimbun*, March 22, 2006.

121. "Kachikan Gaikōwo Suishinsuru Giinrenmei: 'Abe Gaikō' Girenwo Kessei Shin YKK Kensei ka" [A parliamentary group to promote values-oriented diplomacy, formed to counter new "YKK"], *Mainichi Shimbun*, April 3, 2007.

122. "Shasetsu: Kachikan Giren 'Abe Ōendan' no Ayausa" [Editorial: "Value-oriented study group" danger of Abe cheerleaders], *Asahi Shimbun*, May 20, 2007.

123. "Fukuda Shushō: 'Kyōmei Gaikō' Tamesareru Genjitsu Taiōryoku" [Prime Minister Fukuda's synergy diplomacy], *Mainichi Shimbun*, November 25, 2007; "Press Conference by Prime Minister Yasuo Fukuda Following His Visits to the United States and Singapore," Ministry of Foreign Affairs of Japan, November 21, 2007, https://www.mofa.go.jp/region/asia-paci/eas/press0711.html; *Diplomatic Bluebook 2008*, Ministry of Foreign Affairs of Japan, 2.

124. Nobukatsu Kanehara, "Kokka Kokueki Kachito Gaikô Anzenhoshô" [Nation, national interest, value, diplomacy, and national security], in *RonshÛ Nihon no Gaikô to Sôgôteki Anzenhoshô* [Collection of essays: Japanese diplomacy and comprehensive national security], ed. Shotaro Yachi (Tokyo: Wedge, 2011).

125. *National Security Strategy*, December 17, 2013, Kantei, http://japan.kantei.go.jp/96_abe/documents/2013/__icsFiles/afieldfile/2013/12/17/NSS.pdf.

126. Yoichi Kato, "Reaction May Put Strategic Position at Risk," *Asahi Shimbun*, June 28, 2007.

127. Julian Ryall, "Japan PM Dismisses WWII War Crimes Trials as 'Victors' Justice,'" *The Telegraph* [London], March 14, 2013, https://www.telegraph.co.uk/news/worldnews/asia/japan/9930041/Japan-PM-dismisses-WWII-war-crimes-trials-as-victors-justice.html; "Shushō Kōno Danwano Minaoshi Shisan 'Kyōseisei Urazuke Nakatta'" [PM suggests review of Kono statement, saying "No coerciveness was confirmed"), *Sankei Shimbun*, March 2, 2007.

128. Caroline Rose, "The Battle for Hearts and Minds: Patriotic Education in Japan in the 1990s and Beyond," in *Nationalisms in Japan*, ed. Naoko Shimazu (Oxon, UK: Routledge, 2006), 131.

129. Japan Institute for National Fundamentals, "Refute International Criticism of 'Comfort Women,'" September 17, 2014, https://jinf.jp/suggestion/archives/14609; Japan Institute for National Fundamentals, "Verification of Kono Statement Has Not Yet Been Completed," July 17, 2014, https://jinf.jp/suggestion/archives/13516.

130. Alexis Dudden, *Troubled Apologies Among Japan, Korea and the United States* (New York: Columbia University Press, 2008), 57–59.

131. Dudden, *Troubled Apologies*, 57–59.

132. Kevin Michael Doak, *A History of Nationalism in Modern Japan: Placing the People* (Boston: Brill, 2007).

133. Kanehara later expanded on this historical context after leaving Abe's office in *Rekishi no Kyōkun* [The lessons of history] (Tokyo: Iwanami Shoten, 2020); on Professor Haneda, see his profile at: http://www.ioc.u-tokyo.ac.jp/eng/faculty/prof/haneda.html.

134.   *Toward the Abe Statement on the 70th Anniversary of the End of World War II: Lessons from the 20th Century and a Vision for the 21st Century for Japan* (English edition of *Sengo 70 Nen Danwa no Ronten*) (Tokyo: Japan Publishing Industry Foundation for Culture, 2015), iii.

135.   I testified informally to the committee leadership on the international context of their work when they were established. Liberal Democratic Party of Japan, "Submission of Proposal for Restoring Japan's Honor and Trust to Prime Minister Abe," July 30, 2015, https://www.jimin.jp/news/policy/128438.html.

136.   Shinzō Abe, "Statement by Prime Minister Shinzo Abe," August 14, 2015, https://japan.kantei.go.jp/97_abe/statement/201508/0814statement.html (ENG) or https://www.kantei.go.jp/jp/97_abe/statement/2015/0814kaiken.html (JPN).

137.   "Statement by Prime Minister Tomiichi Murayama 'On the Occasion of the 50th Anniversary of the War's End,'" Ministry of Foreign Affairs of Japan, August 15, 1995, https://www.mofa.go.jp/announce/press/pm/murayama/9508.html.

138.   "Yoron Chōsa Abe Danwa 44 Percent Hyōka" [Public opinion polls: 44 percent approve Abe statement], *Kyodo News*, August 15, 2015.

139.   "Sengo 70nen Shushō Danwa Kōmei Daihyōga Hyōka Chūkan Kankei Kaizen ni Tsunagetai" [Komeito chief approves the PM statement, hoping it would lead to a better relationship with China and South Korea], *NHK News*, August 15, 2015.

140.   David Brunnstrom, "U.S. Welcomes Abe's Statement on War Anniversary," Reuters, August 14, 2015, https://www.reuters.com/article/us-ww2-anniversary-usa/u-s-welcomes-abes-statement-on-war-anniversary-idUKKCN0QJ1OP20150814.

141.   "Park Praises Abe's WWII Statement to Certain Extent," *Jiji Press*, August 15, 2015.

142.   "China Raps Abe's War-End Anniversary Statement," *Jiji Press*, August 15, 2015.

143.   "ODA Kentōkai Menbā Kettei Hihanha Zoroi Nijimu 'Abe Karā'" [Members of the ODA commission reflect Abe's color], *Sankei Shimbun*, December 3, 2005.

144.   *Japan's Development Cooperation Policy: Development Cooperation Charter*, Ministry of Foreign Affairs of Japan, November 2, 2015, https://www.mofa.go.jp/files/000406629.pdf#:~:text=Basic%20policies%20of%20the%20development%20cooperation%20of%20Japan,for%20non-military%20purposes%20is%20one%20of%20the%20most.

145.   Ichihara Maiko, "Understanding Japanese Democracy Assistance," Carnegie Endowment for International Peace, March 25, 2013, http://carnegieendowment.org/2013/03/25/understanding-japanese-democracy-%20assistance/ftcg; Ichihara Maiko, *Japan's International Democracy Assistance as Soft Power: Neoclassical Realist Analysis* (Abingdon, Oxon: Routledge, 2017).

146.   "Survey of Japanese Legislators: Attitudes on ODA and Global Health," Japan Center for International Exchange, June 2020, https://www.jcie.org/analysis/jcie-diet-survey-on-global-health-oda/.

147.   "Comments of Ambassador Takasu Yukio at the EAI Online Seminar Enhancing Democratic Partnership in the Indo-Pacific," East Asia Institute, September 18, 2020 (KST), http://www.eai.or.kr/new/en/news/notice_view.asp?intSeq=19997&board=eng_announcement; The Future of Democracy Project, JCIE, http://democracy.jcie.or.jp/.

148. Atsuko Geiger, *Japan's Support for Democracy-Related Issues* (Tokyo: Japan Center for International Exchange, 2019), https://www.jcie.org/wp-content/uploads/2019/10/Japan-Democracy-Survey-2019_FINAL.pdf; Ichihara, *Japan's International Democracy Assistance as Soft Power.* On the rulemaking group, see "Chūgoku Kensei suru Jimingiin Yūshino Ugoki Kappatsuka" [Activities increase among LDP lawmakers to restrain China, proposal on training future leaders in international organizations to be submitted to the government], *Mainichi Shimbun*, August 27, 2020, https://mainichi.jp/articles/20200827/k00/00m/010/255000c.

149. "Mapping the Future of U.S. China Policy," Center for Strategic and International Studies, October 13, 2020, https://chinasurvey.csis.org/.

150. "Japan to Back EU-Led U.N. Resolution on Human Rights in North Korea," *Japan Times*, March 12, 2020, https://www.japantimes.co.jp/news/2020/03/12/national/japan-un-resolution-human-rights-north-korea/. The exception was in 2019, when Abe tried to send an olive branch to Pyongyang in the wake of President Trump's summits with Kim Jong-un, but without any reciprocation, as we shall see in chapter 5.

151. "Japan Rejects Offer to Join Statement Slamming China over Hong Kong Law," *Japan Times*, June 7, 2020, https://www.japantimes.co.jp/news/2020/06/07/national/japan-rejects-offer-join-us-criticizing-china-hong-kong/#:~:text=WASHINGTON%20%E2%80%93%20Japan%20has%20opted%20out%20of%20joining,with%20Beijing%2C%20officials%20from%20countries%20involved%20said%20Saturday.

152. Gen Nakatani, "Jinken Gaikō Giin Renmei" [Parliamentary Federation on Human Rights Diplomacy], Gen Nakatani official website, March 25, 2021, https://nakatanigen.jp/?p=3026 (site discontinued), archived at https://web.archive.org/web/20210921191207/https://nakatanigen.jp/?p=3026.

153. "Japan, U.S. Express Concerns over Myanmar Refugee Crisis," *Japan Times*, September 20, 2017, https://english.kyodonews.net/news/2017/09/886653f29998-japan-us-express-concerns-over-myanmar-refugee-crisis.html#:~:text=Japan%20and%20the%20United%20States%20expressed%20strong%20concerns,reporters%20after%20a%20series%20of%20meetings%20with%20counterparts.

154. "Japan, the United States, and the Future of World Order," Johns Hopkins School of Advanced International Studies, Henry A. Kissinger Center for Global Affairs (remarks of Dr. Kurt M. Campbell, deputy assistant to the president and senior coordinator for Indo-Pacific affairs, National Security Council), March 24, 2021, https://sais.jhu.edu/kissinger/events/us-japan.

155. See, for example, Benjamin Reilly, "Why Is 'Values' the New Buzzword in Australian Foreign Policy? (Hint: It Has Something to Do with China)," *The Conversation*, August 5, 2020, https://theconversation.com/why-is-values-the-new-buzzword-in-australian-foreign-policy-hint-it-has-something-to-do-with-china-143839; *EU-China—A Strategic Outlook*, European Commission, March 12, 2019, https://ec.europa.eu/commission/sites/beta-political/files/communication-eu-china-a-strategic-outlook.pdf.

156. Green and Szechenyi, *Power and Order in Asia*, 18.

157. " 'Wasurerareta Kokusai Jōyaku' ga Hatashita Ōkina Yakuwari / 'Kyū Sekai Chitsujo' wa 'Shin Sekai Chitsujo' ni Tenjita" [Large roles played by "forgotten international

treaties" / "old world order" turned into "new world order"], *Weekly Toyo Keizai*, October 12, 2018.

158. Saori Katada, *Japan's New Regional Reality: Geoeconomic Strategy in the Asia-Pacific* (New York: Columbia University Press, 2020), loc. 333 of 10287, Kindle.

159. Steven K. Vogel, *Japan Remodeled: How Government and Industry Are Reforming Japanese Capitalism* (Ithaca, NY: Cornell University Press, 2006).

160. Katada, *Japan's New Regional Reality*, loc. 1962 of 10287, Kindle.

161. Wu Jiao, "President Xi Gives Speech to Indonesia's Parliament," *China Daily*, October 2, 2013, https://www.chinadaily.com.cn/china/2013xiapec/2013-10/02/content_17007915.htm.

162. "AIIB Zaimusō Tōmen Sanka Miokurino Hōshin Shimesu 'Chūgoku Gawano Setsumei Fujūbun'" [Finance minister says Japan's accession to AIIB will not take place for the time being as China's explanation is insufficient], *NHK News*, March 31, 2015.

163. "'The Future of Asia: Be Innovative'—Speech by Prime Minister Shinzo Abe at the Banquet of the 21st International Conference on the Future of Asia," Prime Minister of Japan and His Cabinet, May 21, 2015, http://japan.kantei.go.jp/97_abe/statement /201505/0521foaspeech.html; "Announcement of 'Partnership for Quality Infrastructure: Investment for Asia's Future,'" Ministry of Foreign Affairs of Japan, May 21, 2015, https://www.mofa.go.jp/policy/oda/page18_000076.html.

164. Daniel F. Runde et al., "Report Launch: Financing and Implementing the Quality Infrastructure Agenda," Center for Strategic and International Studies, September 4, 2018, https://www.csis.org/events/report-launch-financing-and-implementing-quality-infra -structure-agenda; Jonathan Hillman, "'China's Belt and Road Initiative: Five Years Later': Statement Before the U.S.-China Economic and Security Review Commission" (speech, 419 Dirksen Senate Office Building, Washington, DC, January 25, 2018), https://csis-web -site-prod.s3.amazonaws.com/s3fs-public/publication/ts180125_hillman_testimony.pdf.

165. Robin Harding, Avantika Chilkoti, and Tom Mitchell, "Japan Cries Foul After Indonesia Awards Rail Contract to China," *Financial Times*, October 1, 2015, https://www .ft.com/content/eca4af84-67fa-11e5-97d0-1456a776a4f5; "Indoneshia Kōsoku Tetsudō Hakushi Itten Chūgokuan wo Saiyō Kambōchō 'Kiwamete Ikan'" [CCS says "extremely regrettable" in response to Indonesia's decision to adopt China's plan for its high-speed rail], *Nihon Keizai Shimbun*, September 30, 2015; Shang-su Wu, "Is Japan's Rail Diplomacy in Southeast Asia Moving Away from Shinkansen?" *The Diplomat*, October 23, 2019, https://thediplomat.com/2019/10/is-japans-rail-diplomacy-in-southeast-asia-moving -away-from-shinkansen/.

166. See, for example, Agatha Kratz and Dragan Pavlićević, "Norm-Making, Norm-Taking or Norm-Shifting? A Case Study of Sino–Japanese Competition in the Jakarta–Bandung High-Speed Rail Project," *Third World Quarterly* 40, no. 6 (2019): 1113.

167. "Amendment of the JBIC Act," Japan Bank for International Cooperation, May 11, 2016, https://www.jbic.go.jp/en/information/news/news-2016/0511-48128.html. JBIC immediately made use of its greater flexibility in loans to India; see Zhao Hong, "China–Japan Compete for Infrastructure Investment in Southeast Asia: Geopolitical Rivalry or Healthy Competition?" *Journal of Contemporary China* 28, no. 118 (2019): 574, https://www.tandfonline.com/doi/abs/10.1080/10670564.2018.1557946.

168. Jane Perlez, "U.S. Opposing China's Answer to World Bank," *New York Times*, October 9, 2014, https://www.nytimes.com/2014/10/10/world/asia/chinas-plan-for-regional-development-bank-runs-into-us-opposition.html; David Lawder, "After Ex-Im Win, U.S. Conservatives Target Foreign Investment Agency," Reuters, July 13, 2015, https://www.reuters.com/article/us-usa-congress-opic/after-ex-im-win-u-s-conservatives-target-foreigninvestment-agency-idUSKCN0PN0EM20150713.

169. Daniel Runde and Romina Bandura, "The BUILD Act Has Passed: What's Next?" Center for Strategic and International Studies, October 12, 2018, https://www.csis.org/analysis/build-act-has-passed-whats-next.

170. Daniel Runde, Romina Bandura, and Janina Staguhn, "The DFC's New Equity Authority," Center for Strategic and International Studies, April 3, 2020, https://www.csis.org/analysis/dfcs-new-equity-authority.

171. "Joint Statement of the Governments of the United States of America, Australia, and Japan," White House, November 17, 2018, https://www.whitehouse.gov/briefings-statements/joint-statement-governments-united-states-america-australia-japan/ (site discontinued), archived at https://web.archive.org/web/20181118161517/https://www.whitehouse.gov/briefings-statements/joint-statement-governments-united-states-america-australia-japan/;"U.S., Australia, Japan Delegation Travels to Indonesia to Explore Investment Opportunities," U.S. International Development Finance Corporation, August 27, 2019, https://www.dfc.gov/media/opic-press-releases/us-australia-japan-delegation-travels-indonesia-explore-investment; "OPIC to Support World's Longest Subsea Telecommuniations Cable," U.S. International Development Finance Corporation, November 5, 2019, https://www.dfc.gov/media/opic-press-releases/opic-support-worlds-longest-subsea-telecommunications-cable.

172. Christopher K. Johnson, Matthew P. Goodman, and Jonathan E. Hillman, "President Xi Jinping's 'Belt and Road' Forum," Center for Strategic and International Studies, May 9, 2017, https://www.csis.org/analysis/president-xi-jinpings-belt-and-road-forum.

173. "JBIC Signs MOU with China Development Bank," Japan Bank for International Cooperation, October 26, 2018, https://www.jbic.go.jp/en/information/press/press-2018/1026-011525.html.

174. IMF managing director Christine Lagarde noted at a speech during a conference with the IMF and the People's Bank of China (PBC) in Beijing in April 2018: "The Belt and Road Initiative can provide much-needed infrastructure financing to partner countries. However, these ventures can also lead to a problematic increase in debt, potentially limiting other spending as debt service rises, and creating balance of payment challenges." Christine Lagarde, "Belt and Road Initiative: Strategies to Deliver in the Next Phase," International Monetary Fund, April 12, 2018, https://www.imf.org/en/News/Articles/2018/04/11/sp041218-belt-and-road-initiative-strategies-to-deliver-in-the-next-phaseo.

175. "Japan's Infrastructure Development Strategy: Supporting a Free and Open Indo-Pacific," Center for Strategic and International Studies, October 17, 2019, https://www.csis.org/events/japans-infrastructure-development-strategy-supporting-free-and-open-indo-pacific.

176. During a keynote speech at the opening ceremony, Xi Jinping emphasized the high-quality, sustainable infrastructure under BRI. The "high-quality infrastructure" was also mentioned in the joint communiqué. "Xi Delivers Keynote Speech at Second B&R Forum," *China Daily*, April 26, 2019, https://www.chinadaily.com.cn/a/201904/26 /WS5cc26353a3104842260b880d.html; "Joint Communique of the Leaders' Roundtable of the 2nd Belt and Road Forum for International Cooperation," Ministry of Foreign Affairs of the People's Republic of China, April 27, 2019, https://www.fmprc.gov.cn /mfa_eng/zxxx_662805/t1658766.shtml.

177. "China No Match for Japan in Southeast Asia Infrastructure Race," *Japan Times*, June 23, 2019, https://www.japantimes.co.jp/news/2019/06/23/business/china-no-match-japan -southeast-asia-infrastructure-race/.

178. William Choong, *Japan's Indo-Pacific Strategy in Southeast Asia: Floundering, not Foundering*, ISEAS Yusof Ishak Institute, May 6, 2020, https://www.iseas.edu.sg/wp-content /uploads/2020/03/ISEAS_Perspective_2020_40.pdf.

179. Nyshka Chandran, "Japan, Not China, May Be Winning Asia's Infrastructure Investment Contest," *CNBC*, January 23, 2019, https://www.cnbc.com/2019/01/23/belt-and -road-japan-not-china-may-be-winning-investment-contest.html.

180. Koya Jibiki, "Indoneshia, Nihon ni Kousoku Tetsudou Sanka Dashin e Chuugoku Shudou de Okure" [Indonesia to offer Japan participation in Chinese-led high-speed rail project facing delays], *Nihon Keizai Shimbun*, June 7, 2020, https://www.nikkei .com/article/DGXMZO60080710X00C20A6FF8000/.

181. See Midford, *Overcoming Isolationism*.

182. Sheldon Simon, "Deep in South China Sea Diplomacy," *Comparative Connections*, September 2011, http://cc.pacforum.org/2011/09/deep-south-china-sea-diplomacy/; Andrew Quinn, "U.S. Calls for More Clarity on South China Sea Claims," Reuters, July 22, 2011, https://www.reuters.com/article/us-asean-southchinasea/u-s-calls-for-more-clarity -on-south-china-sea-claims-idUSTRE76M0KS20110723.

183. Manuel Mogato, Michael Martina, and Ben Blanchard, "ASEAN Deadlocked on South China Sea, Cambodia Blocks Statement," Reuters, July 25, 2016, https://www.reuters.com /article/us-southchinasea-ruling-asean/asean-deadlocked-on-south-china-sea -cambodia-blocks-statement-idUSKCN1050F6; James Kynge, Leila Haddou, and Michael Peel, "FT Investigation: How China Bought Its Way into Cambodia," *Financial Times*, September 8, 2016, https://www.ft.com/content/23968248-43a0-11e6-b22f -79eb4891c97d.

184. Green and Szechenyi, *Power and Order in Asia*, 7–8.

185. Green and Szechenyi, *Power and Order in Asia*, 16.

186. Myron Brilliant, "Free Trade Agreement Asia Pacific (FTAAP)," U.S. Chamber of Commerce, September 2007, https://www.uschamber.com/free-trade-agreement-asia -pacific-ftaap.

187. Peter Landers, "Japan, the Original Trade Villain, Now Casts Itself as the Hero," *Wall Street Journal*, March 9, 2018, https://www.wsj.com/articles/japan-the-original-trade -villain-now-casts-itself-as-the-hero-1520591404.

188. "The 4th Regional Comprehensive Economic Partnership (RCEP) Summit and RCEP Agreement Signing Ceremony," Ministry of Foreign Affairs of Japan, November 15, 2020, https://www.mofa.go.jp/policy/economy/fta/page1e_000291.html.

189. *RCEP Kyōtei no Keizai Kōka Bunseki* [Analysis of RCEP's economic impact], Government of Japan, March 19, 2021, https://www.mofa.go.jp/mofaj/files/100162437.pdf.

190. Tobias Sytsma, "RCEP Forms the World's Largest Trading Bloc. What Does This Mean for Global Trade?" *RAND Blog*, December 9, 2020, https://www.rand.org /blog/2020/12/rcep-forms-the-worlds-largest-trading-bloc-what-does.html; William Alan Reinsch, Lydia Murray, and Jack Caporal, "At Last, an RCEP Deal," Center for Strategic and International Studies, December 3, 2019, https://www.csis.org/analysis /last-rcep-deal; Cathleen Cimino-Isaacs and Michael Sutherland, "The Regional Comprehensive Economic Partnership: Status and Recent Developments," Congressional Research Service, November 19, 2019, https://crsreports.congress.gov /product/pdf/IN/IN11200. For Japan's perspective and the current statistics, see Shin Kawashima, "Japan's Painful Choice on RCEP," *The Diplomat*, August 3, 2020, https:// thediplomat.com/2020/08/japans-painful-choice-on-rcep/; "RCEP States Make 'Significant' Progress in Trade Talks Without India," *Japan Times*, August 27, 2020, https:// www.japantimes.co.jp/news/2020/08/27/business/economy-business/rcep-states -make-significant-progress-trade-talks-without-india/.

191. A survey conducted by the Chicago Council on Global Affairs in October 2019 showed that 83 percent of Americans thought international trade is good for American companies, and 87 percent said that international trade is good for the U.S. economy, the highest recorded in Chicago Council surveys since the question was first asked in 2004. For more details, see Brendan Helm, Alexander Hitch, and Dina Smeltz, "Record Number of Americans Say International Trade Is Good for the US Economy," Chicago Council on Global Affairs, October 9, 2019, https://www.thechi -cagocouncil.org/research/public-opinion-survey/record-number-americans-say -international-trade-good-us-economy. In the online event with CSIS in September 2020, then defense minister Kono Taro said, "I'm still hoping one day U.S. will come back to TPP and U.S. and Japan could lead rulemaking in this region.... And hopefully like-minded countries could sit down, and United States will be leader of this camp again and we can try to unite global community based on the common values." For the transcript, see "Online Event: Mt. Fuji DC Event: The U.S.-Japan Alliance at 60," Center for Strategic and International Studies, September 9, 2020, https://www.csis .org/analysis/online-event-mt-fuji-dc-event-us-japan-alliance-60. On U.S. business alarm at being left out of RCEP and CPTPP, see Myron Brilliant, "U.S. Chamber Statement on the Regional Comprehensive Partnership Agreement (RCEP)," U.S. Chamber of Commerce, November 16, 2020, https://www.uschamber.com/press-release/us -chamber-statement-the-regional-comprehensive-partnership-agreement-rcep.

192. "Japan Trade Agreement," U.S. Customs and Border Protection, last modified April 5, 2021, https://www.cbp.gov/trade/free-trade-agreements/japan.

193. *Agreement Between the United States of America and Japan Concerning Digital Trade*, Office of the United States Trade Representative, https://ustr.gov/sites/default/files

/files/agreements/japan/Agreement_between_the_United_States_and_Japan_concerning_Digital_Trade.pdf.

194. Reuters, "China Applies to Join Pacific Trade Pact to Boost Economic C Clout," September 17, 2021, https://www.reuters.com/world/china/china-officially-applies-join-cptpp-trade-pact-2021-09-16/

195. "Japan's Successful Participation in the Trans-Pacific Partnership (TPP) Agreement: Preparing for a 21st Century, WTO-plus Agreement," U.S.-Japan Business Council, June 2011, 36.

196. For example, a proposal submitted by Keidanren in April 2011 notes: "No great shift has been observed in Japan's trade strategy . . . while other countries have been tackling trade issues strategically in pursuit of sources of growth and employment. For example, South Korea has signed FTAs with the United States and the EU. . . . On the other hand, there are concerns in Japan about the widening gap with South Korea in conditions of competition." For more details, see "Proposals for Japan's Trade Strategy," Nippon Keidanren (Japan Business Federation), April 19, 2011, https://www.keidanren.or.jp/en/policy/2011/030proposal.html.

197. "EU-Japan Trade Agreement Enters into Force," European Commission, January 31, 2019, https://ec.europa.eu/commission/presscorner/detail/en/IP_19_785.

198. *Waga Kuni no Keizai Renkei Kyōtei (EPA/ FTA) tō no Torikumi* [Our country's efforts in initiatives such as economic partnerships (EPA/FTA)], Ministry of Foreign Affairs of Japan, March 2021, https://www.mofa.go.jp/mofaj/files/000490260.pdf.

199. Shinzō Abe, "Address by Prime Minister Abe at the Seventy-Third Session of the United Nations General Assembly" (speech, September 25, 2018), Prime Minister of Japan and His Cabinet, https://japan.kantei.go.jp/98_abe/statement/201809/_00005.html.

200. A twenty-page report issued by the White House in May 2020 condemns China's "predatory economic practices." For more, see *United States Strategic Approach to the People's Republic of China*, White House, https://www.whitehouse.gov/wp-content/uploads/2020/05/U.S.-Strategic-Approach-to-The-Peoples-Republic-of-China-Report-5.20.20.pdf; "Pompeo says China trade policies 'predatory,'" Reuters, June 18, 2018, https://www.reuters.com/article/us-usa-trade-pompeo/pompeo-says-china-trade-policies-predatory-idUSKBN1JE2QK?il=0.

201. Xi Jinping, "Secure a Decisive Victory in Building a Moderately Prosperous Society in All Respects and Strive for the Great Success of Socialism with Chinese Characteristics for a New Era—Delivered at the 19th National Congress of the Communist Party of China," *Xinhua*, October 18, 2017, http://www.xinhuanet.com/english/download/Xi_Jinping's_report_at_19th_CPC_National_Congress.pdf.

202. See, for example, Alistair Iain Johnstone, "China in a World of Orders: Rethinking Compliance and Challenge in Beijing's International Relations," *International Security* 44, no. 3 (2019): 9–60.

203. "G7 Ise-Shima Summit," Ministry of Foreign Affairs of Japan, May 27, 2016, https://www.mofa.go.jp/ecm/ec/page24e_000148.html.

204. "G-7 Ends in Disarray as Trump Abandons Joint Statement," *BBC*, June 10, 2018, https://www.bbc.com/news/world-us-canada-44427660.

205. Interview with senior MOFA official, June 12, 2018.

206. Jesco Denzel, *Heads of State Attend G7 Meeting—Day Two*, 2018, Bundesregierung, https://www.gettyimages.com/detail/news-photo/in-this-photo-provided-by-the-german-government-press-news-photo/971491304?adppopup=true.

207. Satoshi Sugiyama, "Abe Hails Launch of 'Osaka Track' Framework for Free Cross-Border Data Flow at G20," *Japan Times*, June 18, 2019, https://www.japantimes.co.jp/news/2019/06/28/national/abe-heralds-launch-osaka-track-framework-free-cross-border-data-flow-g20/.

208. *Asia Power Index 2019: Key Findings*, Lowy Institute, https://power.lowyinstitute.org/downloads/Lowy-Institute-Asia-Power-Index-2019-Key-Findings.pdf.

209. *Asia Power Index 2019*.

210. Alex Oliver, "2018 Lowy Institute Poll," June 20, 2018, https://www.lowyinstitute.org/publications/2018-lowy-institute-poll.

211. "Opinion Poll on Japan," Ministry of Foreign Affairs of Japan, March 18, 2020, https://www.mofa.go.jp/press/release/press4e_002784.html.

212. Sharon Seah, Hoang Thi Ha, Melinda Martinus, and Pham Thi Phuong Thao, *The State of Southeast Asia: 2021 Survey Report*, ISEAS Yusof Ishak Institute, February 10, 2021, https://www.iseas.edu.sg/wp-content/uploads/2021/01/The-State-of-SEA-2021-v2.pdf.

213. Dong-Hun Lee, "Nation Brands, 2011 Survey Results," *SERI Quarterly* 5, no. 2 (April 2012): 97–102.

214. *Asia Power Index 2019*. Lowy downgraded Japan for ending ODA to China, which seems like a wise decision in relative power terms rather than a loss of actual power, but the warning about Japanese aggregate power resonates all the same.

5. KOREA

1. For example, the 2014 poll conducted by CSIS shows that Japanese and Korean respondents share the understanding that promoting good governance is important for the region (Japan 97 percent, Korea 92 percent), collapse of North Korea poses challenges to national security (Japan 7.4, Korea 8.3), lack of common values (Japan 7.2, Korea 6.8) and uncertainty about a rising China (Japan 8.6, Korea 7.3) are obstacles for building community in East Asia, and both expect continued U.S. leadership in East Asia over the next decade (Japan 79, Korea 82). For more, see Michael J. Green and Nicholas Szechenyi, *Power and Order in Asia: A Survey of Regional Expectations*, Center for Strategic and International Studies, July 2014, https://csis-website-prod.s3.amazonaws.com/s3fs-public/legacy_files/files/publication/140605_Green_PowerandOrder_WEB.pdf. These results were paralleled in the 2020 CSIS survey on China policy; see: https://chinasurvey.csis.org/.

2. Mark R. Peattie, introduction to *The Japanese Colonial Empire, 1895–1945*, ed. Ramon Hawley Myers and Mark R. Peattie (Princeton, NJ: Princeton University Press, 1984), 15.

3. Most international organizations and the United States Board on Geographic Names refer to the waters as the Sea of Japan or Japan Sea, but Japan and Korea continue to

dispute the nomenclature in the United Nations and other international forums. See: https://www.usgs.gov/core-science-systems/ngp/board-on-geographic-names.

4. Hans J. Morgenthau, *Politics Among Nations: The Struggle for Power and Peace*, 2nd ed. (New York: Knopf, 1967), 117.

5. Samuel Jay Hawley, *The Imjin War: Japan's Sixteenth-Century Invasion of Korea and Attempt to Conquer China* (Seoul: Royal Asiatic Society, Korea Branch, 2005), 45; Arata Hirakawa, *Sengoku Nihon to Daikōkai Jidai Hideyoshi Ieyasu Masamune no Gaikō Senryaku* [Sengoku-era Japan and the Age of Exploration: Diplomatic strategy of Hideyoshi, Ieyasu, and Masamune] (Tokyo: Chuo Koron Shinsha, 2018).

6. Park Cheol Hee, *Strategic Estrangement Between South Korea and Japan as a Barrier to Trilateral Cooperation*, Atlantic Council, November 2019, https://www.atlanticcouncil .org/wp-content/uploads/2019/12/Strategic-Estrangement-Report-web.pdf.

7. Victor D. Cha, *Alignment Despite Antagonism: The United States-Korea-Japan Security Triangle* (Palo Alto, CA: Stanford University Press, 1999), 10.

8. Scott A. Snyder, *South Korea at the Crossroads: Autonomy and Alliance in an Era of Rival Powers* (New York: Columbia University Press, 2018), 122.

9. For example, see Chaesung Chun, "South Korea's Middle Power Strategy as a Foreign Strategy," *American Studies* 37, no. 2 (December 2014): 45–80, http://210.101.116.16/kiss61 /download_viewer.asp (site discontinued), archived at https://web.archive.org/web /20200710014757/https://s-space.snu.ac.kr/bitstream/10371/93894/1/%EB%AF%B8% EA%B5%AD%ED%95%99%2037-2-2..pdf; Jongryn Mo, "South Korea's Middle Power Diplomacy: A Case of Growing Compatibility Between Regional and Global Roles," *International Journal* [Toronto] 71, no. 4 (December 1, 2016): 587–607.

10. "Paku Gaikō Yūsen Juni wa 'Bei Chū tsugini Nichiro' Gaishō Kōho ga Kenkai" [For Park diplomacy the order of priority is "the U.S., China, followed by Japan and Russia"], *Yomiuri Shimbun*, March 1, 2013.

11. "Kankoku 'Nihon Hazushi' Gaikō Kaigi ya Senryaku Taiwa Beichū nomini Dashin Nihon Seifu Fukaikan" [Korean diplomacy to remove Japan, suggesting conferences and strategic dialogue only to the United States and China; Japanese government showing annoyance], *Yomiuri Shimbun*, May 14, 2013; "Bei Kokumushō Iijimashi Hōchō 'Kōkan no Hōnichiji ni Shōsai Kiku'" [U.S. Department of State on Mr. Iijima's North Korea visit "will ask in detail when the senior official visits Japan"], *Nihon Keizai Shimbun*, May 15, 2013.

12. "CSIS Experts Participate in Seoul 'Track 1.5' Dialogues," Center for Strategic and International Studies, July 22, 2013, https://www.csis.org/news/csis-experts-participate -seoul-%E2%80%9Ctrack-15%E2%80%9D-dialogues; "Bei Chū Kan de Anpo Kaigi 22nichi Kaisai e Kankoku 'Nihon Hazushi' de Shin Wakugumi" [U.S.-China-Korea security conference to be held on the 22nd—Korea to create a new framework without Japan], *Kyodo News*, July 19, 2013.

13. *Diplomatic Bluebook 2015*, Ministry of Foreign Affairs of Japan, 28, https://www .mofa.go.jp/files/000106464.pdf (site discontinued), archived at https://web.archive .org/web/20210921192052/https://www.mofa.go.jp/files/000106464.pdf; *Diplomatic Bluebook 2018*, Ministry of Foreign Affairs of Japan, 26, https://www.mofa.go.jp/files/000401242

.pdf (site discontinued), archived at https://web.archive.org/web/20201217090515/https://www.mofa.go.jp/files/000401242.pdf.

14. Ian Rinehart and Bart Elias, "China's Air Defense Identification Zone (ADIZ)," Congressional Research Service, January 30, 2015, 18–21; Victor Cha, *Korea's Mistake on China's ADIZ Controversy*, CSIS Korea Chair Platform, December 2, 2013, https://www.csis.org/analysis/korea%E2%80%99s-mistake-china%E2%80%99s-adiz-controversy, https://fas.org/sgp/crs/row/R43894.pdf.

15. "The Japan–South Korea Joint Public Opinion Poll 2019," Genron NPO, June 12, 2019, https://www.genron-npo.net/en/opinion_polls/archives/5489.html.

16. Narushige Michishita, "Changing Security Relationship Between Japan and South Korea: Frictions and Hopes," *Asia-Pacific Review* 21, no. 2 (2014): 24, https://www.tandfonline.com/doi/abs/10.1080/13439006.2014.970327.

17. Michishita, "Changing Security Relationship," 26.

18. See, for example, *Mapping the Future of U.S. China Policy*, https://chinasurvey.csis.org/.

19. See, for example, David C. Kang and Jiun Bang, "The Pursuit of Autonomy and Korea's Atypical Strategic Culture," in *Strategic Asia 2016–17: Understanding Strategic Cultures in the Asia-Pacific*, ed. Michael Wills, Ashley J. Tellis, and Alison Szalwinski (Seattle: National Bureau of Asian Research, November 2016), https://www.nbr.org/publication/the-pursuit-of-autonomy-and-south-koreas-atypical-strategic-culture/.

20. "Sōru de Nichibeikan Bōei Jitsumusha Kyōgi" [Japan-U.S.-Korea defense working-level talks in Seoul], *Asahi Shimbun*, April 24, 1998; "Sōru de Nichibeikan Bōei Kyōgi" [Japan-U.S.-Korea defense talks in Seoul], *Nihon Keizai Shimbun*, October 20, 1998.

21. "Trilateral Statement Japan, Republic of Korea, and the United States," Office of the Spokesman, U.S. Department of State, December 6, 2010, https://2009-2017.state.gov/r/pa/prs/ps/2010/12/152431.htm.

22. "Living History with Ambassador Chun Yung-woo" (CSIS Korea Chair oral history interview), August 9, 2017, https://beyondparallel.csis.org/living-history-ambassador-chun-yung-woo/.

23. Brad Glosserman and Scott A. Snyder, *The Japan–South Korea Identity Clash: East Asian Security and the United States* (New York: Columbia University Press, 2015), 97.

24. Chung Min-uck, "Lawmakers Express Concern over Korea-Japan Military Pact," *Korea Times*, July 11, 2012; Mark Manyin, Emma Chanlett-Avery, et al., *U.S.-South Korea Relations*, Congressional Research Service, May 23, 2017, 8, https://fas.org/sgp/crs/row/R41481.pdf.

25. Choe Hang Sun, "South Korea Fires Top Presidential Aide over Pact with Japan," *New York Times*, August 5, 2012, https://www.nytimes.com/2012/07/06/world/asia/south-korean-aide-offers-to-resign-over-pact-with-japan.html.

26. Michael J. Green, *Japan's Reluctant Realism: Foreign Policy Challenges in an Era of Uncertain Power* (New York: Palgrave Macmillan, 2001), 118.

27. James Schoff, *Tools for Trilateralism: Improving U.S.-Japan-Korea Cooperation to Manage Complex Contingencies* (Institute for Foreign Policy Analysis, Cambridge, MA: Potomac, 2005), http://www.ifpa.org/pdf/Tools.pdf; Yul Sohn, "Relocating Trilateralism in a Broader Regional Architecture: A South Korean Perspective," National

Bureau of Asian Research, March 25, 2016, https://www.nbr.org/publication/relocating-trilateralism-in-a-broader-regional-architecture-a-south-korean-perspective-brief/.

28. "Nihon Gaikō Henka to Mosaku (Jō) Kitachōsen tono Himitsu Kōshō" [Change and search of Japanese diplomacy (first part): Secret negotiation with North Korea—reliance on Tanaka deciding the outcome], *Nihon Keizai Shinbun*, December 22, 2002.

29. "Seijōka Kōshō Nicchō Raigetsu Saikai e Rachi Kazoku Kikoku Kecchaku nara" [Japan-DPRK negotiations for normalization to restart next month; families of abductees to return home if settled], *Nihon Keizai Shimbun*, May 16, 2004; "Abductions of Japanese Citizens by North Korea," Ministry of Foreign Affairs of Japan, August 6, 2021, https://www.mofa.go.jp/region/asia-paci/n_korea/abduction/index.html; "Abductions of Japanese Citizens by North Korea," https://www.rachi.go.jp/; "Seiji Jinji Tai Kitachōsen Kyōkoha no Yachi Fukuchōkanho Gaimu Jimujikan ni Irei no Fukki" [Government personnel: A North Korea hardliner Assistant Chief Cabinet Secretary Yachi to be vice minister for foreign affairs, an unusual return], *Mainichi Shimbun*, December 28, 2014.

30. Choe Sang-Hun, "South Korea's Leader Will Be Odd Man Out in Meeting with Trump and Shinzo Abe," *New York Times*, September 20, 2017, https://www.nytimes.com/2017/09/20/world/asia/trump-moon-south-korea.html.

31. "Namboku Yūwa Nihon wa Naze Shimpaigao?" [Why is Japan worried about the North and South Korea's reconciliation?], *Nihon Keizai Shimbun*, May 21, 2018.

32. "Press Conference by President Trump," White House, June 12, 2018, https://www.whitehouse.gov/briefings-statements/press-conference-president-trump/ (site discontinued), archived at https://web.archive.org/web/20180618015801/https://www.whitehouse.gov/briefings-statements/press-conference-president-trump/.

33. John Bolton, *The Room Where It Happened: A White House Memoir* (New York: Simon and Schuster, 2020).

34. "Remarks by President Trump Before Marine One Departure," White House, August 1, 2019, https://www.whitehouse.gov/briefings-statements/remarks-president-trump-marine-one-departure-56/ (site discontinued), archived at https://web.archive.org/web/20190806035553/https://www.whitehouse.gov/briefings-statements/remarks-president-trump-marine-one-departure-56/; "Remarks by President Trump Before Marine One Departure," White House, August 9, 2019, https://www.whitehouse.gov/briefings-statements/remarks-president-trump-marine-one-departure-59/ (site discontinued), archived at https://web.archive.org/web/20190809234506/https://www.whitehouse.gov/briefings-statements/remarks-president-trump-marine-one-departure-59/.

35. "Address by Prime Minister Abe at the Seventy-Third Session of the United Nations General Assembly," Ministry of Foreign Affairs of Japan, September 25, 2018, https://www.mofa.go.jp/fp/unp_a/page3e_000926.html.

36. Min Joo Kim, "North Korea Blows Up Joint Liaison Office, Dramatically Raising Tensions with South," *Washington Post*, June 16, 2020, https://www.washingtonpost.com/world/asia_pacific/north-korea-liaison-office-kaesong-explosion-demolish-dmz/2020/06/16/7c7a2dc0-af9d-11ea-98b5-279a6479a1e4_story.html.

37. Reiji Yoshida, "At G20, Abe Has Held Talks with Several World Leaders and Even a Pop Idol, but Not Moon Jae-in," *Japan Times*, June 29, 2019, https://www.japantimes

.co.jp/news/2019/06/29/national/politics-diplomacy/g20-abe-held-talks-several
-world-leaders-even-pop-idol-not-moon-jae/.

38. Robert King, "Japan and North Korea: Summitry, Missile Fears, and Abductions," Center for Strategic and International Studies, June 19, 2019, https://www.csis.org/analysis
/japan-and-north-korea-summitry-missile-fears-and-abductions.

39. "Opinion Poll Report," *Naikakufu* [Cabinet Office], January 2012, https://survey.gov
-online.go.jp/h23/h23-bouei/index.html.

40. *Defense of Japan 2019* (Tokyo: Japan Ministry of Defense, 2019), https://www.mod.go
.jp/en/publ/w_paper/wp2019/pdf/DOJ2019_Full.pdf.

41. For example, using China as an example, Shogo Suzuki argues that China became a nationalist focal point for both the left and right in Japan, and there is no longer a significant difference between the two groups on policy. Phillip Lipscy and Ethan Scheiner argue that the majoritarian electoral rules in 1994 led to a convergence in the policy positions of the two major political parties. Shogo Suzuki, "The Rise of the Chinese 'Other' in Japan's Construction of Identity: Is China a Focal Point of Japanese Nationalism?" *Pacific Review* 28, no. 1 (2015): 95–116.

    For the polarization in Korea, see: Sook-Jong Lee, "Democratization and Polarization in Korean Society," *Asian Perspective* 29, no. 3 (2005): 99–125; Phillip Lipscy and Ethan Scheiner, "Japan Under the DPJ: The Paradox of Political Change Without Policy Change," special issue, *Journal of East Asian Studies* 12, no. 3 (2012): 311–22.

42. See, for example, Gi-Wook Shin, "South Korea's Democratic Decay," *Journal of Democracy* 31, no. 3 (July 2020): 100–14.

43. Noriyo Isozaki, "Nikkan Shimin Shakai niokeru Sōgoninshiki" [Mutual perceptions in Japanese and Korean civic society], in *Nikkan Kankeishi 1965–2015 III Shakai-Bunka* [History of Japan–South Korea relations, 1965–2015, vol. 3: Society and culture], ed. Noriyo Isozaki and Chong-koo Lee (Tokyo: University of Tokyo Press, 2015), 29–60.

44. Article II of the treaty states: "The High Contracting Parties confirm that the problems concerning property, rights, and interests of the two High Contracting Parties and their peoples (including juridical persons) and the claims between the High Contracting Parties and between their peoples, including those stipulated in Article IV(a) of the Peace Treaty with Japan signed at the city of San Francisco on September 8, 1951, have been settled completely and finally." "Agreement Between Japan and the Republic of Korea Concerning the Settlement of Problems in Regard to Property and Claims and Economic Co-operation," *International Legal Materials* 5, no. 1 (1966): 111–17, https://www.jstor.org/stable/20690013.

45. *Iwayuru Jūgun Ianfu ni tsuite* [On the issue of comfort women], Ministry of Foreign Affairs of Japan, August 4, 1993, https://www.mofa.go.jp/mofaj/area/taisen/pdfs/im_050804.pdf.

46. Min-Ah Cho is one of the more recent scholars on the mobilization of the comfort women. *Statement by the Chief Cabinet Secretary Yohei Kono on the Result of the Study on the Issue of "Comfort Women,"* Ministry of Foreign Affairs of Japan, August 4, 1993, https://www.legal-tools.org/doc/cb4732/pdf/; Min-Ah Cho, "Stirring Up Deep Waters: Korean Feminist Theologies Today," *Theology Today* 71, no. 2 (2014): 236–37, https://doi
.org/10.1177%2F0040573614529788.

47. Norimitsu Onishi, "Abe Rejects Japan's Files on War Sex," *New York Times*, March 2, 2007, https://www.nytimes.com/2007/03/02/world/asia/02japan.html.

48. " 'Gyakusatsu ni Hitoshii Shūdan Reipu' Mogi Saiban de Shōgen Kokuren Sekai Jinken Kaigi" [Testimony a mock trial "Gang rape equivalent to genocide," at the UN World Conference on Human Rights], *Mainichi Shimbun*, June 16, 1993.

49. Brian Knowlton, "Bush Urges Congress to Reject Armenian Genocide Resolution," *New York Times*, October 10, 2007, https://www.nytimes.com/2007/10/10/world/europe/10iht-10turkey.7834745.html.

50. " 'Jūgun Ianfu Mondai' Kishimu Nichibei Kain Ketsugian Hirogaru Sandō" [Squeaky relations between the U.S. and Japan over the "so-called comfort women issue," and growing support for the U.S. House resolution], *Asahi Shimbun*, April 4, 2007; "Moto Ianfu eno 'Owabi' Kyōchō Abe Shushō" [PM Abe emphasized "apology" to the former comfort women], *Yomiuri Shimbun*, March 12, 2007. Abe's March 11 statement on *NHK* took place after my interview on *Yomiuri*: " 'Ianfu' Rekishika ni Makaseyo Maikeru Guriin shi ni kiku" [Let historians handle the comfort women issue, says Michael Green], *Yomiuri Shimbun*, March 4, 2007.

51. The letter was published in the American Historical Association magazine: Alexis Dudden, "Letters to the Editor: Standing with Historians of Japan," *Perspectives on History*, March 1, 2015, https://www.historians.org/publications-and-directories/perspectives-on-history/march-2015/letter-to-the-editor-standing-with-historians-of-japan; Anna Fifield, "U.S. Academics Condemn Japanese Efforts to Revise History of 'Comfort Women,' " *Washington Post*, February 9, 2015. Earlier in 2014, *Asahi Shimbun* admitted to errors in its articles, retracting all stories going back decades that quoted a Japanese man who claimed he kidnapped a group of Korean women and forced them to work at wartime Japanese military brothels; see Reiji Yoshida, "Asahi Shimbun Admits Errors in Past 'Comfort Women' Stories," *Japan Times*, August 5, 2014, https://www.japantimes.co.jp/news/2014/08/05/national/politics-diplomacy/asahi-shimbun-admits-errors-in-past-comfort-women-stories/.

52. Youmi Kim and Mike Ives, "A Harvard Professor Called Wartime Sex Slaves 'Prostitutes.' One Pushed Back," *New York Times*, February 6, 2021, https://www.nytimes.com/2021/02/26/world/asia/harvard-professor-comfort-women.html.

53. "Court Says Seoul's Inaction over Former 'Comfort Women' Unconstitutional," *Yonhap News Agency*, August 30, 2011, https://en.yna.co.kr/view/AEN20110830007951315.

54. "Ianfu Mondai Kamiawanu Nikkan" [On comfort women issue, Japan and Korea talk past each other], *Asahi Shimbun*, August 31, 2012; "S. Korea Demands Japan Take 'Fundamental Measures' on Wartime Sex Slavery," *Yonhap News Agency*, March 9, 2012, https://en.yna.co.kr/view/AEN20120309006500315.

55. *Statesmen's Forum: Shinzo Abe, Prime Minister of Japan*, Center for Strategic and International Studies, February 22, 2013, https://csis-website-prod.s3.amazonaws.com/s3fs-public/event/132202_PM_Abe_TS.pdf.

56. "Report on the Review of the Korea Japan Agreement of December 28, 2015 on the Issue of Comfort Women Victims," Ministry of Foreign Affairs of Republic of Korea, December 27, 2017, 6, https://www.mofa.go.kr/viewer/skin/doc.html?fn=20180226052509505

.pdf&rs=/viewer/result/202109; Gilbert Rozman, *Changes in the Japan–South Korea National Identity Gap*, Joint U.S.–Korea Academic Studies, Korea Economic Association of America 2016, 127–42, http://keia.org/sites/default/files/publications/joint_us -korea_2016_-_identity_gap.pdf.

57. In a 2017 *JBpress* article, the journalist Komori Yoshihisa describes the Korean Council for Justice and Remembrance for the Issues of Military Sexual Slavery by Japan as "anti-US, anti-Japan, and pro-North Korea." Yoshihisa Komori, "Ianfu ga Kankoku de Kyarakutā Bijinesu ni?" [In Korea comfort women have become character business?], *JBpress*, January 16, 2017, https://jbpress.ismedia.jp/articles/-/48928. A 2020 *Sankei Biz* article mentions that North Korea backed the same organization on their allegations of misappropriation of donations. "Kitachōsen Kifu Ryūyō nadono Giwaku de Kachū no Kankoku no Moto Ianfu Shiendantai to Zen Rijichō wo Yōgo" [North Korea backs the Korean former comfort women support organization and its chairman in the midst of allegations on misappropriation of donations], *Sankei Biz*, June 3, 2020, https://www.sankeibiz .jp/macro/news/200603/mcb2006031233019-n1.htm.

58. Kim Tong-Hyung, "Court Orders Japan Company to Pay 4 Koreans for Forced Labor," Associated Press, October 30, 2018, https://apnews.com/474886c44d2c498e94e90c0a8abc5f6d.

59. Simon Denyer, "New South Korean Court Ruling Angers Japan, Deepening Crisis Between America's Closest Pacific Allies," *Washington Post*, November 29, 2018, https:// www.washingtonpost.com/world/s-korea-court-orders-japans-mitsubishi-to-pay -compensation-for-wartime-forced-labor/2018/11/28/4f0a6616-f37e-11e8-9240-e8028a62c722 _story.html.

60. "Former President Park Refuses to Be Questioned over Judicial Power Abuse Scandal," *Yonhap News Agency*, January 9, 2019, https://en.yna.co.kr/view/AEN20190109007000325?

61. Kan Kimura, "South Korea's Botched Handling of the Forced Labor Issue," *The Diplomat*, July 9, 2019, https://thediplomat.com/2019/07/south-koreas-botched-handling -of-the-forced-labor-issue/.

62. Mayumi Negishi and Eun-Young Jeong, "Japan Curbs Exports to South Korea, Hitting Global Chip Makers," *Wall Street Journal*, July 1, 2019, https://www.wsj.com/articles /japan-restricts-exports-to-south-korea-as-bilateral-ties-fray-11561953854.

63. "Speaker Submits Bill on Compensation for Japan's Wartime Forced Labor," *Korea Herald*, December 18, 2019, http://www.koreaherald.com/view.php?ud=20191218000918.

64. Moon was one of the first leaders that Suga talked with after his appointment as prime minister. On the issue of forced labor, according to the Blue House spokesperson, Moon said that the two governments differ on the issue but should seek an optimum solution, although Suga acknowledged that the forced labor issue is in an "extremely difficult situation." With the presidential election coming up in March 2022, Moon may face domestic pressure to take a firmer stance on the issue in the coming months. Matthew Goodman, "Japan and Korea: Rising Above the Fray," Center for Strategic and International Studies, August 6, 2019, https://www.csis.org/analysis/japan-and-korea-rising-above -fray; Ryotaro Nakamaru, "FOCUS: Japan-S. Korea Feud Set to Flare over Wartime Labor Row," *Kyodo News*, August 5, 2020, https://english.kyodonews.net/news/2020/08 /a93a8dec49df-focus-japan-s-korea-feud-set-to-flare-over-wartime-labor-row.html;

Chang-Ran Kim and Sangmi Cha, "Japan's New PM Calls for Better Ties with South Korea, Cooperation on North Korea," Reuters, September 23, 2020, https://www.reuters .com/article/us-southkorea-japan/japans-new-pm-calls-for-better-ties-with-south -korea-cooperation-on-north-korea-idUSKCN26F09Z?il=0; Hiroshi Minegishi, "Tokyo and Seoul Struggle for Compromise on Wartime Labor Issue," *Nikkei Asia*, September 26, 2020, https://asia.nikkei.com/Spotlight/Comment/Tokyo-and-Seoul-struggle -for-compromise-on-forced-labor-issue. South Korean Court Dismissses Wartime Labor Case against 16 Japanese Companies, *Japan Times*, June 7, 2021, https://www. japantimes.co.jp/news/2021/06/07/national/crime-legal/south-korea-wartime-labor -japan-lawsuit-dismissed/

65. The 2019 survey conducted by Genron NPO showed that 49.9 percent of respondents in both Japan and South Korea said the impression of the other country is bad or somewhat bad. For more information, see "The Japan-South Korea Joint Public Opinion Poll 2019."

66. "South Korea's Spy Chief Meets Suga amid Protracted Dispute over Wartime Forced Labor," *Korea Herald*, November 10, 2020, http://www.koreaherald.com/view.php? ud=20201110000923.

67. Josh Wingrove and Isabel Reynolds, "Trump Bemoans Request to 'Get Involved' in Seoul-Tokyo Dispute," *Bloomberg*, July 19, 2019, https://www.bloomberg.com/news /articles/2019-07-19/trump-bemoans-request-to-get-involved-in-seoul-tokyo-dispute.

68. Reiji Yoshida and Satoshi Sugiyama, "GSOMIA Survives as South Korea Reverses Decision to Exit Intel Pact with Japan," *Japan Times*, November 22, 2019, https://www .japantimes.co.jp/news/2019/11/22/national/politics-diplomacy/japan-south-korea -gsomia-talks/.

69. "Abe May Settle for Return of Just 2 Out of 4 Northern Territories from Russia," *Mainichi Shimbun*, November 23, 2018, https://mainichi.jp/english/articles/20181123 /p2a/00m/0na/006000c; Robin Harding and Henry Foy, "Russia and Japan Push to Resolve Kuril Islands Dispute," *Financial Times*, November 28, 2018, https://www .ft.com/content/763b2eb2-f2f4-11e8-ae55-df4bf40f9d0d.

70. Keiichi Yamaguchi, "Abe Presents 8-Point Economic Cooperation Plan to Putin," *Nikkei Asia*, May 7, 2016, https://asia.nikkei.com/Politics/Abe-presents-8-point-economic-cooperation-plan-to-Putin; "Japan-Russia Summit Meeting," Ministry of Foreign Affairs of Japan, May 7, 2016, https://www.mofa.go.jp/erp/rss/northern/page4e_000427.html.

71. "Japan Jets Scramble at Cold-War Levels as Chinese and Russian Incursions Increase," Reuters, April 16, 2015, https://www.reuters.com/article/us-japan-airforce -scramble/japan-jets-scramble-at-cold-war-levels-as-chinese-and-russian-incursions -increase-idUSKBN0N60ST20150416; "Russia Deploys Surveillance Drone to Japan-Claimed Isles off Hokkaido, Report Says," *Japan Times*, April 9, 2019, https://www .japantimes.co.jp/news/2019/04/09/national/politics-diplomacy/russia-deploys-surveillance -drone-japan-claimed-isles-off-hokkaido-report-says.

72. "A Conversation with KOICA President Kim Young-mok," Asia Foundation, June 17, 2015, https://asiafoundation.org/2015/06/17/a-conversation-with-koica-president-kim -young-mok/; Koh Byung-joon, "KOICA to Promote Democracy, Rights, Gender

Equality in Overseas Development Projects," *Yonhap News Agency*, December 15, 2017, https://en.yna.co.kr/view/AEN20171214011300315.

73. Green, *Japan's Reluctant Realism*, 133–37.
74. Michishita, "Changing Security Relationship."
75. Michishita, "Changing Security Relationship."

6. INTERNAL BALANCING

1. Kenneth N. Waltz, *Theory of International Politics* (Reading, MA: Addison-Wesley, 1979), 168–70.

2. Waltz, *Theory of International Politics*; *Asia Power Index 2019: Key Findings*, Lowy Institute, https://power.lowyinstitute.org/downloads/Lowy-Institute-Asia-Power-Index-2019 -Key-Findings.pdf.

3. Karel G. van Wolferen, "The Japan Problem," *Foreign Affairs* 65, no. 2 (Winter 1986/1987): 289; Kent E. Calder, "Japanese Foreign Economic Policy Formation: Explaining the Reactive State," *World Politics* 40, no.4 (1988).

4. Peter W. Rodman, *Presidential Command: Power, Leadership, and the Making of Foreign Policy from Richard Nixon to George W. Bush* (New York: Vintage, 2008).

5. "Tsugi no shushou: Suga-shi 46 percent Honsha Zenkoku Yoronchousa" [The next prime minister: Suga at 46 percent in national poll], *Yomiuri Shimbun*, September 7, 2020, 10.

6. Jonathan Steinberg, *Bismarck: A Life* (New York: Oxford University Press, 2011), 16, 191, 198, 211, 245, 267–68, 303–4, 310.

7. Kenneth Pyle, *Japan Rising: The Resurgence of Japanese Power and Purpose* (New York: Public Affairs, 2007), 25.

8. Bernd Martin, *Japan and Germany in the Modern World* (Providence, RI: Berghahn, 1971), 18.

9. Frances McCall Rosenbluth and Michael F. Thies, *Japan Transformed : Political Change and Economic Restructuring* (Princeton, NJ: Princeton University Press, 2010), 36–37; Masako Shibata, "Controlling National Identity and Reshaping the Role of Education: The Vision of State Formation in Meiji Japan and the German Kaiserreich," *History of Education* 33, no. 1 (2004): 75–85.

10. Yamamura Kōzō, "Success Illgotten? The Role of Meiji Militarism in Japan's Techno-logical Progress," *Journal of Economic History* 37, no. 1 (March 1977): 113; Kobayashi Ushisaburō, *Military Industries of Japan* (New York: Oxford University Press, 1922), 161; Richard Samuels, *Rich Nation, Strong Army* (Ithaca, NY: Cornell University Press, 1996), 34.

11. Peter Duus, *Party Rivalry and Political Change in Taisho Japan* (Cambridge, MA: Harvard University Press, 1968), 2.

12. Andrew Gordon, *Modern History of Japan: From Tokugawa Times to the Present* (New York: Oxford University Press, 2003); James Fulcher, "The Bureaucratization of the State and the Rise of Japan," *British Journal of Sociology* 39, no. 2 (1988): 228–54.

13. See, for example, Eri Hotta, *Japan 1941: Countdown to Infamy* (New York: Vintage, 2013).

14. Pyle, *Japan Rising*, 123–24; William G. Beasley, *Japanese Imperialism* (New York: Oxford University Press, 1985), 35.

15. John W. Dower, *Embracing Defeat: Japan in the Wake of World War II* (New York: Norton, 1999), 75, 82, 529.

16. Tomohito Shinoda, *Contemporary Japanese Politics: Institutional Changes and Power Shifts* (New York: Columbia University Press, 2013), 15.

17. Kenji Hayao, *The Japanese Prime Minister and Public Policy* (Pittsburgh, PA: University of Pittsburgh Press, 1993); Terry Edward MacDougall, *Political Leadership in Contemporary Japan* (Ann Arbor: Center for Japanese Studies, University of Michigan, 1982), 14; Rosenbluth and Thies, *Japan Transformed*, 112.

18. Alisa Gaunder, *Political Reform in Japan: Leadership Looming Large* (London: Routledge, 2007), 6–7.

19. Seizaburo Sato, Ken'ichi Koyama, and Shunpei Kumon, *Postwar Politician: The Life of Former Prime Minister Masayoshi Ohira* (Tokyo: Kodansha International, 1990), 445–46.

20. Sōgō Anzen Hoshō Kenkyū Gurūpu [Comprehensive Security Study Group], *Sōgō Anzen Hoshō Senryaku* [Comprehensive Security Strategy] (Tokyo: Ōkurasho Insatsukyoku, 1980).

21. Michael J. Green, *Arming Japan: Defense Production, Alliance Politics, and the Postwar Search for Autonomy* (New York: Columbia University Press, 1995), 53–71.

22. Tomohito Shinoda, *Koizumi Diplomacy: Japan's Kantei Approach to Foreign and Defense Affairs* (Seattle: University of Washington Press, 2017), 26.

23. Shinoda, *Koizumi Diplomacy*, 28.

24. Gotoda Masaharu, *Naikaku Kambōchōkan* [Chief cabinet secretary] (Tokyo: Kōdansha, 1989), 56; Sassa Atsuyuki, *Waga Jōshi Gotōda Masaharu* [Our boss, Gotōda Masaharu] (Tokyo: Bungei Shunju, 2000).

25. Sassa Atsuyuki, *Poritiko Miritari no Susume* [Recommendatinos on political military issues] (Tokyo: Shinkosha, 1994).

26. "Kokka Anzen Hoshō Kaigi Secchihō" [National Security Council Enactment Law], *E-Gov*, https://elaws.e-gov.go.jp/search/elawsSearch/elaws_search/lsg0500/detail?lawId=361AC0000000071; "Wagakunino Jōhōkinō Himitsu Hozen" [Our country's intelligence function and security], *Sangiin*, December 2013, https://www.sangiin.go.jp/japanese/annai/chousa/rippou_chousa/backnumber/2013pdf/20131202015.pdf.

27. Michael J. Green and Igata Akira, "The Gulf War and Japan's National Security Identity," in *Examining Japan's Lost Decades*, ed. Yōichi Funabashi and Barak Kushner (London: Routledge, 2015), 158–75.

28. Glen Fukushima, "The Great Hanshin Earthquake," Japan Policy Research Institute Occasional Paper no. 2 (March 1995), http://www.jpri.org/publications/occasionalp28apers/op2.html (site discontinued), archived at https://web.archive.org/web/20070301183810/http://www.jpri.org/publications/occasionalpapers/op2.html; "Ōmu Kienu Shōgeki Chikatetsu Sarin Jiken 25nen" [Twenty-five years since the Tokyo subway sarin attack:

Indelible shock of Aum Shinrikyo], *Nihon Keizai Shimbun*, March 20, 2020; "Backgrounder: Aum Shinrikyo," Council on Foreign Relations, June 19, 2012, https://www.cfr.org/backgrounder/aum-shinrikyo.

29. Ichiro Ozawa, *Blueprint for a New Japan: The Thinking of a Nation* (New York: Kodansha International, 1994), 24.

30. "Kenshō Gaimushō Kikōkaikaku 'Senryakuteki Gaikō' Zenmen ni" [Foreign ministry reform: "Strategic diplomacy" at the forefront], *Yomiuri Shimbun*, March 31, 1993; "Sōgō Gaikō Seisakukyoku Gaimushōga Shinsetsu e" [Ministry of Foreign Affairs to newly establish a Comprehensive Foreign Policy Bureau], *Nihon Keizai Shimbun*, July 27, 1993.

31. See Cabinet Law Article 15 for the role of deputy chief cabinet secretary for crisis management: "The Cabinet Law (Law No. 5 of 1947, as Amended)," *Kantei*, http://www.kantei.go.jp/foreign/constitution_and_government_of_japan/cabinet_law_e.html; "Michi Nakabano Kikikanri Kyōka Hanshin Daishinsai kara Sannen Osaka" [Osaka: Three years after the Great Hanshin Earthquake, halfway through the strengthening of crisis management], *Asahi Shimbun*, January 16, 1998.

32. "Naikakufu Secchihō" [Act for establishment of the Cabinet Office], *E-Gov*, https://elaws.e-gov.go.jp/search/elawsSearch/elaws_search/lsg0500/detail?lawId=411AC0000000089.

33. Rosenbluth and Thies, *Japan Transformed*, 96–97.

34. Ryūtaro Hashimoto, *Vision of Japan* (Tokyo: Besuto Serazu, 1993).

35. Internal *Asahi Shimbun* exit polls shared with the author at the time.

36. On abduction issues, while Fukuda pursued a behind-the-scene negotiation, Abe sought a more assertive position toward North Korea. " 'Rachi' Kaiketsuni 'Kitakaze' to 'Taiyō' " ["The north wind and the sun" surrounding the abduction issue], *Sankei Shimbun*, March 27, 2002. Their differences became evident during the LDP leadership elections in 2006. "('06 Jimin Sōsaisen) Abe Fukuda Ryōshi Tairitsujiku Senmeini" [Differing positions become evident between Abe and Fukuda in the 2006 LDP leadership election], *Asahi Shimbun*, June 1, 2006.

37. Major newspapers from a broad ideological spectrum—*Nikkei, Asahi, Yomiuri*—published editorials critical of Tanaka between June and August 2001. "Shasetsu: Tanaka Gaikō Koreijōno Teitaiwa Yurusarenai" [Editorial: No more stagnation allowed for Tanaka diplomacy], *Yomiuri Shimbun*, June 10, 2001; "Shakumei Dakeno Tabidewa Nai Tanaka Gaishō Hōbei: Shasetsu" [Editorial: Foreign Minister Tanaka's visit to the U.S.: The visit should be more than just giving explanations], *Asahi Shimbun*, June 17, 2001; "Tsugiwa Tanaka Gaishōno Tekikakuseiga Towareru: Shasetsu" [Editorial: This time Foreign Minister Tanaka's competence will be questioned], *Nihon Keizai Shimbun*, August 4, 2001.

38. "Beikoku Dōji Tahatsu Tero Shushō Kanteide Anzen Hoshō Kaigi" [In light of the 9/11 attack, the NSC meeting held at Kantei], *Mainichi Shimbun*, September 12, 2001; "Beini Zenmen Terokōgeki Nihonseifuga Taisaku Hombu Secchi" [In response to the full-scale terrorist attack on the U.S., Japanese government set up a countermeasure headquarters], *Sankei Shimbun*, September 12, 2001; Shinoda, *Koizumi Diplomacy*, 91.

39. The Law Concerning the Special Measures on the Humanitarian and Reconstruction Assistance Activities (Iraq Special Measures Law) (August 1, 2003); The Law to Protect People's Rights (June 18, 2004); The Law to Facilitate U.S. Military Actions (June 18, 2004); The Law on the Use of the Public Facilities (June 18, 2004).

40. Shinoda, *Koizumi Diplomacy*, 112.

41. The vision for that strategy was articulated just before the 2000 election in Richard L. Armitage, Joseph A. Nye, et al., *The United States and Japan: Advancing Toward a Mature Partnership*, Institute for National Strategic Studies Special Report, October 11, 2000, https://spfusa.org/wp-content/uploads/2015/11/ArmitageNyeReport_2000.pdf.

42. Richard J. Samuels, *Special Duty: A History of the Japanese Intelligence Community* (Ithaca, NY: Cornell University Press, 2019), 174.

43. This was right after Koizumi had expelled opponents of his postal savings reform plans from the Diet and then triumphed over them and the opposition parties in a massive victory at the polls, so domestic politics were also very much at play.

44. Kitaoka Shinichi, "A 'Proactive Contribution to Peace' and the Right of Collective Self-Defense: The Development of Security Policy in the Abe Administration," *Asia-Pacific Review* 21, no. 2 (2014): 1–18, doi:10.1080/13439006.2014.985237.

45. I met several times with Koike and her group to discuss models for NSC structures around the world. "Nihonban NSC 'Shushōni Kawari Shudō' Koike Hosakanga Tsuyoi Iyoku" [Advisor Koike showing strong interests in "leading a Japanese-style NSC" in the prime minister's place], *Nihon Keizai Shimbun*, October 2, 2006. Koike also visited the United States and United Kingdom to gather information on the formation of Japan's NSC. "Nihonban NSC Setsuritsu Koike Hosakan Ei Jōhō Soshikiwo Shisatsude Chōsei" [To establish a Japanese-style NSC, advisor Koike scheduled to visit British intelligence organization], *NHK News*, October 25, 2006.

46. Takashi Uesugi, *Kantei Hōkai Abe Seiken Meisōno Ichinen* [The collapse of Kantei—A year of Abe administration's straying off course] (Tokyo: Shinchōsha, 2007), 126.

47. "Kantei Kinō no Kyōka Senryakushitsu no Gutaizō Shushō Hatsugen de Meisō" [Strengthening of Kantei function and the specific images of strategy department getting off the track due to the prime minister's comment], *Yomiuri Shimbun*, August 25, 2010.

48. Nikkei on Renho and Shiwake.

49. See, for example, Ken Jinbo, "Gaikō Anpo: Rinen Tsuikyū kara Genjitsu Rosen e" [Diplomacy and national security: From pursuit of ideals to pragmatic approach], in *Minshutō Seiken Shippai no Kenshō: Nihon Seiji wa Nani wo Ikasu ka* [Examining the failure of the DPJ: What can Japanese politics learn?], 125–58, Nihon Saiken Inishiatibu [Rebuild Japan Initiative Foundation] (Tokyo: Chuo Kōron Shinsha, 2013); Kiyoshi Kurokawa, *Kisei no Toriko: Gurūpu Shinku ga Nihon wo Horobosu* [Regulatory capture: Groupthink will destroy Japan] (Tokyo: Kodansha, 2016); "DPJ Cabinet's 3 Years of Instability—Hatoyama, Kan and Noda," *Nihon Keizai Shimbun*, November 18, 2012; "Editorial: Resignation of PM Kan—Sin for his short-lived cabinet," *Mainichi Shimbun*, August 27, 2011.

50. Kitaoka, "A 'Proactive Contribution to Peace,'" 4. "National Defense Program Guidelines for FY2011 and Beyond," Japan Ministry of Defense, https://worldjpn.grips.ac.jp/documents/texts/JPSC/20101217.O1E.html.

51. Kitaoka, "A 'Proactive Contribution to Peace,'" 28.

52. The law that passed in November is called "Anzen Hoshō Kaigi Secchihō Nadono Ichibuwo Kaiseisuru Hōritsu 'Gian Jōhō'" [Information on bills], House of Councillors, National Diet of Japan, December 4, 2013, https://www.sangiin.go.jp/japanese/joho1/kousei/gian/185/meisai/m18503183075.htm.

53. "Japan's Proactive Contribution to Peace," Cabinet Public Relations Office, Government of Japan, Spring 2014, https://www.japan.go.jp/tomodachi/2014/spring2014/japans_proactive_contribution_to_peace.html.

54. For the full NSS in English, see National Security Strategy, Kantei, December 17, 2013, http://japan.kantei.go.jp/96_abe/documents/2013/__icsFiles/afieldfile/2013/12/17/NSS.pdf; in Japanese, see Kokka Anzen Hoshō Senryakuni Tsuite [On the National Security Strategy], Kantei, December 17, 2013, https://www.cas.go.jp/jp/siryou/131217anzenhoshou/nss-j.pdf.

55. Defense of Japan 2017 (Tokyo: Japan Ministry of Defense, 2017), 216, https://www.mod.go.jp/e/publ/w_paper/pdf/2017/DOJ2017_3-1-1_web.pdf; "1947 National Security Act," Office of the Director of National Intelligence, https://www.dni.gov/index.php/ic-legal-reference-book/national-security-act-of-1947; see also Kotani Ken, "Nihon-ban Kokka Anzen Hoshō Kaigi (NSC) no kinōteki tokuchō" [Japan-style National Security Council (NSC) and its functional features], Kokusai Anzen Hoshō, March 2015, 61–75, 61–62; Kaneko Masafumi, "Iyoiyo shidō Nihon-ban NSC" [Finally . . . Japan-style NSC starts], PHP Kenkyūjo, 2013, https://thinktank.php.co.jp/kaeruchikara/939/; Adam P. Liff, "Japan's Security Policy in the 'Abe Era': Radical Transformation or Evolutionary Shift?" Texas National Security Review 1, no. 3 (2018): 20.

56. "Naikaku Jinjikyoku Hossoku Ichinen Kanryō Jinji Tsuyomaru Kanteishoku" [One year since the creation of the Cabinet Bureau of Personnel Affairs: Personnel affairs for bureaucrats to be more affected by the cabinet], Yomiuri Shimbun, May 30, 2015; "Suga Kambōchōkan no Zaishoku Rekidai Yoni ni Chikarano Gensuiwa Kanryō Shōaku to Jōhōmō" [CCS Suga in power for the fourth longest time: His power coming from managing bureaucrats and information networks], Kyodo News, May 9, 2015.

57. Giulio Pugliese, "Japan's Henry Kissinger? Yachi Shotaro, the State Behind the Curtain," Pacific Affairs 90, no. 2 (2017): 231–51.

58. Giulio Pugliese, "Kantei Diplomacy? Japan's Hybrid Leadership in Foreign and Security Policy," Pacific Review 30, no. 2 (2017): 152–68, DOI:10.1080/09512748.2016.1201131.

59. "Nichibei NSC Kimmitsu ni Renkei Yachishi Bei Kakuryōrato Kaidan" [For close cooperation between the American and Japanese NSC, Mr. Yachi met with U.S. cabinet secretaries], Nihon Keizai Shimbun, January 18, 2014, https://www.nikkei.com/article/DGXNASFS18005_Y4A110C1MM0000/; "Nichibei Anpo Tantō Kaidan Nichibei Dōmeino Kyōka e Renkei Shinka wo Kakunin" [U.S.-Japan National Security Staff meeting, confirming closer cooperation to strengthen the U.S.-Japan alliance], Mainichi Shimbun, March 1, 2017, https://mainichi.jp/articles/20170301/k00/00e/030/225000c.

60. Liff, "Japan's Security Policy in the 'Abe Era,'" 20; "Kanryo ga Kantei no Kaoiro Mite Shigoto: Fukuda Moto Shusho Abe Seiken Hihan" [Bureaucrats taking cues from Kantei: Former PM Fukuda criticizes Abe administration], *Tokyo Shimbun*, August 3, 2017.

61. Katsuya Hirose, *Kanryō to Gunjin Bummin Tōseino Genkai* [Bureaucrats and soldiers: Limits of civilian control] (Tokyo: Iwanami Shoten, 1989).

62. "New LDP Chief May Spell End to Reign of Economy Ministry," *Asahi Shimbun*, September 6, 2020, http://www.asahi.com/ajw/articles/13702805; Kosuke Takeuchi, "All Abe's Men: Japan's Economy Ministry Sidelined Under Suga," *Nikkei Asia*, September 17, 2020, https://asia.nikkei.com/Politics/Japan-after-Abe/All-Abe-s-men-Japan-s-economy-ministry-sidelined-under-Suga; "Dai niji Abe Naikaku Hossoku Kanteini Hishokan Futari Makikaeshi Nerau Keisanshō TPP Ene Seisakude" [Second Abe cabinet to inaugurate: METI sends two secretaries to Kantei, aiming to roll pushback with TPP and energy policy], *Mainichi Shimbun*, December 27, 2012.

63. "Gaikō Anpo Sokkin Atsumeru Shushō NSS Kyokuchō Kōtai Kitamurashi ni" [PM gathers his close aides on foreign policy and national security, NSS director to be replaced with Kitamura], *Asahi Shimbun*, September 23, 2019; "Suga Gaikō Gaimushō Shudōni Kaikika" [Suga diplomacy to return to MOFA-led diplomacy], *Asahi Shimbun*, October 10, 2020; "Keisanshōno Sonzaikan Teika Seiken naino Rikigakuni Henka Suga Naikaku" [The declining METI presence, change of power dynamics within the administration under Suga cabinet], *Jiji Press*, September 21, 2020.

64. Brad Glosserman, "NSC Change Prepares Japan for New Global Realities," *Japan Times*, April 1, 2020, https://www.japantimes.co.jp/opinion/2020/04/01/commentary/japan-commentary/nsc-change-prepares-japan-new-global-realities/; "Kokka Anpo-kyokuni Keizaihan Hossoku Shingata Korona Taiōmo Kyūmu" [Economy section established within NSS: Emergent matters involve response to COVID], *Nihon Keizai Shimbun*, April 1, 2020.

65. Richard J. Samuels, *Special Duty: A History of the Japanese Intelligence Community* (Ithaca, NY: Cornell University Press, 2019), 205.

66. "Jimintō Shunō wa Bōei Himitsu Hōan no Kon Kokkai Teishutsu wo Miokurukotowo Kimeta" [LDP leaders decided not to submit the defense secrets act to the current Diet session], *Mainichi Shimbun*, February 20, 1988. I recall the effort well, as I was working as a staffer for an LDP Diet member at the time and was grabbed out of the hallway and pushed into a conference room with other random staffers to give the impression to the cameras that the bill had broad support—which it did not. I was ordered to sit in the front of the room by desperate staffers so that the cameras would not show empty seats for the discussion on the unpopular bill.

67. "Mondai ōi Supai Bōshi Hōan: Shasetsu" [Editorial: An antispy law with many problems], *Nihon Keizai Shimbun*, June 5, 1985.

68. "Himitsu Hogo eno Kenen Kaishōni Saranaru Doryoku wo: Shasetsu" [Editorial: Further efforts needed to resolve concerns surrounding the Secrets Law], *Nihon Keizai Shimbun*, October 15, 2014.

69. "Editorial: Enforcement of Security of Information Legislation—Danger of Being Unspecific," *Asahi Shimbun*, December 10, 2014; "Editorial: Security of Information

Legislation in Effect—Necessary for Information Sharing with Foreign Governments," *Yomiuri Shimbun*, December 10, 2014.

70. "Passing of Security of Information Legislation—Steamrolling by the Ruling Parties," *Kyodo News*, December 6, 2013.

71. A CSIS report in 2018 called for the inclusion of Japan in the Five Eyes: *More Important than Ever: Renewing the U.S.-Japan Alliance for the 21st Century*, Center for Strategic and International Studies, October 2018, https://www.csis.org/analysis/more-important-ever.

72. Samuels, *Special Duty*, 216–40.

73. Mark Cancian, "Goldwater-Nichols 2.0," Center for Strategic and International Studies, March 4, 2016, https://www.csis.org/analysis/goldwater-nichols-20.

74. "National Defense Program Outline in and After FY 1996," Ministry of Foreign Affairs of Japan, December 1995, https://www.mofa.go.jp/policy/security/defense96/.

75. Yuki Tatsumi and Andrew L. Oros, eds., *Japan's New Defense Establishment: Institutions, Capabilities, and Implications* (Washington, DC: Henry L. Stimson Center, 2007), https://www.stimson.org/wp-content/files/file-attachments/Japan's%20New%20Defense%20Establishment.pdf.

76. Neil Melvin, "The Foreign Military Presence in the Horn of Africa Region," Stockholm International Peace Research Institute, 2019, 10–11, https://www.sipri.org/publications/2019/sipri-background-papers/foreign-military-presence-horn-africa-region; Sugio Takahashi, *Ballistic Missile Defense in Japan: Deterrence and Military Transformation*, Asie. Visions 59, Proliferation Papers 44 (Paris: Institut Francais des Relations Internationales, 2012), 12–13, https://www.ifri.org/sites/default/files/atoms/files/pp44av59takahashi.pdf.

77. *Defense of Japan 2015* (Tokyo: Japan Ministry of Defense, 2015), 219, https://www.mod.go.jp/e/publ/w_paper/pdf/2015/DOJ2015_2-4-3_web.pdf.

78. "Kaisei Bōeishō Secchihō ga Seiritsu Sebirogumi to Seifukugumi Taitōni" [Enactment of amended Act of Establishment of the Ministry of Defense, placing the civilian officials and uniformed personnel on equal footing], *Yomiuri Shimbun*, June 10, 2015; Mina Pollmann, "Japan's Defense Ministry Seeks to Roll Back Civilian Control," *The Diplomat*, February 28, 2015, https://thediplomat.com/2015/02/japans-defense-ministry-seeks-to-roll-back-civilian-control/.

79. *Defense of Japan 2017* (Tokyo: Japan Ministry of Defense, 2017), 317, https://www.mod.go.jp/e/publ/w_paper/pdf/2017/DOJ2017_3-1-1_web.pdf.

80. Nobuhiro Kubo and Tim Kelly, "Japan Activates First Marines Since WW2 to Bolster Defenses Against China," Reuters, April 7, 2018, https://www.reuters.com/article/us-japan-defence-marines/japan-activates-first-marines-since-ww2-to-bolster-defenses-against-china-idUSKCN1HE069.

81. "US-Japan Advance New Amphibious Capability," *Military News*, October 6, 2018, https://www.militarynews.com/news/us-japan-advance-new-amphibious-capability/article_a8165d68-c995-11e8-ad32-0b2be5d5a42b.html.

82. Richard J. Samuels, " 'New Fighting Power!' Japan's Growing Maritime Capabilities and East Asian Security," *International Security* 32, no. 3 (2007): 84–112.

83. "Mr. Sato to Be Appointed as the First Uniformed Chief of Coast Guard," *Sankei Shimbun*, July 18, 2013.

84. Lyle J. Morris, "Blunt Defenders of Sovereignty: The Rise of Coast Guards in East and Southeast Asia," *Naval War College Review* 70, no. 2 (2017): 91.

85. "Admiral Kawano Unprecedentedly Having the 3rd Extension of Mandatory Retirement Age," *Jiji News*, May 25, 2018.

86. Trent Scott and Andrew Shearer, *Building Allied Interoperability in the Indo-Pacific Region: A Case Study in Joint Command and Control for the Japanese Self-Defense Forces*, Center for Strategic and International Studies, December 2017, https://csis-website -prod.s3.amazonaws.com/s3fs-public/publication/171215_Shearer_BuildingAllied -Interoperability2_Web.pdf.

87. Barry Posen, *The Sources of Military Doctrine: France, Britain, and Germany Between the World Wars* (Ithaca, NY: Cornell University Press, 2014), 40.

88. Michael W. Chinworth, *Inside Japan's Defense: Technology, Economics and Strategy* (Sterling, VA: Brassey's, 1992), 8.

89. "Shinrai Dekiru wa Jietai Toppu" [SDF top of trustworthiness according to Nikkei mail survey], *Nihon Keizai Shimbun*, January 21, 2019, https://www.nikkei.com/article /DGXMZO40237230Q9A120C1905M00/.

90. Yuichi Hosoya, "Kokumin Anzen Hoshō' no Mondai wo Tetteiteki ni Kangaetemita" [Thinking thoroughly on the issue of national security], *Toyo Keizai Online*, September 20, 2019, https://toyokeizai.net/articles/-/301541?page; Yuichi Hosoya, *Gunji to Seiji: Nihon no Sentaku* [Military and politics: Japan's choices] (Tokyo: Bungei Shunju, 2019).

91. "Beikoku-sei Mujinki, Chōtatsu Chūshi mo Seifu, Kosuto-zō Kenen de Saikentō— Gurōbaruhōku Sanki" [Government reconsidering cancellation of U.S.-developed unmanned aerial vehicle procurement due to cost increase—three Global Hawk aircraft], *Jiji Press*, August 14, 2020, https://www.jiji.com/jc/article?k=2020081300689&g=pol.

92. Yuki Tatsumi, "Japan Wants to Streamline Its Defense Industry," *The Diplomat*, October 2, 2015, https://thediplomat.com/2015/10/japan-wants-to-streamline-its-defense-industry/.

93. Patrick Buchan and Benjamin Rimland, "Japan's F-2 Fighter Replacement Program and the Politics of Alliance Management," Center for Strategic and International Studies, April 3, 2020, https://www.csis.org/analysis/japans-f-2-fighter-replacement-program -and-politics-alliance-management; Tim Kelly, "Exclusive: Japan Favors Home-Grown Design for Next-Generation Fighter After Rejecting Foreign Plans: Sources," Reuters, March 27, 2020, https://www.reuters.com/article/us-japan-defence-fighter-exclusive /exclusive-japan-favors-home-grown-design-for-next-generation-fighter-after-rejecting -foreign-plans-sources-idUSKBN21E137.

94. Mike Yeo, "Japan's Defense Industry Continues to Grow. But Is It In for Rough Seas?" *Defense News*, August 15, 2018, https://www.defensenews.com/top-100/2018/08/15 /japans-defense-industry-continues-to-grow-but-is-it-in-for-rough-seas/.

95. For details, see Green, *Arming Japan.*

96. Ying Yu Lin, "The Early Returns of China's Military Reforms," *The Diplomat*, January 13, 2018, https://thediplomat.com/2018/01/the-early-returns-of-chinas-military-reforms/.

97. For details, see Michael J. Green and Katsuhisa Furukawa, "Japan: New Nuclear Realism," in *The Long Shadow: Nuclear Weapons and Security in 21st Century Asia*, ed. Muthiah Alagappa, 347 (Stanford, CA: Stanford University Press, 2008).

98. See, for example, Hugh White, "No Regional Security Without a Secure Japan," The Interpreter, The Lowy Institute, July 18, 2008, https://archive.lowyinstitute.org/the-interpreter /no-regional-security-without-secure-japan (site discontinued), archived at https://web .archive.org/web/20210921205956/https://archive.lowyinstitute.org/the-interpreter/no -regional-security-without-secure-japan.

99. Llewelyn Hughes, "Why Japan Will Not Go Nuclear: International and Domestic Constraints on the Nuclearization of Japan," *International Security* 31, no. 4 (Spring 2007): 67–96.

100. In *NHK* polling conducted for respondents eighteen and nineteen years old in 2017, 86 percent of respondents said Japan should not possess nuclear weapons. "Zenkoku no 18sai to 19sai Shūsen no hi 'Shiranai' 14 percent NHK Yoron Chōsa" [Fourteen percent of 18- and 19-year-olds nationwide "do not know" the anniversary of the end of World War II, according to the *NHK* public opinion poll], *NHK News*, August 9, 2017.

101. "Three Non-Nuclear Principles," Ministry of Foreign Affairs of Japan, https://www .mofa.go.jp/policy/un/disarmament/nnp/. For examples of Diet resolutions regarding the Three Non-Nuclear Principles, see "Hikaku Sangensoku ni Kansuru Kokkai Ketsugi" [Diet resolutions on the Three Non-Nuclear Principles], Ministry of Foreign Affairs of Japan, https://www.mofa.go.jp/mofaj/gaiko/kaku/gensoku/ketsugi.html.

102. Michael Green and Katsuhisa Furukawa, "New Ambitions, Old Obstacles: Japan and Its Search for an Arms Control Strategy," *Arms Control Today*, July/August 2000, https:// www.armscontrol.org/act/2000-07/features/new-ambitions-old-obstacles-japan-its -search-arms-control-strategy.

103. Emma Chanlett-Avery and Mary Beth Nikitin, *Japan's Nuclear Future: Policy Debate, Prospects, and U.S. Interests*, Congressional Research Service, February 19, 2009, https://fas.org/sgp/crs/nuke/RL34487.pdf.

104. See Green and Furukawa, "Japan: New Nuclear Realism," 347–72.

105. "Transcript: Donald Trump Expounds on His Foreign Policy Views," *New York Times*, March 26, 2016, https://www.nytimes.com/2016/03/27/us/politics/donald-trump-transcript .html.

106. *Defense of Japan 2017*, 233.

107. SIPRI Military Expenditure Database 2020, https://www.sipri.org/databases/milex.

108. Liff, "Japan's Security Policy in the 'Abe Era,'" 23.

109. Japan Ministry of Defense, *Medium Term Defense Program (FY2019–FY2023)*, December 18, 2018, http://www.mod.go.jp/j/approach/agenda/guideline/2019/pdf/chuki_seibi31-35 _e.pdf; Tim Kelly and Nobuhiro Kubo, "Exclusive: Japan's Far-Flung Island Defense Plan Seeks to Turn Tables on China," Reuters, December 17, 2015, https://www.reuters .com/article/us-japan-military-china-exclusive-idUSKBN0U107220151218.

110. Franz-Stefan Gady, "Japan's Ministry of Defense Confirms Plans to Procure New Stand-Off Missiles," *The Diplomat*, February 4, 2020, https://thediplomat.com/2020/02/japans -ministry-of-defense-confirms-plans-to-procure-new-stand-off-missiles/.

111. "Looking for a New Term for Teki Kichi Kogeki (Enemy Base Attack)—Differentiation from Preemptive Strike," *Nihon Keizai Shimbun*, July 8, 2020; "Is Teki Kichi Kogeki Noryoku (Enemy Base Attack Capability) Necessary?" *Sankei Shimbun*, June 29, 2020;

"PM Abe Leading Discussion on Teki Kichi Kogeki (Enemy Base Attack)—Urging to Fill the Vacuum of Defense Policy," *Jiji Press*, June 19, 2020; "Defense Minister Kono Says It Is Natural to Discuss the Possession of Teki Kichi Kogeki Noryoku (Enemy Base Attack Capability)," *Asahi Shimbun*, July 9, 2020.

112. See, for example, Masafumi Iida, "China's Security Threats and Japan's Responses," in *Strategic Japan 2021: The Future of Japan-China Relations*, Center for Strategic and International Studies, April 2021, https://www.csis.org/programs/japan-chair/strategic-japan-working-papers#2021.

113. "Uchū Kihon hō" [Basic Space Law], *E-Gov*, https://elaws.e-gov.go.jp/search/elawsSearch/elaws_search/lsg0500/detail?lawId=420AC1000000043.

114. "Japan and U.S. Agree to Boost Defense Cooperation in Outer Space," *Japan Times*, August 27, 2020, https://www.japantimes.co.jp/news/2020/08/27/national/abe-meets-u-s-space-force-chief/.

115. *Defense of Japan 2017*, 338–39.

116. "Jieitai Chihōni Hatsuno Saibā Butai Chūgoku Nentō" [SDF to position a new cyber defense unit with China in mind], *Asahi Shimbun*, June 11, 2019, https://www.asahi.com/articles/ASM67645CM67UTFK01N.html.

117. Grant Newsham, "Time to Be Honest About Japan's Defense Deficiency," *Asia Times*, October 13, 2020, https://asiatimes.com/2020/10/time-to-be-honest-about-japans-defense-deficiency/.

118. Jeffrey R. Hornung, *Japan's Potential Contributions in an East China Sea Contingency*, RAND Corporation, 2020, https://www.rand.org/pubs/research_reports/RRA314-1.html?utm_source=WhatCountsEmail&utm_medium=NPA:2636:6578:Dec%2014,%202020%207:41:15%20AM%20PST&utm_campaign=NPA:2636:6578:Dec%2014,%202020%207:41:15%20AM%20PST.

119. "Three Barriers on the Road to Prosperity," Japan Center for Economic Research, May 31, 2013, https://www.jcer.or.jp/jcer_download_log.php?f=eyJwb3N0X2lkI-jo1MTcwNywiZmlsZV9wb3N0X2lkIjo1MTcwOH0=&post_id=51707&file_post_id=51708.

120. *Emergency Economic Measures for the Revitalization of the Japanese Economy*, Government of Japan, January 11, 2013, https://www5.cao.go.jp/keizai1/2013/130111_emergency_economic_measures.pdf.

121. *New Framework for Strengthening Monetary Easing*: "*Quantitative and Qualitative Monetary Easing with Yield Curve Control*," Bank of Japan, September 21, 2016, https://www.boj.or.jp/en/announcements/release_2016/k160921a.pdf.

122. "Pump-priming," *The Economist*, December 30, 2014, https://www.economist.com/finance-and-economics/2014/12/30/pump-priming?zid=309&ah=80dcf288b8561b012f603b9fd9577f0e.

123. "Council for the Realization of Work Style Reform," *Kantei*, September 27, 2016, https://japan.kantei.go.jp/97_abe/actions/201609/27article2.html; "Abenomics' 'Third Arrow' Key to Revitalizing Japan's Economy," Organisation for Economic Co-operation and Development, April 15, 2015, https://www.oecd.org/newsroom/abenomics-third-arrow-key-to-revitalising-japans-economy.htm; Prime Minister's Office of Japan,

"Opening Speech by Prime Minister Shinzo Abe at the World Assembly for Women in Tokyo: WAW! 2015," *YouTube*, June 1, 2017, https://www.youtube.com/watch?v=K4 QiuT88i9Y.

124. Kaori Kaneko and Leika Kihara, "Japan May Slide Toward Recession as 'Abenomics' Impact Fades," Reuters, November 14, 2019, https://www.reuters.com/article/us-japan -abe-economy-analysis/japan-may-slide-toward-recession-as-abenomics-impact -fades-idUSKBN1XO2YN; "Abenomics Provides a Lesson for the Rich World," *Financial Times*, November 21, 2019, https://www.ft.com/content/f4326dba-0ba5-11ea-bb52 -34c8d9dc6d84; Motonao Uesugi, "Has Abenomics Run Out of Steam?" *Nikkei Asia*, January 12, 2020, https://asia.nikkei.com/Spotlight/Comment/Has-Abenomics -run-out-of-steam; William Pesek, "Coronavirus Fallout Highlights Failure of Japan's Womenomics," *Nikkei Asia*, June 18, 2020, https://asia.nikkei.com/Opinion/Coronavirus -fallout-highlights-failure-of-Japan-s-womenomics.

125. Akira Kawamoto, "Moving the Nation Beyond Abenomics," *Japan Times*, March 8, 2020, https://www.japantimes.co.jp/opinion/2020/03/08/commentary/japan-commentary /moving-nation-beyond-abenomics/; Kathy Matsui, Hiromi Suzuki, and Kazunori Tatebe, *Womenomics 5.0: 20 Years On*, Goldman Sachs, April 2019, https://www.goldmansachs .com/insights/pages/womenomics-5.0/multimedia/womenomics-5.0-report.pdf.

126. Yuri Kageyama, "Japan's Economy Shrinks at Record Rate, Slammed by Pandemic," Associated Press, August 16, 2020, https://apnews.com/article/virus-outbreak-global-trade -ap-top-news-world-war-ii-financial-markets-d10ca239b0e6ffafc5a2c7deafd23d85.

127. See, for example, Akira Kawamoto, "Moving the Nation Beyond Abenomics," *Japan Times*, March 8, 2020, https://www.japantimes.co.jp/opinion/2020/03/08/commentary /japan-commentary/moving-nation-beyond-abenomics; "Abenomics Provides a Lesson for the Rich World," *Financial Times*, November 21, 2019, https://www.ft.com/content /f4326dba-0ba5-11ea-bb52-34c8d9dc6d84.

128. See, for example, "Japan's Problem Is Not Enough Abenomics," *Financial Times*, February 18, 2020, https://www.ft.com/content/17607a42-517a-11ea-8841-482eed0038b1.

129. Emiko Jozuka and Yoko Wakatsuki, "Answering the Call: The Women on the Front Lines of Japan's Defense," *CNN*, February 3, 2019, https://www.cnn.com/2019/01 /23/asia/japan-self-defense-force-recruitment-intl/index.html; "Women Taking On More Frontline Roles in Japan's Self-Defense Forces," *Kyodo News*, October 14, 2018, https://english.kyodonews.net/news/2018/10/7eca2543f9e6-feature-women-taking -on-more-frontline-roles-in-japans-self-defense-forces.html. The U.S. advisory board is DACOWITS—Defense Advisory Committee on Women in the Services; see: https:// dacowits.defense.gov/.

130. "20nen Haru Nyūshō no Kokka Kōmuin Josei wa Kako Saikōno 37 percent" [Of civil servants entering the ministries in spring 2020, women constitute 37 percent, the highest in history], *Nihon Keizai Shimbun*, May 29, 2020, https://www.nikkei.com/article /DGXMZO59741270Z20C20A5EA3000/.

131. "Shutsunyūkoku Kanri Oyobi Nanmin Nintei hō Oyobi Hōmushō Secchihō no Ichibu wo Kaisei suru Hōritsu" [Bill to amend a part of Immigration Control and

Refugee Recognition Act and the Act for Establishment of the Ministry of Justice], House of Representatives, Japan, http://www.shugiin.go.jp/internet/itdb_housei.nsf /html/housei/19720181214102.htm; Simon Denyer and Akiko Kashiwagi, "Japan Passes Controversial New Immigration Bill to Attract Foreign Workers," *Washington Post*, December 7, 2018, https://www.washingtonpost.com/world/japan-passes-controversial -new-immigration-bill-to-attract-foreign-workers/2018/12/07/a76d8420-f9f3-11e8 -863a-8972120646e0_story.html; Takehiro Masumoto, "Japan's Open to Foreign Workers: Just Don't Call Them Immigrants," *South China Morning Post*, June 30, 2018, https:// www.scmp.com/week-asia/business/article/2152880/japans-open-foreign-workers -just-dont-call-them-immigrants.

132.   Oguma Eiji, as quoted in Martin Gelin, "Japan Radically Increased Immigration—and No One Protested," *Foreign Policy*, June 23, 2020, https://foreignpolicy.com/2020/06/23 /japan-immigration-policy-xenophobia-migration/; "Revised Immigration Control and Refugee Recognition Law—No Settlement in the Countryside Expected Despite the Expansion in Accepting Foreign Nationals, Government Lacking Clear Policy," *Mainichi Shimbun*, December 26, 2018; Chris Burgess, "A Japanese Multicultural Society Still Far Off," *East Asia Forum*, October 13, 2016, https://www.eastasiaforum .org/2016/10/13/a-japanese-multicultural-society-still-far-off/.

Recent examples of conservative LDP politicians embracing immigration in some form include Nukaga Fukushiro and Inada Tomomi. "Konbini mo 'Tokutei Ginō ni' Gaikokujin Ukeire de Jimin Teigen" [LDP proposes to add convenience store to the "specific skilled industry" list for accepting foreigners], *Nihon Keizai Shimbun*, June 13, 2020.

133.   Tomoko Kamata, "PM Suga's Digital Mission," *NHK World-Japan*, September 24, 2020, https://www3.nhk.or.jp/nhkworld/en/news/backstories/1304/; Taiga Uranaka and Yuki Hagiwara, "Japanese Banks Expect Digital Shift to Accelerate Under Suga," *Bloomberg*, September 17, 2020, https://www.bloomberg.com/news/articles/2020-09-17/japanese -banks-expect-digital-shift-to-accelerate-under-suga.

134.   The numbers increased from one unicorn in 2018 to three in 2019; see Kazuyuki Okudaira, "Japan's Unicorn Population a Shadow of Those in the US and China," *Nikkei Asia*, August 4, 2019, https://asia.nikkei.com/Business/Startups/Japan-s-unicorn-population-a-shadow-of-those-in-the-US-and-China. However, tech executives based in Japan have told me that they now see dozens of *potential* unicorns in the tech sector.

135.   The survey of experts and investors found an uptick in eighteen of nineteen indicators of strong governance of the economy in October 2020: Jack Lambert et al., *Gatehouse Governance Tracker: Japan Q3 2020*, Gatehouse Advisory Partners, October 21, 2020.

136.   Carol Gluck, "Patterns of Change: A 'Grand Unified Theory' of Japanese History," *Bulletin of the American Academy of Arts and Sciences* 48, no. 6 (March 1995): 38.

137.   Mireya Solís, "The Underappreciated Power: Japan After Abe," *Foreign Affairs* 99, no. 6 (November/December 2020): 124.

138.   Cabinet Office, "Heisei 29 nen-do Yoron Chōsa" [2017 public opinion polling], Government of Japan, https://survey.gov-online.go.jp/h29/h29-life/zh/z02-2.html.

CONCLUSION: THE END OF THE YOSHIDA DOCTRINE

1. "Japan Communist Party Slams China in First Platform Change Since 2004," *Japan Times*, January 18, 2020, https://www.japantimes.co.jp/news/2020/01/18/national/politics-diplomacy/japanese-communist-party-china-platform/.

2. Michael J. Green, *By More than Providence: Grand Strategy and American Power in the Asia Pacific Since 1783* (New York: Columbia University Press, 2017), 548.

3. Usually attributed to the *Sunday Telegraph*, February 9, 1964.

4. Green, *By More than Providence*, 314.

5. *Mapping the Future of U.S. China Policy*, https://chinasurvey.csis.org/.

6. See, for example, Hiroyuki Akita, "Time for Japan and Europe to Fill Void Left by US on World Stage: A Biden Win Would Not Mean an Immediate Return as Global Leader," *Nikkei Asia*, November 1, 2020.

INDEX

Japan (*continued*)
challenges, 6–7; Supreme Court of, 84–85; tapering Chinese dependence, 69–70; technology transforming, 19–21; as third maritime power, 30–31; Three Non-Nuclear Principles, 209; as tier one power, 2; trade of, 156; "Twelve Grades of Cap Rank," 20; U.S. factor in strategic competition, 74–76; U.S. reliance, 226–28; U.S.-Japan alliance, 35–40; unicorns, 216; United Nations admittance, 124; Versailles gains, 112; vulnerability of, 26–27. *See also* Beijing; China; Free and Open Indo-Pacific (FOIP); internal balancing; Republic of Korea (ROK); line of advantage; United States
Japan Air Self-Defense Force (JASDF), 57, 211–12
"Japan-Australia Joint Declaration on Security Cooperation," 128
Japan Bank for International Cooperation (JBIC), 67, 102, 148–49, 150, 159
Japan Center for International Exchange (JCIE), 144
Japan Communist Party (JCP), 219–20
Japan Institute of International Affairs (JIIA), 127–28, 30
Japan International Cooperation Agency (JICA), 143
Japan Maritime Self-Defense Force (JMSDF), 56, 204–6
Japan Self-Defense Forces (JSDF), 201, 205–7; A2/AD capabilities of, 210; Cyber Defense Group, 212; economic growth and, 215
Japan-China Treaty of Peace and Friendship, 66, 74
Japan's Bank for International Cooperation (JBIC), 67, 102, 148–50, 59
Japan's New Regional Reality, 147
Japan's Reluctant Realism (Green), 8
Jiang Zemin, 50–51, 66
Jidai Hideyoshi, 24, 164

Jinnō Shōtōki (Chronicle of gods and sovereigns), 22
Joint Declaration on Security, 128, 136

Kaifu Toshiki, 87, 190
Kaihatsu Kyōryoku Hakusho, 131
Kaikoku Heidan (Discussion concerning military matters of a maritime nation), 25–26
Kaiyō Kokka Nihon no Kōsō (The concept of Japan as a maritime nation), 38
Kamiya Fuji, 37
Kamiya Matake, 35–36
Kan Naoto, 89–90
Kanehara Nobukatsu, 17, 103, 129, 138–39
Kanemoto Toshinori, 193–94
Katsu Kaishū, 28–29, 42
Kawano Katsutoshi, 206
Keidanren, 67, 122, 127, 156
Kelly, James, 39–40
Kim Dae Jung, 179–81
Kim Jong-il, 169, 101
Kim Jong-un, 169–70, 178, 180, 272n150
Kim Sung-hwan, 167
Kishi Nobusuke, 16, 34–35, 218
Kishida Fumio, national security strategy of, 221
Kitaoka Shinichi, 133
Kohl, Helmet, 3
Koike Yuriko, 194, 198, 200; national security strategy of, 221
Koizumi Junichirō, 2, 9, 41, 70, 127,137–38, 199, 213; baseball knowledge of, 157–58; creating new global role, 124–25; 9/11 response, 87–88, 93, 192–93; revolution of, 192–96; seizing LDP leadership, 51–52; visiting North Korea, 169; War Bereavement Association (Nippon Izokukai), 51
Komatsu Ichirō, 92–94,
Kōmeitō Party, 67, 95–96, 142
Kondō Hisaku (Secret strategy for expansion), 27

CPSIA information can be obtained
at www.ICGtesting.com
Printed in the USA
JSHW021126190722
28278JS00001B/69

9 780231 204675